Praise for *American Federalism Today*

"Federalism is a creature of many parts. In *American Federalism Today*, some of the nation's wisest scholars and practitioners of American democracy offer insights into the different parts. The result is a fascinating journey through the complex jumble that American federalism most certainly is."

—**Larry Kramer**, president and vice chancellor,
London School of Economics

"In every generation, some scholar or politician claims that federalism is dead. The contributions [in this book] will convince you that federalism has evolved greatly and that it has a great deal of sticking power. The authors come to conflicting conclusions. But their writings convince me that we still do not fully understand the political robustness of federal arrangements. This volume is an important contribution to the effort to learn from America's partly national and partly federal experience."

—**John Ferejohn**, professor of law and politics,
New York University School of Law

"This excellent volume is rich in the history, theory, and contemporary practice of American federalism. A fascinating through line of many chapters involves American federalism's unsettled and hence regularly contested distribution of powers, which demands engagement from practitioners and highlights the importance of continual study by historians, economists, political scientists, and legal scholars alike. There's much inside to stimulate both new and continuing students of federalism, including longtime researchers."

—**Jeff Clemens**, associate professor of economics,
University of California–San Diego

"We're at a governance moment: the loci of policy are moving to state and local governments. We have here the guidance we need. *American Federalism Today* offers the how and why to manage the conflicts that now are so limiting to national policymaking. *American Federalism Today* is the book for the moment."

—**Robert P. Inman**, professor emeritus of finance, economics,
and public policy, University of Pennsylvania, and coauthor of *Democratic Federalism: The Economics, Politics, and Law of Federal Governance*

"This impressive volume studies US federalism from a variety of perspectives, including economics, political science, law, and history. It also includes comments from three innovative former governors about their own experiences—Mitch Daniels of Indiana, Jeb Bush of Florida, and Jerry Brown of California. As the essays in this volume make clear, American federalism has gone through many phases, so it cannot be understood from just one perspective. This is a volume that every scholar of federalism will want to read."

—**Barry R. Weingast**, Ward C. Krebs Family Professor
of political science, Stanford University

AMERICAN FEDERALISM TODAY

The Hoover Institution gratefully acknowledges the Koret Foundation for its significant support of this publication.

AMERICAN FEDERALISM TODAY

Perspectives on Political and Economic Governance

EDITED BY Michael J. Boskin

HOOVER INSTITUTION PRESS

STANFORD UNIVERSITY | STANFORD, CALIFORNIA

hoover.org

Hoover Institution Press Publication No. 737

Hoover Institution at Leland Stanford Junior University, Stanford, California 94305-6003

First printing 2024

30 29 28 27 26 25 24   7 6 5 4 3 2 1

Manufactured in the United States of America
Printed on acid-free, archival-quality paper

Library of Congress Cataloging-in-Publication Data
Names: Boskin, Michael J., editor. | Hoover Institution on War, Revolution, and Peace, organizer.
Title: American federalism today : perspectives on political and economic governance / edited by Michael J. Boskin.
Other titles: Hoover Institution Press publication ; 737.
Description: Stanford, California : Hoover Institution Press, Stanford University, 2024. | Series: Hoover Institution Press publication ; no. 737 | Proceedings of a conference held by the Hoover Institution in September 2023. | Includes bibliographical references and index. | Summary: "Expert scholars and practitioners examine the relationship between the US federal and state and local governments, in political theory and in practice, applied to current social, economic, and fiscal issues"– Provided by publisher.
Identifiers: LCCN 2024017418 (print) | LCCN 2024017419 (ebook) | ISBN 9780817926359 (cloth) | ISBN 9780817926366 (epub) | ISBN 9780817926380 (pdf)
Subjects: LCSH: Federal government–United States–Congresses. | Intergovernmental fiscal relations–United States–Congresses. | United States–Politics and government–Congresses. | LCGFT: Conference papers and proceedings.
Classification: LCC JK311 .A46 2024–(print) | LCC JK311 (ebook) | DDC 320.473–dc23/eng/20240515
LC record available at https://lccn.loc.gov/2024017418
LC ebook record available at https://lccn.loc.gov/2024017419

Contents

Foreword   ix
Condoleezza Rice

Preface   xi
Michael J. Boskin

Introduction   1
Michael J. Boskin

Part 1: Federalism Principles and Perspectives

1   Why States Rather Than a Single Consolidated Nation?
The Framers' View   9
Michael W. McConnell

    Discussion   32

2   Public Attitudes toward Federalism and the Scope
of National Power   33
Morris P. Fiorina and Alice Yiqian Wang

    Discussion   63

3   The Phases and Faces of Federalism   65
David M. Kennedy

Discussant Remarks and Discussion   73
Discussants: Thad Kousser and Daniel L. Rubinfeld

Part 2: The Current State of Federalism

4   The Budgetary Impact of the Abandonment of Federalism   83
     John F. Cogan

     Discussion   113

5   COVID Federalism   119
     David Brady, Jacob Jaffe, and Douglas Rivers

     Discussion   143

6   Recessions and Ratchets: Federal Funds and Public-Sector
     Employment   145
     Jonathan Rodden

Discussant Remarks and Discussion   171
Discussants: Daniel L. Rubinfeld and Thad Kousser

Part 3: Federalism in Key Areas of Policy

7   Some Evolving Issues in K–12 Education   179
     Eric A. Hanushek

     Discussion   203

8   Infrastructure in a Federal System   205
     Michael J. Boskin and Valentin Bolotnyy

9   Federalist System of Healthcare Financing in America   231
     Thomas MaCurdy and Jay Bhattacharya

     Discussion   286

10   When Are State Liabilities Federal Liabilities?
     Social Insurance and Federalism   291
     Joshua Rauh and Jillian Ludwig

11   Is the United States Still a Competitive Federal System?   321
     Paul E. Peterson and Carlos X. Lastra-Anadón

12   Monetary Aspects of, and Implications for, Federalism   347
     John B. Taylor

Discussant Remarks and Discussion   357
Discussants: Thomas Nechyba and Dennis Epple

Part 4: Practitioners' Perspectives

Governor Mitch Daniels, introduced by Paul E. Peterson   375

Governor Jeb Bush, introduced by Condoleezza Rice   383

Governor Jerry Brown, introduced by Michael J. Boskin   397

About the Editor   407

About the Conference Participants   409

Index   419

Foreword

The following is adapted from Dr. Rice's introductory remarks at the Hoover Institution's Federalism Conference, held September 15, 2023.

In September 2023, Dr. Michael J. Boskin and his colleagues put together an extraordinary conference on a topic of critical importance for the Hoover Institution: the state of federalism. The essential work of augmenting the study of federalism requires an attentive eye toward the challenges of this framework and potential solutions for its improvement.

I was recently in London and was asked a very interesting question by an interviewer, who happened to be Hoover's own Niall Ferguson. Niall asked, "What is it that people around the world do not get about the United States of America?" I replied, "The United States of America is more than Los Angeles, San Francisco, and New York. It's more than Washington, DC." And herein lies the genius of the American system. The framers of the Constitution thought it was awfully important to have most of the power in government reserved for the places that were closest to the people; and they acted on it by enumerating powers for the federal government while leaving all else under the purview of states or the people. As it turned out, it was actually hard to get the framers to stay in the capital that they had created between the swampland in Virginia and the swampland in Maryland, for they much preferred their state houses where they thought governing would really happen.

Since our founding, it has been in our DNA that the locus of activity and the real excellence of government should be at the state level. Over the years, the federal government, in size and in function, has grown. The writ of that growth originated from America's role as a global power and the need for a centralized bureaucracy. Consider national defense: it is infeasible to ask the opinion of every state in responding to a nuclear attack. So the presidency collected more and more power in the federal government, both at the expense of the other branches and to the detriment of the states. The need for states to cooperate with the Interstate Commerce Commission became a critical way to essentially compel cooperation between the states. One of the odd moments I experienced as secretary of state was finding myself signing an agreement between the State of North Dakota and the State of Montana. I asked why I was doing this, and my advisers responded, "Before there was the notion of interstate commerce, this was actually done as a matter of foreign affairs by the Secretary of State."

We have experienced an evolution from the framers' vision of the states as the locus for activity to an expanded role and the increasing encroachment of the federal government. The American people have more trust in the levels of government that are closer to them, where they feel that they have some control. Of course, federalism has experienced its share of setbacks, including the recent disjointed patchwork of COVID-19 policies across the country.

I remember going to work for George W. Bush, who had been the governor of Texas. When we arrived in Washington, he was both stunned and a little put out by the fact that he could not do what he had done in Texas, which was to call together the Democratic Speaker of the House and the Democratic Lieutenant Governor and "horse trade" for solutions to fix this or that problem. He learned very quickly that that was not how Washington, DC, worked, and it was a source of frustration. We find that some of the need for bipartisanship that we talk a lot about at the federal level is actually practiced at the state level as a matter of necessity. With the example of practitioners like Mitch Daniels, Jeb Bush, and Jerry Brown, hopefully, not only will we improve federalism and the ability of the states to perform, but we can also apply some of the lessons of federalism to the federal system.

Advancing the study of state and local governance has been a pillar of the Hoover Institution's research initiatives; the importance of this publication in meaningfully augmenting the work of federalism truly cannot be overstated.

Condoleezza Rice
Tad and Dianne Taube Director
Thomas and Barbara Stephenson Senior Fellow on Public Policy
Hoover Institution, Stanford, California

Preface

After many hours of discussion exploring our shared belief that strong and clear federalist principles, institutions, and policies had an important role to play in improving our prospects for the nation's future, George Shultz and I decided to launch a small Hoover project on federalism. We began the project a year or so before the arrival of COVID-19 and the subsequent lockdowns. They caused a two-year pause but also provided a timely and painful reminder of, indeed an experiment demonstrating, the importance of the relationships among the federal government, state and local governments, and the private sector.

Our goal was to bring together leading experts on the subject, thinkers and practitioners, to discuss, debate, and illuminate various aspects—legal, economic, historical, and political—of America's federal experiment. By doing so, we hoped to contribute to the understanding of federalism's strengths and weaknesses and the opportunities and challenges that it faces in the nation's political and economic governance.

I had noted in some previous writing that relationships between central and subnational governments seemed to be growing ever more strained. At one extreme were calls for secession. French-speaking Quebec had been quiet for a long period, but in many other areas there was more recent contention. The Scots demanded, and received, considerable devolution of authority from Westminster. While they have voted once not to secede from the United Kingdom, they periodically threaten to conduct another referendum. In Spain, Catalonia attempted to secede, but the movement was quashed and its leaders arrested, although a recent political deal will grant them amnesty. Venice and the Veneto have raised secession threats in Italy. And in the process of seceding from the European Union, a supranational institution, Brexit revealed many analogous tensions.

In the United States, there are periodic calls to break up the state of California into two to six separate states (a movement sometimes referred to as Calexit); and seven eastern Oregon counties, unhappy with governance from Salem, want to leave and become part of Idaho. And at an apparent dramatically increasing rate over the course of the last three federal administrations, attorneys general of states controlled by the other dominant political party than the one in the White House have repeatedly sued the federal government over its policies. A prime current example is a bitter fight over the Biden administration's failure to secure the southern border, with border states taking things into their own hands.

While George's passing soon after his one-hundredth birthday prevented him from seeing the Hoover project on federalism to its completion, his imprint on it is immense. After promising him two weeks before his passing that I would bring it home, I consider the September 2023 conference and the essays and presentations by prominent experts in this volume as very much a joint product of our collaboration. That imprint, as with the innumerable other remarkable contributions he made in government, business, and academe, endures and hopefully shines in these pages.

*   *   *

A book such as this does not get into print—and the conference upon which these papers and presentations are based does not occur, let alone run smoothly—without the diligence of many talented people. I would like to especially acknowledge the participants whose papers and presentations contributed to a spirited and insightful series of discussions.

The staff at Hoover covered every detail of the conference and publication, from facilities and catering to sound, videoconferencing connectivity, substantive note-taking, audiovisual recording, transcription, copyediting, and book production, all superbly. Included in alphabetical order are: Barbara Arellano, David Fedor, Julie Gontijo, Joel Gonzalez, Kristin Halle (Culinary Eye Catering), Danica Michels Hodge, Lisa Kohara, Alison Law, Abel Mendoza II, Sharyn Nantuna, and Janet Smith. I would also like to thank Beverly Michaels for her superb copyediting expertise, proofreader Susan Richmond, and Emily Weigel for the engaging cover design. Special thanks to my executive, research, and administrative assistants, Kelli Nicholas, Garrett Te Kolste, and Jennie Tomasino, who kept the project—and me—on track, with grace.

Michael J. Boskin
Stanford, California

Introduction

Michael J. Boskin

Long an exemplar of successful political and economic governance, democratic capitalism is facing renewed critiques and challenges, both internal and external. Externally, it is argued that democratic capitalism is in decline, sclerotic, unable to make important decisions quickly enough given internal squabbling and excessive focus on material reward. The argument continues that it will be replaced by a more authoritarian state-directed system, sometimes labeled state capitalism.

Internally, battles have emerged over the legitimacy of democratic capitalism, particularly the United States' constitutional republic and its institutions. Calls to pack the Supreme Court, add new states to get more senators, and abolish the Electoral College have risen in frequency and volume.

America's system of governance differs from most advanced democratic capitalist societies, which rely primarily on a parliamentary system with fewer internal checks and balances. The American system, founded in rebellion against the British monarchy, created an intricate series of institutions designed to balance various interests. Equal representation in the Senate combined with proportional representation in the House; a constitution with separation of powers among the executive, legislative, and judicial branches; and the Tenth Amendment expressly limiting the scope of federal powers.

America relies relatively more heavily on subnational governments than most other nations, and the scale and scope of the federal government has grown over time. The debates about the proper role of governmental versus private and, within governmental, national versus state and local, have been among the most defining of the American experience, from ratification of the Constitution through the Civil War and responses to World War I, the Great Depression, World War II, and beyond. Thus, the subject of federalism lies at the core of American economic and political governance.

The distinction as to what is federal and what is subnational contains many nuances. For example, many federal government programs are executed by sending funds to state and local governments to provide services or to disburse; the federal government imposes many regulations and mandates on state and local governments; and states are constantly suing the federal government seeking judicial relief from federal diktats.

The papers, presentations, and discussions in this volume, individually and collectively, from some of the nation's most eminent scholars and practitioners, provide perspectives on and analysis of American federalism, and prescriptions and policies to improve it.

Legal scholar Michael W. McConnell leads off by discussing why the framers chose a partly national, partly federal structure for the new nation. As McConnell notes, "This contemplated a genuinely national government, with representation from the people (and not just the states) and power to enforce its own laws through a vigorous executive and an independent judiciary, but the states would retain political autonomy and authority over the issues most significant to ordinary life. The powers of this national government would be confined to certain enumerated objects, primarily foreign affairs and interstate commerce. This was an innovation; there were no precedents in world history for such a mixed system."

Political scientists Morris P. Fiorina and Alice Yiqian Wang trace historical and contemporary trends in public opinion about federalism and the scope of national power. They document that public attitudes toward federalism respond to partisan orientations and perceptions of changes in the scope of federal power. They uncover evidence that the 2020 COVID-19 pandemic shifted public attitudes toward circumscribing the scope of national power.

Historian David M. Kennedy recasts the conventional historical wisdom of "American federalism as a story of successive phases that added up to a cumulative advance of central at the expense of peripheral power." Kennedy concludes that it is historically more accurate to view "the coevolution of the two that has amplified the overall presence of governments (plural) in many sectors of American life. Indeed, federal power has often been the factor driving the scope and scale of state governments."

Economist John F. Cogan traces this evolution through the spending powers of the federal government. He concludes that the originally intended, and perhaps still perceived, sharp division between federal and state government responsibilities no longer exists. "Indeed, the breadth of federal spending is so large that it is hard to think of a state or local government activity that isn't also financed by the federal government." He describes vigorous debate in the early history of the republic, which generally adhered to Madison's view of limiting federal spending. He notes the barrier separating state and local activities from federal spending started to fray when Congress funded internal improvements within state boundaries. The federal budget remained a small percentage of GDP (gross domestic product) and federal budgets were generally balanced, at least over time, with surpluses reducing debt accumulated in wartime and economic downturn. Shortly before World War I, state and local spending in the aggregate exceeded federal spending and the total was modest. Cogan traces the rising share of federal outlays on what were traditional state and local activities from the 1950s to 2019, a share that more than tripled. Among several interesting counterfactual experiments he describes "what the budget would have looked like if all non–social insurance revenues were applied to financing Madison budget expenditures." Madison budget expenditures would have declined from 13 percent to 6 percent of GDP, and the federal government would have had budget surpluses except during wartime and recessions, patterns similar to the early decades of the republic. He observes that while the Constitution gave Congress the power of the purse, presidents have played an influential role in either restraining or expanding federal spending.

Political scientists David Brady, Jacob Jaffe, and Douglas Rivers utilize a series of YouGov polls from March to October of 2020, the early months of the COVID-19 pandemic lockdown and recession, to answer a series of questions, including how much partisanship affected trust in government, whether it was different across different levels of government, and did it seem to respond to the competence of government. They conclude that measurable performance, not just partisanship, played a role in evaluating the competence of the federal government and that partisans were "much more likely to approve of government performance where the relevant level of government was controlled by a copartisan."

Political scientist Jonathan Rodden studies the effect of federal funds on public-sector employment by examining the ratcheting up of federal support for states with each recession. He documents that "recessions are associated with significant increases in reliance on intergovernmental transfers among state governments, but declining aid from states to local governments." The effect has been particularly pronounced in large states.

Economist Eric A. Hanushek details America's complex governance and fiscal structure for K–12 education. While the states predominate, local districts on average "generate an equal amount of funding to the state," but "the details of the state-local split vary dramatically across the states." Federal funds focus primarily on poor children and those with special needs. He documents the relatively poor performance of US schools in terms of achievement, and he also concludes by raising the question of the relative roles of parents and school districts. "Over time, various types of school choice have expanded, signaling an increased role of parents. At the same time, the number of school districts has declined precipitously, leading to larger school districts that place decision making farther from individual parents."

Economists Michael J. Boskin and Valentin Bolotnyy discuss the role of infrastructure in the federal system. They inventory America's vast array of types of infrastructure, where "sometimes ownership is public, sometimes it's private, and sometimes it's something in between." With the impending large infusion of additional federal infrastructure spending, they lay out principles that would enable higher social returns from the spending. These include establishing greater capabilities and incentives for rigorous, nonpolitical, cost-benefit analysis; financing through user fees wherever possible; planning for technological change; and focusing federal policy on proper incentives. They debunk the idea that federal infrastructure spending is effective short-run economic stimulus and discuss the poor incentives and fiscal crosshauling in infrastructure matching grants.

Economists Thomas MaCurdy and Jay Bhattacharya analyze the complex federalist system of healthcare financing. They provide a comprehensive overview of healthcare funding and insurance, the growth of government healthcare financing, the large and growing role of healthcare financing in the federal budget, and policy options for addressing the impending fiscal crisis in public financing of healthcare. They conclude that while there are valuable opportunities to increase consumer-directed healthcare—competitive bidding in Medicare, state Medicaid reform, and allowing states greater flexibility in regulating private health insurance—the funding gap will remain immense unless more radical reforms limiting spending are adopted.

Economists Joshua Rauh and Jillian Ludwig analyze "the increasing federal financing of state-run programs," with special reference to unemployment insurance and Medicaid. They explore whether there has been "greater implicit centralization of state and local government debt and unfunded pension liabilities." They conclude that "many state liabilities have become de facto federal liabilities." They analyze not only longer-term trends, but the effects of crises, especially the 2008–9 global financial crisis and the

COVID-19 pandemic, during which the federal government's role expanded dramatically as state and local systems came under financial pressure.

Political scientists Paul E. Peterson and Carlos X. Lastra-Anadón analyze the system of competitive federalism. Competition among state and local governments can generate greater efficiency by providing services, taxation, and regulation according to local preferences, while redistribution is carried out by the federal government. Analyzing data over three decades, they show that this division of responsibilities remains more or less intact, but since 2021, "changes in the intergovernmental system," including enlarged grant programs, "posed a challenge to the structure of competitive federalism."

Economist John B. Taylor discusses macroeconomic aspects of, and implications for, federalism. While at first glance federalism seems to be primarily about microeconomics, the macroeconomic framework against which the roles and responsibilities, the taxes and spending, the deficits and debt of subnational governments play out is immensely important. For example, stronger economic growth will increase revenues and decrease the demand for some social programs such as unemployment insurance. Inflation and monetary policy influence interest rates, including that paid on state and municipal bonds. Importantly, the macroeconomy and monetary policy affect the federal budget and the availability and desirability of federal grants to state and local governments. Against this conceptual backdrop, Taylor shows the implications of a preferred path to normalization of monetary and fiscal policy, especially because the federal budget will require considerable consolidation in future years due to unsustainable deficits and debt levels and additional pressures for funding Social Security, Medicare, and defense. How fiscal and monetary normalization occurs will have dramatic impacts on the future of state and local budgets and federalism.

These essays are buttressed by the insights and critiques of four prominent economists and political scientists strongly versed in the subject of federalism: Daniel L. Rubinfeld, Thad Kousser, Dennis Epple, and Thomas Nechyba, and by the discussion elicited by the papers and their commentary.

Finally, the collection of essays and insights is complemented by presentations by, and discussions with, three of the nation's most seasoned and respected practitioners in our federal system. Former governors Mitch Daniels of Indiana, Jeb Bush of Florida, and Jerry Brown of California relay their insights, achievements, and frustrations in dealing with federal-state and state-local relations in their time as governor and beyond. With their experience spanning states from different regions, with different political orientations (Florida was a swing state when Bush was governor), the governors reveal real-world factors influencing decision making in areas from education to infrastructure to taxation and more. They also bring to light limitations on, and avenues for strengthening, American federalism.

The confluence of ideas and action represented in the essays and presentations in this volume constitute a valuable multidisciplinary resource for all who seek to understand, evaluate, and improve American federalism and the important role it has played, and continues to play, in America's economic and political governance.

Part 1

Federalism Principles and Perspectives

1

Why States Rather Than a Single Consolidated Nation? The Framers' View

Michael W. McConnell

When the delegates to the Constitutional Convention gathered in Philadelphia in the summer of 1787, they faced three broad choices regarding the relation of the states to the Union. First, they could create a single consolidated nation along the lines of England or France—perhaps preserving existing state governments as administrative units, perhaps breaking them up and drawing new boundaries of more equal dimensions. Only a few delegates openly supported this approach, most notably Alexander Hamilton and George Read of Delaware, though Anti-Federalists typically claimed that the Constitution came as close to a consolidated nation-state as the delegates dared.

Second, they could stick with a confederation, in which states are the primary units of government. States would each send delegates to a central congress, which would have authority only over issues of national concern, such as foreign affairs, war, and international and foreign commerce—and even then would depend on the states to enforce national decisions. This was the system that prevailed under the Articles of Confederation and had been recommended by the sage Montesquieu. A strong minority of the delegates wished to preserve the basic structure of the Articles government, while giving the union additional powers and a potent executive branch. The New Jersey Plan was the most explicit attempt to follow this model.

The delegates devised a third option, described by James Madison as "partly national, partly federal." This contemplated a genuinely national government, with representation from the people (and not just the states) and power to enforce its own laws through a vigorous executive and an independent judiciary, but the states would retain political autonomy and authority over the issues most significant to ordinary life. The powers of this national government would be confined to certain enumerated objects, primarily foreign affairs and interstate commerce. This was an innovation; there were no precedents in world history for such a mixed system. As Madison described it in *The Federalist*, No. 45:

> The powers delegated by the proposed Constitution to the federal government, are few and defined. Those which are to remain in the State governments are numerous and indefinite. The former will be exercised principally on external objects, as war, peace, negotiation, and foreign commerce; with which last the power of taxation will, for the most part, be connected. The powers reserved to the several States will extend to all the objects which, in the ordinary course of affairs, concern the lives, liberties, and properties of the people, and the internal order, improvement, and prosperity of the State.[1]

The fierce struggle over ratification centered on these questions, forcing both supporters and opponents of the proposed Constitution to think more deeply than ever before about what federalism is for. As Madison pointedly inquired in *Federalist* 45:

> If . . . the Union be essential to the happiness of the people of America, is it not preposterous to urge as an objection . . . that such a government may derogate from the importance of the governments of the individual States? Was, then, the American Revolution effected, was the American Confederacy formed, was the precious blood of thousands spilt, and the hard-earned substance of millions lavished, not that the people of America should enjoy peace, liberty, and safety, but that the government of the individual States, that particular municipal establishments, might enjoy a certain extent of power and be arrayed with certain dignities and attributes of sovereignty?[2]

Madison's question was directed to "adversaries to the plan of the convention."[3] It might as aptly be directed to the adversaries of our present centralized government: Why forego national measures, thought to promote the well-being of the people, merely because they intrude upon the "certain extent of power" traditionally reserved to the governments of the individual States? Why do we care about federalism?

The "natural attachment" of the people in 1787 to their States was powerful—far more so than today. But the framers of the federalist system were not content to rest on natural attachments alone. They offered practical and theoretical arguments about how the new system of dual sovereignty would promote three complementary objectives: (1) "to secure the public good," (2) to protect "private rights," and (3) "to preserve the spirit and form of popular government." Achievement of these ends, according to Madison, was the "great object" of the Constitution.[4] To understand the founders' design we must look again at those arguments—not just in the mouths of the Federalists, who prevailed, but of the Anti-Federalists, too. As the people of the twenty-first century, we must evaluate these arguments in light of modern experience and knowledge about political decision making. Many of the arguments of 1787 stand up remarkably well, but others do not.

To "Secure the Public Good"

Rejecting both pure confederation and consolidation, the "Federal Farmer" (a particularly able and influential Anti-Federalist pamphleteer) argued that a "partial consolidation" is the only system "that can secure the freedom and happiness of this people." He reasoned that "one government and general legislation alone, never can extend equal benefits to all parts of the United States: Different laws, customs, and opinions exist in the different states, which by a uniform system of laws would be unreasonably invaded."[5] Three important advantages of decentralized decision making emerge from an examination of the founders' arguments and the modern literature. First, decentralized decision making is better able to reflect the diversity of interests and preferences of individuals in different parts of the nation. Second, allocation of decision making authority to a level of government no larger than necessary will prevent mutually disadvantageous attempts by communities to take advantage of their neighbors. And third, decentralization allows for innovation and competition in government.

Responsiveness to Diverse Interests and Preferences

The first, and most axiomatic, advantage of decentralized government is that local laws can be adapted to local conditions and tastes, while a national government must take a uniform approach. One size does not fit all. So long as preferences for government policies are unevenly distributed among the various localities, more people can be satisfied by decentralized decision making than by a single national authority. This was well understood by the founding generation. A noted pamphleteer, "The Impartial Examiner," put the point this way: "For being different societies, though blended together in legislation, and having as different interests; no uniform rule for the whole seems to be practicable."[6]

For simplicity's sake, let us imagine a hypothetical model of two states, with equal populations of 100 each. Assume further that 70 percent of State A, and only 40 percent of State B, wish to ban sports betting. The others are opposed. If the decision is made on a national basis by a majority rule, sports betting will be banned; 110 people will be pleased and 90 displeased. If a separate decision is made by majorities in each state, the rule will be different in the two states; 130 will be pleased and only 70 displeased. By allocating decision-making discretion to the local level, we increase social satisfaction. The level of satisfaction will be still greater if some gamblers in State A decide to move to State B, and some antigamblers in State B decide to move to State A.[7] In the absence of economies of scale in government services,[8] significant externalities,[9] or compelling arguments from justice, this is a powerful reason to prefer decentralized government. States are preferable governing units to the federal government, and local government to states. Modern public choice theory provides strong support for the framers' insight on this point.

Destructive Competition for the Benefits of Government

A second consideration in designing a federal structure is more equivocal. The unit of decision making must be large enough so that decisions reflect the full costs and benefits, but small enough that destructive competition for the benefits of central government action is minimized. In economic language, this is the problem of externalities.[10]

Externalities present the principal argument for centralized government: If the costs of government action are borne by the citizens of State C, but the benefits are shared by the citizens of States D, E, and F, State C will be unwilling to expend the level of resources commensurate with the full social benefit of the action.[11] This was the argument in *Federalist* 25 for national control of defense.[12] Because a Minuteman III missile in Pennsylvania will deter a Russian or Chinese attack on Connecticut and North Carolina as well as Pennsylvania, optimal levels of investment in Minutemans require national decisions and national taxes. Similarly, because expenditures on water pollution reduction in Kentucky will benefit riparian zones all the way to New Orleans, it makes sense to regionalize or nationalize decisions about water pollution regulation and treatment. Thus, as James Wilson explained to the Pennsylvania ratifying convention, "Whatever the object of government extends, in its operation, *beyond the bounds* of a particular state, should be considered as belonging to the government of the United States."[13]

That significant external effects of this sort provide justification for national decisions is well understood—hence federal funding of defense, interstate highways, national parks, and medical research; and federal regulation of interstate commerce, pollution, and national labor markets. It is less well understood that nationalizing decisions where the impact is predominantly local has an opposite effect. If states can obtain federal funding for projects of predominantly local benefit, they will not care if total cost exceeds total benefit; the cost is borne by others. The result is a "tragedy of the commons" for Treasury funds.[14] The framers' awareness that ill consequences flow as much from excessive as from insufficient centralization is fundamental to their insistence on enumerating and thus limiting the powers of the federal government. Hence, the other half of Wilson's explanation: "Whatever object of government is confined in its operation and effect, *within the bounds* of a particular State, should be considered as belonging to the government of that State."[15] This stands in marked contrast to the modern tendency to resolve doubts in favor of federal control. Washington provided about $3.5 billion in seed money for California's ill-fated high-speed rail project, an entirely intrastate project, which Californians eagerly accepted. Now that cost estimates have soared above $128 billion, all or most to come from state revenues, Californians have soured on the project.[16] If the federal government continued to foot the bill, no doubt the state would happily continue it, no matter what the cost.

Nobel laureate James Buchanan demonstrated that centralized decision making about projects of localized impact will result in excessive spending—excessive meaning more than any of the communities involved would freely choose if they bore both costs and benefits.[17] Each community would be better off if they could agree in advance (as they thought they did in the Constitution) to confine federal attention to issues of predominantly interstate consequence.

Article I, § 8, clause 1 of the Constitution grants Congress the power "to lay and collect Taxes, Duties, Imposts and Excises, to pay the Debts and provide for the common Defense and general Welfare of the United States." The meaning of this provision was the subject of a significant debate between Madison and Hamilton. Madison argued that spending for the "general welfare" is confined to spending for purposes elsewhere enumerated in the Constitution.[18] Hamilton articulated a more functionally valuable interpretation: "The object to which an appropriation of money is . . . made [must] be *General* and not *local*; its operation extending in fact, or by possibility, throughout the Union, and not being confined to a particular spot."[19] This construction is a persuasive reading of the term "general welfare" (the word "general" is frequently used in the debates to signify "national"[20]), and it guards against precisely the fiscal tragedy of the commons discussed above. Early debates in Congress, such as that over a proposal to provide $15,000 for the relief of survivors of a fire in Savannah, Georgia, support Hamilton's view that the constitutional line was understood to be drawn between objects of a predominantly local, as opposed to a general or national, impact.[21]

The point is general. It applies to lawmaking and regulation no less than to taxing and spending. A major effect of regulation is to shift burdens from one region or locality to another. Consider California's ban on the sale of pork from pigs raised in conditions thought (by Californians) to be inhumane.[22] Californians get to bask in the glow of their own superior morality, while farmers and consumers in other states bear the vast majority of the cost. This is an example of one state effectively regulating a national market. More common is the example of the federal government regulating local markets in ways that shift costs and benefits among regions. Consider the federal government's decision to combat air pollution by requiring coal-burning plants to use the best available technology rather than by directly regulating the amount of sulfur-oxide emissions. The effect was to favor eastern producers of "dirty coal" over western producers of lower sulfur-oxide coal, shifting costs from East to West and making pollution reduction more expensive for everyone.[23] Federal milk marketing orders, in the name of protecting "orderly markets," increase the price of milk to consumers for the benefit of higher-cost producers outside of the Midwest.[24]

Taxation, too, can produce a scramble by representatives of politically powerful states to find ways to inflict the tax burden to taxpayers of other states. As one Anti-Federalist writer noted, a single national mode of taxation will result in each state endeavoring "to raise a revenue by such means, as may appear least injurious to its own interest."[25] To give one example: Congress's decision, recently largely reversed, to allow taxpayers to deduct state and local taxes from their income for purposes of federal income benefited not just wealthy taxpayers but those from high-taxing states, mostly controlled by Democrats. Nearly a third of the benefit flowed to voters in California and New York.[26] Tariffs are notoriously manipulable in these ways.

These are just a few examples of the deleterious consequences that predictably occur when there is a mismatch between the locus of costs and benefits.

Innovation and Competition in Government

A final reason why federalism may advance the public good is that state and local governmental units will have greater opportunity and incentive to pioneer useful changes.[27] Justice Louis Brandeis put the point most famously: "It is one of the happy incidents of the federal system that a single courageous State may, if its citizens choose, serve as a laboratory; and try novel social and economic experiments without risk to the rest of the country."[28] A consolidated national government has all the drawbacks of a monopoly: it stifles choice and lacks the goad of competition.

Lower levels of government are more likely to depart from established consensus simply because they are smaller and more numerous. Elementary statistical theory holds that a greater number of independent observations will produce more instances of deviation from the mean. It follows that a smaller unit of government is more likely to have a population with preferences that depart from that of the national majority. If innovation is desirable, it follows that decentralization is desirable.[29]

Perhaps more important is that smaller units of government have an incentive, beyond the mere political process, to adopt popular policies. If a community can attract additional taxpayers, each citizen's share of the overhead costs of government is proportionately reduced. Since people are better able to move among states or communities than to emigrate from the United States, competition among governments for taxpayers will be far stronger at the state and local than at the federal level. Since most people are taxpayers, this means that there is a powerful incentive for decentralized governments to make things better for most people. In particular, the desire to attract taxpayers and jobs will promote policies of economic growth and expansion. This observation is most closely associated with the economist Charles Tiebout, and is usually called "the Tiebout effect."[30]

To be sure, the results of competition among states and localities will not always be salutary. State-by-state determination of the laws of incorporation likely results in the most efficient forms of corporate organization,[31] but state-by-state determination of the law of products liability seems to have created a liability monster. This is because each state can benefit in-state plaintiffs by more generous liability rules, the costs being exported to largely out-of-state defendants; while no state can do much to protect its in-state manufacturers from suits by plaintiffs in the other states. Thus, competition among the states in this arena leads to one-sidedly pro-plaintiff rules of law.[32]

The most important example of this phenomenon is the effect of state-by-state competition on welfare and other redistributive policies. In most cases, immigration of investment and of middle-to-upper-income persons is perceived as desirable, while immigration of persons dependent on public assistance is viewed as a drain on a community's finances. Yet generous welfare benefits paid by higher taxes will lead the rich to leave and the poor to come. This creates an incentive, other things being equal, against redistributive policies. Indeed, it can be shown that the level of redistribution in a decentralized system is likely to be lower even if there is virtually unanimous agreement among the citizens that higher levels would be desirable.[33] This is an instance of the free rider problem: even if every member of the community would be willing to vote for higher welfare benefits, it would be in the interest of each to leave the burden of paying for the program to others. Presumably, that is why advocates of a more generous social safety net tend to push for expansion of federal programs, while advocates of the opposite policy tend to favor state-oriented solutions.

Thus, the competition among states has an uncertain effect: often salutary but sometimes destructive. There are races to the bottom as well as races to the top. And it is often impossible to know which is which; this will depend on substantive policy preferences.

To Protect "Private Rights"

At the time of the founding, defenders of state sovereignty most commonly stressed a second argument: that state and local governments are better protectors of liberty. Patrick Henry went to the heart of the matter when he told the Virginia ratifying convention:

> You are not to inquire how your trade may be increased, nor how you are to become a great and powerful people, but how your liberties can be secured; for liberty ought to be the direct end of your Government.[34]

The most eloquent of the opponents of the Constitution, Henry declared that in the "alarming transition, from a Confederacy to a consolidated

Government," the "rights and privileges" of Americans were "endangered."[35] He was far from alone in this fear.[36]

Madison's most enduring intellectual contribution to the debate over rati-fication is his challenging argument that individual liberties, such as property rights and freedom of religion, are better protected at the national than the state level. The argument, presented principally in *Federalist* 10,[37] is familiar to all:

> If a faction consists of less than a majority, relief is supplied by the republican principle, which enables the majority to defeat its sinis-ter views by regular vote. It may clog the administration, it may con-vulse the society; but it will be unable to execute and mask its violence under the forms of the Constitution. When a majority is included in a faction, the form of popular government, on the other hand, enables it to sacrifice to its ruling passion or interest both the public good and the rights of other citizens.[38]

Madison's argument, greatly simplified, is that the most serious threat to individual liberty is the tyranny of a majority faction. Since any given faction is more likely to be concentrated in a particular locality, and to be no more than a small minority in the nation as a whole, it follows that factional tyr-anny is more likely in the state legislatures than in the Congress of the United States. This argument is supplemented by others, based on the "proper struc-ture of the Union"[39]—deliberative representation, separation of powers, and checks and balances—that also suggest that the federal government is a supe-rior protector of rights. Here I shall concentrate on the argument from the "extent . . . of the Union." Madison's argument blunted the Anti-Federalists' appeal to state sovereignty as the guarantor of liberty. It was, however, only partially successful. Why?

Madison's theory gains support from robust modern social science evi-dence that homogeneous groups will tend to adopt policies more radical than those that individual members of the groups previously supported. Anyone who has been in a one-sided political gathering (such as a faculty meeting) will recognize the phenomenon. The best empirical evidence comes from studies of three-member courts. Courts with three members of the same party will reach more radical results; even a single member from the opposing party mutes this effect.[40] One-party states tend to go to unreason-able extremes. Certain states (California, Mississippi) are overwhelmingly dominated by one political party. The United States as a whole is very closely divided. Hence, the enduring plausibility of Madison's thesis. If we are concerned about the rights of politically unpopular minorities, we should locate rights protection at the national level.

Public choice theory has, however, cast some doubt on elements of Madison's theory. In particular, Madison's assumption that the possibility of minority tyranny is neutralized by majority vote requirements and that minority factions are inherently vulnerable to majority tyranny is undermined by studies showing that a small, cohesive faction intensely interested in a particular outcome can exercise disproportionate influence in the political arena.[41] If these theories are correct, Madison underestimated both the dangers of minority rule and the defensive resources of minority groups.

Moreover, some observers have suggested that the conditions of modern federal politics—especially the balkanized, issue-oriented conjunction of bureaucratic agencies and committee staffs—is especially susceptible to factional politics. Political scientist Keith Whittington thus argues that decentralization may be preferred because federal politicians are too responsive to special interest groups—the modern equivalent of Madison's "factions."[42]

But even taking Madison's fundamental insight as correct—and surely it has much to commend it—the argument on its own terms cautions against total centralization of authority in Washington. It points instead to a hybrid system in which states retain a major role in the protection of individual liberties. There are three basic reasons.

Liberty through Mobility

Madison's argument demonstrates that factional oppression is more likely to occur in the smaller, more homogeneous jurisdictions of individual states. But it does not deny that oppression at the federal level, when it occurs, is more dangerous. The lesser likelihood must be balanced against the greater magnitude of the danger. The main reason oppression at the federal level is more dangerous is that it is more difficult to escape. If a single state chooses, for example, to prohibit marijuana, a person wishing to indulge a taste for marijuana could move to other states where his or her desires can be fulfilled. Similarly, a person with an aversion to the culture of marijuana can move the other direction. It is harder to escape laws at the federal level because international migration is harder and more costly than interstate.[43] We are seeing this effect in the case of abortion after the Supreme Court's decision in *Dobbs*, returning legislative authority over the divisive issue of abortion to the states. (Unlike most such examples, the abortion example only goes one way because fetuses in pro-abortion states are unable to flee to more protective jurisdictions.)

Recognition of this feature of decentralized decision making does not depend on any particular ideological understanding of the content of "liberty." All it takes is policy diversity, which America has in spades. Some may move to avoid high taxes, some to avoid anti-transgender laws, some to escape coercion to join a union, some to be eligible for welfare, some to be able to carry guns, some to get protection from crime, some to live under more sensible pandemic regulations (whatever those may be), some to find freedom to express themselves, some to get an abortion. If a particular policy matters enough, people will migrate to states that they find more congenial. The liberty that is protected by federalism is not the liberty of the apodictic solution, but the liberty that comes from diversity coupled with mobility. If these policies were set at the national level, there would be nowhere to move. Except maybe Australia.

Self-Interested Government

Madison pointed out that there are two different and distinct dangers inherent in republican government: the "oppression of [the] . . . rulers" and the "injustice" of "one part of the society against . . . the other part."[44] The first concern is that government officials will rule in their own interests instead of the interests of the people. The second is that some persons, organized in factions, will use the governmental powers to oppress others. Significantly, while Madison argued that the danger of factions is best met at the federal level (for the reasons familiar from *Federalist* 10), he conceded that the danger of self-interested representation is best tackled at the state level. "As in too small a sphere oppressive combinations may be too easily formed against the weaker party; so in too extensive a one, a defensive concert may be rendered too difficult against the oppression of those entrusted with the administration."[45] Consequently, while powers most likely to be abused for factional advantage ought to be vested in the federal government, powers that are most likely to be abused by self-aggrandizing officials should be left in the states, where direct popular control is ostensibly stronger.

This insight strikes this author as more questionable. As an abstract proposition, it is hard to know where the danger of entrenched, unrepresentative rule is worst. The idea of a "deep state" is likely exaggerated and to a degree paranoid, but it is hard to deny that the federal bureaucracy has its own interests and commitments, which are persistent over time and largely impervious to elections. On the other hand, most big cities have been in the grip of one-party rule for decades. Local journalism, and with it the likelihood of popular accountability for city governments, has atrophied. Particular ideological and economic factions seem to dominate at both levels. Which are worse? (It is possible that states are the sweet spot: large enough to have diverse interests, but small enough to be responsive to voters. State governors tend to be the most popular elected officials.)

Diffusion of Power

Madison himself did not view his argument as establishing the superiority of a consolidated national government; rather he presented his famous arguments about the tyranny of factions in favor of the intermediate, federalist solution of dual sovereignty. In *Federalist* 51, he underscored that "the rights of the people" are best protected in a system in which "two distinct governments," federal and state, "will control each other."[46] The diffusion of power, in and of itself, is protective of liberty. In Alexis de Tocqueville's evocative words, "Municipal bodies and county administrations are like so many hidden reefs retarding or dividing the flood of the popular will."[47]

That the framers and ratifiers of the Constitution were not wholly persuaded that individual liberties are safer in the hands of the central government is evident from their provision of explicit protections for certain cherished liberties in the Bill of Rights—freedom of speech and religion, the right of compensation for takings of property, due process of law, criminal procedure protections, and so forth. For example, if Madison's theory of factions is correct, it suggests that governmental authority over religion is more safely lodged in the federal government, where the multiplicity of religious sects will guarantee against oppression, than in the states, where a single religious denomination often enjoys majority support. Indeed, Madison used the example of religious sects to demonstrate his point in *Federalist* 10 and 51.[48]

The actual treatment of individual rights in the Constitution is, however, the opposite. State authority over basic liberties, including freedom of religion, was left intact. Madison proposed an amendment that "No State shall violate the equal right of conscience,"[49] even commenting that this (along with speech, press, and jury trial rights against the states) was "the most valuable" of his proposed amendments to the Constitution.[50] Notwithstanding his plea, the proposal was rejected by the Senate.[51] By contrast, the federal government was forbidden to pass any law "*respecting* an establishment of religion"—that is, either establishing or disestablishing a religion—or prohibiting the "free exercise thereof."[52] The same was true of the other rights listed in the Bill of Rights. The founders thus opted for a "states' rights" approach to individual liberty; it left decisions "respecting" the establishment of religion and other freedoms almost wholly to the states.[53]

This decision was understandable, even if contrary to Madisonian theory. While it was more likely that individual states would erect a religious establishment (indeed, at that time, six of the thirteen states had an establishment of some sort), a national establishment would have been far more threatening to religious liberty. Religious dissenters were free to travel to more tolerant states, and did; moreover, the example of the more tolerant states generated pressure on the more restrictive states to modify their policies. By 1834, the last state establishment had been repealed. A national establishment would have been far more difficult to eradicate. Moreover, religious minorities are more likely to have influence in an individual state where they are concentrated, and thus more likely to have their rights respected, than at the national level. As "Philadelphiensis" said of Quakers who feared the loss of their religious exemption from compulsory military service if control over the military were vested in Congress instead of the state legislature: "Their influence in the state of Pennsylvania is fully sufficient to save them from suffering very materially on this account; but in the great vortex of the whole continent it can have no weight."[54]

The religious freedom example illustrates that, right or wrong, the framers of the Constitution and Bill of Rights believed that state governments were, in some vital respects, safer repositories of power over individual liberties than the federal government. It is thus no accident that the police power—the protection of public health, safety, welfare, and morals—was left to the states, with the federal government entrusted with less sensitive powers like those over interstate and foreign commerce. Given the diversity of views about issues of morality, and the potential for oppression, it is natural that lovers of liberty would be inclined toward decentralized decision making.

At this point, an important qualification is in order. The arguments from the "public good" and from "private rights" make sense only if one presupposes that the decision in question is appropriate to democratic decision making at *some* level, be it state or federal. Some issues are so fundamental to basic justice that they must be taken out of majoritarian control altogether. This is why both state and federal governments are prohibited, for example, from passing ex post facto laws and bills of attainder.[55] These issues are thus subject to a single national rule; the reason, however, has nothing to do with federalism. Federalism is a system for allocation of democratic decision making power. For those few but important matters on which democracy itself cannot be trusted, neither the public good nor the private rights argument for state autonomy can hold sway.

Even as to compelling matters of justice, however, federalism remains important as a tactical consideration, at least until a just national consensus emerges. Prior to a national majority against slavery, abolitionists would prefer state-by-state decision making, since there would be at least some free states. Upon emergence of an anti-slavery national majority, abolitionists would prefer national legislative power. Once a substantial national consensus developed on the ashes of the Civil War—manifested in two-thirds of both Houses of Congress and three-quarters of the states—it became time to move all authority over the issue to the national level. These judgments would not be principled decisions about federalism; they would be tactical judgments about abolitionism.

To Preserve "the Spirit and Form of Popular Government"

It was an article of faith among many framers that republicanism could survive only in a small jurisdiction. As stated by the prominent Anti-Federalist essayist, Brutus, "a free republic cannot succeed over a country of such immense extent, containing such a number of inhabitants, and these increasing in such rapid progression as that of the whole United States."[56] They believed consolidated national government would lead to oligarchic or despotic rule. Their reasons may be reduced to three major themes: (1) enforcement of laws, (2) nature of representation, and (3) cultivation of public spiritedness.

Enforcement of Laws

Obedience to the law can arise from two different sources: fear of punishment and voluntary compliance. A republican government, which has a minimal coercive apparatus, must rely predominantly upon the latter. As Brutus explained, in a free republic "the government must rest for its support upon the confidence and respect which the people have for their government and laws."[57] To the advocates of decentralized government, this necessarily implied that the units of government must be small and close to the people. "The confidence which the people have in their rulers, in a free republic," according to Brutus, "arises from their knowing them, from their being responsible to them for their conduct, and from the power they have of displacing them when they misbehave."[58] This confidence, he said, is impossible in a country the size of the United States:

> The different parts of so extensive a country could not possibly be made acquainted with the conduct of their representatives, nor be informed of the reasons upon which measures were founded. The consequence will be, they will have no confidence in their legislature, suspect them of ambitious views, be jealous of every measure they adopt, and will not support the laws they pass.[59]

This proposition seems consistent with public choice theory, since in a smaller setting it is more likely that a strategy of cooperation will overcome the "prisoner's dilemma," which in this context holds that the optimal strategy for each citizen is to violate the law while all others abide by it. In a smaller jurisdiction, there is greater likelihood of monitoring and of stigmatization or retaliation, hence greater incentive to abide by legal and other ethical norms.[60]

It is not clear, however, that states or even metropolitan areas are small enough for this kind of direct popular accountability to exist. Moreover, the consolidation of media markets and the advent of national social media as principal venues for debate over political issues may have rendered much of Brutus's argument obsolete. Unfortunately, the new reality is probably not that popular accountability has shifted from one level of government to another, but that popular accountability has ceased to be operative in any genuine sense at any level. Republicanism suffers when citizens cannot monitor what their government is doing, with the ensuing loss of trust in the fairness and wisdom of governing institutions.

Nature of Representation

One of the principal arguments for substantial state autonomy was that representatives in a smaller unit of government will be closer to the people. Patrick Henry, for example, warned in the Virginia ratifying convention that "throwing the country into large districts . . . will destroy that connection that ought to subsist between the electors and the elected."[61] Assuming representative bodies of roughly the same number, any given representative will have fewer constituents and a smaller district at the state or local level. Each citizen's influence on his representative, therefore, will be proportionately greater, and geographically concentrated minorities are more likely to achieve representation. For this reason, some reformers today advocate a substantial increase in the size of the House of Representatives, which would entail a substantial reduction in the size of most districts.[62] This marks a return to a debate among delegates to the Constitutional Convention in 1787. Indeed, the last change to the Constitution, on the last day of the Convention, was to increase the size of the House.[63]

Because federal electoral districts must of necessity be larger and more populous than state legislative districts, representation is likely to be skewed in favor of the well-known few.[64] The Federal Farmer argued that increasing the number of representatives would make the nation "more democratical and secure, strengthen the confidence of the people in it, and thereby render it more nervous and energetic."[65] However, the sheer size of the United States makes it impossible to increase the number of representatives sufficiently without turning the Congress into what Madison called "the confusion of a multitude."[66]

Moreover, if representatives to the national government are required to spend much of their time at the distant national capital, they are likely to lose touch with the sentiments of their constituents, and instead come to identify themselves with the interests of the central government.[67] Even Madison realized that "within a small sphere, this voice of the people could be most easily collected, and the public affairs most accurately managed."[68]

Cultivation of Public Spiritedness

Critics of governmental centralization warned that public spiritedness— then called "public virtue"[69]—could be cultivated only in a republic of small dimensions. Republicanism, it was thought, depended to an extraordinary degree on the willingness of citizens to submerge their own passions and interests for the common good.[70] The only substitute for public virtue was an unacceptable degree of coercion, compatible only with nonrepublican forms of government.

There were two reasons many founders believed that a centralized government would undermine republican virtue. First, public spiritedness is a product of participation in deliberation over the public good. If the citizens are actively engaged in the public debate, they will have more of a stake in the community. The federal government is too distant and its compass too vast to permit extensive participation by ordinary citizens in its policy formulations. By necessity, decision making will be delegated to agents. But as they are cut off from active participation in the commonwealth, the citizens will become less attached to it and more inclined to attend to their private affairs.

Second, the natural sentiment of benevolence,[71] which lies at the heart of public spiritedness, is weaker as the distance grows between the individual and the objects of benevolence. Individuals are most likely to sacrifice their private interests for the good of their family, and then for their neighbors and, by extension, their community. They are unlikely to place great weight upon the well-being of strangers hundreds of miles away. It is unlikely, therefore, that citizens of a nation as large as the United States will assume an attitude of republican virtue toward national affairs.

Do these arguments still hold weight? It is a matter of contention. Are smaller towns places of public virtue and political accountability, as the Anti-Federalists thought, or of narrow-mindedness and prejudice, as Madison's theory might suggest? We are still debating this—as the popular country song by Jason Aldean, "Try That in a Small Town," illustrates.[72] These debates will not be resolved by consensus. They are opposite sides of the same coin. The very features that make smaller units of government closer to the people are also the features that make minorities within those communities uncomfortable. We can have effective, responsive, majoritarian democracy or we can have maximal latitude for minority deviation from majority norms, but we cannot have both—except, perhaps, by the device of lodging power at one level for one kind of decision and another level for other decisions.

Conclusion

The argument for substantial state and local autonomy was powerful at the time of the founding and remains so. Even though some Supreme Court decisions over the last generation evince a greater respect for the constitutional principles of federalism—marking a modest recovery from an all-time low[73]—it is unclear the extent of their purchase. But there continues to be a revival of interest, across the political spectrum, in devolution of governing authority to state, city, and community levels. Due to a combination of political paralysis in the national legislature and the sorting of citizens into more homogeneous "red states" and "blue states," the locus of policy debate seems to be moving in a stateward direction.

Consideration of the reasons for decentralized political decision making strengthens the case for why we may wish to retain or return to the founders' political design. But a thorough analysis of federalism today would require, as well, a more systematic appraisal of the arguments for a centralized national authority. Moreover, if these historical contentions are to have any practical effect, much more thinking needs to be done about the appropriate role of the judiciary, the Congress, and the states themselves. The vision that the Supreme Court, having been informed of the founders' intentions, now has it in its power to restore the original constitutional scheme, is fanciful, and would not necessarily be desirable even if it were less so. The Constitution is everyone's responsibility, and not just the Supreme Court's. Restoration of the constitutional order requires more than a history lesson directed to the Court. It requires a renewed sense by the people of the relation of state sovereignty to the public good, individual liberty, and popular government.

Whatever our chosen theory of interpretation, it is good to cast our minds back to the time of the founding, when popular attention was directed, uniquely in our history, to the issues of self-government. It is the only way to recall, and perhaps recapture, what we may have lost.

The author wishes to thank Charles Edward Power for valuable research assistance.

Notes

1. THE FEDERALIST No. 45, at 292–93 (Madison) (C. Rossiter ed., 1961).

2. THE FEDERALIST No. 45 (James Madison), *supra* note 1, at 288–89.

3. *Id.* at 288.

4. THE FEDERALIST No. 10 (James Madison), *supra* note 1, at 80.

5. THE COMPLETE ANTI-FEDERALIST (Herbert Storing ed., 1981), Vol. 2, at 2.8.13–14.

6. 5 THE COMPLETE ANTI-FEDERALIST, *supra* note 5, at 5.14.6. *See also* ALEXIS DE TOCQUEVILLE, DEMOCRACY IN AMERICA 161 (J.P. Mayer ed., 1969), at 161 ("In large centralized nations the lawgiver is bound to give the laws a uniform character which does not fit the diversity of places and of mores.").

7. Under certain extreme assumptions, a sufficiently decentralized regime with full mobility could perfectly satisfy each person's preferences even with no voting at all. *See* ROBERT P. INMAN & DANIEL L. RUBINFELD, DEMOCRATIC FEDERALISM: THE ECONOMICS, POLITICS, AND LAW OF FEDERAL GOVERNANCE 37–75 (2020); DENNIS C. MUELLER, PUBLIC CHOICE III 182–206 (2003); DAVID L. SHAPIRO, FEDERALISM: A DIALOGUE 76–106 (1995); Charles M. Tiebout, *A Pure Theory of Local Expenditures*, 64 J. POL. ECON. 416 (1956).

8. H. Geoffrey Moulton, Jr., *Federalism and Choice of Law in the Regulation of Legal Ethics*, 82 MINN. L. REV. 73, 141 (1997) (arguing decentralization is undesirable if it frustrates efforts to achieve economies of scale). Economies of scale may not be a major issue in actual practice. Small units of government are able to contract with one another or with private service providers so as to achieve economies of scale without sacrificing decision-making autonomy. *See* Jens Blom-Hansen, Kurt Houlberg, &

Søren Serritzlew, *Size, Democracy, and the Economic Costs of Running the Political System*, 58 AM. J. POL. SCI. 790, 797–801 (2014) (discussing the effects of scale in government efficiency). *Compare* Gordon Tullock, *Federalism: Problems of Scale*, 6 PUB. CHOICE 19, 21 (Spring 1969), *with* JEROME ROTHENBERG, *Local Decentralization and the Theory of Optimal Government, in* THE ANALYSIS OF PUBLIC OUTPUT 31, 33 (Julius Margolis ed., 1970).

9. *See* Jacques LeBoeuf, *The Economics of Federalism and the Proper Scope of the Federal Commerce Power*, 31 SAN DIEGO L. REV. 555, 565–74 (1994).

10. *See generally* RICHARD A. POSNER, ECONOMIC ANALYSIS OF LAW § 27.1 (9th ed. 2014); ROBERT P. INMAN & DANIEL L. RUBINFELD, *The Political Economy of Federalism, in* PERSPECTIVES ON PUBLIC CHOICE: A HANDBOOK 73–105 (Dennis C. Mueller ed., 1997).

11. *See* THE PRACTICE OF FISCAL FEDERALISM: COMPARATIVE PERSPECTIVES 8 (Anwar Shah ed., 2007); Mancur Olson, Jr., *The Principle of "Fiscal Equivalence": The Division of Responsibilities among Different Levels of Government*, 59 AM. ECON. REV. 479, 482 (1969).

12. THE FEDERALIST No. 25 (Alexander Hamilton), *supra* note 1, at 163.

13. James Wilson, Speech to the Pennsylvania Convention (Nov. 24, 1787). *See also* Jill Elaine Hasday, *Interstate Compacts in a Democratic Society: The Problem of Permanency*, 49 FLA. L. REV. 1, 6–7 (1997) ("Interstate compacts, with larger and more flexible jurisdictions, are better equipped to counter externalities than an individual state's laws, particularly given the general assumption that externalities are a constantly diminishing function."); *cf.* WILLIAM ANDERSON, THE NATION AND THE STATES, RIVALS OR PARTNERS? 149 (1955) (stating that, "on grounds of greater efficiency," one level of government may be better suited than another to perform a given function).

14. *See* Garrett Hardin, *The Tragedy of the Commons*, 162 SCIENCE 1243 (1968); *see also* Brett M. Frischmann, Alain Marciano, & Giovanni Battista Ramello, *Retrospectives: Tragedy of the Commons after 50 Years*, 33 J. ECON. PERSPECTIVES 211 (2019).

15. Wilson, *supra* note 13. Wilson's formulation was widely echoed in the debates of the period. *See, e.g.,* 3 THE COMPLETE ANTI-FEDERALIST, *supra* note 5, at 3.14.8 (essays of "A [Pennsylvania] Farmer"). According to Tocqueville, a similar model was employed for the allocation of power between states and townships. *See* TOCQUEVILLE, *supra* note 6, at 67 ("In all that concerns themselves alone the townships remain independent bodies, and I do not think one could find a single inhabitant of New England who would recognize the right of the government of the state to control matters of purely municipal interest.").

16. *See* California High-Speed Rail Authority, *Capital Costs and Funding*, https://hsr.ca.gov/about/capital-costs-funding/.

17. JAMES M. BUCHANAN & GORDON TULLOCK, THE CALCULUS OF CONSENT 135–40 (1962). *See also* Olson, *supra* note 11, at 482–83; Gordon Tullock, *Comment, in* THE ANALYSIS OF PUBLIC OUTPUT 65 (Julius Margolis ed., 1970).

18. A close look at the language of Article I, § 8, clause 1 suggests that it does not empower Congress to spend, but only to tax for certain purposes. Spending, according to this Madisonian view, is permitted only as "necessary and proper" to the other enumerated objects of Article I, § 8.

19. 10 THE PAPERS OF ALEXANDER HAMILTON 303 (Harold C. Syrett ed., 1966).

20. *See, e.g.,* 2 THE COMPLETE ANTI-FEDERALIST, *supra* note 5, at 2.8.78 (letters from the "Federal Farmer") ("In a federal system we must not only balance the parts of the same government, as that of the state, or that of the union; but we must find a balancing influence between the general and local governments.").

21. 6 ANNALS OF CONG. 1712–27 (Joseph Gales ed., 1834) (Dec. 28, 1796).

22. National Pork Producers Council v. Ross, 143 S. Ct. 1142, 1144 (2023).

23. *See* BRUCE ACKERMAN & WILLIAM HASSLER, CLEAN COAL/DIRTY AIR, OR HOW THE CLEAN AIR ACT BECAME A MULTIBILLION-DOLLAR BAIL-OUT FOR HIGH-SULFUR COAL PRODUCERS (1981).

24. Haley H. Chouinard, David E. Davis, Jeffrey T. LaFrance, & Jeffrey M. Perloff, *Milk Marketing Order Winners and Losers,* 32 APPLIED ECONOMIC PERSPECTIVES AND POLICY 59–76 (2010).

25. *See* 5 THE COMPLETE ANTI-FEDERALIST, *supra* note 5, at 5.14.6 (the "Impartial Examiner").

26. *See* Jared Walczak, *The State and Local Tax Deduction: A Primer* (2017), https://taxfoundation.org/research/all/state/state-and-local-tax-deduction-primer/.

27. *See* Craig Volden, *States as Policy Laboratories: Emulating Success in the Children's Health Insurance Program,* 50 AM. J. POL. SCI. 294, 294–95 (2006) (finding that more successful state children's health insurance programs tend to be emulated); Brett M. Frishmann & Mark A. Lemley, *Spillovers,* 107 COLUM. L. REV. 257, 269 (2007) (imposing uniform federal standards may have undesirable effects because it impedes the "virtuous cycle" of state copycat innovation). *But see* William Magnuson, *The Race to the Middle,* 95 NOTRE DAME L. REV. 1183, 1186, 1213 (2020) (arguing that federalism dynamics spark a "race to the middle" that leads to states trying not to "distinguish[] themselves from the crowd" but rather to fit into it).

28. New State Ice Co. v. Liebmann, 285 U.S. 262, 311 (1932) (Brandeis, J., dissenting). The irony is that Brandeis's dissent favored a particularly stupid piece of local special-interest regulation.

29. There is also the separate argument that federalism incentivizes beneficial competition between the states and federal government. *See* Todd E. Pettys, *Competing for the People's Affection: Federalism's Forgotten Marketplace,* 56 VAND. L. REV. 329, 333 (2003) ("With two separate governments vying to win their trust, the Framers reasoned, the people would be free continually to assess the sovereigns' conduct.").

30. *See* Tiebout, *supra* note 7, at 416.

31. *See* Jonathan H. Adler, *Interstate Competition and the Race to the Top,* 35 HARV. J.L. & PUB. POL'Y 89, 89 (2012) (arguing that "robust interjurisdictional competition facilitates the enactment of better public policy at the state level" for corporate

law); Judge Ralph Winter, *Private Goals and Competition among State Legal Systems*, 6 HARV. J.L. & PUB. POL'Y 127 (1982). *But see* Marcel Kahan & Ehud Kamar, *The Myth of State Competition in Corporate Law*, 55 STAN. L. REV. 679, 685 (2002); Lucian A. Bebchuk, *Federalism and the Corporation: The Desirable Limits on State Competition in Corporate Law*, 105 HARV. L. REV. 1435 (1992).

32. *See* Michael W. McConnell, *A Choice-of-Law Approach to Products-Liability Reform*, 37 PROC. ACAD. POL. SCI. 90 (1988).

33. Posner, *supra* note 10; WALLACE E. OATES, FISCAL FEDERALISM 6–8 (1972); *see also* PAUL E. PETERSON, CITY LIMITS (1981).

34. 5 THE COMPLETE ANTI-FEDERALIST, *supra* note 5, at 5.16.2.

35. *Id.*

36. *See, e.g.*, 1 FEDERAL CONVENTION, *supra* note 63, at 340–41 (Luther Martin); 2 THE COMPLETE ANTI-FEDERALIST, *supra* note 5, at 2.3.7 (Robert Yates and John Lansing, Jr.); *id.* at 2.9.22 (Brutus). Compare Tocqueville's analysis: "Local institutions are to liberty what primary schools are to science; they put it within the people's reach; they teach people to appreciate its peaceful enjoyment and accustom them to make use of it. Without local institutions a nation may give itself a free government, but it has not got the spirit of liberty." TOCQUEVILLE, *supra* note 6, at 63.

37. Madison put the argument forward earlier in an essay entitled "Notes on the Confederacy," written in April 1787. *See* 1 LETTERS AND OTHER WRITINGS OF JAMES MADISON 325–28.

38. THE FEDERALIST NO. 10 (James Madison), *supra* note 1, at 80.

39. *Id.* at 84.

40. Cass R. Sunstein et al., *Ideological Voting on Federal Courts of Appeals: A Preliminary Investigation*, 90 VA. L. REV. 301, 306 (2004); Thomas J. Miles, *The Law's Delay: A Test of the Mechanisms of Judicial Peer Effects*, 4 J. LEGAL ANALYSIS 301, 302 (2012); Pauline T. Kim, *Deliberation and Strategy on the United States Courts of Appeals: An Empirical Exploration of Panel Effects*, 157 U. PA. L. REV. 1319, 1323–24 (2009).

41. *See generally* MANCUR OLSON JR., THE LOGIC OF COLLECTIVE ACTION (1965); JAMES Q. WILSON, POLITICAL ORGANIZATIONS (1973); Bruce A. Ackerman, *Beyond Carolene Products*, 98 HARV. L. REV. 713 (1985); John M. de Figueiredo & Brian Kelleher Richter, *Advancing the Empirical Research on Lobbying*, 17 ANN. REV. POL. SCI. 163 (2014) (discussing the current state of empirical research on lobbying's effects).

42. Keith E. Whittington, *Dismantling the Modern State? The Changing Structural Foundations of Federalism*, 25 HASTINGS CONST. L.Q. 483, 508–10 (1998); *see also* Richard B. Stewart, *Madison's Nightmare*, 57 U. CHI. L. REV. 335 (1990).

43. *See, e.g.*, Richard A. Epstein, *Exit Rights under Federalism*, 55 L. & CONTEMP. PROBS. 47 (1992); Gregory v. Ashcroft, 501 U.S. 452, 458 (1991) (observing that federalism "makes government more responsive by putting the States in competition for a mobile citizenry"); ALBERT O. HIRSCHMAN, EXIT, VOICE, AND LOYALTY: RESPONSES TO DECLINE IN FIRMS, ORGANIZATIONS, AND STATES 16–17, 34 (1970) (explaining that dissatisfied consumers often have "exit options" and "voice options";

that economists tend to believe exit is the most powerful means of expressing unhappiness; and that, when exit is not a viable alternative, "voice must carry the entire burden of alerting management to its failings."); Heather K. Gerken, *Exit, Voice, and Disloyalty*, 62 DUKE L.J. 1349 (2013) (reprising Hirschman's classic work).

44. THE FEDERALIST NO. 51 (James Madison), *supra* note 1, at 323; *see also* 1 LETTERS AND OTHER WRITINGS OF JAMES MADISON at 325–28.

45. Letter from James Madison to Thomas Jefferson (Oct. 24, 1787), *in* 10 THE PAPERS OF JAMES MADISON 214 (Robert A. Rutland et al. eds., 1973).

46. THE FEDERALIST NO. 51 (James Madison), *supra* note 1, at 323.

47. *See* TOCQUEVILLE, *supra* note 6, at 263. *Compare* Andrzej Rapaczyski, *From Sovereignty to Process: The Jurisprudence of Federalism After Garcia*, 1985 SUP. CT. REV. 341, 389, *with* Akhil Reed Amar, *Of Sovereignty and Federalism*, 96 YALE L.J. 1425, 1429–1519 (1987); *see also* Roderick M. Hills, Jr., *Is Federalism Good for Localism? The Localist Case for Federal Regimes*, 21 J.L. & POL. 187, 187–88 (2005).

48. THE FEDERALIST NO. 10 (James Madison), *supra* note 1, at 84; THE FEDERALIST NO. 51 (James Madison), *supra* note 1, at 324.

49. 1 ANNALS OF CONG., *supra* note 21, at 452 (June 8, 1789).

50. *Id.* at 458.

51. *Id.* at 86 (Sept. 21, 1789).

52. U.S. CONST. amend. I.

53. *See* Michael W. McConnell, *Establishment and Disestablishment at the Founding, Part I: Establishment of Religion*, 44 WM. & MARY L. REV. 2105, 2109 (2003); *see also* WILBUR G. KATZ, RELIGION AND AMERICAN CONSTITUTIONS 8–11 (1964); William W. Van Alstyne, *What Is "An Establishment of Religion?,"* 65 N.C. L. REV. 909 (1987).

54. 3 THE COMPLETE ANTI-FEDERALIST, *supra* note 5, at 3.9.12.

55. U.S. CONST. art. I, § 9, cl. 3; *id.*, § 10, cl. 1.

56. 2 THE COMPLETE ANTI-FEDERALIST, *supra* note 5, at 2.9.11.

57. *Id.* at 2.9.18. *See also* GORDON S. WOOD, THE CREATION OF THE AMERICAN REPUBLIC: 1776–1787 66 (1969).

58. 2 THE COMPLETE ANTI-FEDERALIST, *supra* note 5, at 2.9.18.

59. *Id.*

60. *See* ROBERT AXELROD, THE EVOLUTION OF COOPERATION 1 (1984); Jenna Bednar & William N. Eskridge, Jr., *Steadying the Court's "Unsteady Path": A Theory of Judicial Enforcement of Federalism*, 68 S. CAL. L. REV. 1448, 1449 (1995).

61. 5 THE COMPLETE ANTI-FEDERALIST, *supra* note 5, at 5.16.27. The Federal Farmer argued, similarly, that "a small representation can never be well informed as to the circumstances of the people, the members of it must be too far removed from the people, in general, to sympathize with them, and too few to communicate with them." *Id.* at 2.8.99.

62. *See* Lee Drutman et al., *The Case for Enlarging the House of Representatives* (Amer. Acad. of Arts and Sciences 2021), https://www.amacad.org/ourcommonpurpose/enlarging-the-house.

63. 2 MAX FARRAND, THE RECORDS OF THE FEDERAL CONVENTION 644 (Sept. 17, 1787) (1911).

64. *See, e.g.*, 5 THE COMPLETE ANTI-FEDERALIST, *supra* note 5, at 5.6.2 (Patrick Henry); *id.* at 2.8.158 (Federal Farmer); *id.* at 6.12.16 (Melancton Smith).

65. *Id.* at 2.8.158.

66. THE FEDERALIST NO. 10 (James Madison), *supra* note 1, at 82. For a modern discussion, see ALBERTO ALESINA & ENRICO SPOLAORE, THE SIZE OF NATIONS (2005); and ROBERT A. DAHL & EDWARD R. TUFTE, SIZE AND DEMOCRACY (1973).

67. *Compare* 2 THE COMPLETE ANTI-FEDERALIST, *supra* note 5, at 2.6.27 (Letters of Cato), *with* Tullock, *supra* note 8, at 25 ("The longer the chain of officials that runs between the voter making the choice and the actual provision of the product, the more noise is introduced into the process by the individual bureaucrats who have their own preference functions and by the problems of information transmission.").

68. 10 THE PAPERS OF JAMES MADISON, *supra* note 45, at 212. *See also* JEFFREY M. BERRY, THE REBIRTH OF URBAN DEMOCRACY 49 (1993) (describing the relationship between size and effectiveness of neighborhood self-government); SIDNEY VERBA, PARTICIPATION AND POLITICAL EQUALITY: A SEVEN-NATION COMPARISON 269–85 (1978) (finding lower rates of political participation in urban than in rural areas); ROBERT A. DAHL & EDWARD R. TUFTE, SIZE AND DEMOCRACY 73–88 (1973) (suggesting the ability of officials elected from smaller constituencies to make contact with constituents and generate voter satisfaction).

69. *See* WOOD, *supra* note 57, at 68.

70. For the connection between this doctrine of public virtue and the framers' conception of religious liberty, see Michael W. McConnell, *Accommodation of Religion*, 1985 SUP. CT. REV. 1, 14–22; and THE COMPLETE ANTI-FEDERALIST, *supra* note 5, at 22–23.

71. *See* ADAM SMITH, THE THEORY OF MORAL SENTIMENTS (D. D. Raphael ed., 1976).

72. *See, e.g.*, Emily Olson, *How Jason Aldean's "Try That in a Small Town" Became a Political Controversy*, NPR (July 20, 2023), https://www.npr.org/2023/07/20/1188966935/jason-aldean-try-that-in-a-small-town-song-video.

73. FERC v. Mississippi, 456 U.S. 742 (1982); Garcia v. San Antonio Metropolitan Transit Authority, 469 U.S. 528 (1985); South Dakota v. Dole, 483 U.S. 203 (1987).

PAUL E. PETERSON: There was one thing you didn't mention at the beginning, and that was the effort to make sure that we would have a common market, which I think was, the states couldn't interfere with trade. I think that was an incredibly important thing that was done at the convention.

Although states have autonomy within the American federal system, they cannot erect trade barriers that prevent a large common market. The Constitution struck down the barriers that had arisen under the Articles of Confederation. Europeans are still struggling to achieve a common market that Americans take for granted.

2

Public Attitudes toward Federalism and the Scope of National Power

Morris P. Fiorina and Alice Yiqian Wang

Introduction

The proper distribution of state versus federal authority affects nearly every policy domain—from environmental regulation to immigration policy—in American politics today. With the COVID-19 pandemic, the subject of federalism received renewed attention as policymakers across different levels of government jockeyed over the "appropriate" policy response and their inherent authority to carry out that response (Fiorina 2023). These recent developments make it even more important to understand how the public views the proper allocation and scope of state versus national power. Is the public's attitude toward federal authority driven by their normative preferences over centralized or decentralized governance? Or is the public just as "unprincipled" as political elites when it comes to their support for federal power? Moreover, has the public's experience of the recent COVID-19 pandemic shaped their federalism preferences? And if so, are such attitudinal changes likely to become more permanent fixtures of the American political landscape?

To provide preliminary answers to these questions, we begin by describing public attitudes toward federalism and federal power. In particular, we focus on the extent to which attitudes toward state and local governments are either reflections of or conceptually distinct from public attitudes toward the federal government. We then examine how the public's attitudes toward federalism— as measured by their preferences over the scope of federal power—have changed from the early 2000s onward. By examining time trends data across these past two decades, we find evidence to suggest that attitudes toward federalism are responsive to respondents' partisan orientations as well as to their perceptions of actual changes in the scope of federal power.

Next, we turn toward perceptions of trust in local, state, and federal governments. While we find that trust in local and state governments has remained relatively stable over time, trust in the federal government has varied substantially across the past two decades. One important structuring factor appears to be the ideological orientations of respondents: those whose partisanship matched those of the incumbent administration reported higher levels of trust in the federal government than those whose partisanship did not. This correspondence paints a potentially pessimistic picture in which political expediency overrides any principled concerns over federal overreach. The effects of partisanship alignment on public attitudes are less pronounced for state and local governments, however.

Following our discussion of partisanship match/mismatch and the possibility of an unprincipled public, we turn toward how this relationship plays out across different states. To analyze this, we compare public attitudes toward *state* governments when there is a partisan match (the party affiliations of the respondent and their state governor are the same) and when there is a partisan mismatch (the affiliations of the respondent and their state governor are different). Using 2022 Cooperative Election Study (CES) data, we find that respondents are systematically less confident and trusting of their state governments when their personal party affiliation differs from that of their state governor. Building on our discussion of how public attitudes appear to be strongly structured by partisanship as well as by actual changes in federal policy, we focus specifically on the extent to which the COVID-19 pandemic has altered prior attitudinal trends. Leveraging high-frequency Google Trends data from 2017 to 2022, we find some preliminary evidence that the public's experiences with the pandemic might be correlated with greater interest in circumscribing the scope of national power. However, that increase in interest is not particularly large.

In the final section, we speculate about the permanence of the attitudinal changes induced by the COVID-19 pandemic.

Drivers of Public Attitudes toward Federalism

Theoretical explanations for the drivers of public trust in local and state institutions typically fall into two general categories. On the one hand, the determinants of public confidence in state and local governments may be distinct from the determinants of public confidence in the national government (Jennings 1998). Because subnational governments hold different roles and responsibilities than their national counterpart, the manner in which they are evaluated by the public may diverge as well. This view taps into the public's core political beliefs—including attitudes toward the distribution of federal authority—that are more ingrained and less prone to change than attitudes toward, say, short-term economic conditions (Green and Guth 1989; Arceneaux 2006; Wolak 2016).

On the other hand, given the ongoing nationalization of American politics (Hopkins 2018), and the decline in regional and local news outlets (Hayes and Lawless 2021), confidence in state and local governance may be largely a reflection of attitudes toward national government. Public attitudes are less attributable to individual evaluations of subnational governments as such, but are more structured by their evaluations of other levels of government (Hetherington and Nugent 2001). In this case, the determinants of public confidence in subnational governments remain similar to those for the national government. Likely factors would include approval of legislative and executive performance as well as broader changes in economic prosperity. Public approval (or disapproval) of the national government will then "spill over" into the public's evaluations of subnational governments (Uslaner 2001).

Public opinion toward the federal and state governments' recent pandemic responses is illustrative. Reflecting broader trends in the early stages of the pandemic with respect to bipartisan agreement over federal relief aid, 89 percent of Republicans and 89 percent of Democrats expressed support for the 2020 economic aid package (Pew Research Center 2020). As the pandemic wore on, more Republicans than Democrats expressed confidence in the ability of the Trump administration and the federal government to combat COVID-19. With the transition to the Biden administration in early 2021, this dynamic was reversed, as more Democrats expressed confidence in the federal government's capacity to efficiently tackle the pandemic.

Indeed, when communities become dissatisfied with the federal government's pandemic response, they may begin to express greater support for their state's response, especially when the restrictiveness (or the lack of restrictiveness) of the latter's response comports with their personal preferences. Take, for instance, state-level responses in California and Florida. Relative to the Trump administration's federal-level response, California's state-level response was arguably more robust during the early stages of the COVID-19 pandemic in 2020. Following Governor Gavin Newsom's declaration of a State of Emergency on March 4, 2020, his office would issue a statewide stay-at-home order on March 19, 2020. Not only was California slow to "reopen" in 2021, but the governor did not end the state's COVID-19 State of Emergency until several years later, on February 28, 2023.

In contrast, Florida governor Ron DeSantis charted an altogether different path. Although Governor DeSantis issued a statewide stay-at-home order on April 1, 2020, in which he limited activities within the state to essential services, he would lift business capacity restrictions by September of that year. Also, in September 2020, Governor DeSantis issued additional executive orders (see, for example, Executive Order 20-244) that limited the extent to which local governments and private businesses were permitted to adopt their own COVID-19 mitigation policies. In short, if residents in California and Florida were more supportive of their state's pandemic response relative to the federal government's, we might expect those attitudes to translate into general satisfaction with their state government or greater support for devolved authority.

Public Attitudes toward Federalism
Contemporary Attitudes toward Federalism
With these two general frameworks in mind, we now turn toward contemporary preferences concerning the scope of state versus federal power. Our data suggest that ebbs and flows in public preferences for the scope of federal power are structured not only by the political orientation of the respondent but also by the preexisting political context. Please note that as this paper is primarily concerned with trends across time and observed empirical associations, we do not seek to make causal claims; rather, we simply note some theoretical possibilities.

With that said, figure 2.1 shows the percentage of respondents who reported that the federal government wields "too much" power. Overall, the percentage of respondents who reported this belief has increased relatively steadily from 2002 until 2013, before decreasing from that year onward. However, since our Gallup data only begins in 2002, we cannot determine whether this trend began in 2002 or in an earlier year. In particular, it could be that this trend began earlier in 2001. Since the Bush administration and the 107th Congress passed a series of executive orders and legislative reforms, respectively, that expanded the scope of federal power after the September 11th attacks, it is plausible that this observed increase reflects the public's response to those new policy measures.

Do you think the federal government today has too much power, has about the right amount of power, or has too little power?

Percent of survey respondents reporting the federal government has "too much" power

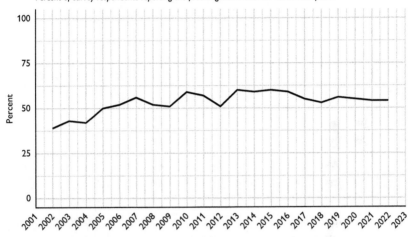

Figure 2.1 Attitudes toward the scope of federal power (2002–2022)
Source: Data from Gallup Poll Social Series, 2022.

Once we disaggregate public attitudes toward the scope of federal power by party, strong partisan trends emerge (figure 2.2). During the first and second Bush presidencies (from 2001 to 2009), the percentages of Democrats, Republicans, and independents who reported that the federal government holds too much power all increased. However, the percentage of Republicans who reported this view continued to increase into the Obama presidency while the percentage of Democrats decreased. Throughout Obama's two terms, the percentage of Republicans who reported that the federal government is too powerful hovered around 80 percent and exhibited minimal variation (only shifting 2 to 3 percentage points) across eight years. Among Democrats, that same percentage increased, on average, during Obama's first term in office, then decreased steadily during his second term.

In 2016, we observed another strong partisan effect after the November elections. The percentage of Democrats who reported that the federal government wields too much power increased steadily—from 30 to 50 percentage points—during the Trump presidency. However, two trends suggest that it is not just partisan preferences driving attitudes toward the federal government; rather, substantive changes in the powers of the federal government seem to factor into respondents' assessments as well.

Do you think the federal government today has too much power, has about the right amount of power, or has too little power?
Percent of survey respondents reporting the federal government has "too much" power

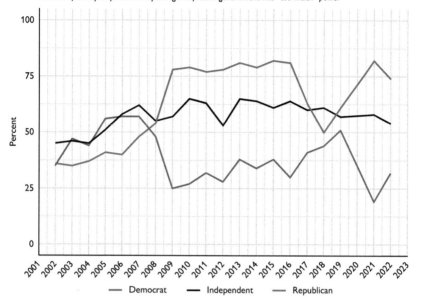

Figure 2.2 Attitudes toward the scope of federal power (by party)
Source: Data from Gallup Poll Social Series, 2022.

First, we observe that the average percentage of Democrats who believed the federal government holds too much power during the Trump period is roughly equal to the percentage of Democrats who reported similar sentiments during the Bush administration. Given that Democratic attitudes toward the Trump administration were more negative than Democratic attitudes toward both Bush administrations, we might expect the percentage of Democrats who reported the federal government to have too much power to be higher during the Trump administration than during either Bush administration if it was solely partisan preferences that drove respondents' attitudes. The fact that this did not obtain suggests Democrats also considered other factors, such as the extent to which federal power actually expanded during the two Bush administrations.[1] This interpretation is also supported by the fact that the percentages of both independents and Republicans who stated that the federal government holds too much power also increased throughout this period.

Second, the percentage of Republicans who reported that the federal government holds too much power increased drastically in 2019, during a Republican administration. Again, this suggests that Republicans' attitudes toward the federal government are structured partly by policy changes at the national level and not just by their personal political orientation. While we cannot identify what policy changes in 2019 motivated attitudinal changes among Republican respondents, this trend in attitudes toward federal power continues into 2020 with the COVID-19 pandemic. Interestingly, however, we do not see any significant increases among independents on this same metric.

One possible explanation might be that Republicans react more strongly to expansions of governmental power under Republican administrations. Because Republican Party platforms tend to emphasize smaller government, Republican voters may react more negatively when Republican administrations seemingly "go back" on their campaign promises once in power. In contrast, the proportion of Democrats who reported that the federal government holds "too much" power decreased steadily from 2019 to 2021 before increasing sharply in 2021. Here, the prevailing trend speaks against mere partisan sentiments. Despite their general opposition to the Trump administration, Democrats were less inclined to report that the scope of the federal government was too vast during the second half of the Trump administration than during the first. One possible explanation for this unexpected shift downward is the COVID-19 pandemic. As Democrats might have desired a more robust public health response at the federal level, it is plausible that some of those sentiments spilled over into their evaluations of the federal government's proper authority.

As noted earlier, the percentage of independents who reported that the federal government wields too much power increased during both the first and the second Bush presidencies. However, unlike attitudes among their Republican and Democrat counterparts (which continued to increase and decrease, respectively), attitudes toward the federal government among independent-identifying respondents remained relatively unchanged after peaking in 2007. From 2007 onward, approximately 60 percent of independents on average would report that the federal government wields too much power.

Historical Attitudes toward Federalism

How do contemporary trends in federalism preferences compare to their historical counterparts? From the 1960s onward, the proportion of respondents who expressed concerns that the federal government is "too powerful" has generally increased.

In the first half of the 1970s, we observed a steady increase in the proportion of respondents who reported that the federal government is too strong; this increase may be, plausibly, in response to the significant civil rights legislation that was adopted at the federal level. Starting in 1980, the percentage of respondents who reported that the federal government is too powerful decreased and would hover in the mid- to high 30s throughout the next two decades.

Once we disaggregate the above data by respondents' political affiliations, we observe an interesting divergence between *historical* partisan attitudes and *contemporary* partisan attitudes toward the federal government. Principally, we observe that the historical attitudinal gap between Democratic and Republican respondents who believe the federal government is "too strong" (or alternatively, not too strong) is *smaller* than the contemporary attitudinal gap. Take, for instance, the proportion of respondents who reported that the federal government is too strong. From 1964 to 2000, the gap between Democratic and Republican attitudes hovered around 18 percent. In other words, approximately 18 percent more Republicans on average reported that the federal government was too powerful. However, during the first Obama presidency, this attitudinal gap between Democrats and Republicans would increase to a little more than 50 percent.

Figure 2.3 reflects the percentage of respondents who reported that the federal government is indeed "too powerful." Similar to the trends we observed previously, variations in partisan attitudes tend to track one another rather closely. Although the magnitude of the change might differ across political affiliations, increases (or decreases) in the proportion of Democrats, Republicans, and independents who reported that the federal government is "too powerful" tended to proceed along very similar lines from 1964 to 2000.

Public Attitudes toward Local, State, and Federal Governments
Trust and Confidence in Local Governments

We now turn toward public confidence in local, state, and federal governments. Trust in local governments (i.e., the percentage of respondents who reported that they hold a "great deal" or a "fair amount" of confidence in their local governments to handle local problems) has remained relatively stable—though trending upward—across the past two decades, with aggregate support hovering around the 65 to 75 percentage point range. In 2021, however, there is a 6-point decline in overall trust in local governments, a fairly significant decrease. Indeed, the 6 percent drop in 2021 is the largest change in

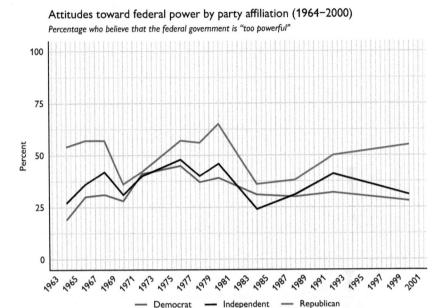

Attitudes toward federal power by party affiliation (1964–2000)
Percentage who believe that the federal government is "too powerful"

— Democrat   — Independent   — Republican

Figure 2.3 Federal government is "too powerful" (by party)
Source: Data from American National Election Studies (ANES) Time Series, 2000.

local government trust from 2001 to the present, matched only by a 6-point increase in public confidence in local governments from 2011 to 2012.

Despite the occasional volatility in public opinion, confidence and trust in local governments remained relatively stable across time as a general matter. In the period from 2002 to 2022, confidence trended upward by approximately 3 percent on average.

Once we disaggregate respondents' confidence in their local governments by party affiliation, we observe noticeable partisan trends. As we see in figure 2.4, Republican respondents tend to report higher levels of trust and confidence in their local governments than either independent or Democratic respondents across nearly all years (with the exception of 2004). One possible explanation is that Republican ideology tends to favor policymaking at lower levels of governance rather than at higher levels, a core belief that then carries over into their evaluations of their local governments.

We might expect partisan attitudes toward local governments to reflect the partisanship of the national executive and legislative branches. If the partisanship of respondents is opposite to that of the national executive, we might expect those individuals to place more confidence in the ability of

How much trust and confidence do you have in the local governments
in the area where you live when it comes to handling local problems?
Percent of survey respondents reporting a "great deal" or a "fair amount"

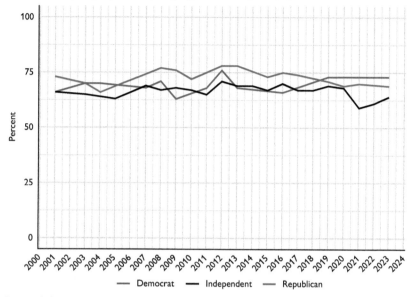

Figure 2.4 Attitudes toward local governments (by party)
Source: Data from Gallup Poll Social Series, 2023.

their local governments to do what they believe the national government
will not (or cannot) do. This favoring of their local government over the
federal one might be especially pronounced when the partisanship of the
former is more closely aligned with the respondent's personal political
preferences.

Despite such expectations, however, partisan differences in trust and confidence in local governments do not appear to follow any discernible pattern.
Take, for example, President Bush's and President Obama's terms in office. We
might expect Democrats' confidence in their local governments to increase or
at least remain constant throughout the Bush administrations.

However, while we observe a 4-point increase during the first Bush administration, we observe a 2-point *decrease* followed by a 3-point increase during the second Bush term. Contrary again to expectations, we observe an
8-percentage-point *decrease* in Democrats' confidence in their local governments at the beginning of the first Obama presidency, but then a 15-point
jump from 2009 to 2012.

Trust and Confidence in State Governments

Public trust and confidence in state governments exhibit more variation than confidence in local governments, though they remain less variable overall when compared to attitudes toward the federal government. On the whole, public trust decreased by 12 percentage points during the first half of the Bush presidency before rebounding during the second half. During Bush's second term in office, trust in state governments remained stable at 67 percent.

With the transition to the Obama administration in 2008, we see a similar dynamic play out. Trust in state governments decreased by 16 percentage points from 2008 to 2009, then increased by 13 points from 2009 to 2012. During Obama's second term, public trust hovered around 62 percent on average. Although trust decreased by 7 percentage points during the first half of his second term, it increased by 5 percentage points from 2015 to 2016. Following 2016, the percentage of respondents who stated that they had a "great deal" or a "fair amount" of trust in their state governments held steady at 63 percent. Only in 2019 did the percentage of respondents in this

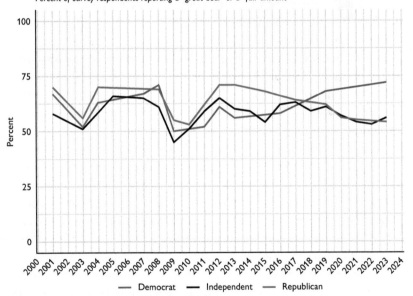

How much trust and confidence do you have in the government of the state where you live when it comes to handling state problems?

Percent of survey respondents reporting a "great deal" or a "fair amount"

Figure 2.5 Attitudes toward state governments (by party)

Source: Data from Gallup Poll Social Series, 2023.

category begin to decline, further decreasing from 63 percent in 2019 down to 52 percent in 2021.

As figure 2.5 shows, changes in trust for state governments by party affiliation initially track one another but then begin to diverge in 2013. For both Democrat and Republican respondents, trust in state governments decreased during the first Bush presidency before steadily increasing in the second. Surprisingly, trust among Democrats and Republicans both decreased in the first half of the Obama presidency, increased after the 2010 midterm elections, then decreased again after Obama's reelection in 2012. Starting in 2013, Democrats' trust in their state governments continued to rise throughout the last half of Obama's second term as well as throughout the Trump administration. In contrast, after 2013, Republicans' trust in their state governments declined throughout both subsequent Democratic and Republican administrations.

Trust and Confidence in the Federal Government

Across the past two decades, trust in the federal government has decreased from an artificial high of 66 percent in 2002 to a low of 37 percent in 2021.[2] In contrast to the aforementioned dynamics observed with respect to local and state governments, partisan attitudes toward the federal government are more strongly structured by the ideological orientation of the incumbent executive. Put differently, matches (or mismatches) between the political orientation of the respondent and that of the executive tend to induce increases (decreases) in trust of greater magnitude than those we had observed with respect to subnational forms of government.

We next turn to a discussion of contemporary public attitudes, which are captured in figure 2.6. Among Republicans, trust in the federal government reached a high of 83 percent in 2004 and remained in the mid- to high 70s throughout Bush's second term in office. Following Obama's historic victory in 2008, Republicans' trust in the federal government would decrease substantially before reaching a low of 27 percent during the 2010 midterm year. Throughout the period from 2008 to 2016, trust in the federal government among this group remained less than 35 percent. After Trump's election in 2016, trust in the federal government among Republicans increased to the mid-60s. Contrary to past trends, Republican respondents' trust in the federal government decreased sharply in 2020 despite an incumbent Republican president. It is unclear whether this decrease was in response to the Trump administration's handling of the COVID-19 pandemic, suspicions of federal health agencies, or other factors.

How much trust and confidence do you have in our federal government in Washington when it comes to handling domestic problems?

Percent of survey respondents reporting a "great deal" or a "fair amount"

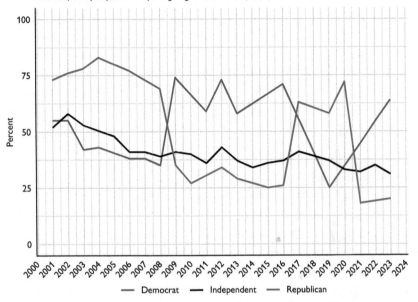

Figure 2.6 Contemporary attitudes toward the federal government (by party)

Source: Data from Gallup Poll Social Series, 2023.

Democratic respondents show the opposite movements. Trust in the federal government remained low throughout the first and second Bush administration, then increased during the Obama period before decreasing again after Trump's election in 2016. For both Republicans and Democrats, trust in the federal government increased once an executive of the same political orientation took office; in instances where the partisanship of the respondent and of the executive aligned, the public's level of trust tended to increase at the beginning of that president's term, decrease during his (first) term in office, then increase slightly before and after the next midterm elections. Following the same pattern, trust decreases again after the midterms before increasing again in the period preceding the next presidential election. Overall, voters' attitudes toward the federal government are substantially less stable than their attitudes toward their local and state governments. While changes in trust in local and state governments tend to remain within a 10-percentage-point range of each other, trust in the federal government exhibits much higher volatility of 40 percentage points or more.

Once again, we see that independent respondents' attitudes toward the federal government remained unaffected by electoral cycles—they remained generally stable regardless of whether there was an upcoming midterm or presidential election. However, independents' trust in the federal government appears to trend downward throughout the entire period under study—decreasing from the mid-50s in the early 2000s to the low 30s in 2021.

While the Gallup survey discussed above is not directly comparable to the American National Election Studies (ANES) Trust in Government Index, the latter may still prove helpful in contextualizing the former. Measured on a 100-point scale from "least trusting" to "most trusting," the ANES Trust in Government Index is an aggregate measure of governmental trust built from four standard ANES questions.[3] Overall, with the exception of three temporary peaks in 1966, 1986, and 2002, public confidence in the federal government has declined at a steady pace since the postwar period (figure 2.7).

Although today's decrease in public confidence appears to be a continuation of historical trends, these similarities end once we disaggregate respondents by their political affiliation. From the postwar period until the early 2000s, the ebbs and flows in partisan attitudes toward the federal government tend

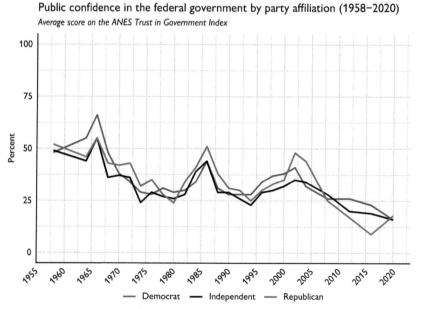

Figure 2.7 Historical attitudes toward the federal government (by party)
Source: Data from American National Election Studies (ANES) Time Series, 2020.

to track one another closely. When Democrats lose confidence in the federal government, so do Republicans and independents. And when Republicans regain their confidence in the federal government, so do their Democratic and independent counterparts. This represents a substantial difference relative to partisan attitudes in the contemporary period, where an increase in confidence among members of one party is marked by a concurrent decrease in confidence among members of the other.

Trust and Confidence by Party: A More Granular Look

To better understand how partisan dynamics structure attitudes toward different levels of governance, we now shift toward a more fine-grained account of the public's federalism preferences. Drawing from recent YouGov survey data on public confidence and trust in local, state, and federal governments,[4] we compare the public's federalism preferences across three states: Arizona, California, and Texas. For our purposes, these three states are especially instructive given their general political orientations. While California and Texas are viewed as reliably Democratic and Republican strongholds, respectively, Arizona is better characterized as a "purple" state. This state-level variation in partisan orientations allows us to better illustrate the role of party (mis)match in shaping the public's trust/confidence in different levels of government.

Trust among Californian respondents adheres to clear partisan distinctions (figure 2.8). California Republicans overwhelming trust their local government the most (at 80.17 percent); perhaps surprisingly, they trust the California state government (9 percent) even *less* than they trust the national government (11 percent). On the surface, this pattern appears to run contrary to a supposedly core Republican belief: that policymaking is best conducted at lower levels of governance. One possible explanation is that California Republicans' concerns for political expediency outweigh their more principled concerns over federal overreach. Not only is California's governor a Democrat, but both of the state's legislative chambers are controlled by the Democratic Party in 2024. Even though the US presidency and the Senate remain under Democratic control, Californian Republicans might still find some solace—and confidence—in the Republican-controlled House.

Meanwhile, California Democrats appear to trust their local and state governments in equal proportions (at 40 percent and 40 percent, respectively). Their trust in the national government is lower, at 20 percent, however. The underlying reason for Democrats' decreased trust in the federal government

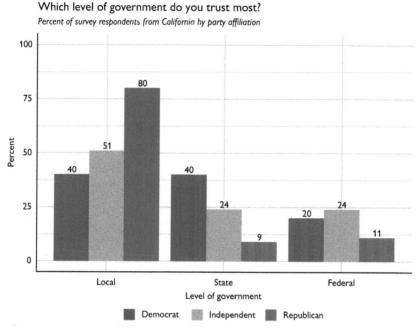

Figure 2.8 California: Attitudes toward different levels of government
Source: Data from YouGov, 2022.

is likely the same as that for Republican's decreased trust in the California state government. While California Democrats might find confidence in the Democratic governor and Democrat-controlled state legislature, their trust in the federal government might be moderated downward by the existence of a Republican-controlled House. Finally, independent respondents do not appear to adhere to any partisan trends. Instead, independent respondents' confidence in the three levels of government progressively decreases across the local, state, and federal governments.

Much of the aforementioned dynamics we observed in California are further evident in Texas (figure 2.9). Among Republican respondents, 57 percent indicated that they trusted their local government the most. This was followed by the Texas state government (at 36 percent) and the federal government (at 7 percent). Like Texas Republicans, Texas Democrats also trust their local government the most, relative to the state or the federal government. While 41 percent of Texas Democrats stated that they trust the federal government the most, that number decreases to 14 percent for the Texas state government.

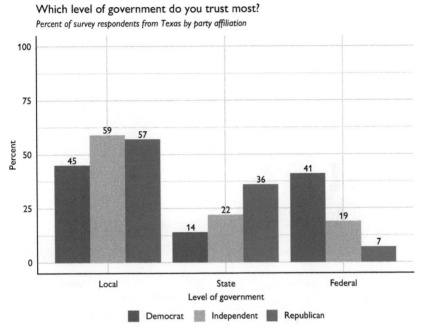

Figure 2.9 Texas: Attitudes toward different levels of government
Source: Data from YouGov, 2022.

Just as in California, independents in Texas do not adhere to any party-specific trends. Rather, the proportion of independent respondents who indicated that they trust the government decreases as they move from their local government to their Texas state government, then finally to the federal government.

Concluding with Arizona (figure 2.10), a solidly "purple" state, we see that Republicans overwhelmingly trusted their local governments more (at 74 percent) than either their state or local governments (at 19 and 7 percent, respectively). This aligns with our prior observations that Republican-identifying respondents tend to have the highest levels of trust in their local governments. Meanwhile, we see that a higher percentage of Democrats indicated they trust the federal government than either Republican or independent respondents did; this, again, seems to point toward the influence of partisanship mis(match) in shaping attitudes toward the federal government.

Interestingly, we see that Democratic, Republican, and independent attitudes toward Arizona's state government appear to be roughly equal—while

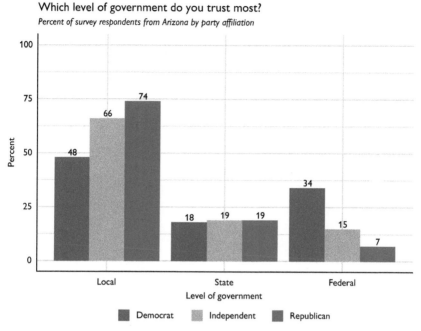

Figure 2.10 Arizona: Attitudes toward different levels of government
Source: Data from YouGov, 2022.

18 percent of Democrats stated that they trusted their state government the most, 19 percent of independents and 19 percent of Republicans stated they did so as well. Here, we can interpret the relative congruence between Democratic, Republican, and independent attitudes toward their state government as supporting the importance of party affiliation for structuring federalism attitudes. While Arizona's governor is from the Democratic Party, both chambers of the Arizona state legislature are under Republican control. In other words, unlike California and Texas, in which one single party dominated both the state executive and legislature, Arizona is characterized by divided government at the state level. Just as Democratic Arizonans will be able to see their political positions reflected in their state governor, their Republican counterparts will be able to see their own views reflected in their state legislature.

State-Level Partisan (Mis)match
Next, we turn toward a high-level overview of how partisanship match and mismatch plays out across all states. The 2022 CES module asks respondents

about "how much trust [they] have in the government of the state where [they] live when it comes to handling the nation's problems." Respondents are then asked to register their opinion by selecting "a great deal," "a fair amount," or "not at all." Taking this CES data, we sum up the percentage of respondents who reported that they trust their state government "a great deal" and "a fair amount," then aggregate them based on their party affiliation and their state of residence. Then we identify the partisanship of their state governor before noting whether there is a match or mismatch between the respondent's partisanship and their state governor's partisanship.

On average, 54 percent of Republican respondents reported that they held a "great deal" or a "fair amount" of trust in their Republican state governors. Yet when we turn toward states in which there was a Republican mismatch between respondents and their governors in 2022, we see an entirely different story. Here, among Republican respondents residing in a state with a Democrat governor, only 20 percent indicated that they trust their state government a "great deal" or a "fair amount." In comparison to their Republican match counterparts, Republican respondents in "mismatched" states are substantially less confident in their state governments (by 34 percent). This nontrivial gap in state confidence suggests that the public might be less principled over their federalism preferences than previously assumed.

Figure 2.11 sums up this approval gap in states controlled by Republican governors. While this general trend (of Republicans expressing more confidence in their state governments than their Democratic counterparts) tends to hold across most states, we observe some notable outliers. In Maryland, Massachusetts, and Vermont, more Democratic respondents expressed confidence in their Republican-controlled state governments than Republican respondents within those same states. This is likely a function of the unique political environment across those three states, whereby nominally Republican governors tend to be more moderate than the typical Republican governors in other states.

We now engage in the same exercise, but with Democratic respondents. On average, 61 percent of Democratic respondents living in states held by Democratic governors expressed support in the performance of their state governments. Interestingly, the average percentage of Democratic respondents in Democratic states who expressed confidence in their state governments (61 percent) is *greater* than the average percentage of Republican respondents in Republican states who expressed those same attitudes (54 percent). While this initially seems to run contrary to expectations and

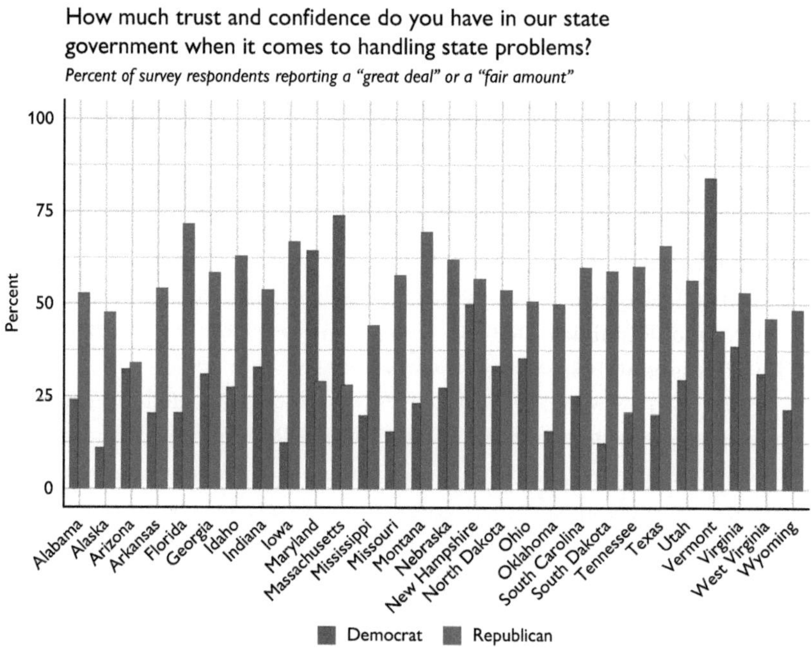

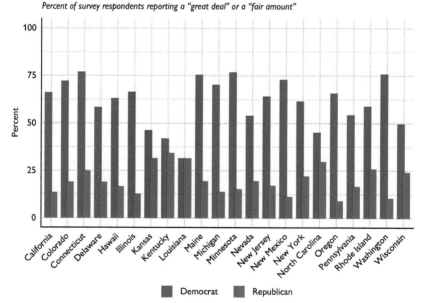

How much trust and confidence do you have in our state
government when it comes to handling state problems?

Percent of survey respondents reporting a "great deal" or a "fair amount"

Democrat ■ Republican

Figure 2.11 Public confidence in Republican match states

Source: Data from Cooperative Election Study, 2022.

How much trust and confidence do you have in our state
government when it comes to handling state problems?

Percent of survey respondents reporting a "great deal" or a "fair amount"

Democrat ■ Republican

Figure 2.12 Public confidence in Democratic match states

Source: Data from Cooperative Election Study, 2022.

received wisdom that Republicans tend to value devolved governance, that might not necessarily be the case. Rather, Republicans might simultaneously prefer devolved governance while maintaining a healthy skepticism of government in general.

Here, the 54 percent of Republican respondents in Republican states who expressed confidence in their state governments might reflect their general skepticism (relative to Democrats) of government in general. Moreover, that 54 percent of Republicans is likely higher than the percentage of Republicans who express confidence in the *federal* government.

Among states in which there was a Democratic mismatch between respondents and their governors in 2022, the percentage of respondents who expressed confidence in their state governments drops down sharply to 31 percent. Moreover, as figure 2.12 illustrates, unlike with states controlled by Republican governors, we do not observe any instances in which Republicans expressed *more* approval of their Democrat-controlled state governments than Democrats did within those same states. With that said, respondents in Louisiana came close. While 32 percent of Democrats expressed confidence/trust in the Louisiana state government, 31 percent of Republicans did so as well.

COVID-19 and Federalism

Has the COVID-19 pandemic altered patterns of party affiliation and federalism preferences? There is some evidence to suggest that this is the case. For instance, communities that have, historically, taken a more negative stance on governmental prerogatives have shifted their position toward a more agreeable one. As Mueller et al. (2020) note, rural communities that historically expressed stronger opposition to government spending have tempered some of those attitudes in response to the pandemic. They report that 79 percent of respondents approved of increasing spending for small businesses, while another 64 percent approved of increasing spending on healthcare. However, the findings by Mueller et al. do not disaggregate across local, state, and federal levels of government spending, so they are of limited value for our paper. Even though rural respondents might be more amenable to governmental spending as a whole, their specific preferences might remain highly conditional on the level of government at which that spending occurs. And even if the *absolute* levels of support for government spending have increased throughout the pandemic, the *relative* difference in support for local/state versus federal government spending may have remained the same.

Experimental survey evidence has also helped disentangle the relationship between the pandemic and the public's federalism preferences. Rendleman and Rogowski (2022) find that attitudes toward federalism reflect both evaluations of government performance during the COVID-19 pandemic and the public's ideological commitments. Respondents who were either (1) satisfied with their state's response to the pandemic or (2) more satisfied with their state's response relative to the federal government's response were more likely to express a preference for greater state powers. Overall, they find evidence to suggest that it is ideological orientations—not political allegiances—that determine support for devolved government. Along similar lines, Jacobs (2021) finds that the American public's preferences for governmental intervention—whether at the state or federal level—were generally independent from their particularized, lived experiences with pandemic virulency. After taking stock, Jacobs concludes that the public's attitudes toward government performance and authority during the pandemic were largely structured by their party affiliation.

Google Trends and Public Attitudes toward Federalism

To complement existing survey research into how COVID-19 has induced shifts in federalism preferences, we leverage observational search data from Google Trends to consider how the pandemic response influences the public's perceptions of federal overreach. Collected in real time by the Google News Initiative, Google Trends data is a measure of the key terms and phrases that the public searches for during any given week. So far, existing research has demonstrated that Google Trends strongly correlates with racial animus (Stephens-Davidowitz 2014), anti-Asian attitudes during the pandemic (Huang et al. 2023), immigration attitudes (Chykina and Crabtree 2018), disease outbreaks (Carneiro and Mylonakis 2009, Ginsberg et al. 2009), and other related health outcomes (Ayers et al. 2012). To that end, we collected Google Trends data on public searches relating to federalism broadly and to the scope of federal power specifically; we then consider the onset of the COVID-19 pandemic as an exogenous shock to the public's federalism preferences in 2020.

Our investigation takes national Google Trends queries from a five-year period from 2017 to 2022. We adopt this five-year timeframe for two reasons. First, this five-year timeframe allows us to determine whether any observed changes in federalism preferences are due to seasonality effects rather than to the pandemic itself. Second, by limiting our investigation from 2017 to early 2022, we are able to avoid unintentionally capturing events that are unrelated to the pandemic but may have induced public concerns over the scope of federal power. In particular, by stopping our investigation in early 2022, we avoid the Supreme Court's decision in *Dobbs v. Jackson Women's Health Organization* on June 24, 2022 (the draft decision was leaked on May 2, 2022). This stopping point is crucial because, by reverting the power to regulate abortion access back to the states, *Dobbs* may have similarly spurred public interest in state versus federal power.

We view the advantages of Google Trends to be twofold. First, relative to survey data, respondents are likely to be more forthcoming with their Google search results than when answering either online or face-to-face surveys. Although the public's preferences toward federalism is not an inherently sensitive topic (in contrast to, say, racial prejudice or previous engagements in illicit markets), there might still be some downward pressure for respondents to answer in a "socially acceptable" manner. For instance, one can imagine a scenario in which right-leaning respondents living in a more left-leaning area feel some social pressure to express federalism preferences that do not wholly reflect their own sincerely held preferences (though, admittedly, the magnitude of this effect will likely be small). Second, since Google Trends queries are collected on a weekly basis, they are relatively high-frequency data points that give the researcher a sense *across time* of the public's expressed interest in federalism and federal power. Relative to retrospective survey questions that may ask respondents to report their behavior or attitudes at some unspecified time in the past, Google Trends does not suffer from recall bias.

Google Trends: Searches for "Federalism"

The following section displays Google Trends for the following search terms and phrases: "federalism," "states' rights," and "state sovereignty." We first turn toward the "federalism" Google Trend. Figure 2.13 displays the "popularity" of the search term "federalism" month by month from 2017 to 2022.

To start, we observe in figure 2.13 an interesting seasonality with respect to Google searches for "federalism." While overall interest in federalism slowly decreases from January onward, we see an annual spike in public interest in September, which then decreases to "normal" levels of interest by the end of each year. In 2020 (as denoted by the green line), Google searches for "federalism" were at a five-year high in April and September of that same year. While it is difficult to identify exactly what events or conditions prompted these interest peaks, two cases are instructive. First, the small peak in April

Google search trends for "federalism"
Relative search volume for the keyword "federalism" from 2017 to 2022

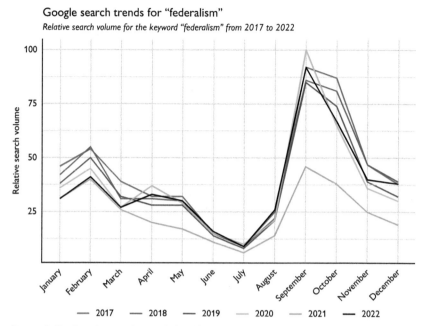

Figure 2.13 Google search trends for "federalism" (by year)
Source: Data from Google Trends, 2022.

coincided with the Trump administration's decision to extend the voluntary
nationwide shutdown until April 30. Second, the peak in September coincided with when COVID-related mortality numbers in the United States sur-
passed 200,000. If these two explanations hold, it is interesting to note that
the reasons underlying the public's interest in federalism at either of these
two times seem to run in opposite directions. In April, the public's interest in
federalism was presumably motivated by concerns over federal overreach and
whether the Trump administration was exceeding its authority to extend the
voluntary nationwide shutdown order. Yet in September, the public's interest
in federalism was likely motivated by their concern that the federal government was not doing enough to stem the COVID-19 crisis.

Put differently, while the above Google Trends tells us that public interest
in federalism increased somewhat in 2020, it does not allow us to determine
the reasons associated with that change. A user might search for "federalism"
because she is dissatisfied with the federal government's limited response
and desires her state government to step in and implement more stringent
pandemic restrictions, but this search behavior would be observationally

equivalent to that of another user who thought the federal government had overstepped its legal prerogatives, and who desired an even more limited response.

Google Trends: Searches for "States' Rights" and "State Sovereignty"
In order to more precisely determine whether the public preferred a more limited or more expansive federal pandemic response, we refine our search terms to "states' rights" and "state sovereignty." The Google Trends associated with each of these two phrases are as follows:

As figures 2.14 and 2.15 illustrate, public interest in states' rights and state sovereignty was unusually high in 2022 (as denoted by the black line). However, as previously noted, this surge in interest was likely in response to discontent over reproductive rights and the Supreme Court's *Dobbs* decision, rather than resulting from any sustained concerns over pandemic restrictions. We will return to this question of attitudinal permanence in a later section.

As expected, public interest in states' rights and state sovereignty was particularly high in 2020 (as again denoted by the green line). Following

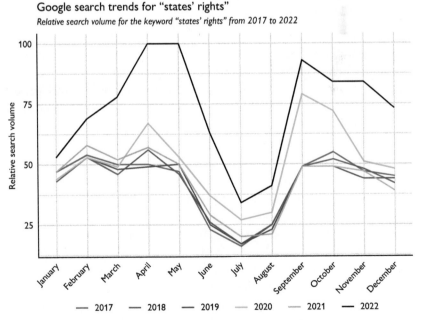

Google search trends for "states' rights"
Relative search volume for the keyword "states' rights" from 2017 to 2022

Figure 2.14 **Google search trends for "states' rights" (by year)**
Source: Data from Google Trends, 2022.

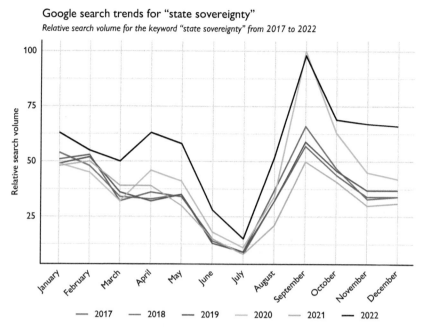

Figure 2.15 Google search trends for "state sovereignty" (by year)
Source: Data from Google Trends, 2022.

March 2020, "states' rights" was a more popular Google search term across all remaining months of that year than it was during comparable months in 2017, 2018, 2019, and 2021. In 2020, Google searches for "states' rights" peaked slightly in April of that year before decreasing steadily until September. In September 2020, Google searches for the term peaked again. We observe a similar trend—with similar peaks in April and September 2020—with respect to Google searches for "state sovereignty," though this trend is not as pronounced. Notably, these April and September 2020 peaks for "states' rights" and "state sovereignty" mirror those previously observed for "federalism."

Google Trends: Searches for "Lockdown," "Mask Mandate," and "Vaccine Mandate"

By comparing when the public tends to concentrate their searches on keywords such as "federalism" and "state sovereignty" with when the public searches for phrases such as "lockdown" or "mask mandate," we are able to gain a preliminary sense of whether the former might be operating as an underlying worry for the public with regard to the latter.

With that question in mind, we first turn to Google search trends for "lockdown" and "stay at home" before moving forward to search trends in "mask mandate" and "vaccine mandate." Unsurprisingly, Google searches for the key terms "lockdown" and "stay at home" spiked in March and April 2020, before tapering off with a brief peak in late 2020. Likewise, searches for "mask mandate" were marked by three distinct spikes in May 2021, August 2021, and February 2022. And finally, "vaccine mandate" searches remained relatively stable at the start of the pandemic, which is unsurprising given (1) the lack of a suitable vaccine at the time as well as (2) the absence of public discourse over recommended or mandatory vaccinations. Overall, Google searches for "vaccine mandate" began in earnest in late 2021 before spiking rapidly from September 2021 to January 2022.

As these Google Trends demonstrate, there is not much outward correlation between (1) searches for federalism and its associated key terms, and (2) searches for pandemic-related restrictions and regulations. As the above-mentioned Google Trends do not necessarily map onto one another, one plausible interpretation is that the public did not make core distinctions between the levels at which pandemic restrictions were implemented. If so, this seems to mirror existing experimental evidence that "Republicans prove to be just as outcome-oriented as Democrats in their support or opposition to a face mask and vaccination requirement, regardless of which level of government proposes the policy" (Jacobs 2021).

Of course, our Google Trends data has several obvious limitations. First, we cannot make any substantive claims concerning whether it was individuals' experiences of the pandemic that induced changes in their attitudes toward national power. Second, we cannot be certain that Google Trends queries are representative of the national population. It might very well be the case that those who feel most strongly about states' rights and circumscribed national power are those who engaged in the most internet searches for those key terms.

Conclusion

We conclude with three brief observations. Though we have seen shifts in public attitudes toward federalism as a function of the COVID-19 pandemic, it is unclear if the pandemic induced more permanent changes in popular preferences toward federal versus state authority. Now three years since the onset of the pandemic, we have some evidence to suggest the *impermanence* of these changes to the public's federalism preferences. While Google searches for "states' rights" and "state sovereignty" were at a five-year high in 2020, the public's interest in both concepts would decrease to "normal" levels by the next year. And indeed, the public's interest in "state sovereignty" in particular was occasionally at its lowest monthly levels during 2021.

Although this paper thus far has not extensively discussed Google Trends data in 2022, it is worthwhile noting that Google searches for "states' rights" peaked during the week of May 1 to May 7, then increased once again during the week of June 19 to June 25. As expected, these two peaks coincided with the leak of the *Dobbs* decision (on May 2) and the release of Court's finalized *Dobbs* decision (on June 24). In both *Dobbs*-related peaks, the increase in public interest over time was *higher* than during previous COVID-19 related peaks. While we cannot draw strong conclusions from these observed trends, this difference appears to suggest that federalism and states' rights were more in the forefront of the public's consciousness with respect to reproductive rights than with respect to the COVID-19 pandemic.

Finally, we note the unfortunate scarcity of disaggregated data on federalism attitudes. While there exist comprehensive time series data on trust/confidence in the federal government, the presidency, Congress, and the Supreme Court, there is very little longitudinal data that is disaggregated by different levels of government. Given this lack of disaggregated time series data, we are left with "snapshot" survey experiments that do now allow us to draw conclusions about the evolution of attitudes toward federal power across time. To advance our understanding of the public's federalism preferences, a more robust data collection effort would be essential.

Notes

1. This would include, among others, an executive order establishing military commissions and mass surveillance programs, as well as the creation of the US Department of Homeland Security.

2. An artificial high because according to longer time series such as the American National Election Studies, trust spiked in the aftermath of 9/11 before falling back to more normal levels. https://electionstudies.org/data-tools/anes-guide/anes-guide .html?chart=trust fed govt.

3. The four ANES questions comprising the Trust in Government Index are as follows: (1) How much of the time do you think you can trust the government in Washington to do what is right—just about always, most of the time, or only some of the time?; (2) Would you say the government is pretty much run by a few big interests looking out for themselves or that it is run for the benefit of all the people?; (3) Do you think that people in the government waste a lot of money we pay in taxes,

waste some of it, or don't waste very much of it?; (4) Do you think that quite a few of the people running the government are (1958–72: a little) crooked, not very many are, or do you think hardly any of them are crooked (1958–72: at all)?

4. Our many thanks and deepest appreciation to David Brady and Doug Rivers for sharing their survey data.

References

Arceneaux, Kevin. 2006. "The Federal Face of Voting: Are Elected Officials Held Accountable for the Functions Relevant to Their Office?" *Political Psychology* 27, no. 5 (October): 731–54.

Ayers, John W., Benjamin M. Althouse, Jon-Patrick Allem, Daniel E. Ford, Kurt M. Ribisl, and Joanna E. Cohen. 2012. "A Novel Evaluation of World No Tobacco Day in Latin America." *Journal of Medical Internet Research* 14, no. 3 (May/June): e77.

Carneiro, Herman Anthony, and Eleftherios Mylonakis. 2009. "Google Trends: A Web-Based Tool for Real-Time Surveillance of Disease Outbreaks." *Clinical Infectious Diseases* 49, no. 10 (November): 1557–64.

Chykina, Volha, and Charles Crabtree. 2018. "Using Google Trends to Measure Issue Salience for Hard-to-Survey Populations." *Socius* 4: 2378023118760414.

Farrell, Justin, J. Tom Mueller, Kathryn McConnell, Paul Berne Burow, Katie Pofahl, and Alexis A. Merdjanoff. 2020. "Impacts of COVID-19 on the Rural West: Material Needs, Economic Recovery, and Changes in Political Attitudes." Executive Summary of Research Findings. New Haven, CT: Yale School of the Environment.

Fiorina, Morris P., ed. 2023. *Who Governs? Emergency Powers in the Time of COVID.* Stanford, CA: Hoover Institution Press.

Ginsberg, Jeremy, Matthew H. Mohebbi, Rajan S. Patel, Lynnette Brammer, Mark S. Smolinski, and Larry Brilliant. 2009. "Detecting Influenza Epidemics Using Search Engine Query Data." *Nature* 457, no. 7232 (February 19): 1012–14.

Green, John C., and James L. Guth. 1989. "The Missing Link: Political Activists and Support for School Prayer." *Public Opinion Quarterly* 53, no. 1 (Spring): 41–57.

Hayes, Danny, and Jennifer L. Lawless. 2021. *News Hole: The Demise of Local Journalism and Political Engagement.* Cambridge: Cambridge University Press.

Hetherington, Marc J., and John D. Nugent. 2001. "Explaining Public Support for Devolution: The Role of Political Trust." In *What Is It about Government that Americans Dislike?*, edited by John R. Hibbing and Elizabeth Theiss-Morse, 134–51. Cambridge: Cambridge University Press.

Hibbing, John R., and Elizabeth Theiss-Morse. 2001. *What Is It about Government that Americans Dislike?* Cambridge: Cambridge University Press.

Hopkins, Daniel J. 2018. *The Increasingly United States: How and Why American Political Behavior Nationalized.* Chicago: University of Chicago Press.

Huang, Justin T., Masha Krupenkin, David Rothschild, and Julia Lee Cunningham. 2023. "The Cost of Anti-Asian Racism during the COVID-19 Pandemic." *Nature Human Behaviour* 7, no. 5 (May): 682–95.

Jacobs, Nicholas. 2021. "Federalism, Polarization, and Policy Responsibility during COVID-19: Experimental and Observational Evidence from the United States." *Publius: The Journal of Federalism* 51, no. 4 (Fall): 693–719.

Jennings, M. Kent. 1998. "Political Trust and the Roots of Devolution." In *Trust and Governance*, edited by Valerie Braithwaite and Margaret Levi, 218–44. New York: Russell Sage Foundation.

Mueller, J. Tom, Kathryn McConnell, Paul Berne Burow, Katie Pofahl, Alexis A. Merdjanoff, and Justin Farrell. 2020. "Impacts of the COVID-19 Pandemic on Rural America." *Proceedings of the National Academy of Sciences* 118(1): 2019378118.

Pew Research Center. 2020. "Positive Economic Views Plummet; Support for Government Aid Crosses Party Lines," April 21.

Rendleman, Hunter, and Jon C. Rogowski. 2022. "Americans' Attitudes toward Federalism." *Political Behavior*, published online September 2.

Stephens-Davidowitz, Seth. 2014. "The Cost of Racial Animus on a Black Candidate: Evidence Using Google Search Data." *Journal of Public Economics* 118 (October): 26–40.

Uslaner, Eric M. 2001. "Is Washington Really the Problem?" In *What Is It about Government that Americans Dislike?*, edited by John R. Hibbing and Elizabeth Theiss-Morse, 118–33. Cambridge: Cambridge University Press.

Wolak, Jennifer. 2016. "Core Values and Partisan Thinking about Devolution." *Publius: The Journal of Federalism* 46, no. 4 (Fall): 463–85.

MICHAEL J. BOSKIN: It does look like, for everybody, confidence at lower levels is higher than at the federal level. I think that's important as well as the partisan differences.

MICHAEL W. McCONNELL: You don't have that by copartisans, though?

ALICE YIQIAN WANG: No, we don't. No.

McCONNELL: Any way to tell the difference between large, urban cities versus small towns?

WANG: Not in the Gallup or the ANES [American National Election Studies] data I was able to find. I think they were, at least for the Gallup data, it was more just what it was at the national level. Wasn't able to find the specific metropolitan region or specific city that these respondents were at.

MORRIS P. FIORINA: As Alice mentioned, there are long time series on confidence in the federal government, in the presidency, in the Supreme Court, the Congress, but surprisingly little asked about levels of government. That was a surprise to us.

MICHAEL T. HARTNEY: How important do you think the political sophistication of the people answering the question matters here? Because I'd imagine there are a lot of people out there who think the president is the reason it takes a long time to get through the line at the DMV. So I wonder if maybe you've broken this out, controlling for—they're imperfect—but some of the questions on political knowledge, that sort of thing.

WANG: That's a great idea in terms of, if you go ask the average person, "Hey, can you define federalism for me?" Maybe that isn't necessarily a point of reference for them, that's always at the forefront of their minds. Or thinking about if there is a political problem, yes, that's something that they're going to attribute to the executive, the federal government, rather than the local one. I think your question is probably something that we're going to look to further in the future, but not something we considered here.

BOSKIN: That's a great idea, Michael [Hartney]. I would just make a quick comment that this project is related, but there's a separate umbrella project at Hoover called the Tennenbaum Program for Fact-Based Policy. Doug Rivers and I are trying to figure out what people know about a subject, which I think, Doug informed me, is depressing when you look at the data. What they think they know, but also what they think other people would benefit from knowing more factual knowledge about. And that's been pretty fascinating. So we'll look forward to engaging with some of you. This may be an area that makes some sense for you to dig deeper and we can do some additional polling.

BRUCE E. CAIN: There's an interesting point here about whether the confidence that you see in local government is structural or whether it's political, and here's how I'll define it. Okay? Structural might be that local government is closer to the people, smaller in units, delivers services that are more visible. Political would be that maybe you have more people—particularly in the West and the Midwest—that are elected on nonpartisan tickets. And so you don't have partisan signals and you don't have the national media exposure, etc. So the nice thing about this time series is you could control at the state level, whether you have split government, united government, copartisans, that kind of stuff over time. But I think you could also have some of the structural stuff in terms of the size of the government, test and see whether [with] smaller governments there's more confidence, etc.

3

The Phases and Faces of Federalism

David M. Kennedy

A word about the title of my paper. It departs rather substantially from the assigned title ("What Ever Happened to Previous Calls for a 'New Federalism?'"), as well as the prior assumptions with which I began work on this project. That original title fitted comfortably with what might be called a standard historical approach: review past incidents of change, whether proposed or actuated, and chronicle the evolution of the principle, practice, or institution in question. With respect to federalism, a version of the conventional historical wisdom long conformed to that formulation, assessing American federalism as a story of successive phases that added up to a cumulative advance of central at the expense of peripheral power. The path to that destination was usually signposted as Civil War, Progressive Era, World War I, New Deal, World War II, Great Society.

But on closer consideration, it seemed that the character of America's federal experiment, with some partial exceptions noted below, was less a matter of evolution than it was of stasis—or, perhaps more accurately, cyclicity. The historical record reveals stubbornly persistent confusion and argument about the legitimacy, logic, value, and very meaning of *imperium in imperio* and endless, repeated, Groundhog Day–like contestation and frequent reversal of positions both ideological and pragmatic about its actual operation. Indeed, the rationale for this Hoover Institution project testifies to the continuing lack of agreement on federalism's nature in either theory or practice.

The Founders themselves had difficulty specifying the precise meaning of federalism. The term does not appear in the Constitution, though all the framers understood that they were building a political edifice in which power, authority, and loyalties were somehow to be shared between the central and state governments. Yet they differed sharply over the nature of that relationship, about the precise valence of those competing claims in the larger scheme of "checks and balances" that characterize the Constitution's overall architecture.

Thomas Jefferson, for example, thought that "it is not by the consolidation, or concentration of powers, but by their distribution, that good government is affected. Were not this country already divided into states, that division must be made, that each might do for itself what concerns itself directly, and what it can so much better do than a distant authority."[1]

That's about as concise a case for the virtues of federalism as could be imagined. Yet as on so many matters, Alexander Hamilton strenuously disagreed:

> Who can seriously doubt, that if these States should either be wholly disunited, or only united in partial confederacies, the subdivisions into which they might be thrown would have frequent and violent contests with each other. To presume a want of motives for such contests, as an argument against their existence, would be to forget that men are ambitious, vindictive and rapacious . . . [and to anticipate that we would be] splitting ourselves into an infinity of *little, jealous, clashing, tumultuous commonwealths, the wretched nurseries of unceasing discord* and the miserable objects of universal pity or contempt.[2]

That, in turn, is among the most trenchant cases for the superiority of central power. And of course—and by no means incidentally—Hamilton asserted not only the supremacy of the national or central government, but the paramountcy of the executive branch within it: "A feeble executive implies a feeble execution of the government. A feeble execution is but another phrase for a bad execution: And a government ill executed, whatever it may be in theory, must be in practice a bad government."[3]

Even James Madison, arguably the most astute and thoughtful of the framers, was uncharacteristically obscure when he turned to the subject in *The Federalist*, No. 39:

> The proposed Constitution, therefore, is, in strictness, *neither a national nor a federal Constitution*, but a composition of both. In its foundation it is *federal, not national*; in the sources from which the ordinary powers of the government are drawn, it is *partly federal and partly national*; in the operation of these powers, it is *national, not federal*; in the extent of them, again, it is *federal, not national*; and, finally, in the authoritative mode of introducing amendments, *it is neither wholly federal nor wholly national*.[4]

Whatever else might be said about that tortured definition, it could not be described as a model of clarity—or a practical guide as to how the concept of federalism might take on institutional and operational consistency. Madison himself was conspicuously inconsistent. A nationalist at Philadelphia in 1787, he was a states' righter in 1798 when he authored the Virginia Resolution opposing the federal Alien and Sedition Acts: "In case of a deliberate, palpable, and dangerous exercise of other powers [the states] have the right, and are in duty bound, to interpose for arresting the progress of evil."[5] As Jack Rakove has summarily noted, "Whether the framers of the Constitution anticipated a progressive widening in the effective scope of federal action thus remains one of the most elusive of the many questions asked about their intentions."[6]

A half century after the birth of the republic, yet another uncommonly insightful political analyst—Alexis de Tocqueville—registered a similarly incongruous, even self-contradictory, appraisal of American federalism: "No one can appreciate the advantages of a federal system more than I," he wrote in *Democracy in America*. "I hold it to be one of the most powerful combinations favoring human prosperity and freedom. I envy the lot of the nations that have been allowed to adopt it.... [But]," he added, "clearly we have here not a federal government but an *incomplete national government*."[7]

"States' rights," infamously and inextricably entangled with the "peculiar institution" of slavery, agitated American politics for decades until at last submitting to the arbitrament of arms in the Civil War. The war and the three Reconstruction amendments that followed supposedly settled the question of where ultimate authority lay. But the incompleteness of the national government that Tocqueville remarked on was vividly in evidence in the decades following Appomattox. Though it became commonplace to say that before 1861 the United States *were*, and after 1865 the United States *was*, reality made a mockery of that tidy formulation. Despite the Union's conclusive military victory, the Jim Crow system that emerged in the postwar years demonstrated the southern states' considerable residual power to constrict the political, economic, and social circumstances of their black citizens, often in open and unapologetic defiance of federal statutes as well as constitutional mandates. Jim Crow endured for a century. Its gross and often violent transgressions gave the concept of "states' rights" a bad name from which it has yet to recover.

The Fourteenth Amendment may have lain dormant for generations, but it eventually proved a potent weapon against racism and discrimination— and by its very nature that weapon was owned and operated by the federal government, which has been the great, if sometimes sputtering, engine of our national ideal of equality. Yet even the achievements of the "Second Reconstruction" in the 1960s, notably including the Civil and Voting Rights Acts, which asserted federal authority at long and overdue last over basic political and social rights, did not once and for all settle the matter, as demonstrated in the 2013 Supreme Court decision in *Shelby County v. Holder*.[8]

On the other hand, in the larger economic realm, the postbellum Gilded Age saw repeated instances of the feebleness of individual states' capacities in the face of national and even international concentrations of corporate power—until the 1886 *Wabash* case reasserted federal supremacy over interstate transportation, commerce, and other economic activities.[9] *Wabash* effectively submerged the states' rights rock on which previous federal efforts to regulate the economy had repeatedly foundered. An early consequence was the Interstate Commerce Commission, created in 1887 as the first federal regulatory agency.

It was the patent obsolescence of states' capacities in the new industrial order that gave rise to further early- and mid-twentieth-century federal initiatives that eventually transformed the nation's economic landscape. In almost all cases, the states came begging for federal assistance; they did not have it roughly shoved down their throats. *Wabash* reaffirmed Justice John Marshall's 1824 pronationalist ruling in *Gibbons v. Ogden*, but shifted its logic in the different historical context of the late nineteenth century.[10] It was no longer sufficient to check state control over commerce and replace it with nothing. The dominant concern now was not how to release entrepreneurial energies but how to tame the formidable energies concentrated in behemoth corporations. Here is one instance where the historian can in fact see the fairly consistent evolution of a reality-reckoning sort in favor of the growth of national over state power.

Theodore Roosevelt can stand as the most articulate champion of that development, as he explained in his 1912 presidential campaign:

> There once was a time in history when the limitation of governmental power meant increasing liberty for the people. In the present day the limitation of governmental power . . . means the enslavement of the people by the great corporations who can only be held in check through the *extension* of governmental power. . . . The people of the United States have but one instrument which they can efficiently use against the colossal combinations of business—and that is the Government of the United States.[11]

For much of the remainder of the twentieth century the Commerce Clause underwrote that Rooseveltian assertion of federal supremacy. But even that apparently settled constitutional doctrine was sharply challenged in 1995 when the Supreme Court struck down a federal gun control statute in *United States v. Alfonso D. Lopez, Jr.*[12]

Here it should be added that Roosevelt, like Hamilton, asserted not only the supremacy of the central government, but an expanded concept of presidential power within it—as did Roosevelt's nemesis, Woodrow Wilson, who notoriously asserted that "the President is at liberty, both in law and conscience, to be as big a man as he can."[13] (It's worth noting that in the same treatise Wilson declared that "the *question* of the relation of the states to the federal government is the cardinal *question* of our constitutional systems." Note the repetition of the word *question*, one more among the countless reminders that federalism remains an ever-contested proposition without a fixed definition.)

The related preferences for central over state authority and for greater presidential power evince alike the chronic yearning for more efficient, orderly, uniform, and consistent governance than is easily achieved in America's purpose-built constitutional contraption conceived in the peculiar circumstances of the postrevolutionary late eighteenth century. As Henry Adams once observed about that formative moment: "The great object of terror and suspicion to the people of the thirteen provinces was power; not merely power in the hands of a president or a prince, of one assembly or several, of many citizens or few, but power in the abstract, wherever it existed and under whatever form it was known."[14]

With Adams's keen insight in mind, it is appropriate to note that federalism American style, with its dispersal of authority and chronic disputation over the precise relation of *imperium* to *imperio*, is a luxury, a labile, malleable arrangement affordable only in circumstances of guaranteed national security, abundant economic resources, and assured social peace. When all—or any—of those conditions are absent, pressure arises, like a law of nature, for unitary leadership from the center. As Tocqueville knew, this is what had happened in the French revolutionary era, when foreign invasion, economic disruption, and the prospect of protracted civil war compelled the concentration of power even in the midst of a democratic revolution.

The federal architecture peculiar to the United States has not only historically impeded efforts to secure commercial uniformity and financial stability, and underwritten flagrant violations of rights supposedly guaranteed in the

Constitution—it has also facilitated outright evasion of responsible engagement with issues of great moral and ethical consequence by deliberately scattering decision making and accountability to several jurisdictions. Stephen Douglas's notoriously futile effort to elide the slavery problem with the doctrine of "popular sovereignty," as embodied in the Kansas-Nebraska Act of 1854, is a prominent example.

In an entirely different setting, US Army Provost Marshal Enoch Crowder somewhat cynically captured the essence of Douglas's logic with respect to the local draft boards set up by the Selective Service System in World War I: "They became the buffers between the individual citizen and the Federal Government, and thus they attracted and diverted, like local grounding wires in an electric coil, such resentment or discontent as might have proved a serious obstacle . . . had it been focused on the central authorities. Its diversion and grounding at 5,000 local points dissipated its force."[15]

In short, even while it has assuredly allowed experimentation and accommodation to American society's manifest diversity (respecting such matters as religion, education, environmental quality, and lifestyle choices concerning recreational drugs, assisted death, and so on), federalism has also often allowed Americans to avoid coming to grips with some vexedly weighty issues. Some may call this a safety valve; others will deem it an escape hatch. The current fifty-state controversy over abortion rights, occasioned by the Supreme Court's 2022 *Dobbs* decision, is a case in point, a twenty-first-century replay of Stephen Douglas's approach to slavery, with perhaps predictably similar results.[16]

As with so many things, so too with federalism, where you stand depends on where you sit. When one party or ideology dominates in Washington, DC, the minority seeks refuge or scope for initiative at the state level. And when the situation reverses, so do the players' preferences and tactics. The liberal embrace of federalism in states like California in the environmental and welfare sectors in response to conservative federal dominance in the late twentieth century is a case in point, as richly documented in Richard Nathan's informative 2006 article, "There Will Always Be a New Federalism."[17]

A concluding observation: Something remains of that venerable assessment that the long-term history of federalism is a tale of federal aggrandizement—but with an important qualification, best captured in Morton Grodzins's distinction between "layer cake" and "marble cake" federalism (figure 3.1).[18]

As Grodzins and others have argued, I believe correctly, the real cumulative effect of federalism in practice over more than two centuries has not been

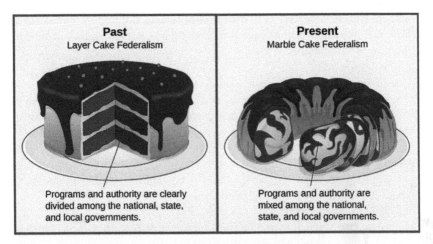

Past	Present
Layer Cake Federalism	Marble Cake Federalism
Programs and authority are clearly divided among the national, state, and local governments.	Programs and authority are mixed among the national, state, and local governments.

Figure 3.1 "Layer cake" federalism and "marble cake" federalism

Source: Glen Krutz and Sylvie Waskiewicz, *American Government 3e* (Houston: OpenStax, 2021), https://openstax.org/books/american-government-3e/pages/3-2-the-evolution-of-american-federalism. Textbook content produced by OpenStax is licensed under a Creative Commons Attribution License.

simply the steady aggrandizement of central power and the relentless diminution of state power, but the coevolution of the two that has amplified the overall presence of governments (plural) in many sectors of American life. Indeed, federal power has often been the factor driving the scope and scale of state governments. Prominent examples include Title III (unemployment insurance) of the 1935 Social Security Act; the Interstate Highway System; and Medicaid. As Nathan puts it summarily: "The dominant effect of U.S. federalism is to expand the scope and spending of the domestic public social sector."[19]

Yet within that framework, controversy continues—and in all probability forever will. Thus it's more appropriate to speak not of several distinct historical *phases* of federalism, but of its several enduring though constantly mutating *faces*, persistent features of our living constitutional system—and of our endlessly contentious society.

Notes

1. Thomas Jefferson, *Autobiography* (1821) Works 1:120–22. In *The Works of Thomas Jefferson*, collected and edited by Paul Leicester Ford, Federal Edition, 12 vols. (New York and London: G. P. Putnam's Sons, 1904–5), text available at https://press-pubs.uchicago.edu/founders/documents/v1ch8s44.html.

2. Alexander Hamilton, *The Federalist*, nos. 6 and 9, in *The Federalist Papers* (New York: New American Library, 2003), ed. Clinton Rossiter, intro. and notes by Charles R. Kesler. Emphasis added.

3. *The Federalist*, no. 70.

4. *The Federalist*, no. 39. Emphasis added.

5. James Madison, "Virginia Resolution" (1798), text available at the Bill of Rights Institute, https://billofrightsinstitute.org/primary-sources/virginia-and-kentucky-resolutions.

6. Jack Rakove, "The Legacy of the Articles of Confederation," *Publius* 12 (Fall 1982): 62.

7. See Ralph C. Hancock, "Tocqueville on the Good of American Federalism," *Publius* 20 (Spring 1990): 89–108. Emphasis added.

8. Shelby County v. Holder 570 U.S. 529 (2013).

9. Wabash, St. Louis & Pacific Railway Company v. Illinois, 118 U.S. 557 (1886).

10. Gibbons v. Ogden, 22 U.S. (9 Wheat.) 1 (1824).

11. Theodore Roosevelt, Address at the Coliseum, San Francisco, September 14, 1912, text available at The Ohio State University, https://ehistory.osu.edu/exhibitions/1912/1912documents/LimitationofGovernment. Contrast that Hamiltonian vision with Ronald Reagan's unqualifiedly Jeffersonian (and constitutionally arguable) assertion in his first inaugural address: "It is my intention to curb the size and influence of the Federal establishment and to demand recognition of the distinction between the powers granted to the Federal Government and those reserved to the States or to the people. All of us need to be reminded that the Federal Government did not create the States; the States created the Federal Government." Inaugural address, January 20, 1981, text available at Ronald Reagan Presidential Library & Museum, https://www.reaganlibrary.gov/archives/speech/inaugural-address-1981.

12. United States v. Alfonso D. Lopez, Jr., 514 U.S. 549 (1995).

13. Woodrow Wilson, *Constitutional Government in the United States* (New York: Columbia University Press, 1908), 66. Wilson's claim was quoted approvingly by John F. Kennedy at the National Press Club, Washington, DC, January 14, 1960, during his presidential campaign. Text available at John F. Kennedy Presidential Library and Museum, https://www.jfklibrary.org/archives/other-resources/john-f-kennedy-speeches/presidency-in-1960-19600114.

14. Henry Brooks Adams, "The Session," *North American Review* 111, no. 228 (July 1870): 29–62.

15. Enoch H. Crowder, *The Spirit of Selective Service* (New York: Century, 1920), 78–84.

16. Dobbs v. Jackson Women's Health Organization, No. 19-1392, 597 U.S. 215 (2022).

17. Richard Nathan, "There Will Always Be a New Federalism," *Journal of Public Administration Research and Theory* 16, no. 4 (October 2006): 499–510.

18. American Assembly, *Goals for Americans: Programs for Action in the Sixties* (Englewood Cliffs, NJ: Prentice Hall, 1960).

19. Nathan, "New Federalism," 505.

Federalism Principles and Perspectives

Discussants: Thad Kousser and Daniel L. Rubinfeld

THAD KOUSSER: Thank you so much for the invitation and the chance to learn from these great papers. I'm going to talk about the David Kennedy and the [Alice] Wang and [Morris] Fiorina papers. On David Kennedy's paper, I'm thrilled to see that he takes on this traditional narrative of the course of federalism in American history. The textbook story of federalism is that it's been a monotonic increase in greater and greater national power and greater and greater national spending over the history of time, but it's been more complicated than that. In Jonathan Rodden's paper, we will trace some of that at the financial level, but in the realm of state power, I think David is absolutely right to focus on cycles, to talk about this aggregate trend that has over time generally increased the realm of national authority and national spending.

But there have been these periods where states have challenged the federal government. They've challenged it with policies, challenged it in the courts, and of course challenged it on the battlefield. You see it in the Supreme Court, where you see a landmark case on federalism just about every session, right? So it's always being renegotiated; this question of what falls under a state's autonomy and what's a national power is America's great unresolved argument. We started this fight in Philadelphia, and we haven't ended it. And thinking through David's paper, there's one point I want to make and then one question I want to raise.

The point is that he terms this history as this story of "stubbornly persistent confusion and argument." And I want to make the point that this is much more argument than confusion. Woodrow Wilson, he's quoted as saying that this is the great unfinished, unanswered question.

An unanswered question is something that you can resolve with logic and with better or worse argument. But instead, this is really a battle. It's a battle that's been fought through political, legal, and sometimes even military power.

So he quotes James Madison talking about this federal and state combined power, and Kennedy characterizes him as this uncharacteristically obtuse version of Madison trying to spell out where the division is. And I think the reason he can't spell it out is that it's not an answerable intellectual question. It's something that has to be argued and negotiated and renegotiated over time consistently. And the people who are talking about it in that state and federal realm aren't speaking of it in obtuse or uncertain terms. They're always making clarion calls.

So for instance, one of the practitioners who we're going to hear from later today, Governor Jerry Brown: five years ago, Attorney General Jeff Sessions came to Sacramento in part of this federalism war. Sessions was there to castigate the state for passing a sanctuary state law that said essentially that state and local law enforcement could not cooperate with federal immigration authorities when it came to people convicted of misdemeanors. And Jerry Brown said that Sessions was initiating a "reign of terror" and that this is basically going to "war" against the state of California. Sessions ramped it up, called the state radical extremists. And was this overheated? Well, this is a really, truly important issue for the people who were part of it, but I think what this shows is that [it's] an argument fought in really strident terms continuously and still today between the state and national government.

The question I want to raise is that in this argument, is anyone ever making a principled argument? Certainly in Philadelphia there were principled arguments, and Michael [McConnell] laid them out beautifully. And there's kind of an evolution of those arguments. So I think today, a political theorist who believes in state power would say that philosophical commitment to decentralization is all about innovation in a Brandeis manner, and also having greater responsiveness, a greater match to local preferences and power. So if you're a Californian during the Trump era, you get the policies that you want, at least at the state level. You get the sanctuary state. If you're a Floridian during the Biden era, you get Ron DeSantis's version of how to address COVID and that better fits. And so that's the state argument.

And there's a principled argument on the other side, which is that this patchwork of policies is not internally cohesive, creates externalities that spill over, and one state's problem rubs off on another. And also, that there are certain important rights that need to be guaranteed federally. I think Madison won that debate that you were talking about, between whether local or national government is the better protector of fundamental rights. But I don't think anyone who's engaged in these debates is actually following these principles, right? If you look, no one's consistent. There is no party that is the consistent party of state power. If you look at what Democrats have supported, liberals have wanted national power when it comes to healthcare programs, right? The ACA [Affordable Care Act] with both the individual mandate and the Medicaid expansion, those were big pushes for national power.

On the environment, Obama had the Clean Power Plan that was held up by a deadlocked Supreme Court. That would've required every state to have a plan to decarbonize its energy grid. That would've been a huge expansion of national power. The preservation of voting rights, H.R. 1 that Congress was focused on last year, that would've had a national way to run an election. Guarantees of LGBTQ rights, preserving federal gun controls, keeping immigration a federal issue, and striking down things like California's Prop 187—Democrats have wanted all that. But Democrats have also wanted state rights when it comes to sanctuary state laws, when it comes to the environment. California always pushes for Clean Air Act amendments that exempt California.

And exactly as Michael was talking about with this Pork Producers Act, California legislators now are very intentionally trying to use California's market power to affect the way that other states govern themselves. So no party has been consistent; the parties have shifted on the question of which level should govern abortion. People who were saying abortion should be a state issue now want to pass a federal ban on abortion. So no party is consistent philosophically on federalism. And so I think, that doesn't mean that we as academics don't have to bring principled arguments. And I think David brings at the end of this a very forceful argument, that it's futile, that Stephen Douglas's argument for popular sovereignty is futile. It's just a way to kick the can down the road for the weighty issues of the day. So other academics— Jake Grumbach has a recent book called *Laboratories against Democracy*, Jamila Michener's *Fragmented Democracy*—they've criticized federal power, and I think that's where we need to have the argument.

So in two minutes, I'll talk about the very helpful Wang and Fiorina paper that brings comprehensive data on mass attitudes across time to this question. And I read it through the lens of this question that David Kennedy raises, which is: Does the public have a principled view of federalism, or is the public just as unprincipled as our politicians? So you very helpfully break things down by parties. And you look at people's views on the role of the federal government. And what you see is that when Democrats are in power in Washington, DC, Democrats in the mass public want federal power. When Donald Trump wins, they back away from that. And you see this perfect fluctuation depending on who's in power in Washington, DC.

So people are basically having the same views on trust in government, on the role of the federal government. And I bet if you looked at presidential approval, it would just essentially track that, right? But then if that's the case, then it raises this question of, "Is there a substance behind that public opinion?" There's a question that [Douglas] Rivers, [David] Brady, and [Jacob] Jaffe, their paper is also going to bring up. And so I think that's where, as you revise this, you take this wealth of data to use, the question that David [Kennedy] was asking, like, do people who are local winners, who have copartisans in the governor's office, do they favor state powers? Is there a way to look at particular issues—abortion, gun control—to see where people want power exercised? And really, at the end of the day, is there any substance to this issue? Or are we all just reasoning from our views on policies and projecting that into arguments on federalism? Thanks.

DANIEL L. RUBINFELD: So I'm going to work my way back to Michael McConnell's paper, which I thought was wonderful. What's interesting to me is that the McConnell paper offers views that are in near agreement with my recent book with Robert Inman [*Democratic Federalism*]. However, while McConnell offers a wonderful development, I disagree with him with respect to several of the policy issues. Interestingly, the source of our likely areas of disagreement comes out of the work Bob Inman and I began at the Center for Advanced Study only thirty years ago. It eventually led to our book, which came out in paperback in 2022.

Inman and I were trying to develop a coherent, primarily normative, theory of federalism. And the only natural place to start was with small governments, which, for a lot of reasons, the founders discussed extensively. The benefits of small governments included, one, fostering political participation; two, protecting individual rights and liberties; and three, matching citizen preferences to service levels.

It's very powerful from a normative perspective to think about the nature of the ability to have competition among local governments and to have liberty as well as participation benefits. And that goes way beyond the underlying pure economics. The hard question for me, with which the McConnell discussion is really helpful, is to understand the normative role for states.

The early economics literature flipped between local activities and the center and said nothing about the appropriate role for intermediaries—the states. Yet there's a natural role for states, which goes beyond economic federalism to cooperative federalism. Here you start thinking about the treatment of various externalities that are best treated at the local level if possible. If not purely local, there is a role for the states. States are able to manage the inefficiencies that result from local provision while protecting against tyranny by the center and promoting and protecting a stable democracy.

And once you start to think about the role of states, you can read, I think, a fair amount of this into the founders' debate, which McConnell discusses. That debate included a discussion of the benefits—and costs—of a system of constitutional federalism in which there is direct representation in the center. Our empirical analysis suggests that this system is preferable to a system of de facto federalism in which politically independent lower-tier governments operate without direct representation at the center. To complete the federalism story, I note that what is missing from Michael's essay, which would just complement it further, is the fact that many externalities have been handled by the creation of special districts. Today, there are over fifty thousand special districts in the US that handle all kinds of externalities that wouldn't otherwise make sense at the state level, let alone the federal level. The founders didn't talk about special districts, but it's a natural consequence of growth or economy. In my view, there are powerful arguments for the efficiencies that flow from some form of decentralization. US economist Caroline Hoxby's papers are very supportive in that regard. If you go back to the work I did back about thirty years ago, there are clearly efficiencies with respect to the provision of K–12 public education, bearing in mind, of course, the compelling show by Rick [Eric] Hanushek that dollars spent on education are not necessarily productive.

So Inman and I went back and looked empirically at what we would describe as federal states in the world, of which the US is, I'd say, the prominent, most successful example. But there are many less-prominent forms of government. And when you look at the data over about a thirty- or forty-year period and look at various measures of success, the federal design we have in the US has been successful. If you look at measures of success, including basic measures like output per worker, the US framework does well. The more interesting political question is why other systems did not do as well. To illustrate, Inman and I have a chapter on the European federal state, which is an example of what I think some of the founders of the US Constitution had in mind for an ideal federal state. But the EU has failed significantly on many dimensions, and in our chapter we highlight some of those. Those failures have to do with the ineffectual nature of the European Parliament and with macro issues, where the monetary system there does not function very well. To sum up, all of these other federal systems do reasonably well compared to more traditional centralized systems, but none do as well as the US.

Now my disagreement, if there is one, with McConnell comes when we start to look at some of the practical debates about what makes sense at the center and what doesn't. And there, Inman and I have, I think, an interesting discussion of the work we did in South Africa, where a World Bank–led team helped South Africa to design a decentralized system.

With respect to issues of decentralization, there is an important, extensive legal and economic literature surrounding the so-called state action exemption doctrine. The question at issue is when the federal government should trump the activities of state and local governments. And the raisin producers cartel example in *Parker v. Brown* is noteworthy. That case is all about the California raisin cartel that controlled a market where it produced almost all the raisins, while Californians consumed almost none. *Parker v. Brown*, from my point of view, was a wrongly decided case, and the reason is a failure to account for this significant externality when the benefits and costs are not appropriately aligned at a local-state level.

Unfortunately, that is still true today. If you look at the case law relating to state action, the emphasis is on the ability of states or localities to promulgate their own regulations and to enforce them but not to account for the significant externalities they had created. Our suggestion is to create a federalism impact statement, which would basically be a system that would require a formal federalism analysis before regulatory activities are put in place.

If Alice Rivlin [former director of the US Office of Management and Budget] were still with us, I would ask her to take charge of an analysis by the Congressional Budget Office or some other appropriate organization that would seriously trade off the pros and cons of what should be centralized and what should not be centralized. So even if we take *Dobbs* [*Dobbs v. Jackson Women's Health Organization*], which was mentioned earlier by McConnell, the subject, about which there are very strong views, could be evaluated within our federalism impact framework.

Finally, a few comments on David Kennedy's paper. Kennedy offers an insightful commentary on how the framers viewed the concept of a federal system of government. The key, he points out, is an appropriate sharing of powers between the states and the center. Kennedy properly emphasizes the importance of the Commerce Clause—it offers a grant of congressional authority and a restriction on the regulatory authority of the states. I did find the reference to Madison's discussion in *The Federalist*, No. 39 to be of interest —where, if I recall, Madison describes the proposed constitution as neither a national nor a federal constitution.

Part 2

The Current State of Federalism

4

The Budgetary Impact of the Abandonment of Federalism

John F. Cogan

In most high school and college courses on American government, students are taught that the federal powers are limited and that there is a sharp division between federal and state government responsibilities. When it comes to federal spending, nothing could be further from the truth. No state or local activity is beyond the reach of the federal government's check-writing machine. The original limitations on the scope of federal spending power no longer exist. Indeed, the breadth of federal spending is so large that it is hard to think of a state or local government activity that isn't also financed by the federal government.

Each year, Congress grants federal funds to states for highways, medical care, social services, educational instruction, nutrition assistance, and welfare. It regularly finances activities that are at the core of local government responsibilities, including municipal parks and playgrounds, local pedestrian bike paths and hiking trails, city sidewalks, bus stops, railroad crossings, traffic signs and stoplights, and beautification projects for all the above. It provides funds for such activities regardless of a community's income or wealth and regardless of local jurisdictions' financial capacity. Recent federally funded local projects include a museum celebrating high-tech CEOs in Palo Alto, California (a city with a median household income of $174,000), a bike-share program to support casino-to-casino transit in Las Vegas, a soccer field in Anaheim, California, a baseball field in Lowell, Massachusetts, a ski jump in New Hampshire, and sewers in Peoria, Illinois.

As numerous as these projects are, they constitute only a small fraction of federally financed activities that were once exclusively under the jurisdiction of state or local governments. The lion's share of such expenditures is made through a host of entitlement programs that provide cash or in-kind transfer benefits to individuals.

The breadth of modern-day federal spending on state and local activities is light-years from the original concept of federalism in fiscal matters. This concept, envisioned by James Madison and practiced by Congress during its first thirty years, held that federal spending is constrained to activities that are necessary and proper to carry out the Constitution's enumerated powers. Congress could appropriate federal funds to raise and support armed forces, to regulate commerce, to collect tax revenue, and so forth. But it could not fund grants to states for such activities as healthcare, community development, and social services. Nor could it provide financial or in-kind assistance to individuals unless that aid was compensation for federal service. As emphasized by the Tenth Amendment, these activities were reserved for the states and individuals. Congress adhered to this view from 1789 to 1817 by limiting its appropriations to activities that were justified by an enumerated power and consistently rejecting proposals to fund activities that were outside of those powers.

The original concept of fiscal federalism began to erode in the 1820s, continued to erode throughout the nineteenth and early twentieth centuries, and was abandoned entirely in the 1930s.[1]

This paper examines the impact of the abandonment of federalism on federal expenditures, revenues, and the federal budget deficit. The period of analysis is from 1950 to 2019. It uses the original concept of fiscal federalism to distinguish between expenditures on national versus state and local activities. The former category may be thought of as a "Madison budget" because it includes only those expenditures necessary and proper to carry out the Constitution's enumerated powers.

The analysis reveals that federal spending on activities originally regarded as state and local increased from 2 percent of GDP in 1950 to 14 percent in 2019, accounting for more than the entire growth in federal spending during the period. It now constitutes two-thirds of all federal expenditures. The analysis also shows that the nearly continuous string of federal budget deficits since the 1960s is due to Congress's failure to raise revenues sufficient to finance the growth in federal spending on state and local activities. Since the 1930s, the federal government has, in effect, chosen to take on additional responsibilities and has been persistently unwilling to finance them with tax revenues. Instead, it has financed them with debt.

A balanced federal budget was one of the many benefits of the original concept of fiscal federalism. During the nineteenth and early twentieth centuries, Congress balanced the annual federal budget after allowing for surpluses to reduce the outstanding debt, except during wartime and economic recessions. Since 1950, the Madison budget has followed the same behavior. Annual federal revenues, excluding social insurance tax revenues used to finance social insurance programs, such as Social Security and Medicare, have exceeded annual Madison budget expenditures, except during the Korean and Vietnam Wars, the defense buildup during the Reagan administration, and the economic recessions of 1990–91 and 2008–9.

This paper is divided into four sections: an examination of Congress's original concept of fiscal federalism as developed from 1789 to 1817; an outline of the steady erosion and eventual abandonment of this original concept; an analysis of the budgetary impact of the abandonment from 1950 to 2019; and some concluding remarks.

The Original Idea of Federalism: 1789–1817

The original idea of fiscal federalism is inexorably linked to the Constitution's limits on the federal spending power. The ink on the Constitution's parchment was barely dry when two distinctly different interpretations of the scope of federal spending power arose. James Madison held the view that the spending power was limited to activities to carry out the federal government's enumerated powers. All other activities were the responsibility of state and local governments and the people. The Tenth Amendment reinforced this view. Alexander Hamilton believed that the spending power also included spending to promote the general welfare on activities that were national, as opposed to local, in purpose, and to "create" commerce through commercial subsidies.

The two views defined two different systems of fiscal federalism. In the Madison view, specific grants of authority defined a boundary line between federal and state and local functions that the federal government could not cross in its decisions on how to spend federal funds. The Hamilton view was much broader. The federal government could not only finance improvements in commerce, it could also fund any activity that Congress deemed to be in the national interest.

From 1789 to 1822, Congress largely adhered to the Madison view and, in doing so, established the original concept of fiscal federalism. This adherence occurred despite numerous attempts to break from the Madison view. During this formative period, members of Congress offered numerous spending proposals that pushed against the limits imposed by Madison's enumerated powers doctrine. With only a few exceptions, Congress denied these proposals; burying some in committee while rejecting others after vigorous debate. More than a dozen proposals were introduced to fund road and canal construction within or between state boundaries, including the famous Erie Canal. For example, an 1809 bill proposed that a portion of the profits of a soon-to-be-created national bank system "be appropriated for the general welfare in the construction of public roads and canals."[2] Congressional majorities consistently rejected these proposals on the grounds that internal improvements were a state and local government responsibility. The only exception to this pattern was the Cumberland Road, which, as we will see later, was financed under unique circumstances involving the state of Ohio's entry into the Union.[3]

Numerous proposals for commercial subsidies in the form of loans, cash subsidies, or governmental purchases of company stock were offered based on the Commerce Clause, the general welfare clause, or on vaguer terms of national interest. For example, in 1791 a loan to a glass manufacturer was proposed on the basis that the federal government was "vested with a general power to encourage the arts and manufacturers of the United States."[4] The bill was defeated after constitutional objections were raised. Later proposals to use federal funds for similar purposes, including aiding a silk manufacturer, a mine and metal company, a fire insurance company, and a company with a new technique for abating rat and mice infestations were likewise rejected.[5]

Proposals to fund a national university based on the power "to promote the useful arts" was rejected by three different Congresses. The committee report on an 1811 proposal noted the national importance of expanding knowledge and the value of training future teachers. But the committee rejected the proposal on the grounds that the Constitution reserved research and education activities to state and local governments. The previously mentioned National Bank Bill proposed to use a portion of its proceeds for "the establishment of seminaries for education throughout the United States." The proposal was similarly rejected.[6]

Local disaster relief was also regarded as a state and local responsibility. The debate over a bill to assist fire victims in Savannah, Georgia, in 1796 illustrates this well. Virginia representative Robert Rutherford claimed that "policy, humanity, and justice should prompt the House to a noble action." Fellow Virginian John Nicholas countered that "the General Government had no power but what was given to it, but the state Governments had all power for the good of their several States." Representative Nicholas's argument carried the day and the bill was defeated. Proposals to aid victims of fires and other local disasters in New York City, Charlestown and Georgetown, South Carolina, and Beaumont, Georgia, faced a similar fate during this period.[7]

More generally, Congress regarded grants to states for any purpose as beyond its constitutional power. From the First Congress to the Fourteenth, grants-to-states proposals were rare and not one was enacted into law. This fact alone serves as an indication that most members of Congress regarded such grants as beyond the federal government's power. One such bill proposed to provide $2 million in grants to states to assist the poor and justified the expenditure as promoting the general welfare. Congressional debate records do not record any floor debate; only that the bill was rejected with a relatively few supporters.[8]

Congress was willing to finance similar activities if they could be justified by an enumerated power or another constitutional provision. Thus, Congress appropriated funds for military roads and canals within the federal territories and in the District of Columbia. Also, from 1789 onward, Congress regularly funded the construction of lighthouses and beacons, but only after the land upon which the structure was built was ceded by the state to the federal government.

Although Congress was unwilling to provide federal funds for persons suffering losses from fire and other natural disasters, it was willing occasionally to provide such assistance through the tax code. For example, Congress delayed tax payments due on goods destroyed by fires in Portsmouth, New Hampshire, in 1803. On numerous occasions Congress appropriated funds to compensate private individuals for losses suffered in service to the federal government. Payments to persons who assisted government officials during the Whiskey Rebellion and pensions awarded to Revolutionary War veterans are two notable examples.[9]

In a few instances, Congress stretched an enumerated power to enact a popular bill. These "work-arounds" are further evidence that Congress sought to adhere to the enumerated powers doctrine.[10] A 1794 bill to aid refugees from Santo Domingo stands out as an early example. Earlier that year, three thousand French refugees landed in Baltimore and overwhelmed the city's resources. Representative Elias Boudinot argued that Congress had a responsibility to provide the city with aid "by the law of Nature, by the law of Nations—in a word, by every moral obligation that could influence mankind." Representative William Giles countered "Gentlemen appeal to our humanity. . . . [The question is] whether, organized as we are, under the Constitution, do we have the right to make such a grant?" The relief bill was enacted only after the House overcame the constitutional objections by stipulating in law that since the beneficiaries were French citizens, the aid was a loan to the French government.[11] In 1813, Congress authorized a vaccine agent to collect vaccination materials and distribute them to individuals upon request through the postal service.[12]

During the Republic's early years, federal spending remained small and exhibited little growth. Except during the War of 1812, federal spending hovered around 2 percent of GDP. The vast majority of appropriations from 1789 to 1817, 93 percent, were devoted to four main activities: maintaining an army and navy; conducting foreign affairs; interest payments on the national debt; and financing the salaries and related expenses of executive branch departments, the judiciary, and members of Congress. Appropriations for activities that were arguably beyond—or stretched—the enumerated powers constitute the remaining 7 percent. The bulk of these appropriations, 6.5 percent of the budget, financed purchases of the Bank of the United States stock and the Louisiana Territory. The remaining appropriation of $700,000 consisted of appropriations to build the Cumberland Road and to distribute a portion of the proceeds of lands to newly created states.[13]

These latter appropriations, which occurred under unique circumstances, warrant a brief discussion. The precedent for both types of appropriations was a compact between the federal government and Ohio when that state was admitted to the Union in 1802. Under the compact, a portion of the proceeds from the sale of federal lands within the state would be returned to the state for the construction of roads within the state and for roads leading from the state to the navigable waters emptying into the Atlantic Ocean. In return, the new state exempted federal land sales within its borders from taxation.

At the time, supporters justified the compact by Article 4 of the Constitution, which authorized the federal government to dispose of federal land in ways that were beneficial to the country. Ohio's agreement not to tax remaining federal land within its border improved the value of the remaining federal land within the state. Thus, supporters argued, the federal government was acting as a "prudent proprietor" of the federal domain.

In 1806, Congress authorized the Cumberland Road to carry out the compact's provision for a road from the waters emptying into the Atlantic Ocean to Ohio. The so-called National Road would run through the states of Virginia, Maryland, and Pennsylvania. During debate over the bill, the only controversial issue was whether the consent of these states was required. It was decided in the affirmative. The Cumberland Road, which received appropriations for thirty-one years, was unique. No other federally financed road was constructed within state boundaries for more than a century, except military roads for the transport of troops and supplies. The 1806 law also established a special fund to distribute 3 percent of the proceeds of federal lands sales within Ohio to the state. This latter provision served as a model for newly admitted states in the future.[14]

Two of the more important debates on federal spending power's constitutional limits occurred at the bookends of this first period. In 1792, the House extensively debated the issue of whether, under the general welfare clause, Congress could appropriate federal funds for direct relief to individuals. At issue was the method of providing relief to fishermen suffering from the impact of a previously enacted import tax on salt. The Tariff Act of 1789 had imposed a duty on salt and, to limit the financial harm done to fishermen who used salt to cure their fish, the law also provided an allowance "in lieu of a drawback," on exports of fish products. But the allowance mainly benefited export merchants, not fishermen who paid the salt tax. The initial version of the 1792 bill sought to remedy this perceived unfairness by repealing the allowance on fish products and replacing it with direct payments to fishermen from the Treasury, termed bounties.[15]

The bill, coming on the heels of the publication of Alexander Hamilton's "Report on Manufactures," sparked an extensive and well-recorded debate in the House of Representatives over the government's power to spend to promote the general welfare. Mr. Hamilton had argued that payments from the Treasury, termed "bounties," were the most efficacious means of encouraging industry and were justified under the general welfare clause. Representative Abbott Laurence supported the Hamilton view by arguing that if an expenditure enhances the national wealth, it is in the general welfare. As Mr. Laurence put it, "The general welfare is inseparably connected with any object or pursuit which in its effects adds to the riches of the country."[16]

The bill's opponents, led by James Madison in the House of Representatives, argued that granting bounties was a precedent-setting constitutional breach. Madison famously and prophetically warned:

> If Congress can apply money indefinitely to the general welfare, and are the sole and supreme judges of the general welfare, they may take the care of religion into their hands; they may establish teachers in every state, county, and parish, and pay them out of the Public Treasury; they may take into their own hands the education of children, establishing

in like manner schools throughout the Union; they may undertake the regulation of all roads, other than postroads. In short, everything from the highest object of State legislation down to the most minute object of police, would admit the application of money, and might be called, if Congress pleased, provisions for the general welfare.[17]

William Giles added a moral dimension to the argument against direct payments to individuals from the Treasury by remarking that "the product of one man's labor is transferred to the use and enjoyment of another. This can be justified only under the proposition that the entire product of an individual's work is the real property of the government."[18]

Finally, Representative Hugh Williamson of North Carolina warned that the payment of bounties to fishermen would inevitably expand to others who would be deemed no less worthy of government aid by saying:

> Establish the doctrine of bounties, set aside that part of the Constitution which requires equal taxes and demands similar distributions, destroy this barrier, and it is not a few fishermen that will enter, claiming ten or twelve thousand dollars, but all manner of persons—people of every trade and occupation—may enter at the breach, until they have eaten up the bread of our children.[19]

After vigorous debate, members agreed to provide the desired relief in a way that satisfied the constitutional concerns of Madison and others. The bounty was stricken from the bill and was replaced by an allowance. The bit of wordsmanship permitted the relief to be considered as a rebate against taxes paid. Also, the bill's purpose was to make clear that it was to provide relief from the salt tax, not bounties to promote the cod fishing industry.[20]

A second important congressional debate over the breadth of the federal spending power took place in 1817 over a bill to finance a national transportation system. The bill was in response to increased demands for improved commercial transportation, which had accelerated following settlement of the western lands obtained by the Louisiana Purchase. The so-called Bonus Bill proposed to use the proceeds from the Bank of the United States to finance a block grant to states to construct an interconnected system of roads and canals. Its chief sponsor, John C. Calhoun, argued that the bill was needed to bind the nation together: "The more enlarged the sphere of commercial circulation, the more extended that of social intercourse; the more strongly are we bound together; the more inseparable are our destinies."[21] He defended the constitutionality of his plan by appeal to the general welfare clause.[22] Others, including Henry Clay, supported the bill's constitutionality on the Commerce Clause. Still others invoked the government's authority to build postal roads and the need for military roads for national defense.

Opponents challenged all but the last of these justifications. The general welfare clause did not give the government the open-ended power to spend funds on any projects that in its view improved the nation's welfare. The Commerce Clause did not give the government the power to create commerce by building roads and canals, only to regulate it in certain ways. The postal power did not give the government the power to construct postal roads, only to designate existing roads as postal.

Aside from constitutional concerns, the Calhoun bill faced other obstacles. The block grant approach avoided the thorny issue of whether the federal government had the authority to build roads within a state without the state's permission. More than a decade earlier, Congress passed the Cumberland Road bill only after it required the permission of the states through which the road ran. Little had changed in the years since. But the block grant approach would not necessarily produce a nationally interconnected system. States would be free to use the funds instead to build roads and canals that suited local purposes.

The bill passed both chambers by slim margins. President Madison, like President Jefferson before him, supported federal funding of internal improvements, but believed that the Constitution had to be amended first to permit it.[23] President Madison vetoed the bill on his last day in office. In his veto message, Madison argued that permitting the expenditure

> would be contrary to the established and consistent rules of interpretation, as rendering the special and careful enumeration of powers, which follows the clause, nugatory, and improper. Such a view of the Constitution would have the effect of giving to Congress a general power of legislation, instead of the defined and limited one hitherto understood to belong to them.[24]

In Madison's view, one of the Constitution's fundamental purposes was to establish a clear dividing line between federal and state government jurisdictions. The Supreme Court was responsible for ensuring that the federal government did not extend its activities beyond this constitutional boundary. Madison's veto message noted that the question of whether a particular action served the general welfare involved policy preferences over which the Supreme Court would be unlikely to render judgments. Hence, the Hamiltonian view of the general welfare clause "would have the effect of excluding the judicial authority of the United States from its participation in guarding the boundary between the legislative power of the General and the State Governments."

Although Congress upheld Madison's veto, the vote signaled the beginning of the end of the dominance of the Madison view.[25] For the first time, Congress had passed a bill claiming federal authority to finance the construction of roads and canals within the states. But within Congress, there was no consensus on any particular Constitutional rationale for this authority, nor on how far into other state and local activities it extended.

In summary, from 1789 to the end of the War of 1812, Congress adhered to Madison's view of the limits on federal spending power and its meaning for federalism with few exceptions. Congress vigorously debated and, with one exception, rejected all proposals to fund roads and canals within state boundaries other than those for military purposes. Similarly, Congress rejected all proposals to appropriate funds to provide financial assistance to individuals, except to those who had performed government service. Congress also refused to fund grants-to-states programs for education, aid to the poor, and until 1817, internal improvements. No such grants for any purpose were enacted into law. This adherence to the enumerated powers defines the original idea of federalism in fiscal matters.

Erosion

The barrier separating state and local activities from federal spending began to erode in the 1820s when, in 1823, James Monroe reversed his previous position and held that Congress could federally fund internal improvements within state boundaries. Thereafter, Congress regularly passed legislation appropriating federal funds for river clearance and harbor dredging projects. However, prior to the Civil War there continued to be little agreement as to the constitutional basis for this funding. A minority in Congress and all Democratic presidents continued to regard funding of such projects as unconstitutional. Majority support was divided. The Commerce Clause provided the primary constitutional rationale. The remaining support was split among those who favored roads for military purposes, those who relied on the federal government's responsibility for postal roads, and a few who relied on the general welfare clause. Congress was further divided along regional and party lines. Westerners and Whigs and Republicans generally supported internal improvements, while southerners and Democrats stood in opposition.

Congress was generally more favorably disposed toward internal improvements than pre–Civil War presidents. Congress regularly passed bills that pressed against presidential limitations. Their passage produced an extraordinary series of presidential vetoes. President Jackson vetoed six bills appropriating funds for internal improvements within state borders. President Tyler vetoed the only internal improvement bill presented to him.[26] Presidents Polk and Buchanan each vetoed the two bills they received. Franklin Pierce vetoed a total of six internal improvement bills. Congress sustained these vetoes until the 1850s, when it overrode five of President Pierce's vetoes.

After the Civil War, Democratic Party opposition faded as federal funds became an important source for financially strapped Southern states whose transportation infrastructure had been severely damaged during the war. Constitutional concerns were overwhelmed by self-interest and the strong force of precedents that had been established by previously enacted bills. For the remainder of the nineteenth century and thereafter, Congress regularly passed river and harbor appropriations bills with little opposition.

Although river and harbor bills were important to the erosion of the original concept of fiscal federalism, spending on these projects never amounted to a significant part of federal spending. From the 1820s to the end of the nineteenth century, rivers and harbors expenditures constituted only 4 percent of the budget. Their percentage peaked at only 8 percent in the early 1830s.[27]

Prior to the Civil War, Congress was remarkably unwilling to extend its spending beyond internal improvements to other state and local activities. The only significant exceptions are the single-year distribution of large budget surpluses to states in 1837 and 1841, the publication of agricultural information and the distribution of seeds to farmers in the 1840s and 1850s, and a onetime appropriation to study the chemistry of vegetables in 1850.

From the Civil War to the 1930s, Congress steadily expanded its spending power into areas that had previously been the exclusive province of state and local governments. The expansion was slow initially. Congress created the Departments of Agriculture in 1862 and Education in 1867, but it limited their activities mainly to collecting and disseminating information to farmers and educators, respectively. In 1887, Congress appropriated federal funds for agricultural experiment stations at land-grant colleges. This act, coming nearly a hundred years after the Republic began, was the federal government's first grants-to-states program other than the grants of federal land sale revenues to newly admitted states. Three years later, and after rejecting two decades of proposals for federal funding of elementary and secondary schools, Congress enacted the first appropriations for education. The second Morrill Act of 1890 provided federal funds for teacher salaries and operational expenses at land-grant colleges. Perhaps most consequential for the future, Congress in 1874 appropriated funds for relief of victims of a flood along the Mississippi River. This was the first time Congress provided direct cash payments to individuals for economic relief. It opened the door for similar disaster relief bills. During the 1880s and 1890s, Congress appropriated funds, or the president used previously appropriated funds, to provide aid to individuals suffering primarily from floods, but also tornadoes, cyclones, and fires within the states on fifteen separate occasions.

Despite these expansions, the original idea of fiscal federalism still retained its strong hold on Congress. This hold was instrumental in limiting federal spending to a small percentage of the economy and producing balanced budgets. From the beginning of the Republic to the Civil War, federal spending averaged only 1.7 percent of GDP. From the Civil War to the nineteenth century's end, it averaged only 2.7 percent. The federal budget ran annual surpluses except during wartime and economic downturns. The surpluses were used to reduce the outstanding public debt.

During the early years of the twentieth century, the pace of federal funding of what were originally state and local affairs accelerated. The main vehicles were so-called 50-50 programs for highway construction, vocational education and rehabilitation, cooperative agriculture extension services, and maternal and child health, which provided federal matching payments to state programs. Along with federal funds came requirements for states to adhere to federal rules and regulations. Through these requirements, the federal government began to influence not only the level of state expenditures in certain areas, but also where within the state and how these expenditures were made. Congress also broke new ground by extending federally financed credit assistance to farmers, first by providing federal financing to nonfederal land banks in 1916, then by providing credit directly to farmers in the 1920s. Subsidies for shipbuilding followed in the wake of this aid.

By 1930, federal spending on activities that were originally reserved to states, local governments, and individuals ballooned to 18 percent of the noninterest federal budget. Remarkably, in 1930 the federal government was spending more on these activities than it spent on all its other non-defense-related national functions.

But more important, by 1930 the federal government had breached large sections of the constitutional barrier that separated states and individuals from federal authorities. The 50-50 laws had opened a new avenue for federal involvement in state and local government affairs. The provision of credit to farmers could be extended to other commercial enterprises. Federal funding of rivers, harbors, and highways could be extended to other state and local infrastructure projects. Most important, relief to persons suffering economic hardship from natural disasters could be extended to persons suffering similar economic distress from economic disasters and, more generally, to persons suffering economic hardship through no fault of their own. Thus, by 1930, all the precedents for a dramatic expansion of the federal role in state, local, and private individuals' activities were in place.

The collapse of asset values and widespread unemployment during the Great Depression reduced state and especially local government revenues. The federal government, with its greater taxing authority and, more importantly, its greater borrowing capacity, stepped in. President Roosevelt's New Deal followed President Hoover's more limited response with emergency measures to provide federal loans and deposit insurance for banks, expanded loans to farmers and commercial enterprises, local public works and conservation projects, crop insurance and direct payments to farmers, and the creation of the Tennessee Valley Authority to generate electric power for households and business in its region of operation.

These emergency measures were followed by programs with a more permanent purpose. The 1935 Social Security Act's matching payments for state public assistance programs, its funding of administrative expenses of state unemployment insurance programs, and its signature retirement program put the federal government firmly in the income support business, an area into which it had not ventured previously in its 146-year existence.

These measures were a natural extension to the relief Congress had been providing to persons suffering from natural disasters.[28] The human misery caused by widespread unemployment was hardly different from the human misery caused by natural disasters, and the more than half century of federal funding on the latter established the precedent for funding on the former.

Two years later, the Supreme Court famously ruled that Congress had the power to spend to promote the general welfare on activities that were national, rather than local, in scope. Furthermore, according to the Court, the authority to determine whether an activity was national or local rested solely with Congress. All along, Hamilton had been right and Madison wrong. The ruling effectively removed the Court from its role as guardian of the boundary line between federal and state jurisdiction on spending matters, just as Madison had warned it would in 1817. The original idea of fiscal federalism was now a dead letter.[29]

With no constraint on the scope of federal spending power, the Truman administration made the New Deal emergency programs for housing, urban renewal, and nutrition assistance for schoolchildren permanent. The federal government extended itself further into state and local affairs, creating a new federal-state matching program for impoverished disabled workers and extending matching payments to states for medical care for public assistance recipients. The Eisenhower administration continued this expansion by making Social Security coverage universal, by increasing funding for urban renewal programs, and by establishing a new Social Security disability program and a new national highway program.

By the advent of the Great Society, only a few areas of state and local activities remained free from federal funds and the regulatory requirements attached to them. By the Great Society's end, there were no areas left. In the span of ten years, from 1964 to 1973, Congress enacted new 100 percent federally financed programs providing medical care to seniors, nutrition assistance to low-income households, financial assistance to college students, and grants and loans to all colleges and universities, not just land-grant colleges. It extended subsidies to cities for elementary and secondary schools, mass transit, community development, and clean water infrastructure projects. It reached down into city neighborhoods and rural communities to fund preschool programs, health clinics, legal aid services, youth employment, job training, and social service programs.

Thus, by the mid-1970s, the federal government was at least partially funding almost every—if not every—function that the Constitution had originally reserved to the states and individuals. Since then, further extensions have been marginal. These extensions have included new programs to assist households with home heating and weatherization expenses, to subsidize individual purchases of phones and monthly phone bills, and to earmark funds for local construction projects.

Impact of Federal Government Spending on State and Local Activities

This section examines the impact of abandoning the original concept of fiscal federalism on the federal budget from 1950 to 2019. The examination uses the Madison view of federal spending power's scope to separate federal

expenditures into those on national activities and those which Congress originally considered state and local activities.

Dividing federal budget expenditures between the two types of activities
might seem like an impossible task. The federal budget contains more than
three thousand federal programs and, because of societal changes and technological advances, many current programs carry out activities that were hardly
imaginable during the Republic's early days. Moreover, many programs have
both federal and local attributes.

But given the highly concentrated character of federal spending, the task is
not as difficult as it first might seem. Federal expenditures on four categories:
national defense–related expenditures, interest on the public debt, direct cash
and in-kind transfer payments to individuals, and grants to states for healthcare, education, transportation, and other similar purposes, currently account
for 96 percent of federal spending. In 1950, they accounted for 92 percent.
This high concentration serves as the basis for allocating federal spending to
national activities and those which would be regarded in a Madison budget
as state and local. Once agreement is reached on the classification of these
categories into national versus state and local activities, differences of opinion
on the remaining programs has only a marginal effect on the allocation.

Table 4.1 shows the amounts spent on each of the four major expenditure
categories and how they are classified in the last and first years of our analysis:
2019 and 1950. The top bank of numbers shows expenditures that are designated as national. The middle bank shows those that are designated as state
and local. The lower numbers are the remaining expenditures that could be
allocated between national and state and local after a more detailed analysis.

National defense–related expenditures, which include all national defense
outlays (function 050), the Department of Veterans Affairs outlays (function
700), and outlays for military retirement, constitute the largest component
of "national" expenditures. All international affairs outlays (function 150)
are also classified as national.[30] All interest payments on the public debt are
considered as national, even though a portion is likely to have been incurred
on debt issued to finance state and local expenditures. Public debt is not
issued on a program-by-program basis, so interest payments cannot be allocated to individual programs. The approach taken here to classify all interest
payments as national errs on the side of understating expenditures on state
and local activities. The same approach to understating these expenditures is
taken throughout the classification process.

The lion's share of aid to individuals and grants to states are classified as
state and local expenditures. Aid to individuals includes expenditures on

the major federal entitlement programs, such as Social Security, Medicare, Disability Insurance, Unemployment Insurance, the Supplemental Nutrition Assistance Program (SNAP), child nutrition programs, student loans, Supplemental Security Income, Affordable Care Act subsidies, the Earned Income Tax Credit, and other refundable tax credits that exceed income taxes owed.[31] It excludes entitlement program payments to individuals for government service, in particular the aforementioned payments to veterans and military retirees. Federal employee retirement benefits are also excluded and are included instead in the unallocated portion of expenditures. Social insurance program expenditures, which are financed by dedicated revenues, are shown separately from those that are financed by general fund revenues. As we will see later, the distinction between the two is important to understanding the impact that federal spending on state and local activities has had on federal budget deficits.

Federal grants-to-states programs include all federal grants for education, social services, healthcare, transportation, community development, and welfare services. State grants that the budget classifies in the national defense or international affairs functions are excluded.

As the table shows, in 2019, 66 percent of federal spending was on activities that were originally considered to be the responsibility of state and local governments or private-sector entities such as charitable organizations. In 1950, that amount was only 15 percent. Aid to individuals accounts for 80 percent of this increase, grants to states the remaining 20 percent.

The following set of charts uses this classification scheme to show trends in federal spending on state and local activities and how they have impacted the federal budget. In these charts, expenditures in the "all other" category in table 4.1 are assigned to spending on "national" activities and as a result, the amount of spending assigned to state and local activities is understated.

Figure 4.1 displays federal spending on state and local activities as a share of total federal spending from 1950 to 2019. The sharp rise in the share from the mid-1950s to the late 1980s reflects the growth and expansion of large social insurance programs, the enactment of the Johnson administration's Great Society and its further liberalization by the Nixon administration. The share reaches 50 percent by the mid-1970s. At this point in time, the network of income-transfer and grants-to-states programs that exists today was nearly fully in place. The share's plateau in the 1980s reflects the Reagan administration's efforts to restrain domestic spending. The growth thereafter is a consequence of the steady expansions of existing income-transfer and

Table 4.1 Federal spending on national versus state and local activities

	1950		2019	
	(2019 $)	(Share)	(2019 $)	(Share)
Madison Outlays				
National Defense	$200	54%	$926	21%
International Affairs	$43	12%	$53	1%
Interest on the Public Debt	$43	12%	$375	8%
Total	$287	77%	$1,354	30%
State and Local Outlays				
Aid to Individuals: Social Insurance	$26	7%	$807	18%
Aid to Individuals: Means Tested	$9	2%	$1,394	31%
Grants to States	$19	5%	$719	16%
Total	$54	15%	$2,920	66%
All Other Spending	$30	8%	$173	4%
Total Outlays	$370	100%	$4,447	100%

Source: Author calculations using data from the Office of Management and Budget, Budget of the United States Government for Fiscal Year 2024 (hereafter US Budget 2024), Historical Tables 3.1, 10.1, 11.2, 11.3, and 12.2.

grants-to-states programs, and the few relatively small new programs created since the early 1990s.

Figure 4.2 displays how the composition of federal spending on state and local activities has changed over time. Aid to individuals has been the dominant form of expenditures on these activities, rising from 60 percent in the 1950s to between 70 and 80 percent since the 1980s. The major changes in shares are mainly due to changes in spending on grants-to-states programs. The rise in the share accounted for by grants to states from the early 1960s to the mid-1970s is due to Great Society expansions. Its decline in the 1980s reflects the Reagan administration's efforts to reduce these programs.

The following charts show how federal spending on state and local government activities has impacted total federal spending and federal budget deficits. Figure 4.3 displays annual federal spending and revenues as percentages of GDP from 1950 to 2019. As the figure shows, total federal spending as a percentage of GDP grew rapidly from the mid-1950s to the mid-1980s. Its decline from the mid-1980s, and especially from the mid-1990s to the early 2000s, is attributable in part to modest spending restraint, but primarily to

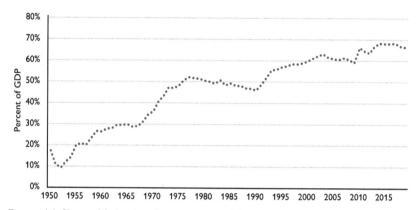

Figure 4.1 Share of federal outlays on state and local activities

Source: Author calculations using data from US Budget 2024, Historical Tables 3.1, 11.2, 11.3, and 12.2.

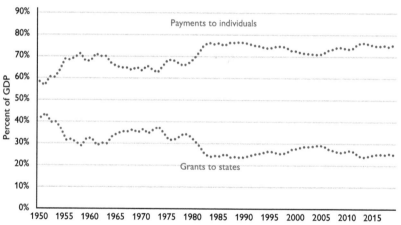

Figure 4.2 Share of spending on state and local activities by type

Source: Author calculations using data from US Budget 2024, Historical Tables 11.2, 11.3, and 12.2.

the rapid growth in GDP sparked by the dot-com bubble. Thereafter, it continued its upward rise with a spike during the great recession in 2008–10.

Meanwhile, federal revenues as a percentage of GDP (in green) have remained remarkably constant since the 1960s, fluctuating mainly within a small range from 17 to 18 percent of GDP. The exceptions are during the dot-com bubble in the mid-to-late 1990s and the great recession. It appears that for the better part of the last seventy years, Congress has been unwilling or

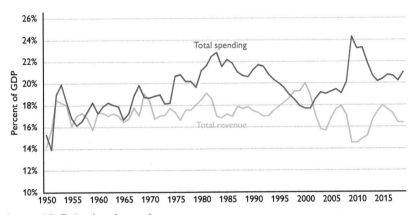

Figure 4.3 **Federal outlays and revenues**

Source: Author calculations using data from US Budget 2024, Historical Tables 2.1, 3.1, and 10.1.

unable to consistently raise or lower taxes as a percentage of GDP significantly outside of this range. The result has been annual budget deficits in all but five years from 1961 to 2019. These chronic budget deficits can be said to be due to a failure of Congress to raise federal revenues sufficiently to meet growing federal expenditures.

Figure 4.4 breaks down total federal spending into expenditures on national activities, termed Madison budget expenditures (the dashed blue line), and those on state and local activities (the dotted blue line). As the chart makes clear, federal spending on state and local activities accounts for more than the entire growth in total federal spending since 1950. Driven mainly by programs that provide aid to individuals, federal spending on these activities has grown from 2 percent of GDP in 1950 to nearly 15 percent in 2019. Meanwhile, the percentage of GDP the federal government spends on national activities has declined to only half of its mid-1950s level. The only interruptions to this long-term decline are the Korean and Vietnam Wars, the Reagan administration's defense buildup, and the great recession.

Figure 4.4 suggests a modification of the conclusion reached from figure 4.3: the chronic budget deficits can be said to be due to a failure of Congress to raise federal revenues sufficiently to meet growing federal expenditures *on state and local activities.*

A more complete picture of the role that federal spending has played in producing budget deficits can be obtained by incorporating the behavior of major social insurance programs, Social Security and Medicare.

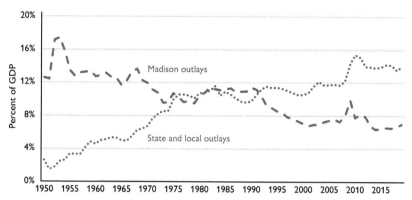

Figure 4.4 Madison outlays vs. state and local activity outlays

Source: Author calculations using data from US Budget 2024, Historical Tables 3.1, 10.1, 11.2, 11.3, and 12.2.

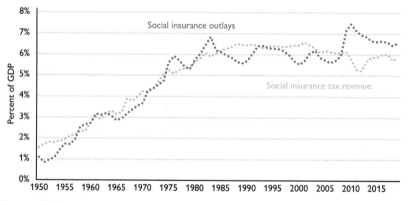

Figure 4.5 Social insurance tax revenue and outlays

Source: Author calculations using data from US Budget 2024, Historical Tables 2.1, 3.1, and 10.1.

As noted earlier, these large social insurance programs are financed by dedicated revenues primarily derived from payroll tax collections. They operate on a pay-as-you-go basis in which annual program revenues are kept roughly in line with expenditures.

Figure 4.5 shows the behavior of social insurance revenues and expenditures as percentages of GDP from 1950 to 2019.

The pay-as-you-go nature of these programs is evident from the relatively close approximation of federal expenditures and revenues (although the relationship has weakened in recent years as the programs are now running cash shortfalls). The figure also shows their remarkable growth. From 1950 to the early 1990s, Congress raised the Social Security payroll tax rate and the level of earnings subject to the tax more than a dozen times and added additional payroll taxes for disability and Medicare on top of this. Taken together, these actions increased payroll tax revenues from 1.5 percent of GDP in 1950 to around 6 percent in the mid-1980s, where it has remained since then.

The large increase in social insurance tax revenues in combination with relatively constant total revenues as a percentage of GDP means that federal revenues from all other sources, mainly individual and corporate income taxes, have declined as a share of the economy. Figure 4.6 shows the extent of this decline since 1950 and its relation to the increase in social insurance tax revenues. The increase in social insurance tax revenues as a percentage of GDP from 1950 is matched by a nearly equal decline in general fund revenues over the same period. There appears to be a one-for-one trade-off between the two revenue sources. The idea of such a trade-off is further supported by the fact that after the early 1990s, when the growth in social insurance tax revenues levels off, the decline in general fund taxes is arrested.

The plausible explanation for these trends is that Congress has been unwilling to raise total federal taxes beyond a certain limit and, as a result, social insurance taxes have crowded out general fund taxes. Federal budget deficits have arisen because remaining general fund revenues have not been sufficient to finance the combined level of federal spending on both national and state and local activities, after social insurance programs have been excluded. The federal government

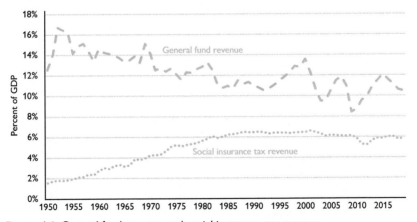

Figure 4.6 General fund revenue and social insurance tax revenue

Source: Author calculations using data from US Budget 2024, Historical Table 2.1.

has resorted to borrowing to finance the excess. The federal budget pools general revenues instead of allocating them to specific programs. So how much of national versus state and local expenditures the non–social insurance revenues would have financed (with taxes versus borrowed funds) cannot be determined.

Nevertheless, it is of some interest to ask what the budget would have looked like if all non–social insurance revenues were applied to financing Madison budget expenditures. Figure 4.7 answers this question by showing Madison budget expenditures (in blue) and revenues available after excluding those from social insurance taxes (in green). As the chart shows, Madison budget expenditures and revenues would have experienced a long-term decline since 1950. From the mid-1950s to 2019, non–social insurance tax revenues declined from 14 percent of GDP to around 10 percent. Madison budget expenditures would have declined slightly faster, from 13 percent to 6 percent. The Madison budget would have experienced chronic budget surpluses instead of chronic budget deficits. Budget surpluses would have existed in all but eleven of the seventy years from 1950 to 2019. The deficit years would have been limited to the Korean War, one year of the Vietnam War, the deepest year of the economic recessions of 1981–83, 1990–91, and the great recession in 2008, and three years of the Reagan administration's defense buildup in 1984–86. In all other years, budget surpluses would have been available to reduce the outstanding national debt.

Remarkably, the behavior of the post–World War II Madison budgets is strikingly similar to the behavior of nineteenth- and early-twentieth-century

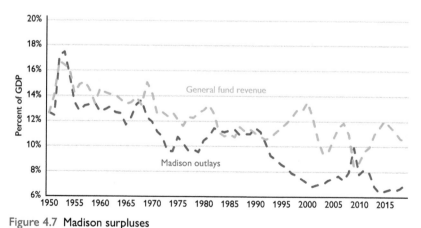

Figure 4.7 Madison surpluses

Source: Author calculations using data from US Budget 2024, Historical Tables 2.1, 3.1, 10.1, 11.2, 11.3, and 12.2.

budgets. During those years, when federal spending was almost exclusively devoted to national activities, federal budget deficits were incurred only during wartime and economic recessions. Surplus revenues during the intervening years were used to reduce the outstanding public debt issued during wars and recessions.

Figure 4.8 shows the extent to which surplus revenue from the Madison budget (orange line) would have financed expenditures on state and local activities excluding social insurance programs (the blue line). Madison budget surpluses are sufficient to fully finance state and local expenditures in only three years during the 1950s and, since the early 1960s, only during the dotcom bubble. In all other years, available revenues fall short and the trend in the revenue shortfall is significantly upward. During the entire period from 1950 to 2019, Madison budget surpluses are sufficient to finance only about one-half of federal spending on state and local activities.

An alternative way to display the deficit impact of federal spending on state and local activities is shown in figure 4.9, which modifies the Madison budget by adding social insurance expenditures and revenues. Although social insurance programs are beyond those necessary and proper to carry out an enumerated power, many observers today regard these programs as national in scope. The solid blue line shows total government spending. The dashed blue line shows Madison budget plus social insurance program expenditures. The difference between the two is federal spending on state and local activities excluding social insurance. The green line shows total federal revenues.

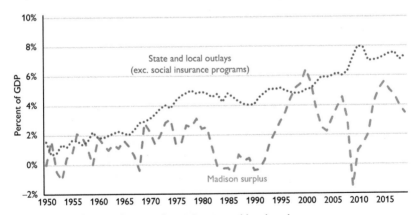

Figure 4.8 Madison budget surplus and state and local outlays

Source: Author calculations using data from US Budget 2024, Historical Tables 2.1, 3.1, 10.1, 11.2, 11.3, and 12.2.

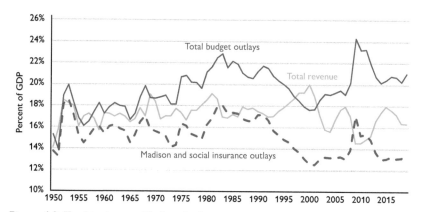

Figure 4.9 Total budget vs. Madison budget

Source: Author calculations using data from US Budget 2024, Historical Tables 2.1, 3.1, 10.1, 11.2, 11.3, and 12.2.

Total revenues exceed Madison plus social insurance expenditures in almost all years. Enhanced Madison budget surpluses occur every year except during the Korean War, in 1983–86, and at the depth of the great recession. These surpluses are similar to those in the Madison budget. The similarity between the enhanced Madison budget and Madison budget surpluses should not be surprising given the pay-as-you-go nature of social insurance programs.

Adding state and local expenditures to the enhanced Madison budget causes total expenditures, excluding social insurance payments (the solid blue line) to exceed total revenues excluding social insurance tax receipts (the green line) in almost all years since the early 1960s. This also should not be surprising, given the pay-as-you-go nature of social insurance programs.

Concluding Observations

This paper has documented the role that the abandonment of federalism in fiscal matters has played in the post–World War II rise in federal spending and chronic federal budget deficits since the early 1960s. All the increase in federal spending as a percentage of GDP since the 1950s, and the budget deficits it has created, is due to rapidly growing spending on activities that Congress originally regarded as state and local. Thus, the fiscal challenge the federal government faces today is a direct consequence of the abandonment of the original idea of fiscal federalism. Its abandonment removed an important constitutional constraint not only on the type of activities funded but also on the level of total federal spending and led to the federal government's $27 trillion public debt.

The paper is not a plea to return to the "good old days" of 1789–1817 when the original concept of fiscal federalism prevailed. The paper's purpose is to improve our understanding of the roots of the federal government's fiscal challenge. Its findings can provide some guideposts to addressing the challenge.

Budgeting is mainly about setting priorities. Maintaining an adequate national defense is the highest priority of any federal government. In contrast to most federally funded activities, no other level of government can provide for the nation's defense. State and local governments can provide income support and social services for the poor, education, local transportation systems, and community development projects. But they cannot adequately finance a national defense. The Founders understood this well when they replaced the Articles of Confederation with the Constitution. Yet, since the 1950s, spending on activities that Congress originally regarded as the responsibility of state and local governments appears to have been Congress's highest priority. Funding this priority has come at the expense of national defense. With rising global tensions, Congressional priorities need to be reversed with national defense as the first priority and spending on state and local activities returned to the states and individuals.

History shows the important influential role presidents play in the use of this power. During the nineteenth century, presidents from James Madison to Grover Cleveland used the veto to restrain federal spending on internal improvements. In the twentieth century, President Reagan used the veto, the bully pulpit, and other means to restrain domestic spending. President Clinton used the power of his office to help enact welfare reform. On the flip side, Presidents Franklin Roosevelt, Lyndon Johnson, and Richard Nixon used their influence for large expansions in federal spending. The Constitution gave Congress the power of the purse, but the president's leadership is essential to meeting the fiscal challenge.

Notes

1. Useful histories of this erosion include Corwin (1923), Warren (1978), Currie (1997, 2001, 2005), and Walker (1995).

2. Annals of Congress, 11th Congress, 690. The debate on the resolution is described in Annals of Congress, 11th Congress, 1st Session, 1378.

3. Similar provisions were included in enabling compacts with Louisiana, Indiana, Mississippi, Illinois, Alabama, and Missouri. See Hibbard (1965) for discussion of federal lands policies. For a comprehensive treatment of the Cumberland Road, see Young (1902).

4. Annals of Congress, 1st Congress, 2nd Session, 1686.

5. Financial aid to a silk manufacturing firm was rejected by the Committee on Commerce and Manufactures (Annals of Congress, 4th Congress, 2nd Session, 825), as was the idea of federal fire insurance (American State Papers [Finance, No. 45]). Aid to a Metal and Mine Co. was rejected by a vote of 36–34 on April 22, 1800 (Annals of Congress, 6th Congress, 1st Session, 678). Congress also rejected support for other commercial ventures, such as Frederich Guyer's venture for the "discovery of the longitude by lunar observation" (Annals of Congress, 7th Congress, 1st Session, 376); and Lewis DuPré's request in 1802 for development of a perpetual motion machine based on his newly discovered "principles of perpetual motion."

6. For the debate on the national university, see Annals of Congress, 4th Congress, 2nd Session, 1197–8, 1600, 1702. The national banking system proposal is described in Annals of Congress, 11th Congress, 1st Session, 1378.

7. Annals of Congress, 4th Congress, 1st Session, see page 1723 for Rutherford quote and for Nicholas quote 1724.

8. Annals of Congress, 14th Congress, 2nd Session, 933. A search of the Annals of Congress reveals eight bills that were explicitly justified on the general welfare clause, all of which were rejected.

9. Dauber (2005) provides a thorough treatment of disaster relief.

10. The most notable of these is the Louisiana Purchase, which is not directly germane to the issue of federal involvement in state and local governments. President Jefferson knew the great importance of the acquisition to the country. But he felt that it was beyond the government's constitutional powers. In a letter to John Dickinson on August 9, 1803, Jefferson wrote that the constitution "has not given it a power for holding foreign territory, and still less of incorporating it into the Union." Jefferson stood by as Congress justified the purchase mainly on the treaty power. In 1828, the Supreme Court ratified the view that the government had the right to purchase territory. In *American Insurance Co. v. Canter*, Chief Justice Marshall declared: "The Constitution confers absolutely on the Government of the Union the powers of making war, and of making treaties; consequently, the Government possesses the power of acquiring territory, either by conquest or by treaty" (26 U.S. 1 Pet. 511 [1828]).

11. For the debate, see Annals of Congress, 3rd Congress, 1st Session, 172–73. The law made $15,000 available. Statutes at Large, chapter 2, 6 Stat. 13 (1794) (Private Relief Act). A similar case, but one not involving state and local government activities, occurred nearly twenty years later in 1812, when Congress provided relief

to victims of an earthquake in Caracas, Venezuela. Congress justified the relief on the foreign policy grounds that Venezuela was a strategic ally on the eve of war with England. See Warren (1978), page 20, and the statement by Representative Rhea, Annals of Congress, 12th Congress, 2nd Session, page 1350.

12. An Act to Encourage Vaccination, Statute II Chapter 37. The Act was repealed in 1822 (Chapter 50), after the agent's error in distributing the vaccine material caused the deaths of ten individuals.

13. These calculations are taken from annual reports of Receipts and Disbursements of the United States.

14. Similar provisions were included in compacts with Louisiana, Indiana, Mississippi, Illinois, Alabama, and Missouri (see Hibbard 1965 for a discussion of federal lands policies). For a comprehensive treatment of the Cumberland Road, see Young (1902).

15. Annals of Congress, 2nd Congress, 1st Session, 364.

16. Hamilton made his case in his Report on Manufactures (1791). For Representative Laurence's quote, see Annals of Congress, 2nd Congress, 1st Session, 385.

17. Annals of Congress, 2nd Congress, 1st Session, 388.

18. Annals of Congress, 2nd Congress, 1st Session, 364.

19. Annals of Congress, 2nd Congress, 1st Session, 381.

20. As Currie (1997) notes, the compromise meant that while the Congress did not have the power to spend to promote the general welfare, it had plenary power to provide relief through the tax code (168–69). The original bill's purpose was "for the immediate encouragement of the said fisheries, while the enacted legislation stated that the law's purpose was 'as a commutation and equivalent therefor' for Tariff Act of 1789 law." Annals of Congress, 2nd Congress, 1st Session, 362–63.

21. Annals of Congress, February 4, 1817, 854.

22. Mr. Calhoun asked, "If the framers had intended to limit the use of the money to the powers afterward enumerated and defined, nothing could be more easy [sic] than to have expressed it plainly" (Annals of Congress, February 4, 1817, 856–57). Calhoun attempted to bolster his case by citing congressional precedents, chief among these were aid to the Santo Domingo refugees, aid to earthquake sufferers in Caracas, and the Cumberland Road, which, as Warren (1978) has pointed out, were not argued on the basis of the general welfare clause (Annals of Congress, February 4, 1817, 857).

23. In his annual message of December 15, 1815, preceding the Bonus Bill debate, Madison argued for a system of "roads and canals which can be best executed under national authority." He noted that the Constitution provided a means for allowing the government to build such a system: "It (is) a happy reflection that any defect of constitutional authority which may be encountered can be supplied in a mode which the Constitution itself has providently pointed out" (Whooley and Peters 2023). The "Bonus Bill" passed by just two votes in the House. The bill was heavily supported

by Middle Atlantic states (New York, New Jersey, and Pennsylvania) and opposed by New England and Southern states. In a harbinger of things to come, the two-vote margin of victory was provided by the western states.

24. Veto message, March 3, 1817 (Whooley and Peters 2023).

25. The vote was 60–56 to override the president's veto—a majority, but well short of the necessary two-thirds. Henry Clay, who in his role as Speaker of the House had previously abstained from voting on legislative bills, exercised his voting right and voted to support the president's veto.

26. President Tyler did so on the grounds that "the application of the revenue of this Government, if the power to do so was admitted, to improving the navigation of the rivers by removing obstructions or otherwise would be for the most part productive only of local benefit. The consequences might prove disastrously ruinous to as many of our fellow-citizens as the exercise of such power would benefit" (Veto Message, June 11, 1844; Whooley and Peters 2023). In a similar vein, President Polk's veto of a massive bill that funded internal improvements in every state in the Union was justified because: "The Constitution has not, in my judgment, conferred upon the federal government the power to construct works of internal improvement within the States, or to appropriate money from the treasury for that purpose." Polk, H. Doc. 493, 70th Congress, 2nd Session, August 3, 1846, 10.

27. US Department of the Treasury, *A Statement of the Receipts and Expenditures of the United States Government from the 4th of March 1789 to the 31st of December, 1819* (H. Doc. 16–75), February 7, 1820; US Department of the Treasury, *Combined Statement of the Receipts and Disbursements (Apparent and Actual) of the United States*, for the fiscal years ended June 30, 1890, and June 30, 1900.

28. This point has been effectively made by Dauber (2005).

29. The Court qualified its ruling that Congress had sole discretion by saying "except when the choice is clearly wrong." Since then, however, the Court has not once declared any federal expenditure to be unconstitutional on the grounds that it is local in character.

30. These expenditures may include some to which Madison would have objected. For example, the defense budget includes some expenditures on military bases and navy shipyards that no longer serve defense purposes and remain operational primarily because they are important to the local communities in which they are located. Our classification is in keeping with our approach of erring on the side of classifying ambiguous expenditures as federal. Also, the international affairs budget includes expenditures, such as contributions to the International Monetary Fund, which the Madison interpretation might regard as not constitutionally permissible. These expenditures are classified as part of Madison's budget only because they are not state and local.

31. Total payments to individuals exclude payments to states for Medicaid, which are included under grants to states and payments to veterans, which are included as a separate entry in the table.

Bibliography

Corwin, Edward S. 1923. "The Spending Power of Congress, Apropos the Maternity Act." *Harvard Law Review* 36, no. 5 (March): 548–82.

Council of State Governments. 1949. *Federal Grants-in-Aid*. Council of State Governments.

Currie, David P. 1997. *The Constitution in Congress: The Federalist Period, 1789–1801*. Chicago: University of Chicago Press.

———. 2001. *The Constitution in Congress: The Jeffersonians 1801–1829*. Chicago: University of Chicago Press.

———. 2005. *The Constitution in Congress: Democrats and Whigs 1829–1861*. Chicago: University of Chicago Press.

Dauber, Michelle Landis. 2005. "The Sympathetic State." *Law and History Review* 23, no. 2 (Summer): 387–442.

Dewey, Davis Rich. 1931. *Financial History of the United States*, 11th ed. New York: Longmans, Greene.

Douglas, Paul. 1920a. "The Development of a System of Federal Grants-in-Aid I." *Political Science Quarterly* 35, no. 2 (June): 255–71.

———. 1920b. "The Development of a System of Federal Grants-in-Aid II." *Political Science Quarterly* 35, no. 4 (December): 522–44.

Hibbard, Benjamin Horace. 1965. *History of Public Lands Policies*. Madison: University of Wisconsin Press.

LaCroix, Alison. 2015. "The Interbellum Constitution: Federalism in the Long Founding Moment." *Stanford Law Review* 67, no. 2 (February): 397–445.

Larson, John Lauritz. 1987. "Bind the Republic Together: The National Union and the Struggle for a System of Internal Improvements." *Journal of American History* 74, no. 2 (September): 363–87.

———. 2001. *Internal Improvement*. Chapel Hill: University of North Carolina Press.

Lee, Gordon Canfield. 1972. *The Struggle for Federal Aid, First Phase: A History of the Attempts to Obtain Federal Aid for the Common Schools, 1870–1890*. New York: AMS Press.

MacDonald, Austin F. 1928. *Federal Aid*. New York: Thomas Y. Crowell Company.

Niskanen, William. 1992. "The Case for a New Fiscal Constitution." *Journal of Economic Perspectives* 6, no. 2 (May): 13–24.

Office of Management and Budget. Budget of the United States Government, Fiscal Year 2024, Historical Tables.

Scott, Ray. 1970. *The Reluctant Farmer*. Urbana: University of Illinois Press.

Studenski, Paul, and Herman Krooss. 1963. *Financial History of the United States*. New York: McGraw-Hill.

US Department of the Treasury. 1820. *A Statement of the Receipts and Expenditures of the United States Government from the 4th of March 1789 to the 31st of December, 1819*. H. Doc. 16–75. February 7.

Valgren, V. N. 1923. "The Agricultural Credits Act of 1923." *American Economic Review* 13, no. 3 (September): 442–60.

Walker, David B. 1995. *The Rebirth of Federalism.* Chatham, NJ: Chatham House Publishers.

Warren, Charles. 1978. *Congress as Santa Claus.* New York: Arno Press.

Whooley, John, and Gerhard Peters. 2023. The American Presidency Project. Accessed June 20. https://www.presidency.ucsb.edu.

Young, Jeremiah. 1902. *A Political and Constitutional Study of the Cumberland Road.* PhD diss., University of Chicago.

Zavodnyik, Peter. 2011. *The Rise of the Federal Colossus.* Santa Barbara, CA: ABC-CLIO.

ERIC A. HANUSHEK: What did you do with payments to individuals? You made some distinction?

JOHN F. COGAN: Yes. The point is that during the years when Madison's view prevailed, Congress rejected spending on individual purposes other than compensation for government services. Grants in states or direct payments to the poor: rejected. Local disaster relief to help individuals: rejected. And so, when looking at the modern era, direct spending on individuals for income support, healthcare, housing, student loans, etc. would be outside of the Madison view, as I've defined it.

HANUSHEK: Did you count that as state and local?

COGAN: Right.

HANUSHEK: And you said you'd excluded veterans?

COGAN: Yes. Veterans are considered defense-related spending. Under the Madison view, Congress has the authority to spend for national defense, and of course veterans' payments are also compensation for government service. So, on those grounds, I've excluded veterans' payments from expenditures on state and local activities.

JOSHUA RAUH: I would just add to that an anecdote. Sometimes when I am in a hurry to read papers, the first thing I do is start looking at figures in the paper. And so I opened up your paper to a figure that you showed in this presentation, which is the share of domestic federal spending on state and local activities, and it's well over 90 percent. I thought, what have I done wrong? I mean, I have been looking at these expenditure data for a long time. I realized, oh, okay, it's because you've redefined state and local activities as ones that were initially under our Constitution—

COGAN: Originally.

RAUH: —left to state governments as opposed to federal government. At that point I realized you had done something very clever, and I learned that as an economist, you should always actually read the paper carefully. Although I do have one question for you after all that. You said you were interested in ideas of identification. What is the causal mechanism you're interested in identifying? What caused this increase?

COGAN: As I indicated in presenting the paper, I have not identified the causal mechanism. In the paper, I tell a story about how partisan politics played a role from the get-go. At the country's beginning, various members of Congress pressed against the Madison limits. These Hamiltonians held the view that the government did have the power to spend on internal improvements. As the United States expanded, so did the demand for transportation systems to be expanded to connect the West with the East, South with the North. So the growing commercial interests, growing agricultural interests, growing size of the country, lead to this high demand for spending on internal improvements, river clearances projects, harbor dredging. The Hamiltonian views that the Congress could spend to "create" or "improve" commerce, or to promote the general welfare, provided a constitutional rationale for expenditures to meet the greater demand.

PAUL E. PETERSON: The slavery question created a major barrier to federal spending on state and local improvements. Southerners did not want the federal government messing around in their neighborhood. And Southern opposition precluded spending on roads and canals until the breakout of the Civil War. Abraham Lincoln was a strong proponent of internal improvements. [Henry] Clay was as well. But they couldn't make any progress on internal improvements until the war breaks out. Once that happens, Congress appropriates money for the intercontinental railroad, we get the Homestead Act, and we get a much different view of what the federal role should be. So, it's not the whole story, but you can't ignore the slavery question.

COGAN: So, I think a little bit differently about the role of the South during the earlier period in internal improvements. Prior to the Civil War, the South opposed internal improvements. And one reason that spending is so limited—as I said, around 4 percent of GDP—is because of Southern opposition. Southerners have a big influence at the national Democratic Party level. Because of Southern influence, the Democratic Party opposes internal improvements throughout this period. But the source of Southern and Democratic Party opposition is objection to the high tariffs that are required to finance a system of internal improvements.

PETERSON: But [John C.] Calhoun was the foremost spokesman for anti-tariffs. And our liberty is so dear. For Southerners, liberty meant the right to own slaves.

COGAN: I don't want to discount slavery during the pre–Civil War period. But slavery, or perhaps it would be better to say, the end of slavery, played a role after the war. After the war, male slaves were given the right to vote. But because they had been enslaved, they had little education, ability, information, or knowledge on the issues of the day. Slavery had deprived them of tools upon which to vote. After the war, the Republican Party pressed for a federal grants-to-states program for elementary and secondary school education. And they pushed their bills for twenty years, from 1870 through 1890. State and local governments in the South were unwilling or financially unable after the war to provide that education. Southern Democrats opposed federal aid, along with the religious schools that were disproportionately located in urban districts. The Republican efforts finally achieved some success in 1890 with the passage of the second Morrill Act to fund land-grant colleges.

So the expansion of federal funding of education is related to slavery, but it's through the desire of the Republicans to have a voting population that is knowledgeable about public affairs. For internal improvements, again, it's the war that made a big difference. After the war, the Southern opposition to internal improvement goes away. It does so because now internal improvement becomes the means of revitalizing the infrastructure of the South. Now there is support for internal improvements by both parties at the national level.

In summary, the war made a major difference in the expansion of the federal government. In the case of education, the end of slavery was important. In the case of internal improvements, federal funding to revitalize a damaged infrastructure was important.

STEVEN J. DAVIS: I want to put two causal stories on the table, which you might dismiss or not. One is that there was always an unmet demand for risk-sharing or redistribution. Let's treat those as the same for the moment. State capacity eventually emerged that made it feasible to meet that demand for risk-sharing and redistribution. I put that story on the table because the phenomenon documented here is happening in rich countries around the world and, to a lesser extent, in middle-income countries. It's not something peculiar to the American political system. That's number one. Number two, maybe more applicable to the pre–New Deal era, is that the US Constitution allocates disproportionate political power to small and sparsely populated states. So I'm wondering, is the character of the expansion in the federal government, especially in the pre–New Deal era, is it tilted in a way that reflects the disproportionate political power of smaller, less populous states? From your description, it sounds like maybe it was. A lot of farming stuff and so on. Anyway, those are two causal stories worth considering.

COGAN: The latter was a good thought. I hadn't thought about that, but that's an excellent thought. I've looked at a little bit of the distribution of rivers and harbors appropriations prior to the Civil War, and I didn't see the smaller states getting a disproportionate share.

DAVID BRADY: John, if that's true, why is it that big-state Democrats like [President] Cleveland are the ones vetoing the spending bills?

COGAN: If what is true?

BRADY: Well, the point is, if the big states, small states, you would expect the big states to be wanting to expand it because they'll get more benefits, right? I guess I don't see how the small state–big state thing quite fits in.

COGAN: Well, it's an empirical question, right? Starting with Andrew Jackson, presidents prior to the Civil War are almost all Democrats. The exceptions are Millard Fillmore and Zach Taylor, and John Tyler, who replaced William Henry Harrison but who is a Southerner; the Democratic presidents and Tyler all opposed internal improvements. After the Civil War, to the nineteenth century's end, all the presidents except Cleveland are Republican. The Republican Party is the party for a bigger, more expansive, more muscular federal government in a lot of areas, including federal spending. Cleveland is a limited-government Democrat and vetoes the Rivers and Harbors Appropriation Bill, an Education Appropriation Bill, and a grants-to-states program which would distribute surplus federal revenues to the states. His vetoes are very consistent with the party story in which the Democratic Party is the conservative party during the nineteenth century. And of course in the twentieth century it changes.

MICHAEL J. BOSKIN: What about the surplus and deficit financial situation of the states and how does that fit in?

COGAN: Yes. So, fairly significantly. I've done a little bit of statistical work on rivers and harbors because it expands greatly in the early 1930s. And those are the years of big surpluses. Surpluses that could be unimaginable today. Revenues exceeding expenditures by 60 percent over a ten-year period. Once the federal government paid down the national debt, the question arose of what was to be done with the excess revenues. Well, rivers and harbors are a natural way to spend the surplus funds. Same thing's true late in the nineteenth century, when big surpluses lead to an expansion in education.

5

COVID Federalism

David Brady, Jacob Jaffe, and Douglas Rivers

Introduction

In the American version of federalism, federal, state, and local governments have overlapping responsibilities and authority. This was nowhere more apparent than in early 2020 when SARS-CoV-2 (COVID-19) spread from China to the United States and the rest of the world. President Trump banned travel from China by foreign nationals on January 31, 2020. Federal agencies regulated virus testing and treatments and funded the development of vaccines. However, most preventive measures, including lockdowns, were undertaken by state governments, with variations in implementation and enforcement mostly at the discretion of local governments, who controlled police, schools, and hospitals. For a while, the president used daily news conferences as a bully pulpit, but he had little actual authority over many areas of pandemic response and quickly got into fights with Democratic governors, who did have authority, over their handling of the pandemic.

The US federal system was famously described by Morton Grodzins as being like a marble cake. Federalism makes it difficult for voters to know who is in charge and whom to credit or blame for policy outcomes, though COVID-19 provided an easier case in this regard. Unlike many policy areas, where most people are not concerned and do not pay much attention, COVID policy was highly salient. In the United States alone, over one million people died from COVID-19 (Mathieu et al. 2023). Lockdowns, mask mandates, and eventually vaccinations became hotly contested issues and involved more than a single level of government. Many Americans declined to follow governmental and public health recommendations throughout (Gaskell et al. 2020).

Grodzins, of course, was writing in an era with much less partisan polarization than today. The COVID-19 pandemic was such a novel event in the recent political history of the United States, and the response to the pandemic was so reliant on mass public adherence to behavioral guidelines, that in many ways the story of the pandemic is a story about trust. Did Americans trust the government to deal with the crisis? While Americans' trust in government tends to be relatively low, it is not homogeneously so. Factors such as demographics, political partisanship, and governmental competence have all been suggested as potential contributors to trust and distrust. We argue that even when people are presented with a novel issue that does not have previous partisan cues but does have metrics to evaluate competence, partisanship grows in importance but fails to overwhelm evaluations of competence. While what does and does not qualify as competence becomes a partisan issue, as examined through stay-at-home orders and school closures here, the impact of COVID-19 case numbers remains, especially when evaluating the federal government.

This is not the first study of how trust in government has been affected by the pandemic and the degree to which Americans trust different levels of government to respond (Suhay et al. 2022). The advantage of this study, however, is in how it leverages a common set of questions asked many times over 2020, combined with COVID-19 policy choices, to measure the impact of competence on American's trust in government with regard to COVID-19.

Our contribution to the literature is based on answering the following questions. First, how large is the effect of partisanship on trust in government during the COVID-19 pandemic? Second, to what degree, if any, does this relationship change across different levels of government? Third, to what degree, if any, did Americans' trust in government respond to the competence of government in a manner that can be distinguished from partisanship?

To answer these questions, we utilize a series of twenty-seven YouGov polls carried out from March 14, 2020, to October 17, 2020. These polls surveyed a cross section of registered American voters.

Questions included basic demographics, rating the performance of the federal, state, and local governments with regard to COVID-19, personal experiences with COVID, and more. Observational data was gathered on daily state-level COVID-19 cases and deaths by the Johns Hopkins Coronavirus Research Center.

Our results show that while partisanship greatly affects how voters interpret new information, Republicans and Democrats do both interpret some signals in the same way. While it may be expected that Democrats have less trust in the federal government to deal with COVID-19, in 2020 both Republicans and Democrats whose states had more COVID-19 cases became less confident in the federal government's ability to manage the pandemic as a result. On the state and local level, however, interpretations were more mixed. While state politics are more national than ever before, state interpretations were a little less polarized. Also, whether voters held the state government responsible for higher rates of COVID cases depended on voter copartisanship with the governor.

Discussion

The manner in which citizens interact with government is necessarily predicated on their evaluations of its competence and trustworthiness. Therefore, for political leadership to be effective, trust is required. Government officials depend on the trust of citizens in order to obtain compliance in government decision making in both the short and long term (Barber 1983; Tyler 2006). A lack of trust leaves coercion as the sole mechanism for the government to ensure adherence, which also limits the ability of the government to make credible long-term commitments. Many of the policies surrounding COVID-19, such as mask mandates or vaccines, depend on the compliance of citizens.

Citizens trust the government when they believe that the goals of government are their goals, and that the government has the competence to effectively pursue those goals (Bangerter et al. 2012). Though there exists some fuzziness about the definition of political trust and how it might differ from intrapersonal trust, it would be normatively positive if there was a relationship between government performance and trust in government. If voters judge the competence of government in a way that is independent of the actual actions of government, it lessens the power of the reelection incentive to improve government performance. For performance to have an impact on trust, citizens must monitor the performance of the president, Congress, and the economy, which there is some evidence they do (Citrin 1974). That said, long-term trends in trust in government do not necessarily reflect apparent trends in government performance (Keele 2007).

This discrepancy may be explained by the influence of partisan polarization, which has been increasing in the aggregate in the United States (McCarty et al. 2016; Iyengar et al. 2019). If perceptions of governmental goals and competence are driven solely by partisanship, the true goals and competence of government have no impact on trust. Indeed, partisan polarization appears to be correlated with substantially decreased out-party trust (Hetherington and Rudolph 2015).

While partisanship may drive trends in trust in government, in a federal system voters may trust different levels of government differently. Indeed, American voters tend to have greater approval and trust in government the "closer" government is to them. For example, voters tend to approve of their congressman much more than Congress as a whole (Fenno 1978). This phenomenon is also observed in election administration, where voters are most confident that their own vote was counted correctly, followed by votes in their county, then votes in their state, and then votes in the country as a whole (Atkeson et al. 2015). The relation between proximity and trust may have several causes. The fewer people a government institution represents, the more representative of them it may be, as the constituency is smaller and likely more homogeneous. More local levels of government may also represent an ideal that is attractive to many voters with preferences for smaller government. There is mixed evidence on whether trust in state government, as distinct from trust in the federal government, depends on state-level performance (Hetherington and Nugent 2001; Wolak 2020), though much current research seeks to distinguish between trust in the various institutions that make up the government of the United States. With regard to COVID-19, state and local governments have an opportunity to distinguish themselves from evaluations of the federal government.

For three reasons, the COVID-19 pandemic provides an important case study on how trust in government varies across levels of government. First, it is the rare example of a truly new issue in American politics. Since COVID-19 was a new disease and neither of the two major parties had a strong previous policy position on the handling of a pandemic, voters did not have strong previous partisan cues to fall back on when evaluating the government's pandemic response. Second, the different levels of the federal system had meaningfully different responsibilities and responses to the pandemic. The federal government was largely responsible for coordinating and supplying resources such as masks and respirators, while state or local governments made decisions about quarantines, school closings, and more. This observable heterogeneity in responsibilities allows voters to potentially distinguish between the performances of different levels of government, a task that is ordinarily exceptionally difficult for voters (Sances 2017; de Benedictis-Kessner and Warshaw 2020). Finally, when evaluating competence with regard to COVID-19, there are relatively clear, observable metrics, such as case numbers and deaths.

Measuring the actual competence of the government in addressing the COVID-19 pandemic is neither feasible nor the actual quantity of interest. We are interested in the perception of competence instead. As described earlier, trust in government requires voters to believe the government is in some way competent. It does not necessarily require that the government is actually competent. Whether or not voters are accurate in assessing the competence of government with regard to COVID-19 is an interesting question, but not one that this paper directly addresses. Things like cases, deaths, knowing someone who has gotten COVID, and school openings or closings may in fact be directly related to government competence, but that is not relevant for the question being studied here. They are relevant because these are the factors voters are most likely to use when constructing their evaluations of government response to COVID.

Over the course of 2020, the performance of the federal government with regard to COVID-19 was highly scrutinized. During this time period, COVID-19 was the lead story almost every single day. If ratings of the federal government's handling of COVID are determined solely by perceptions of competence, we would expect to see ratings move in response to outcomes such as deaths or cases. If ratings are determined by partisanship, we would expect to see significant divergence between partisans on both sides. COVID was not initially inherently polarized, though perceptions of Donald Trump, as leader of the executive branch, were. From the beginning, Trump's role in handling the US response to the COVID-19 pandemic was highly visible, starting with travel bans. Therefore, any partisan differences in evaluations of his role and the role of the federal government were likely to start high and remain high. Given the fairly extreme differences in evaluations of Trump in general and the controversy surrounding the COVID-19 response under Trump, any rally-round-the-flag effect Trump saw as leader during a time of crisis would be expected to be minimal.

Evaluations of state or local governments, on the other hand, are less likely to be immediately governed by partisanship. As previously discussed, state and local governments have significant high-profile responsibilities with regard to handling COVID-19. They are also generally more trusted than the federal government, and are missing the "Trump factor" with regard to partisan polarization. When given more room to distinguish themselves, state and local governments may be able to establish identities outside of the partisanship of the elected officials.

Data

Across the twenty-seven Economist/YouGov surveys, there are 44,456 registered voters. Observations are weighted to match the demographic distribution described in the American Community Survey.

Partisanship is operationalized using a three-category response. For each level of government, respondents rate their handling of the pandemic as *excellent, good, not sure, fair,* or *poor.* Responses are rescaled to a −2 to +2 scale with equal distance between each category.

Observational variables that are likely to affect perceptions of competence are included in the model. The Johns Hopkins Coronavirus Resource Center collected daily data on county-level cases and deaths from COVID-19. That data was aggregated to the state level. Analysis on levels of disaggregated, substate, local governmental approval during COVID is a topic for future research.

The surveys are the source of data on whether respondents know anyone (including themselves) who has gotten COVID, as well as demographic information and trust in government performance during COVID-19.

Methods

Time Trends

We conduct analyses of group averages over time. Public opinion on the handling of the COVID-19 pandemic by the federal government, for instance, clearly changed over the course of 2020. That is apparent from figure 5.1.

The overall trend is that Americans' perceptions of competence decrease over the pandemic. In figure 5.1, we can see that the proportion of respondents rating the federal government's handling of the pandemic as poor explodes from April to October of 2020. On the other hand, the proportion who rate the federal government's handling of the pandemic as good, fair, or not sure decreases. Obviously, this shows a strong general dissatisfaction with the course the federal government charted over this period with regard to the pandemic. This pattern is not completely linear, however, as some hesitation in decrying the federal government's job may indicate a hesitant rally-round-the-flag effect, though that would not last. Additionally, the proportion of respondents rating the federal government as excellent with regard to COVID held more or less steady. This exception from the larger pattern could potentially indicate the presence of partisanship within evaluations as a cadre of supporters continue to back the manner in which former president Trump steered the federal government during this time.

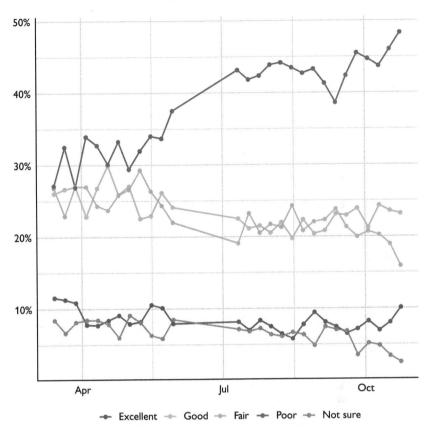

Figure 5.1 Approval of federal handling of COVID-19 over 2020
Source: Data from Economist/YouGov Polling.

We replicate the same analysis in figure 5.2 while restricting our data to respondents who self-identified as Democrats in order to investigate the potential impact of partisanship on evaluations of how the federal government handled COVID-19. While *poor* started as the plurality choice, it was not the majority choice. Nearly 20 percent of Democratic respondents initially graded the federal response as good. By October, that percentage was approximately halved while the percentage rating the federal response as poor had nearly doubled, going from just above 40 percent to just under 80 percent. While Democrats are clearly more negative than the respondents as a whole initially, it is really over the course of the summer of 2020 that a difference develops.

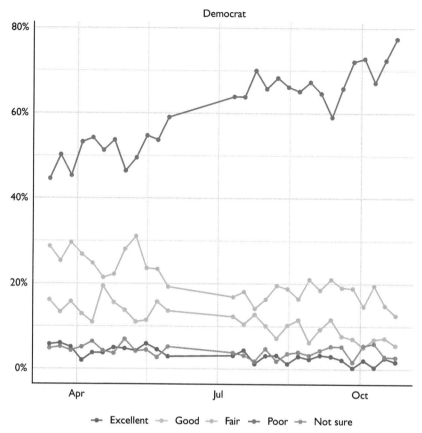

Figure 5.2 Approval of federal handling of COVID-19 among Democrats
Source: Data from Economist/YouGov Polling.

Figure 5.3 shows that from April until the end of September, the percentage of Republicans rating the federal handling of COVID-19 as poor was increasing, which is the same pattern Democrats were undergoing. From mid-July onward, however, the percentage of Republicans rating it as good was increasing. If there are a substantial number of Republicans rating the federal government's handling of the pandemic positively and a substantial number rating it negatively, that may potentially indicate disagreement within the Republican Party.

In figure 5.3, we can see that the pattern among Republicans is different from that of Democrats, but not opposite. While *poor* was the most popular selection among Democrats and only grew over time, *good* (not *excellent*) was the most popular selection among Republicans. *Excellent* only overtook *fair*

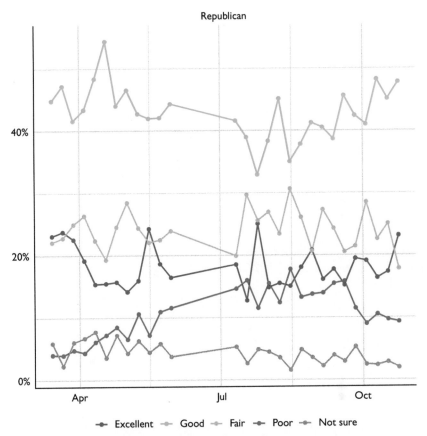

Figure 5.3 Approval of federal handling of COVID-19 among Republicans
Source: Data from Economist/YouGov Polling.

in the final survey included in the data. Indeed, while *good* achieved clear net growth over the period the surveys were collected, *excellent* ended in largely the same position it began.

Finally, figure 5.4 shows how self-identified independents rated the federal government on COVID-19. In it, independents largely appear to be between Democrats and Republicans. Overall, there is a large increase in the proportion of respondents who rate the federal government's response as poor. However, as with the Republican respondents, there is movement over time in the number of respondents selecting *good* or *excellent*. The Democratic respondents, on the other hand, exhibit a simple downward slope in those two categories over time.

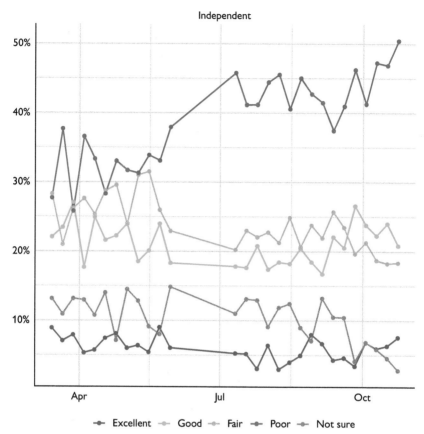

Figure 5.4 **Approval of federal handling of COVID-19** among independents
Source: Data from Economist/YouGov Polling.

The federal government was not the only level of government responsible for COVID-19 response in the United States during the pandemic. State governments were also responsible for a wide range of COVID-19 policy, such as issuing shelter-in-place orders or statewide education policies.

In figure 5.5, we can see how respondents rated their state's handling of the COVID-19 pandemic. Interestingly, the time trends in this figure to some degree mirror the federal time trends shown in figure 5.1. The initial conditions, however, are near opposite. In both cases, the proportion of respondents rating handling as poor grew dramatically, the proportion rating things as good fell, and the proportion rating as excellent fell, but made a recovery. In figure 5.5, *good* starts as the most popular category, not *poor*, and *excellent*

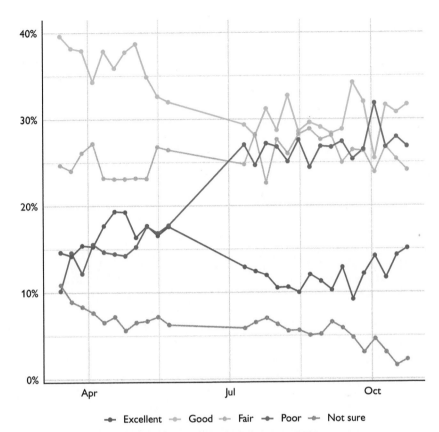

Figure 5.5 Approval of state handling of COVID-19 over 2020

Source: Data from Economist/YouGov Polling.

is initially outpacing poor. Though *poor* grows substantially as a category, it does not end the period as the plurality choice; *good* is the most popular option in the final collection period. There is also minimal net movement in the *excellent* category. For state-based evaluations, and not federal ones, the *fair* category sees minimal net movement, and the degree of the fall seen by the *good* category is much larger than in federal evaluations.

As seen in figure 5.6, Democrats initially become more positive on the state's handling of COVID-19: *excellent* as a category rises to just about 30 percent of respondents, and the next highest category is *good*.

Then, however, both *good* and *excellent* fall over the rest of the period, with *poor* experiencing a corresponding increase. While noisier, this pattern is relatively comparable to the overall graph.

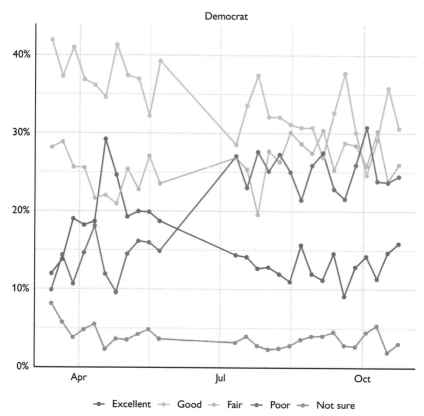

Figure 5.6 Approval of state handling of COVID-19 among Democrats
Source: Data from Economist/YouGov Polling.

In figure 5.7, Republicans display relatively comparable trends, but are overall noticeably more likely than Democrats to rate their state's performance during the COVID-19 pandemic as good. Additionally, there does not appear to be any spike in *excellent* ratings in April 2020 that would correspond to the one for Democrats in figure 5.6.

Interestingly, independents were largely the most negative group toward their state's handling of the pandemic, as seen in figure 5.8. *Poor* as a category had the same climb among independents as it did among Democrats and Republicans, albeit much steeper. In the end, among independents *poor, fair,* and *good* ended in a near three-way tie.

The overall pattern of approval of local handling of the COVID-19 crisis, as seen in figure 5.9, largely mirrors the ratings of state handling of the crisis,

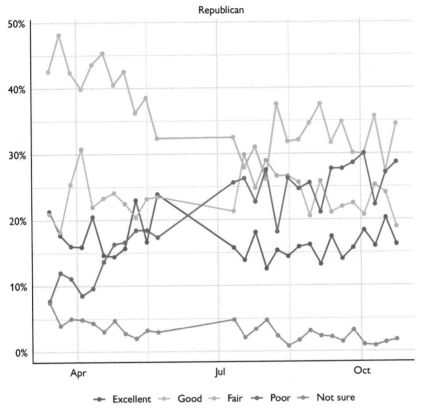

Figure 5.7 Approval of state handling of COVID-19 among Republicans

Source: Data from Economist/YouGov Polling.

albeit more positive. While there is still a growth in the proportion of respondents rating the handling as poor over the course of the survey collection period, it is a markedly less steep growth and ends at a lower level. The same is true of the corresponding decrease in respondents rating things as good.

From figure 5.10 we can see that the aggregate pattern obscures some variability, as Democrats display much more movement than the overall picture does. Visually, it is apparent that Democrats are responsible for the jump in approval in the early part of 2020 shown in figure 5.9, which corresponds to the jump in approval of local governments by Democrats in the same period. This pattern is comparable to how state governments were rated, as shown in figures 5.5, 5.6, and 5.7. It is possible that this indicates that some respondents are grouping state and local governments together and in doing so are

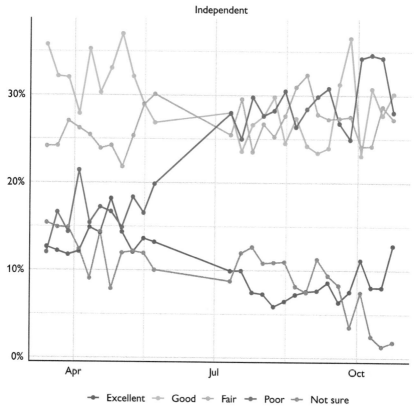

Figure 5.8 Approval of state handling of COVID-19 among independents
Source: Data from Economist/YouGov Polling.

misattributing blame or credit between the two levels of government. It is also possible that the performance of state and local governments were in the aggregate quite positive for Democrats.

Figure 5.11 shows that Republicans experienced a near inverse to the positive spike in confidence reported by Democrats in the local handling of the COVID-19 pandemic. Early in the period, Republicans spiked in the number of respondents rating local handling as fair or poor. That said, the general trend toward more negative ratings is comparable, as in the aggregate and Republican cases. The strength of the trend is much greater in the case of Democratic respondents.

As seen in figure 5.12, independent respondents appear as a combination of Democratic and Republican attitudes. There are offset spikes in positive

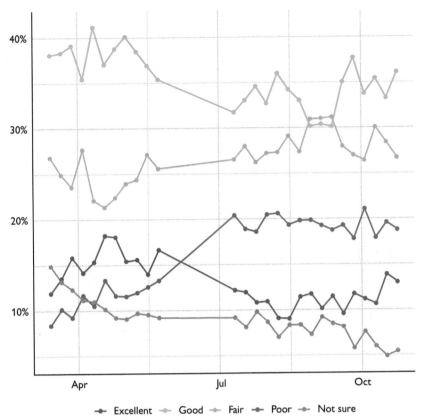

Figure 5.9 Approval of local handling of COVID-19 over 2020
Source: Data from Economist/YouGov Polling.

and negative ratings at different times. The growth in poor ratings appears similar to Democratic respondents, while independents are unique in that the excellent and good ratings rise at the very end of the period.

We have presented substantial evidence that Democratic and Republican respondents have divergent views on how the different levels of government handled COVID-19. In fact, Republicans and Democrats differ most dramatically in their views on the performance of the federal government. Given that difference, and the fact that Republicans controlled the federal government in 2020 through then president Donald Trump, the data suggests that copartisanship with the party in charge is relevant to how respondents rated the handling of COVID-19. With the case of the federal government, copartisanship with the president depends only on the party of the respondent. In the case of

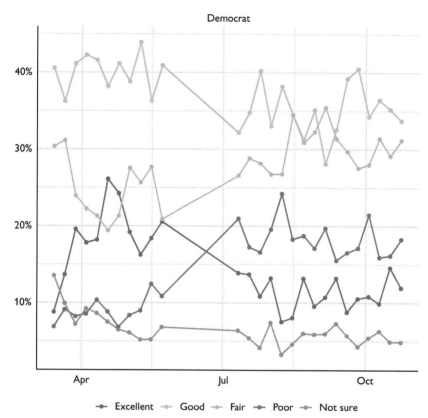

Figure 5.10 Approval of local handling of COVID-19 among Democrats
Source: Data from Economist/YouGov Polling.

the state government, copartisanship depends on the party in charge of state government. We operationalize state control with a three-category variable. States may have a Democratic or Republican trifecta, in which the governorship and both state legislative houses are controlled by the same party, or they may be mixed. Measuring local control is outside the scope of the current paper. In this section of the analysis, individual ratings are collapsed from *not sure, poor, fair, good,* and *excellent* into a single number. Each of those ratings is assigned a value of −2, −1, 0, +1, and +2, respectively, which allows group means to be taken across categories.

We examine states with a Democratic trifecta in figure 5.13. Respondents are separated within the figure by partisanship and LOESS curves are fitted for each group.[1] In Democrat-controlled states, trust started in the same

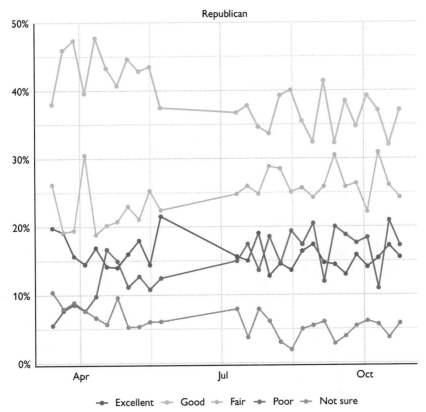

Figure 5.11 Approval of local handling of COVID-19 among Republicans

Source: Data from Economist/YouGov Polling.

place among all three groups before rising among Democrats and falling among Republicans. It fell among all three groups over the summer before rising slightly among independents and rising more substantially among Democrats.

This indicates polarization in respondents, while showing that there are some common patterns as well. The manner in which Republican and Democratic respondents move from parallel trends to opposite trends by late September likely also indicates the increased presence and influence of campaign messaging on perceptions of COVID competence.

Figure 5.14 shows a nearly identical pattern for respondents from states with a Republican trifecta. The largest difference is that all groups, Democrat, Republican, and independent, are shifted downward compared

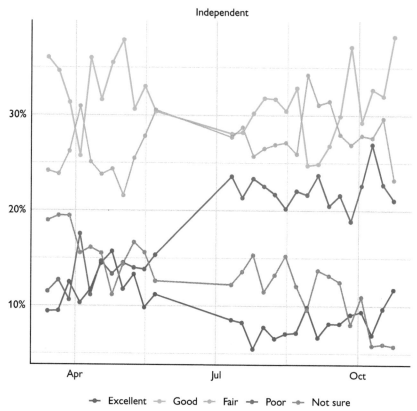

Figure 5.12 Approval of local handling of COVID-19 among independents
Source: Data from Economist/YouGov Polling.

to their peers in other states. Democrats in Republican trifecta states are more negative on the aggregate than Republicans in Democratic states, and the reverse.

Figure 5.15 shows that states without a trifecta are most similar to Democrat-controlled states. Interestingly, independents are slightly more negative and Republicans are slightly less negative in such states at the end of the period. In the middle, Democrats do not rise quite as high on the positive part of the figure. It is not completely clear why this might be the case or if this is a meaningful difference. Overall, we would expect states with mixed control to be battleground-type states, in which partisan messaging around COVID-19 policy in the run-up to the 2020 general election was especially strong. There are exceptions to this pattern in the form of safe states, with

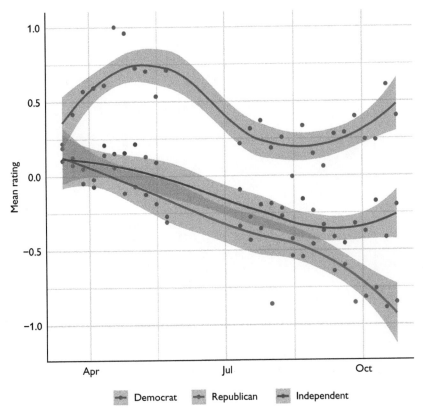

Figure 5.13 Approval of state handling of COVID-19 in Democratic states
Source: Data from Economist/YouGov Polling.

a governor who doesn't match the party of the legislature: Massachusetts, Kentucky, Alaska, Maryland, New Hampshire, Louisiana, and Vermont. Regardless of the presence of partisan messaging, mixed states clearly have some openness to Democratic candidates or ideas.

These charts provide extremely strong visual evidence that partisanship has an effect on how Americans evaluated each level of government during the COVID-19 pandemic. For competence to have an effect on how Americans view their government, however, partisanship cannot be the only thing that Americans used to rate government performance with regard to COVID-19. The most logical factor voters could use to judge how well government was doing during the crisis is the spread of COVID-19 itself.

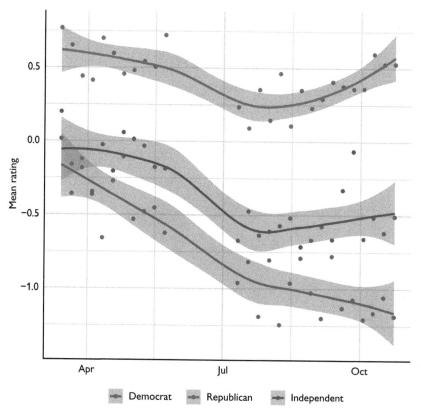

Figure 5.14 Approval of state handling of COVID-19 in Republican states
Source: Data from Economist/YouGov Polling.

To some degree, this is a fraught measure when examining actual government competence. The specific circumstances in some states would lead to
higher rates of COVID-19 infection. Additionally, it was not completely clear
at the time what the impact of any given policy might be, or the degree to
which state government might have any meaningful impact on COVID-19
infections at all. This work is intentionally uninterested in measuring or even
defining actual competence when it comes to governmental response to the
COVID-19 crisis. Instead, we are interested in perceived competence. The
assumption being made in this analysis is that lower levels of COVID cases is
something that people would notice and would use to generate their opinions
on the state of the crisis. We found that using COVID-19 cases vs. deaths
made no difference, so cases are used throughout.

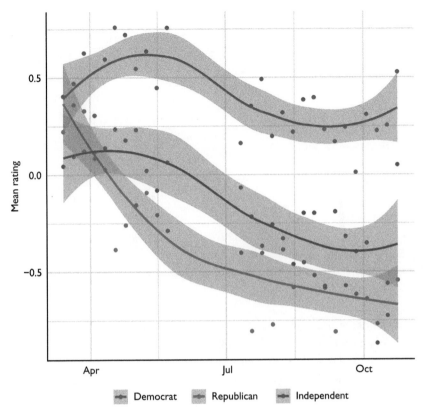

Figure 5.15 Approval of state handling of COVID-19 in mixed states
Source: Data from Economist/YouGov Polling.

Table 5.1 shows the results of running a single predictor regression for the three outcome variables. The federal, state, and local numerical approval variables are regressed on respondent partisanship and the state case rate. As partisanship is a categorical variable, the coefficients can be interpreted as group offsets from the intercept. This is a relatively simple model, which includes the two theoretical causes of perceptions of government competence with regard to COVID-19: the rate of the disease spreading within the state and respondent partisanship. It is clear that partisanship alone does not fully explain the perceived competence of state and local governments. In the model using the federal rating as the outcome variable, the difference between the Democrat and Republican coefficients is the partisan difference and directly comparable to the copartisan governor coefficient in the other models, in which

Table 5.1 Simple regression models

	Dependent Variable		
	Federal (1)	State (2)	Local (3)
Democrat	−0.172* (0.008)		
Republican	0.299* (0.009)		
Copartisan Governor		0.302* (0.009)	0.163* (0.009)
Cases/10k	−1.924e−4* (3.177e−5)	−3.143e−4* (4.019e−5)	−2.300e−4 (4.012e−5)
Observations	41,750	24,787	24,712
R^2	0.299	0.198	0.073

Note: *$p < 0.01$

Source: Data from Economist/YouGov Polling and Mathieu et al. 2023.

independents are excluded. The difference between the Republican and Democrat coefficients is 0.471, significantly larger than the coefficients for the state and local models. While partisanship is clearly of great importance, other factors are also influential for trust in state and local government.

Additional Analyses

This data also lets us take a descriptive look at which states are rated the highest or lowest by respondents. Wisconsin was the state rated lowest by respondents for its COVID response. This is possibly explained by the fact that Wisconsin is an extremely competitive state along partisan lines, and had a highly publicized partisan dispute between the Democratic governor and the Republican legislature over an attempt by the governor to move the date of the Wisconsin presidential primary. Interestingly, Wisconsin Democrats and Republicans both rated the state relatively low for its management of COVID-19. We do not argue that how respondents rate the government's pandemic response is not affected by other factors. On a state level, it may also be impacted by how respondents feel about the state government in general.

Conclusions

While it is clear that partisanship plays a significant, even primary, role in how voters evaluate the competence of the federal government, it is also the case that, at least in the case of COVID-19, actual, measurable performance plays a role. Partisans viewed the performance of the different levels of government differently overall, but they were also much more likely to approve of government performance where the relevant level of government was controlled by a copartisan.

Further work can improve on this analysis in two very clear ways. First, more sophisticated modeling could better integrate the temporal nature of the data used. In this case, although the data was collected using the same question over time, approaches that address the fact that the data was collected at different points in time may be appropriate in the future.

Second, this paper does not utilize possible measures of perceived competence other than case rate. It seems likely that some Americans had preferences with regard to government COVID-19 policy that depended on things other than spread of the virus. During this period, concerns over shelter-in-place orders, school closures, and mask mandates were held by some Americans regardless of impact on case rates. These are also directly measurable policies, while the impact of government performance on case rate is not always clear. As these varied across and occasionally within states, analysis of these differences could also help us gain leverage over the question of misattribution in federalist systems and the factors that contribute to trust and confidence across levels of government.

Note

1. A LOESS curve is a regression in which the curve at each point is fit using a localized subset of the data.

References

Atkeson, Lonna Rae, R. Michael Alvarez, and Thad E. Hall. 2015. "Voter Confidence: How to Measure It and How It Differs from Government Support." *Election Law Journal* 14, no. 3 (September): 207–19.

Bangerter, Adrian, Franciska Krings, Audrey Mouton, Ingrid Gilles, Eva G. Green, and Alain Clemence. 2012. "Longitudinal Investigation of Public Trust in Institutions Relative to the 2009 H1N1 Pandemic in Switzerland." *PLoS One* 7, no. 11 (November 21): e49806.

Barber, Bernard. 1983. *The Logic and Limits of Trust.* New Brunswick, NJ: Rutgers University Press.

Citrin, Jack. 1974. "Comment: The Political Relevance of Trust in Government." *American Political Science Review* 68, no. 3 (September): 973–88.

De Benedictis-Kessner, Justin, and Christopher Warshaw. 2020. "Accountability for the Local Economy at All Levels of Government in United States Elections." *American Political Science Review* 114, no. 3 (August): 660–76.

Fenno, Robert F. 1978. *Home Style: House Members in Their Districts*. Boston: Little, Brown.

Gaskell, Jen, Gerry Stoker, Will Jennings, and Daniel Devine. 2020. "Covid-19 and the Blunders of Our Governments: Long-Run System Failings Aggravated by Political Choices." *Political Quarterly* 91, no. 3 (July–September): 523–33.

Hetherington, Marc J., and John D. Nugent. 2001. "Explaining Public Support for Devolution: The Role of Political Trust." In *What Is It about Government That Americans Dislike?*, edited by John R. Hibbing and Elizabeth Theiss-Morse, 134–51. Cambridge: Cambridge University Press.

Hetherington, Marc J., and Thomas J. Rudolph. 2015. *Why Washington Won't Work: Polarization, Political Trust, and the Governing Crisis*. Chicago: University of Chicago Press.

Iyengar, Shanto, Yphtach Lelkes, Matthew Levendusky, Neil Malhotra, and Sean J. Westwood. 2019. "The Origins and Consequences of Affective Polarization in the United States." *Annual Review of Political Science* 22: 129–46.

Keele, Luke. 2007. "Social Capital and the Dynamics of Trust in Government." *American Journal of Political Science* 51, no. 2 (April): 241–54.

Mathieu, Edouard, Hannah Ritchie, Lucas Rodés-Guirao, Cameron Appel, Daniel Gavrilov, Charlie Giattino, Joe Hasell, Bobbie Macdonald, Saloni Dattani, Diana Beltekian, Esteban Ortiz-Ospina, and Max Roser. 2023. "Coronavirus Pandemic (COVID-19)." Published online at OurWorldInData.org. Accessed September 13. https://ourworldindata.org/coronavirus.

McCarty, Nolan, Keith T. Poole, and Howard Rosenthal. 2016. *Polarized America: The Dance of Ideology and Unequal Riches*. Cambridge, MA: MIT Press.

Sances, Michael W. 2017. "Attribution Errors in Federalist Systems: When Voters Punish the President for Local Tax Increases." *Journal of Politics* 79, no. 4 (October): 1286–301.

Suhay, Elizabeth, Aparna Soni, Claudia Persico, and Dave E. Marcotte. 2022. "Americans' Trust in Government and Health Behaviors during the COVID-19 Pandemic." *RSF: The Russell Sage Foundation Journal of the Social Sciences* 8, no. 8 (December): 221–44.

Tyler, Tom R. 2006. *Why People Obey the Law*. Princeton, NJ: Princeton University Press.

Wolak, Jennifer. 2020. "Why Do People Trust Their State Government?" *State Politics & Policy Quarterly* 20, no. 3 (September): 313–29.

BRANDICE CANES-WRONE: Are you thinking of putting in a policy? So I'm working on a paper with very different data, so I'd be curious. And where we find out that out-partisan approval does respond somewhat to which policies the governors enacted.

DAVID BRADY: When the governor says we're going to open schools, the Republicans like that and Democrats don't like it. So it's fairly partisan and overall it doesn't make much of a difference.

MICHAEL W. MCCONNELL: Question both to the earlier MO [money supply] analysis paper, too. I think one of the most startling facts about modern American politics has been that the ten most popular governors were all Republicans in blue states. And that doesn't seem to correlate with any of this. And it puzzles me.

BRADY: There aren't very many of them.

MCCONNELL: Well, they're all the ten most popular in the country.

BRADY: Ten over how many years? In 2020? How many are there? [Maryland governor Larry] Hogan?

CANES-WRONE: This is the out-partisan effect. I mean, but most of them, in COVID did enact something akin to blue state policy. So this is that out-partisan effect.

DOUGLAS RIVERS: Democratic governor or Republican state, it's variable. So you're going to have to—

CANES-WRONE: Yeah, in Kansas [which had a Democratic governor], they opened. There are some examples such as these that counter.

RIVERS: But they do get elected because they're positive.

CANES-WRONE: Yes, I agree.

RIVERS: Individually, they're not.

6

Recessions and Ratchets: Federal Funds and Public-Sector Employment

Jonathan Rodden

Introduction

Each of the most recent US recessions has spurred the federal government to assemble a large, temporary, ad hoc package of special intergovernmental grants for state governments. For the most part, these grants have not been targeted based on need. Rather, they have been distributed on a per capita basis, but with a very substantial bonus for small states. These packages have created a ratchet effect, such that each time, real per capita federal transfers to state governments stay above pre-recession levels, and states become more dependent on intergovernmental transfers.

A large cross-national literature in political economy observes that when subnational governments receive additional revenues, they tend to spend the vast majority of the windfall rather than reducing taxation or paying down debt. This is known as the "flypaper effect" (Hines and Thaler 1995; Inman 2008; Carlino et al. 2023). A number of studies indicate that a large share of unanticipated revenue windfalls is often spent on public employment (Larraín and Perelló 2019; Caselli and Michaels 2013).

More broadly, Wagner's law states that government activity inevitably increases as economies grow (Wagner 1911). A related literature on "cyclical ratcheting" finds a tendency for the size of government to increase during recessions and to be only partially reduced during expansions (Hercowitz and Strawczynski 2004), in part because it is politically painful to eliminate public-sector employees, especially in the presence of vocal public-sector unions.

In light of these findings, and the fact that federal grants to states are ratcheting upward with each recent recession, we might expect to find that public employment is also ratcheting upward. However, exactly the opposite has occurred. This chapter documents a rather striking contraction of public employment in the United States over the last twenty years in the wake of each successive recession. The sharp decline of the public-sector work-force in the United States stands out relative to other advanced industrial democracies.

Given the well-known political obstacles to cutting public employment, the contraction of the public sector in the United States is an interesting puzzle. This chapter explores the possibility that the explanation lies largely in the nature and operation of American federalism. The vast majority of public employment in the United States occurs at the municipal level, where wages and benefits for public-sector workers make up a large share of expenditures. Especially in relatively poor communities, and especially in the field of education, much of the wage bill is subsidized by grants from state governments to local governments.

For most state governments, recessions bring declining own-source revenue, increasing demands on the social safety net, and large but ostensibly temporary increases in federal grants. Faced with balanced budget requirements, this chapter shows that state governments have chosen to bolster direct expenditures while engaging in large cuts in support for local governments. These cuts, often combined with declining own-source revenues, provide local governments with no choice but to trim the public-sector workforce.

The extent of this phenomenon varies across states. First, declining state aid to localities is more pronounced in the states most adversely affected by recessions. For some states that are less affected by recessions, large federal relief packages are essentially unexpected windfalls, and it has been possible to increase direct state expenditures without making cuts in support for local government. Second, the distribution of federal funds to states during recessions has been strongly biased in favor of small states, which have become increasingly dependent on federal grants with each recession. As a result, the small states have not found it necessary to cut support for local governments during recessions, and they have been able to largely avoid recession-induced cuts to the local public sector. Public-sector employment has always been far greater in small, sparsely populated states than in larger states, and this difference has only grown over time. This chapter begins by placing the most recent recessions in historical perspective, explaining the evolving role of the federal government in funding the activities of the states. It demonstrates that recessions have been important moments in the development of transfer-dependence among state and local governments. Specifically, recessions are associated with significant increases in reliance on intergovernmental transfers among state governments, but declining aid from states to local governments.

The next section focuses on each recession since 1980, exploring the efforts of state governments to balance their budgets on the backs of local governments while expanding their own expenditures. The following section takes a closer look at the difference between small and large states, and the coevolution of transfer-dependence and a large public sector in the small states. The final section discusses avenues for further research and concludes.

Crises, Ratchets, and American Federalism

Military and fiscal crises are the most crucial junctures in the histories of federal systems. In the United States, the lack of federal response to state-level fiscal crises in the 1840s laid the foundation for a system in which US states were viewed by creditors and voters as miniature sovereigns. For the next seventy years, with the exception of the Reconstruction experience in the South, the US system of federalism was quite decentralized in every respect. Federal involvement in the decisions of state governments was quite limited, although a series of early forays of the federal government into financing and regulating the activities of states is documented by John F. Cogan in chapter 4 of this volume.

In the first half of the twentieth century, however, there were three events that led to ratchet-like spikes in federal taxes and expenditures and a more expansive role for the federal government in regulation. Via the War Revenue Act of 1917, World War I led to a sudden and dramatic increase in the federal government's ability to raise and spend money. Figure 6.1 displays the expenditures of the federal government as a share of total expenditures, beginning in 1900, revealing a large spike associated with World War I. The federal government's role in expenditures quickly retreated after the war, but not all the way to its prewar level.

Next, in response to the Great Depression, the New Deal was perhaps the single most important turning point in the history of US federalism. The federal government became involved in a wide range of activities that had previously been considered off-limits, and for the most part, it has not subsequently retreated. After the New Deal, the states became much more involved in implementing federal grant–funded programs, and both layers of government became intertwined in a complex web of activity.

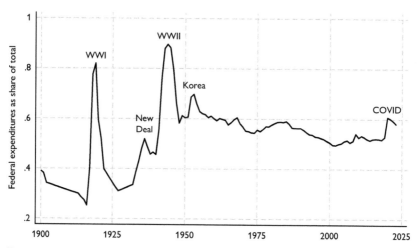

Figure 6.1 Federal expenditures as a share of total (federal, state, municipal) expenditures in the United States, 1900 to present

Source: Author calculations using data from US Census Bureau, *Bicentennial Edition: Historical Statistics of the United States, Colonial Times to 1970;* United States Federal Budget Historical Tables; US Census, Annual Survey of State and Local Finances, all archived by usgovernmentspending.com.

The next big expansion of the federal government relative to the state and local governments was to fund World War II. The spike in the federal government's share of expenditures was large and lasting, in part because it was followed by the Cold War, the arms race with the Soviet Union, and another spike associated with the Korean War.

With each of these major crises, the federal government gained a more prominent role in taxation, and it came to rely increasingly on intergovernmental grants to states and municipalities, often earmarked for specific purposes and with conditions attached. Each case seems consistent with Milton Friedman's quip that "nothing is so permanent as a temporary government program" (Friedman 1984). Responses to crises, often sold as short-term emergency measures, change the nature of the game of American federalism. They alter incentives, create new winners and losers, and generate new coalitions and vested interests.

One might expect the ratchet effect in federal taxation and expenditures to be associated with something similar in public employment. However, this has clearly not been the case. Using data from the Federal Reserve Bank of St. Louis, figure 6.2 displays public-sector jobs per 1,000 people from 1955 to the present. Federal government employment (in black) has steadily fallen as a share of the population over the last seventy years, with temporary spikes associated with each decennial census. Employment in the states (in orange) increased in the early postwar period, but has been relatively flat since the early 1980s.

Figure 6.2 makes it clear that the bulk of the growth in public-sector employment in the postwar period has taken place at the municipal level (in green). Growth was steady and steep until the stagflation recession of the mid-1970s. Growth returned after the recession, but next, the early 1980s recessions led to a steep decline in local public employment. This was followed by another lengthy period of employment growth that lasted until the 2001 recession, when the growth of local government employment started a gentle decline, which then intensified with the onset of the great recession, falling dramatically once again with the COVID recession. Local public employment is at the same level today as in 1985. Total government employment at all levels is at about the level of 1966.

Figure 6.2 suggests that while federal and state-level employment are not very responsive to the business cycle, local employment often falls in the wake of recessions, and since 2000, seems to be ratcheting downward with each recession. These recession-induced cuts in local public employment since 2000 are puzzling, given the rise of the practice of negotiating special

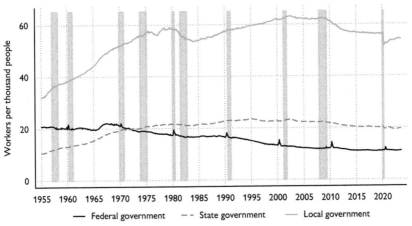

Figure 6.2 Public-sector jobs per 1,000 population by level of government, 1955 to present

Note: Recessions are indicated with vertical gray bars.

Source: Author calculations using data from Federal Reserve Bank of St. Louis.

countercyclical "stimulus" packages with the onset of each recession. The protection of state and local jobs is often front and center in the arguments used to justify rapid passage of these programs during legislative and public debates.

Figure 6.3 plots state and local jobs per thousand people in blue, corresponding to the left axis, and real intergovernmental grants from the federal government to states in orange, corresponding to the right axis. We can see that federal assistance to the states decreased during the early 1980s recessions, but increased modestly for three years after. Each subsequent recession has seen a much larger ratchet in federal grants to states. However, the blue line indicates that if anything, public employment has been leveling off or decreasing with each recession.

Why has this increased federal support associated with recent recessions not insulated the public sector from cuts? The answer may be relatively straightforward: the funds never make it to the local governments and school

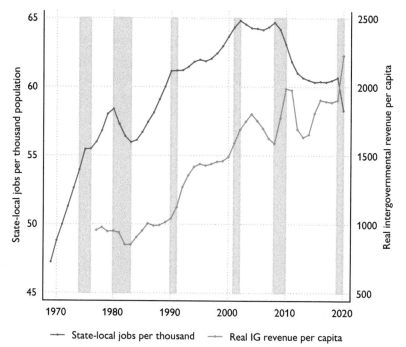

Figure 6.3 State-local public-sector jobs per 1,000 population (left axis) and real federal intergovernmental revenues per capita, 1970 to 2020

Note: Recessions are indicated with vertical gray bars.

Source: Author calculations using data from Bureau of Economic Analysis (BEA) and US Census of Governments via the Willamette Government Finance Database.

districts that are responsible for hiring and firing. Figure 6.4 plots grants from state governments to local governments as a share of state government expenditures. These appear to be ratcheting downward with each recession. Increased federal support for the states associated with recent recessions has clearly not been spent on assistance to local governments.

It is also useful to get a sense of the relative dependence on intergovernmental transfers of both state and local governments. Figure 6.5 plots intergovernmental transfers as a share of revenues for state governments (in blue) and local governments (in green and orange). Starting with the early 1990s recession, transfer-dependence has been ratcheting starkly upward for the states. Each recession ushers in a period of sharply increasing transfer-dependence, which then levels off but never returns to the pre-recession level, ratcheting up again with the next recession.

In general, local governments are more reliant on grants than state governments. During the era of general revenue sharing, they were highly dependent on transfers, but this reliance fell throughout the 1980s after the demise of general revenue sharing. It started to rise slightly again in the 1990s, but beginning with the 2001 recession, transfers as a share of revenues has fallen with recent recessions as state aid has been cut. Transfers from higher-level

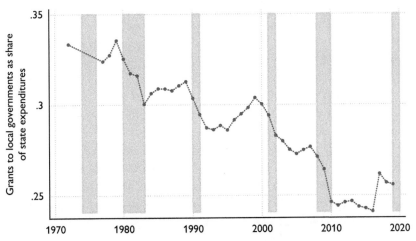

Figure 6.4 Grants from state government to local government as share of total state government expenditures, 1970 to 2020

Note: Gray bars indicate recessions. Data not available for 1973–1976.

Source: Author calculations using data from US Census of Governments via the Willamette Public Finance Database.

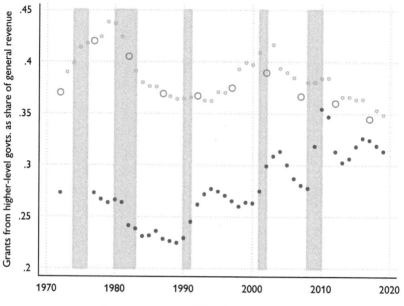

Figure 6.5 Grants from state government to local government as share of total state government expenditures, 1970 to 2020

Note: Gray bars indicate recessions. Data for states unavailable for 1973–1976. Full census of governments taken in years ending in 2 and 7; sample in other years.

Source: Author calculations using data from US Census of Governments via the Willamette Public Finance Database.

governments as a share of local revenue are now lower than at any time since data became available in the early 1970s, and local governments are now almost as reliant on own-source revenues as are the states.

In sum, it appears that something basic has changed in American federalism in recent decades. State governments are learning to expect countercyclical fiscal relief from the federal government during recessions. Local governments, on the other hand, have learned to expect strongly pro-cyclical transfers from their state governments.

A Closer Look at Recessions since 1980

Let us take a closer look at the dynamics associated with the early 1980s double recession, the early 1990s recession, the early 2000s recession, and the great recession. It is important to note that recessions do not affect all states equally. In fact, in each recession a nontrivial number of states continued to experience economic growth throughout the recession.[1] Let us examine those states separately from the states that experienced contraction.

I choose the baseline years of 1980, 1990, 2001, and 2008, and examine real per capita federal grants to states relative to the base year in subsequent years. The evolution of aggregate real federal grants per capita is plotted in figure 6.6, in black for the states with declining GDP per capita during the recession, and in gray for the states with increasing GDP per capita. The early 1980s recession was the last in which states experienced declining real federal grants per capita, although transfers to the most affected states recovered to pre-recession levels by 1985. But in each subsequent recession, real per capita grants increased sharply for several years.

Figure 6.6 also provides an indication of the extent to which fiscal relief in the wake of recessions is poorly targeted. In the 1990s and 2000s, states with increasing GDP per capita during the recession actually received somewhat larger spikes in federal transfers than those whose economies contracted. To examine this further, for each recession, I regressed the percent change in federal grants from the pre-recession fiscal year to the year of the (nation-wide) trough against the percent change in state GDP per capita for the same period. For three of the four recessions, there was no discernible relation-ship, but for the early 2000s recession, the coefficient was positive and signifi-cant, indicating that the states with the strongest growth received the largest increase in federal grants, and those most affected by the recession received the smallest increases.

Next, figure 6.7 examines what happens to real direct state expenditures during recessions; that is to say, expenditures other than those on intergov-ernmental grants to lower-level governments. In each of the three most recent recessions, state governments increased their direct expenditures, even in states where GDP per capita (and hence own-source revenues) declined. In each case, the evolution of direct expenditures closely resembles that of fed-eral grants in figure 6.6.

Figure 6.8 plots intergovernmental grants to lower-level governments. Here, the pattern is quite different. In the 1980s, the states most affected by the recession cut their transfers to local governments for four years. In the early 2000s and again after the great recession, both types of states engaged in a sustained long-term period of cuts in transfers to local governments. In the years after the great recession, these cuts were much deeper for the states most affected by the recession.

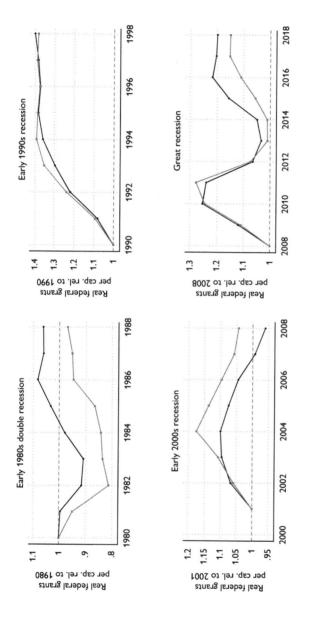

Figure 6.6 Real federal grants per capita relative to base year, growing versus declining states

Source: Author calculations using data from US Census of Governments via the Willamette Government Finance Database.

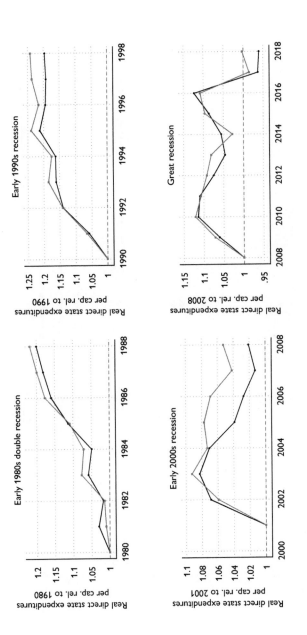

Figure 6.7 Real per capita direct state expenditures relative to base year, growing versus declining states

Source: Author calculations using data from US Census of Governments via the Willamette Government Finance Database.

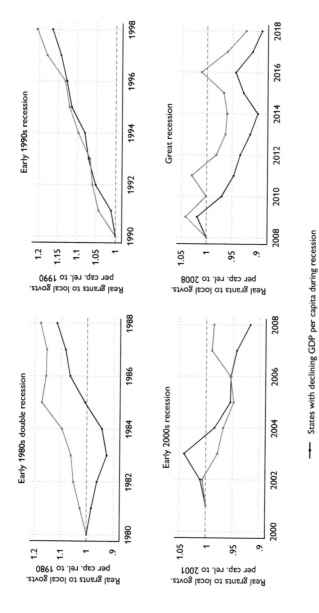

Figure 6.8 Real per capita transfers to local governments relative to base year, growing versus declining states

Source: Author calculations using data from US Census of Governments via the Willamette Government Finance Database.

It appears that states used increased federal transfers to bolster their own direct expenditures. This is not surprising, since those direct expenditures included programs like Medicaid, for which demand was increasing during the recession, and for which some of the increased federal funds were expressly designated (see chapter 10 of this volume by Joshua Rauh and Jillian Ludwig). The federal matching rate for Medicaid creates strong incentives to increase Medicaid spending and make cuts elsewhere.

At the same time, their hands were tied by their obligations to implement cofinanced federal programs, for which demand increases during recessions. Perhaps it is the case that demand for education and other services funded by grants from state governments to municipalities is less correlated with the business cycle, causing these grants to become squeezed during recessions. It may also be the case that governors and state legislators believe they are less likely to be blamed for cuts that will ultimately be carried out by municipal officials. Whatever the reason, with the exception of the 1990s recession, the states carried out large and sustained cuts in transfers to local governments.

Local governments were faced with declining own-source revenues as well as cuts in grants. Figure 6.9 demonstrates the implications for employment. For some years in some states, the BEA employment data do not differentiate between state and local employment, so in order to conduct time-series analysis over the entire period, it is necessary to combine them. State and local employment declined substantially after the early 1980s recessions, mildly after the early 2000s recession (and only for the states experiencing economic decline), and very substantially after the great recession.

Declining aid from state governments seems to be an important part of the story. A useful avenue for further research is to use data on individual local governments and school districts to disentangle the relative importance of declining own-source revenue versus intergovernmental grants in public-sector employment decisions, perhaps contrasting high-income suburban areas with lower-income urban core areas and rural areas, the latter of which tend to be highly dependent on intergovernmental transfers.

Are Small States Different?

An enduring feature of US federalism is that the system of intergovernmental transfers is biased in favor of small states (Lee 2000; Dragu and Rodden 2011). Figure 6.10 plots real federal grants per capita against the log of state population, for 1972 (the first year for which data are available) in red, and for the most recent year, 2020, in black.

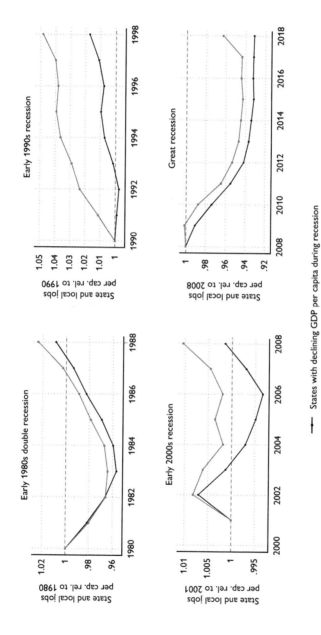

Figure 6.9 State and local employment relative to base year, growing versus declining states

Source: Author calculations using data from BEA.

States with declining GDP per capita during recession

States with increasing GDP per capita during recession

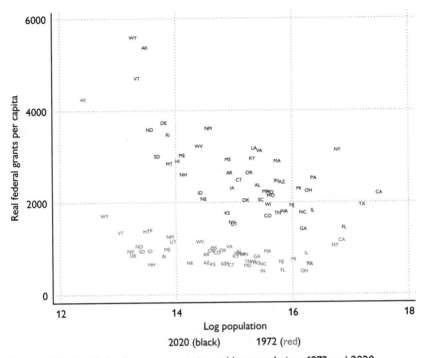

Figure 6.10 Real federal grants per capita and log population, 1972 and 2020

Source: Author calculations using data from US Census of Governments via the Willamette Government Finance Database.

Figure 6.10 shows that there was already a small-state bonus in 1972, but it has grown substantially over the decades. The growth in real federal grants per capita has been much more modest in large states like California or Florida than in small states like West Virginia or Wyoming. On a per capita basis, federal transfers are more than twice as high in Wyoming and Vermont as in Texas and Illinois.

Representatives of smaller states advocate for larger federal transfers on the logic that the per capita cost of providing services is higher in small and especially sparsely populated states. Economies of scale in service provision are very likely an important consideration, and population decline in rural areas may have increased the costs of service provision even further. However, it seems doubtful that the cost differential has grown so substantially over the last fifty years as to explain the pattern in figure 6.10. Some of the small states experiencing dramatic growth in federal grants per capita, like Delaware and Rhode Island, are densely populated. A common claim in the political economy literature is that small states, with two senate seats, are in a better position to bargain for higher transfers in the legislature (Lee 2000).

Whatever its origin, it seems that a norm, or perhaps focal point, in time-pressured negotiations over fiscal relief packages during recessions has emerged, whereby the starting point for discussions about distribution is a per capita scheme with a very generous subsidy for small states. Senators from small states have been vocal in threatening to scuttle proposed packages unless they receive their customary windfall. Legislative bargaining over fiscal relief packages seems to have provided small states with an excellent opportunity to expand their baseline advantage.

Figure 6.11 plots the coefficients from yearly regressions of real per capita federal grants on logged population density. It shows that the small-state advantage (represented by negative coefficients) gradually increased

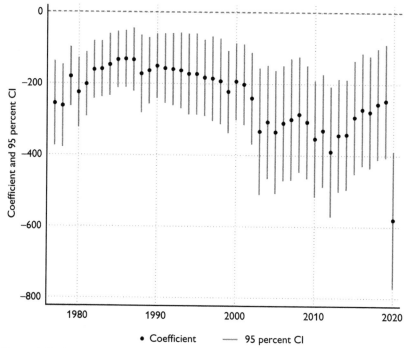

Figure 6.11 Coefficients and 95 percent confidence intervals from regressions of real federal grants per capita on logged state population

Source: Author calculations using data from US Census of Governments via the Willamette Government Finance Database.

during the 1990s, but then ratcheted upward with the rescue package after the 2001 recession, and then again with the rescue package after the great recession. However, the largest increase in small-state advantage came with the first COVID relief package in 2020, which was exceptionally generous to small states.

This system of largesse for small states should make it much easier for them in the aftermath of recessions. Small states should be relatively immune from the constraints that generate large cuts in grants to local governments in larger states and, as a result, less likely to experience large cuts in public employment.

I classify the following states with three or fewer members of the House of Representatives as "small states": Wyoming, Alaska, Vermont, North and South Dakota, Delaware, Montana, Rhode Island, Hawaii, Maine, New Hampshire, West Virginia, New Mexico, Idaho, and Nebraska. As above, I examine the evolution of real per capita transfers from states to local governments, aggregating over all small states and all remaining states, for the most recent recessions.

Figure 6.12 shows that indeed the small states have not cut intergovernmental grants to local governments after the 1980s recession, the early 1990s recession, or the 2001 recession. In the great recession, there were cuts in grants to local governments among the small states, but they were far smaller than those in the larger states.

What are the implications for public employment? Figure 6.13 presents a similar display of the data for state and local jobs per thousand people. It demonstrates that public-sector employment reacts very differently to recessions in small states than in large states. Cuts in public employment were much smaller in small states than in larger states in the 1980s recession. Public-sector job growth was stronger in the small states after the 1990s recession than in the larger states. In the early 2000s, when small states received an especially large boost from the federal government, they went on a public-sector hiring spree, while larger states made cuts. Finally, during the great recession, small states did cut jobs, but those cuts were less than half the size of the cuts in the larger states.

I have also taken an event study approach, regressing real per capita transfers to local governments and state-local public employment on lags and leads of the year of recession onset. This approach shows that larger states react to recessions with lasting cuts, while small states do not.

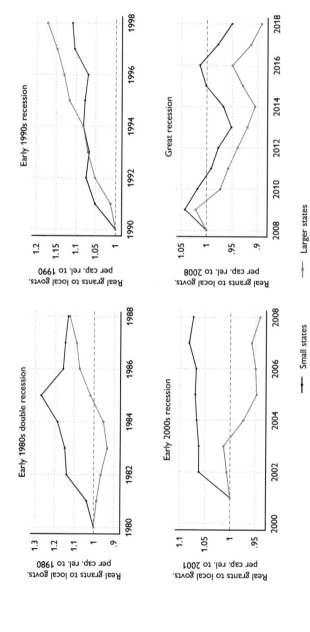

Figure 6.12 Real per capita grants from state governments to local governments relative to base year, small states and larger states

Source: Author calculations using data from US Census of Governments via the Willamette Government Finance Database.

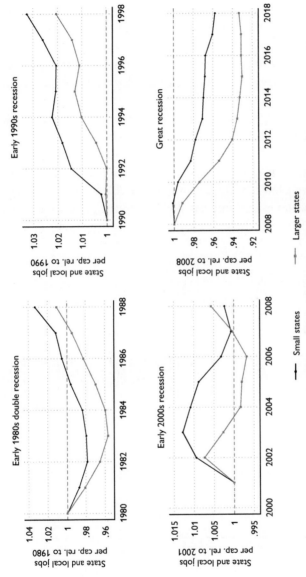

Figure 6.13 Real per capita grants from state governments to local governments relative to base year, small states and larger states

Source: Author calculations using data from BEA.

In short, the role of downturns in trimming the growth of the public sector appears not to apply to small states, for whom recessions can lead to windfalls in federal funds. There has been a strong negative correlation between population size and public employees per 1,000 population since data first became available in 1969. Figure 6.14 displays coefficients from year-by-year regressions of state and local employees per 1,000 people on logged state population, showing that the negative relationship between state size and the level of public-sector employment has grown stronger over time.

This relationship goes against popular perceptions that public employment is especially dominant in large, urbanized states in the Northeast with a history of strong labor unions. Figure 6.15 plots state and local jobs per 1,000 population against logged state population in 2020. Public employment is relatively low in large, urbanized states like Florida, Pennsylvania, and Michigan, and even California. Relative to the population, the public

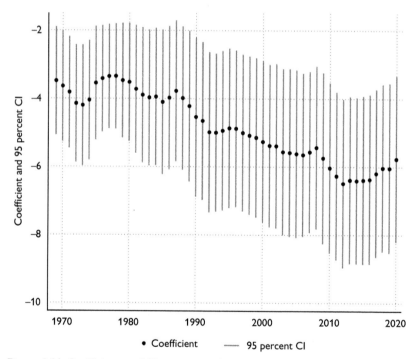

Figure 6.14 Coefficients and 95 percent confidence intervals from regressions of state and local public employees per 1,000 population on logged state population
Source: Author calculations using data from BEA.

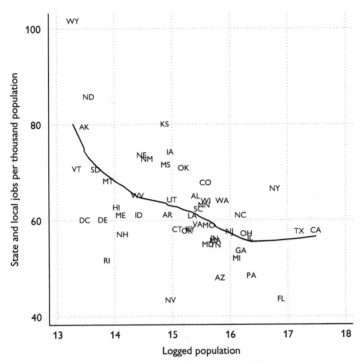

Figure 6.15 State-local employment per 1,000 population and log population, 2020

Source: Author calculations using data from BEA.

sector is almost twice as large in North Dakota as in Florida. State and local public-sector employment per thousand population in Wyoming and North Dakota are larger than for all levels of government in France. In Alaska and Kansas, they are larger than for all levels of government in the UK or Austria. In Florida, Pennsylvania, and Arizona, in contrast, the public sector is substantially smaller relative to population than in any country in Europe.

Surely an important part of the explanation for this relationship is that a larger number of employees per capita is required to provide similar service levels in the small states that are also sparsely populated. Note, for example, that Delaware, Maine, New Hampshire, and Rhode Island are outliers in figure 6.15. The relationship is driven by rural states. However, an interesting question for future analysis is the role of ever-increasing federal grants in loosening the fiscal constraints on small, rural state governments, which have developed exceptionally large public sectors.

Discussion and Conclusion

Recessions and fiscal crises are crucial moments in the evolution of federal systems. In the 1840s, the US federal government famously resisted calls for federal bailouts. However, in the post–New Deal era, as the state governments have become increasingly responsible for implementing aspects of the modern social safety net such as unemployment insurance and Medicaid, legislators and members of the executive branch find it increasingly difficult to ignore the fiscal woes of the states during recessions. Own-source revenues decline and demands on safety net programs increase, and states are unable to borrow.

With each recent recession, federal legislators feel compelled to negotiate a "temporary" package of assistance, usually with a very strong bias in favor of small states. In most states, these additional transfers appear to be used to bolster direct expenditures by state governments. But in order to balance budgets, states have developed a practice of implementing rather large cuts in transfers to local governments, who then have no choice but to reduce the size of the local public sector. In related work, I have shown that the impact of this phenomenon is especially large in rural areas, which are typically more dependent on grants from the state government and rely much more heavily on public employment than suburban or urban areas (Rodden 2023).

In this chapter, I explored a potentially important source of cross-state heterogeneity. For small states—especially those with natural resources or other economic activities that make them less vulnerable to national downturns—a recession can bring about a windfall of federal funds. Perhaps as a result, small states have been less likely to cut their support to local governments after recessions, and less likely to cut public-sector jobs. These states have also developed the highest levels of public-sector employment in the United States.

Future work might pay closer attention to the reactions of individual state governments to the massive expansions in federal assistance associated with recessions. In addition to state size and the severity of recessions, the partisanship of state government might be another interesting source of cross-state heterogeneity. Carlino et al. (2023) show that the marginal propensity to spend additional transfers is higher in states controlled by Democrats than in states controlled by Republicans. If Democratic states respond to additional federal grants with higher expenditures, and Republican states respond with tax cuts, the latter would end up with larger transfers as a share of revenues.

An ongoing political realignment has created a growing aggregate positive state-level (and county-level) correlation between income per capita and Democratic voting, as well as a growing correlation between population density and Democratic voting. Since federal grants favor relatively poor, smaller, and more sparsely populated states, a strong correlation between transfer-dependence, the size of the public sector, and partisanship has appeared in the last two decades. In addition to rurality, perhaps part of the explanation for relatively high levels of public employment in Republican states and counties has to do with legacy costs associated with past generosity in determining benefits. Perhaps it is the case that localities with a long history of government by Democrats tend to spend more on benefits for long-standing employees and retirees, while localities run by Republicans might be able to spend more on new hires. The partisanship of governors and legislators might also have an impact on the strategies chosen by state governments when determining how to cut expenditures during recessions, although preliminary analysis indicates that the reliance on cutting grants to local governments is broadly bipartisan.

Another source of cross-state variation is taxation and the nature of revenue generation in the fifty states. Some states, like California, rely on progressive income taxes, and have experienced large revenue windfalls as high-income state residents have experienced rapid income growth. On the other hand, states without income taxes have not experienced similar growth in own-source revenues during recessions, but have also experienced less volatility over the business cycle.

Another important source of cross-state and time-series variation is in the nature of education finance. In some states, such as California and Michigan, the state government has become far more involved in education finance than in other states. And in several states, far-reaching reforms and orders by state courts have changed the nature of education finance and the role of the state government vis-à-vis school districts over time, providing researchers with valuable quasi-experiments.

Another worthwhile area for future analysis is to zoom in on the specific expenditures and types of employment that municipalities are cutting after recessions. Future work might explore the implications of these cuts, if any, for pupil-to-teacher ratios and educational outcomes. Hanushek (2006) points out that pupil-to-teacher ratios have experienced a long period of decline since the 1980s, although the great recession represented a sudden and sharp deviation from this trend (Evans, Schwab, and Wagner 2019). In some parts of the country, as the population ages and birth rates decline, it may be possible for school districts to employ fewer teachers per capita without increasing the pupil-to-teacher ratio. Moreover, it is possible that some of the recession-induced cuts are made to nonteaching employees. Furthermore, public employment per capita might be declining in part because school districts and municipal governments are relying increasingly on contractors rather than formal employees.

It might also be worthwhile to explore the role of public-sector unions in the wake of declining support from the state after recessions. Perhaps union leaders face incentives to protect the pay and benefits of long-standing members rather than advocate for the maintenance or expansion of the size of the public-sector workforce. In fact, Scott Walker explicitly defended his efforts to curb the power of public-sector unions in Wisconsin as a way to protect public-sector jobs during a period of austerity.[2] It is possible that the specific reaction to budget cuts is different in states with and without strong public-sector unions.

A final area worthy of further study relates to policy reform. Few would advocate in the abstract for a system in which countercyclical fiscal relief for lower-level governments is determined by ad hoc political bargains carried out in a high-pressure environment during fiscal crises. In addition to poor targeting and potential moral hazard, this chapter stresses another, less-appreciated aspect of this system: sharply declining support for the local governments that are responsible for paying the salaries of teachers, healthcare workers, and firefighters.

Notes

1. I differentiate between states that experienced a decline in real GDP per capita from the year of onset to the trough and those that experienced (at least some) growth during that period. In the 1980s, states experiencing growth included New Hampshire, Oklahoma, Colorado, Massachusetts, Texas, Wyoming, New Mexico, North Dakota, Louisiana, Virginia, Connecticut, and Alaska. In the 1990s, they included Delaware, Nebraska, Alabama, Kansas, Utah, Wyoming, West Virginia, New Mexico, Washington, Arkansas, North Dakota, Louisiana, South Dakota, and Hawaii. In the early 2000s, the list was quite long: New Hampshire, Florida, Oklahoma, Delaware, Maryland, Massachusetts, Texas, Nebraska, Arizona, New Jersey, Montana, Maine, Wyoming, Rhode Island, New York, West Virginia, North Dakota, Pennsylvania, Louisiana, Virginia, Connecticut, Alaska, Vermont, and Wisconsin. In the great recession, the list was quite short: Oklahoma, Maryland, New York, West Virginia, North Dakota, South Dakota, Alaska, Vermont.

2. See Scott Walker, "Conservative Reforms Worked Wonders in Blue Wisconsin," *New York Times*, August 26, 2021.

References

Carlino, Gerald, Thorsten Drautzburg, Robert Inman, and Nicholas Zarra. 2023. "Partisanship and Fiscal Policy in Economic Unions: Evidence from US States." *American Economic Review* 113, no. 3 (March): 701–37.

Caselli, Francesco, and Guy Michaels. 2013. "Do Oil Windfalls Improve Living Standards? Evidence from Brazil." *American Economic Journal: Applied Economics* 5, no. 1 (January): 208–38.

Dragu, Tiberiu, and Jonathan A. Rodden. 2011. "Representation and Redistribution in Federations." *Proceedings of the National Academy of Science* 108, no. 21 (May 24): 8601–4.

Evans, William, Robert Schwab, and Kathryn Wagner. 2019. "The Great Recession and Public Education." *Education Finance and Policy* 14, no. 2 (March): 298–326.

Friedman, Milton and Rose. 1984. *Tyranny of the Status Quo*. San Diego, CA: Harcourt Brace Jovanovich.

Hanushek, Eric A. 2006. "School Resources." In *Handbook of the Economics of Education*, vol. 2, edited by Eric A. Hanushek and Finis Welch, 865–903. Amsterdam: North-Holland.

Hercowitz, Zvi, and Michel Strawczynski. 2004. "Cyclical Ratcheting in Government Spending: Evidence from the OECD." *Review of Economics and Statistics* 86, no. 1 (February): 353–61.

Hines, James R., and Richard H. Thaler. 1995. "The Flypaper Effect." *Journal of Economic Perspectives* 9, no. 4 (Fall): 217–26.

Inman, Robert. 2008. "The Flypaper Effect." National Bureau of Economic Research (NBER) Working Paper Series w14579 (November). Cambridge, MA: National Bureau of Economic Research.

Larraín, Felipe, and Oscar Perelló. 2019. "Resource Windfalls and Public Sector Employment: Evidence from Municipalities in Chile." *Economía* 19, no. 2 (Spring): 127–68.

Lee, Frances E. 2000. "Senate Representation and Coalition Building in Distributive Politics." *American Political Science Review* 94, no. 1 (March): 59–72.

Rodden, Jonathan A. 2019. *Why Cities Lose: The Deep Roots of the Urban-Rural Political Divide*. New York: Basic Books.

———. 2023. "The Great Recession and the Public Sector in Rural America." *Journal of Economic Geography* (published online July 12, 2023). https://doi.org/10.1093/jeg/lbad015.

Wagner, A. 1911. "Staat in nationalökonomischer Hinsicht." In *Handwörterbuch der Staatswissenschaften*, vol. 7, edited by Johannes Conrad, Ludwig Elster, Wilhelm Lexis, and Edgar Loening, 727–39. Jena, Germany: G. Fischer.

The Current State of Federalism

Discussants: Daniel L. Rubinfeld and Thad Kousser

DOUGLAS RIVERS: Why don't Delaware and Hawaii and Rhode Island get disproportionate shares? Or is this just due to agriculture?

JONATHAN RODDEN: They do.

RIVERS: It didn't look like it on the graph.

RODDEN: Let's see how . . . Which graph? Oh, the public-sector graph?

RIVERS: Yes.

RODDEN: That's an interesting question. I think this is why, I think when it comes to the public sector, I agree that it has a lot to do with . . . This is not a graph of transfers. If we look at a graph of the transfers, you'll see that Rhode Island does pretty well, and New Hampshire and Maine, but for some reason it doesn't have the same stimulative impact on the public sector. And so that leads to the . . . I think Michael's idea that it has a lot to do with sparsity, but if you just take, you run some regressions and you control for population density, federal transfer still is a pretty good predictor of public sector.

PAUL E. PETERSON: Do you control for percentage of the land in a state that is owned by the federal government? In Wyoming, Utah, Nevada, and other western states, the federal government owns a lot of the land.

MICHAEL J. BOSKIN: Land, a huge amount.

RODDEN: How that affects the state and local public sector, it's not clear to me. I mean, Wyoming runs its own hospital system and there's some other things that are interesting things that are going on in these states.

*   *   *

DANIEL L. RUBINFELD: Three great papers. With respect to Jonathan's paper, I wonder whether some of the phenomenon he's talking about has to do with capital improvements that made the need for employment to be reduced for certain public functions. And also I wonder whether the distinction between who is running the programs and who is funding them is crucial. A good example would be education in California. K–12 education is primarily managed locally, as we know, but over the years, education has been taken over by the state. That disconnect creates an analytical problem from my point of view, and it does suggest that it's a little hard to look at the data. Flipping over to David Brady's paper, what strikes me is that perceptions about the effectiveness of the public sector do matter, at least in the short run. So to the extent to which people are successful in characterizing programs one way or the other, that seems to have a big effect in the short run on how these programs are evaluated. But over time, I think the realities of the effectiveness of the program does make a difference, which is good news from my point of view. Moving on, I have a few things to say about John Cogan's excellent paper. I learned a lot from reading it, but what strikes me—and this is consistent with what I think he said in the paper—is if you put aside the entitlement programs, for lots of reasons revenue raising can be very effective at the federal level. So it's natural to think about growing the center, thereby substantially raising revenues, which in turn would make all these grant programs make sense. One of the examples that I think is worth discussing is a program that has been quite successful, Obamacare. What is interesting about the program is that it's an expansion of Medicaid.

Under Obamacare, Medicaid, as we know, has been given as an option for growth at the state level. Some states liked it, some didn't. But what is interesting is that a number of the states that accepted the expansion of Obamacare had opposed it initially but now are quite happy about it, because it's been very popular.

Now, to focus a little more on the revenue-raising side of the story: I always ponder the flypaper effect, which Jonathan has talked about in his paper. I think one thing we can all agree on is money does tend to stick where it hits. And there is a lot of evidence supporting the view that the fly-paper effect applies to all levels of government. But the curiosity in my mind is the local level, particularly with respect to schools, where there are some efficiencies, despite the fact that the grants tend to stick, thereby effectuating budget cuts.

THAD KOUSSER: I'll try to be as concise as an academic possibly can. And I think I'm going to follow up; I'm reestimating my comments for your paper, and so I'll follow up with written comments. Jonathan Rodden poses this wonderful puzzle that I don't think anyone has brought to the fore before, right? Why has federal aid to the states ratcheted up at the same time over the last two decades that spending and local school employment has ratcheted down? And so of course that begs the explanation, and I think the implicit explanation in this paper is it's a pure federalism power play, right? Local governments are creatures of the states. States can do it to the locals when times are tough. You cut local governments and keep the state employment. That might be going on but let me throw out a few other possible things to explain this.

One is the peculiar structure of federal grants, especially in Medicaid, which is the bulk of the money. This is the eight-thousand-pound gorilla in these intergovernmental transfers, and it's designed in a highly targeted way, where states get matching dollars. California, for every dollar it spends, it gets $1.60 from the federal government in 2010, which is this key moment here. Texas though, because it's poorer, gets $2.44; Mississippi gets $5.61. This could explain why some of the small states, smaller states that are poor, but not Hawaii, and others are taking this big deficit. So what does that mean? That means when times are good, you can spend. When times are good, Mississippi can spend $100 million of state money and get $661 million worth of health-care for its citizens. When times are bad, in order to trim $100 million from its deficit, it has to cut $661 million worth of services. So that distorts state incentives and that takes money. Well then, why don't we cut schools? Because dollar for dollar, a school cut is a lot less painful than healthcare cuts. So that both ratchets healthcare spending up and ratchets education spending down. Also healthcare, welfare, public safety, those are all . . . they have countercyclical demand. When times are bad, there's more demand for them. Schools don't have that dynamic, and so that may make schools easier to cut. And then finally, it could be purely a partisan story. In 2009, when local governments were large, Republicans controlled 43 percent of state lower houses and had nine trifectas of governors and both houses in the legislature. Today, Republicans have 55 percent of statehouse seats and twenty-two trifectas.

MICHAEL T. HARTNEY: I have a question for Jonathan [Rodden] about your paper. More broadly, do you see the role of public-sector unions factoring in at all to what may be going on? And a smaller question was on the graph that everyone was talking about, with the number of workers per capita. I think it'd be interesting to break that one out by local school employees in particular, because when somebody reformulated what you're doing, and saying, Oh, there's been a decrease in school employees, something went off in my mind. And I was saying, well, that denominator there should be students, not necessarily people in the state, because we've had a decrease in enrollment oftentimes and an increase in hires.

RODDEN: Yeah. I guess kind of like Michael McConnell in his presentation earlier, I'm not taking a normative position on what the right number of public employees should be and whether moving it up or down is a good or a bad thing. I'm just trying to understand it. But I think it's right that it should be broken down by employment category, and take a look at how much of it is in education, which I think that's where a lot of the action is.

And then the question about public employee unions. There are a lot of questions that I have about . . . I mean, first, I guess, I would've expected not to see these cuts, given the power of labor unions, but I wonder if that isn't part of the story, in that the states—it's not necessarily the goal of the labor union to maximize the number of employees, it's to take care of the more senior employees among those who are already employed. And so it could be that there's a tension there, that in places where public-sector unions are strong and have traditionally been strong, that the amount of money that's spent on benefits squeezes out the possibility of new hires and makes it harder to retain people. I'd let others who know more about this weigh in on that.

ERIC A. HANUSHEK: But Michael's point is that employment in education hasn't gone down. I mean that, in fact, the population that's being served has gone down much more rapidly than the employment. And so that normalizing education by the population in a state gives a misleading picture that things are shrinking.

RODDEN: Yeah. I am not looking at education employment alone. I am looking at total public-sector employment, so it would be odd to examine public-sector employment per student, and in any case, I am primarily focused on the timing of expansions and contractions relative to recessions.

Again, it could be that the movement is in the proper direction. But it does certainly happen very . . . If it's a good thing, recessions are quite an opportunity to make it happen. If it's a bad thing, then you see it differently.

BOSKIN: In some areas—I don't know about the data on employment—but in some areas there's a lot of documentation of federal spending being partially offset by state and local spending, for example on infrastructure. The CBO estimates about a third of a dollar for every dollar. And in recent years, we've created this expectation that there's going to be explosions of spending in the next crisis, and it creates an incentive for states and localities to wait and get on the gravy train when it happens, which also can't be the most efficient way, especially to plan stuff like infrastructure.

RODDEN: That's really interesting. That'd be interesting to try to show, see empirically how that plays out.

BOSKIN: So I think that's something that's probably worth looking into. But the CBO has done a variety of studies on this, on infrastructure in particular.

THOMAS MACURDY: Hey, Jonathan [Rodden], one point I wanted to make is if you consider federal spending, you have to look at federal contractors. That's where the federal government has really moved a lot of its employment. Civil service laws constrain employment and discourage performance. Government can fire contractors if they do not perform. Consider defense—there's been a huge shift from civil service to federal contractors. If you look in the health area, federal contractors work everywhere. So, I believe it's really a misrepresentation to look only at federal employment. There has been a huge increase in federal government employment paid through private contractors. And the same is not true in states. States' public unions are much more prominent, and a lot of state employment is public employment.

RODDEN: Yeah, this paper, I'm really mainly looking at state and local and not federal. But I think the same . . . I guess what some people are telling me is that it's very different across states but that there is a movement toward—

MaCurdy: Well, there are also differences across states in the amount of employment supported by contractors versus public unions.

Rodden: Yeah. There are aspects of something that you would've hired some people for twenty years ago. You now make a contract with the—

MaCurdy: They've gone to private in some cases and gone to public in others. You must carefully measure and document these trends if you want to understand what's going on.

Boskin: I think that's an important point. It's useful to take a look at a definition that it's employees that are doing stuff because of the state spending. That might include NGOs in some instance, for example. Of course, contractors too.

MaCurdy: Well, there's a lot, but it's hard to acquire the data on this.

Rodden: I would like to gather some ideas about how to examine some case studies. I'm very curious about that. I'd like to get some data on the transition from public employees to contractors.

MaCurdy: That'd be a good area for case studies, because there's a lot of useful information relevant to this topic.

Peterson: The other measurement issue is when you look at percentages of state spending that is going to local governments, there's two sides of the coin. One is: How much is going to the local governments and how much money is being spent by the state themselves? And so if you have a huge increase, say in Medicaid, you're going to have a huge increase in state expenditure. But that could be driving the percentages. You're interpreting that the percentages are all being driven by the size of the grants going to the state and local government. But you're actually looking at the share of state expenditure that's going to state and local governments.

Rodden: I'm mostly looking at real per capita data. I didn't do too much with shares in the paper. This is related to what Thad was arguing earlier. I think it's right, that a lot of the incentives being created by Medicaid direct the resources away from support for state and local governments.

Part 3

Federalism in Key Areas of Policy

7

Some Evolving Issues in K–12 Education

Eric A. Hanushek

In many ways, the US system of K–12 education looks to be a case study in the strengths and weaknesses of having a federalist system of governance and finance. Decisions about education are made at all levels of government. And views on the balance of decision making have changed over time. The question that we need to ask is whether the structure has worked in the sense of delivering educational outcomes that meet societal needs.

No other country in the world has a governance and fiscal structure for K–12 education that is as complex as that in the United States. Overall, the federal government is a minor actor, but this is not true in all areas. The state governments have the primary responsibility for education, but they delegate operation to local districts that in general make all of the operational decisions. Then, of course, learning activities are implemented at the school and classroom level. The overlapping structure of educational decision making in the United States weaves together a complicated set of objectives and governance that is difficult to disentangle.

The results have not been good. While the United States led the world in developing universal education, the rest of the world has now caught up, and the United States is no longer an educational leader. A large number of other countries have both students completing more years of schooling and students that perform better in terms of measured skills. There are also large disparities in performance within the United States—both across family backgrounds and across states.

The overall performance of the system is obviously a very large question that cannot realistically be answered in its broadest sense. This essay will focus on some key features that are currently up for debate. It begins with an overview of the performance of the system in terms of resources and outcomes. The discussion turns to the federal accountability system and to the trend toward more direct citizen choices—two potentially important but very different aspects of the federalist system. The objective is entirely descriptive, highlighting some of the features of the system that seem to be important in making judgments about where education policy might go.

Finance and Outcomes

The overall picture of enrollments, structure of the schools, and funding has significantly changed over time. The aggregate picture also masks an enormous heterogeneity across the states. Because of the central role of states in setting policy and funding the schools, this heterogeneity provides an important backdrop to thinking about how the various parts of the system go together.

It is useful to start with a description of the outcomes of the educational system. This picture of outcomes can then be matched with funding decisions.[1]

Student Performance

The United States has a long tradition of assessing student performance through the National Assessment of Educational Progress (NAEP), which is often called the Nation's Report Card. Going back to 1973, the Long-Term Trend (LTT) assessment of NAEP makes it possible to get representative national data for math and reading performance of students ages 9, 13, and 17.

Figure 7.1 shows math score changes for different age groups relative to the initial scores in 1973. Scores of all age groups improved over the past fifty years, but the improvements were smallest for the seventeen-year-olds, who are the students closest to leaving high school and entering college or careers.

The scores for all age groups have dropped sharply in the most recent years. While COVID was certainly responsible for significant falls in performance, it is important to note that scores began declining before COVID. This longer period of decline is discussed below, because it coincides with the change in federal accountability regimes.

The scores for reading performance (not shown) follow the same pattern except that both the gains and the recent drop were smaller. The recent losses are also apparent on the other version of NAEP testing. Beginning in 1992, a second version of NAEP, called Main NAEP, was started with math and reading testing in grades 4 and 8.[2] While the tests are somewhat different, the recent losses are consistently found there also.

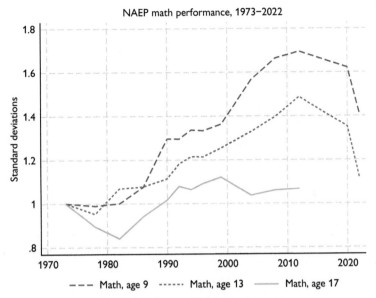

Figure 7.1 Math performance trends since 1973 by student age

Note: Testing of seventeen-year-olds was suspended in 2012.

Source: Data from US Department of Education, Institute of Education Sciences, National Center for Education Statistics, National Assessment of Educational Progress (NAEP), https://www.nationsreportcard.gov (Nation's Report Card).

The achievement changes in figure 7.1 represent total overall changes in student performance. In interpreting these performance data, it is important to note that achievement is a function not only of schools but also of parents, peers, and neighborhoods. Thus, the data obviously do not provide information about the causal impact of schools alone.

The national achievement data mask the fact that there are dramatic differences in achievement across states. Figure 7.2 arrays the eighth-grade math performance on the NAEP tests for each state in 2022. The differences in performance across states is very large. By conventional estimates, the difference in performance between Massachusetts (the top performing state) and New Mexico (the bottom performing state) translates to 2 to 2.5 years of education at the eighth grade.[3]

One related pattern that does take into account some of nonschool factors is the historical evolution of achievement gaps by socioeconomic status (SES). Concerns have been raised that the widening of the US income distribution has led to expanding SES achievement gaps (Reardon 2011). That concern, however, appears unfounded, as test information that is linked over

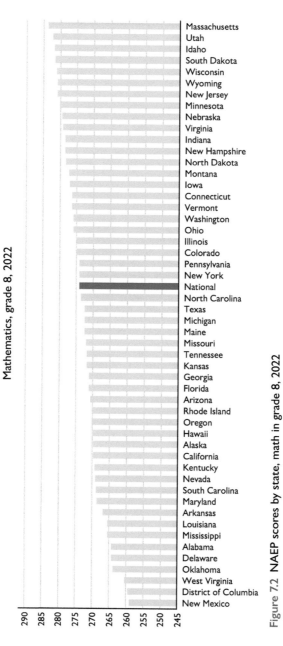

Mathematics, grade 8, 2022

	Massachusetts
	Utah
	Idaho
	South Dakota
	Wisconsin
	Wyoming
	New Jersey
	Minnesota
	Nebraska
	Virginia
	Indiana
	New Hampshire
	North Dakota
	Montana
	Iowa
	Connecticut
	Vermont
	Washington
	Ohio
	Illinois
	Colorado
	Pennsylvania
	New York
	National
	North Carolina
	Texas
	Michigan
	Maine
	Missouri
	Tennessee
	Kansas
	Georgia
	Florida
	Arizona
	Rhode Island
	Oregon
	Hawaii
	Alaska
	California
	Kentucky
	Nevada
	South Carolina
	Maryland
	Arkansas
	Louisiana
	Mississippi
	Alabama
	Delaware
	Oklahoma
	West Virginia
	District of Columbia
	New Mexico

290 285 280 275 270 265 260 255 250 245

Figure 7.2 NAEP scores by state, math in grade 8, 2022

Source: Nation's Report Card.

time shows a slow shrinking of gaps for birth cohorts born between 1961 and 2001 (Hanushek et al. 2022). Figure 7.3 shows the evolution of achievement gaps by socioeconomic status that was created by combining the LTT NAEP and the Main NAEP scores with the international testing of the Trends in International Mathematics and Science Study (TIMSS) and the Programme for International Student Assessment (PISA). The relative comparison of scores in standard deviations (SDs) for the top and bottom quartiles of the SES distribution has shown a slight but steady decline over the past half century.

There is, however, one remaining comparison that is useful to pinpoint the achievement of US students. Figure 7.4 shows the math performance of US fifteen-year-olds compared to those in other countries. US students are being outperformed in math by students in Spain, Italy, and thirty-two other countries. In an absolute sense, this is not a desirable position for US citizens. Because the quality of the labor force is important for long term growth, this outcome for students does not bode well for the future (Hanushek and Woessmann 2012, 2015).

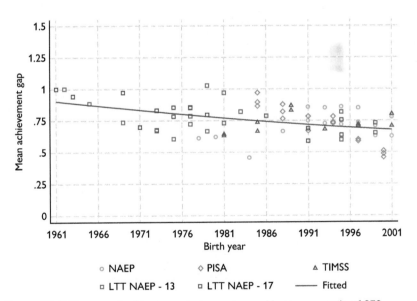

Figure 7.3 Difference of achievement between top and bottom quartile of SES distribution

Source: Hanushek et al. (2022).

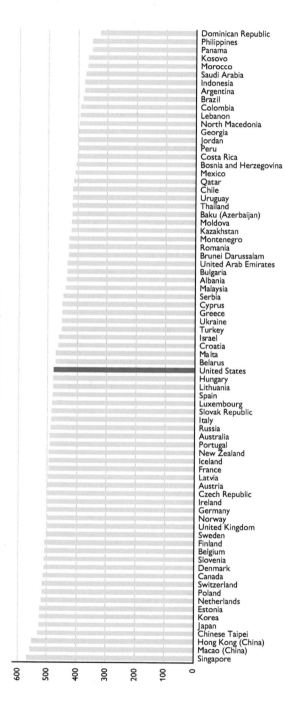

PISA math scores, 2018

Dominican Republic
Philippines
Panama
Kosovo
Morocco
Saudi Arabia
Indonesia
Argentina
Brazil
Colombia
Lebanon
North Macedonia
Georgia
Jordan
Peru
Costa Rica
Bosnia and Herzegovina
Mexico
Qatar
Chile
Uruguay
Thailand
Baku (Azerbaijan)
Moldova
Kazakhstan
Montenegro
Romania
Brunei Darussalam
United Arab Emirates
Bulgaria
Albania
Malaysia
Serbia
Cyprus
Greece
Ukraine
Turkey
Israel
Croatia
Malta
Belarus
United States
Hungary
Lithuania
Spain
Luxembourg
Slovak Republic
Italy
Russia
Australia
Portugal
New Zealand
Iceland
France
Latvia
Austria
Czech Republic
Ireland
Germany
Norway
United Kingdom
Sweden
Finland
Belgium
Slovenia
Denmark
Canada
Switzerland
Poland
Netherlands
Estonia
Korea
Japan
Chinese Taipei
Hong Kong (China)
Macao (China)
Singapore

600   500   400   300   200   100   0

Figure 7.4 Average performance on PISA test, 2018

Source: OECD (2019).

Revenues for US Education

The United States has tried to deal with any schooling problems by adding to the funding of schools—sometimes through specific programs like reducing class sizes and sometimes by just increasing overall funding. Figure 7.5 shows revenues for the public schools from 1960 to 2019. State and local revenues each comprise roughly 45 percent of per pupil funding. The federal share, which began rising in the 1960s as the federal government assumed a larger role in financing schools for disadvantaged students and subsequently for special education students, rose around the 2008 recession and then returned to historic levels. The federal government also contributed large additional amounts of temporary funds (about $190 billion) with the onset of the pandemic in 2020 (not shown).

The steady increase in per pupil funding over the entire period means that public school funding per student in 2019 was over four times that in 1960 in real terms. In fact, except for the dip in school funding after the end of federal support for the 2008 recession, real per pupil spending has risen continuously for over one hundred years (Hanushek and Rivkin 1997). State revenues come from a variety of sources that differ across the fiscal structures of the various states, and that determine where fiscal decisions are being made. Individual states have established their own funding systems that differ widely, although on average, funding responsibilities and decision making

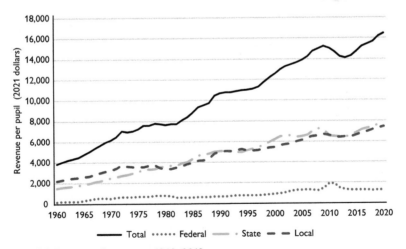

Figure 7.5 Revenues by source, 1960–2019

Source: Data from US Department of Education, Institute of Education Sciences, National Center for Education Statistics, Digest of Education Statistics, Table 235.10 (2022 and prior editions).

Table 7.1 Distribution of funding source makeup with representative states, 2019 (percent)

Revenue Source	Mean	Minimum	Maximum
Local	42.3	2.1 (Hawaii)	92.0 (Washington, DC)
State	50.1	26.6 (Illinois)	90.3 (Vermont)
Federal	8.6	4.1 (New Jersey)	15.4 (Alaska)

Source: Data from Digest of Education Statistics, Table 235.30 (2019).

are almost evenly split between state sources and local sources. At the same time, with few exceptions, local property taxes remain the dominant source of local revenues.

The aggregate data hide the wide variation that is seen across the states. States differ significantly in how revenues are raised and in the level of spending. Table 7.1 shows the extent of compositional differences in school funding. Typically, most of the revenue is derived from state and local sources, with the federal government contributing a smaller portion, but the federal share across states differs, ranging from 4 to 15 percent of funding. For Alaskan schools, 15 percent of the funding comes from the federal government, the highest percentage of all states. States like Hawaii, with its one district, and Vermont provide almost all funding at the state level, while funding for schools in Washington, DC, is provided almost entirely at the local level. Figure 7.6 maps the distribution of state per pupil spending levels in the 2018–19 academic year. Northeastern states spend over $15,000 per student, significantly higher than the $9,000 to $11,000 per pupil spent by the majority of southern states.

The determination of funding levels and the distribution of funding across districts is, however, complicated. While the legislatures in each of the states have primary responsibility for appropriating money for schools, a variety of litigation has pushed many financing decisions of legislatures into the courts.

Court Interventions

The United States is unique in the role that courts have played in school policy decision making. The power of the courts to intervene comes from their authority to enforce certain rights under both federal and state constitutions, such as the right to equal protection of the laws.[4]

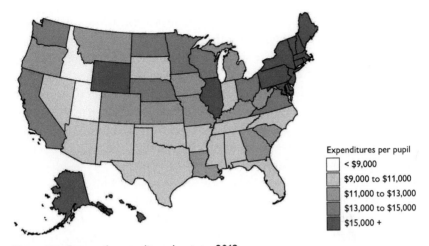

Figure 7.6 Per-pupil expenditure by state, 2019
Source: Data from Digest of Education Statistics, Table 236.65 (2019).

The federal courts have not had any consistent long-run impact on school finance. The more general issues of school finance outside of desegregation considerations were brought into federal courts in 1968. The Texas system of funding schools through local property taxes was challenged in federal court as discriminatory and in violation of the equal protection clause of the Fourteenth Amendment. In 1973, the United States Supreme Court rejected that claim in *San Antonio Independent School District v. Rodriguez*, ruling that school funding did not concern a fundamental right under the federal constitution, which does not mention education in its text. Therefore, education was ruled to be a matter appropriately left to the states.

The claims pursued in the state courts argued that the education funding "pie" should be divided more equally among a state's school districts. These claims (in the language of Coons, Clune, and Sugarman 1970) rested on the premise that the quality of a child's education should not depend upon the wealth of one's neighbors. The earliest of these state court "equity" cases was *Serrano v. Priest*, in which plaintiffs in 1968 challenged California's education funding system. In California, like most other states, the public schools were financed largely through a combination of local property taxes and state revenues. While California employed a foundation formula with student-weighted state funding designed to moderate disparities in local property tax bases, the compensation for differing tax bases was relatively low, leading to wide variation in local revenues.[5]

Equity court cases met varying degrees of success.[6] Ultimately, plaintiffs were successful in less than half of these cases, leaving the prior state funding system unchanged. These setbacks led to a different kind of court case around the concept of "adequacy." These suits had their genesis not in the equal protection clause of state constitutions, but in the education clause of state constitutions. In adequacy cases, the courts are called on to decide what level of education is required under the vaguely worded state constitutions, whether the state provides such an education, and, if not, what needs to be done to remedy the situation.

Through 2022, state courts have been involved in 205 identifiable school funding litigations. These cases have all been brought under the individual state constitutions. There has clearly been an increase in cases over time. While the 1970s and 1980s had fewer than twenty cases per decade, the numbers grew to over fifty per decade in the twenty-first century.

Across all of the state court decisions, 53 percent were decided for the defendants, which in general implies retaining the system of finance in place at the time of the decision. For the decisions based purely on equity, 59 percent ultimately favored retention of the current system. But those cases combining both equity and adequacy yielded 53 percent of decisions for the plaintiffs.

The courts have been very active in school finance, but it is important to keep in mind exactly where they enter into policy discussions. Throughout history, their role has focused on the level and distribution of funds. This role puts the focus solely on bolstering and equalizing inputs, not on maximizing outcomes per se. Yet a central element of much of the litigation has been discussion of how overall funding affects student outcomes. The following sections address this fundamental issue.

Resources and Outcomes

The obvious issue, which comes back to the nature of educational decision making, is whether the focus on funding has been effective. There is an obvious question that comes from putting together the discussion of educational outcomes and the discussion of increases in funding. On the surface, the dramatic increases in funding do not match with the outcomes, but this could hide many things under the surface.

As an overview, it is possible to look across the states to match spending and outcomes. Figure 7.7 relates 2022 NAEP math performance in grade 8 to

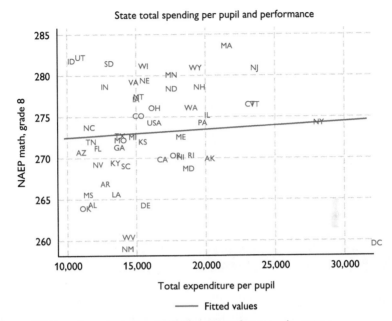

Figure 7.7 Spending per pupil and NAEP math performance by state
Source: Data from Nation's Report Card and Digest of Education Statistics, Table 236.65 (2022).

spending differences across the states. There is simply no clear relationship between NAEP scores and spending. The simple regression shows an insignificant correspondence of state spending and state performance.

This picture of course does not indicate the causal impact of funding decisions. Many other things go into performance, including families and neighborhoods. Addressing the causal impacts of funding has been a contentious field of study. Early reviews of the research summarized an inconsistent relationship of funding and achievement (Hanushek 2003), but there are legitimate concerns about many of the studies included in the review that do not come up to current quality standards.

More recent studies have not, however, provided clear guidance on the relationship of funding and achievement. Reviews and analysis of existing high-quality studies indicate that a positive relationship between funding and outcomes is likely (see the summary in table 7.2). But this "no harm" finding of added funding is insufficient justification for increased government spending (Handel and Hanushek 2023, 2024).

Table 7.2 Distribution of standardized school spending estimates

Outcome	Median	Min	Max	N	N pos.	N significant
Test scores	0.070	−0.244	0.543	16	14	9
Attainment	0.057	0.011	0.850	18	18	14

Notes: For test score estimates, results represent the effect of a 10 percent increase in spending on the change in test scores (in individual standard deviation units). For attainment outcomes, results represent the percent change in the outcome variable for a 10 percent increase in spending. For example, an estimate of 0.05 for graduation indicates that a 10 percent increase in spending led to a 5 percent increase in graduation rates. Estimates are significant if p < 0.05.
Source: Handel and Hanushek (2024).

At an aggregate level, it seems possible to conclude that the governance of education has not led to the best outcomes. Spending on average has been high but results have not matched spending.

The Changing Shape of US Schooling

As an alternative to the pure funding perspective, it is useful to go into more detail about the nature of educational decision making, the changing institutions, and how citizen choices have evolved.

Students are spread very unevenly across states and, within states, across separate local school districts. At the state level, Vermont has a total of 82,000 students while California has six million. The prime operating level is the school district, of which there were 13,452 in 2019, down from 117,408 in 1940. Moreover, the states are broken up into widely varying numbers of local districts. While Hawaii and the District of Columbia each have only one school district, five states have more than one thousand districts.

But even these aggregate variations understate the degree of heterogeneity in the schools. The growing importance of school choice leads to even more decentralized operation of education. The public school district is the prime operating unit, but it does not cover the full provision of educational services. First, beginning in 1991, charter schools were established in Minnesota, and the model spread across the country. Charter schools are public schools that operate with varying degrees of autonomy, depending on the state. Typically, charter schools are free to operate outside of many of the education regulations in a state, and, importantly, they can—independent of local teachers' unions—set their own requirements for teacher preparation, their own salary schedules, and their own personnel rules. They receive public funding, and they are almost always required to take all students who apply, or to randomize admissions if more students apply than they can accommodate. They are required to participate in the state student assessment systems. By 2021, counting the increase during COVID disruptions, charter schools made up 8 percent of the public schools and 7 percent of the public school population.

In addition to the charter schools, students can attend private schools or be homeschooled. Private schools almost always receive no direct public funding, as is the case for homeschooling. These parts of the system are generally very unregulated, and they can set their own curricula and standards. They generally do not participate in state student assessment systems.

Figure 7.8 shows the substantial changes in the structure of US schools in the twenty-first century in terms of parental choices that interact with school finance.[7] There has been a steady rise in charter school attendance with relatively stable homeschool attendance (about 3 percent of the age group) and declines in private schooling (stabilizing at close to 10 percent). The private school attendance is one-quarter nonsectarian and three-quarters religious based, with the religious component evenly split between Catholic and other denominations.

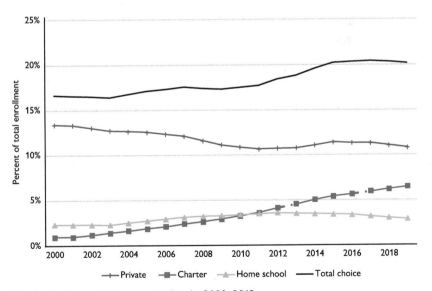

Figure 7.8 Parental choice and schools, 2000–2019

Source: Data from Digest of Education Statistics, Tables 205.15, 206.10, and 206.30 (2021 and prior editions).

Note, however, that the data in the figure are all pre-pandemic. With the pandemic, traditional public school attendance fell while the other options, and particularly homeschooling, increased. Within the public school sector there was also a shift from the traditional public schools to charter schools. The long-run distribution is yet unclear.

These trends show a steady move of the locus of decision moving toward more direct choices of the parents. While states traditionally call on traditional school districts to implement education, that is changing, and it is not clear where the overall pattern of school attendance (and decision making) ends up.

But there is another force that has been surprisingly important over time and that undoubtedly influences educational decision making. There has been a move to consolidate school districts, which has taken us from the more than 119,000 districts seen in 1938 to the current number of somewhat over 13,000 (figure 7.9). This change obviously moves school decisions farther from the average citizen as districts become larger and more bureaucratic.

The arguments for consolidation are that the smaller districts have cost disadvantages or difficulties in offering full programs, or both. Thus the normal subsidiarity arguments are that the disadvantages of having decision making

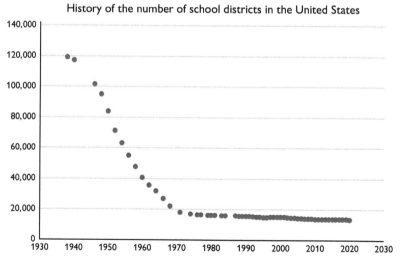

History of the number of school districts in the United States

Figure 7.9 Number of school districts in the United States, 1938–2020

Source: Data from Digest of Education Statistics, Table 214.10 (2022 and prior editions).

at the lowest level are greater than the advantages. But the existing literature has not been very good at disentangling the impacts of consolidation.[8]

An interesting research possibility in this area focuses on consolidations since 1990. Between 1990 and 2019, the number of districts shrank by 13 percent, going from 15,358 to 13,349. Importantly, there were a number of states that introduced regulations or incentives designed to encourage district consolidation. Figure 7.10 shows some the largest changes in the population of districts. Some states have regulations about district size, such as Arkansas, where a 2004 regulation prohibits districts below 350 students. Others have introduced monetary incentives for consolidation, such as Illinois in 2006 and 2010 and Nebraska in 2006. And some states have experienced declines in the number of districts without any apparent regulations or incentives, such as North Dakota.

By looking at experiences between 1990 and 2019, it would be possible to link changes in the number of districts to specific laws and also to understand the impact on spending and on student performance given the NAEP testing. These issues—while justifying various consolidation efforts—have not been adequately evaluated.

Federal Accountability

Perhaps the largest change in the locus of decision making over the past quarter century, however, has been the increased involvement of the federal government in school operations.[9] This change started rather abruptly with the adoption of the No Child Left Behind Act of 2001 (NCLB), which went into effect in 2002. NCLB mandated that all states develop a system of test-based school accountability. The system further had to lead to all students being proficient by 2014. While over half of the states had accountability systems at its introduction, NCLB laid a federal imprint on accountability.

NCLB began with broad bipartisan support in Congress, but support for it waned over time. It was a very complicated Act that introduced a number of components into school accountability that had little precedent. It was supposed to be reauthorized in 2007, at which time the most problematic features could presumably be remedied, but Congress never reauthorized it. The original version simply continued in force.

A variety of criticisms of NCLB accumulated over time, but perhaps the most fundamental criticisms surrounded the high-stakes use of standardized tests. State-developed tests matched to each state's own learning standards were used to judge the performance of each school. Schools not meeting

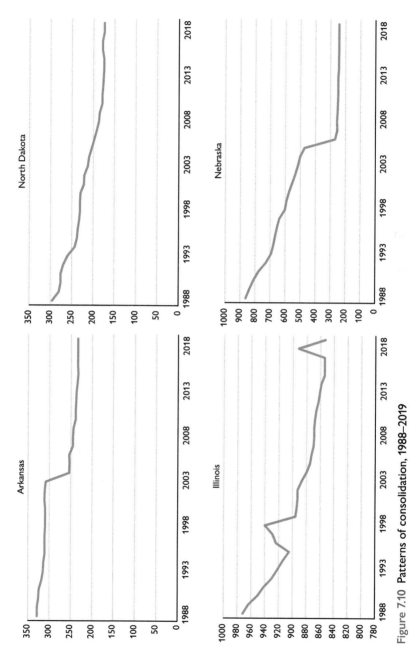

Figure 7.10 Patterns of consolidation, 1988–2019

Source: Data from Digest of Education Statistics, Table 214.10 (2022 and prior editions).

achievement goals (adequate yearly progress or AYP) were subject to a hierarchy of federally prescribed sanctions. Ultimately, the unrealistic goal of having all students reach proficiency led to the broad consensus that NCLB had to be replaced.

From early on, school personnel were concerned that the test results might be used to assess the performance of teachers. Because the accountability systems focused on status measures, or the level of performance, the observed scores necessarily conflated family and neighborhood factors with the impacts of schools and teachers.

The idea of employing the existing testing regimes for teacher evaluations was elevated in policy and legislative circles with the development of the Race to the Top program (RTT) in 2009 under President Obama. As an extension of federal involvement in school accountability, the Race to the Top program was a competitive grant program at the state level, where states were invited to enter a competition for funds. The guidelines included a variety of elements for the state grants, but the two most important were adoption of the Common Core curriculum and the use of value-added measures for teacher evaluations.

RTT provided state grants in three separate waves, but educators and decision makers in many states objected to the curriculum component and to being pushed toward teacher evaluations based on student performance. Coupled with the competitive grant aspect, which also was a source of annoyance, the adverse reactions to RTT added to the pressures against NCLB.

Crafting a new federal accountability regime clearly involved making substantial changes. Congress, which had not been able to reauthorize NCLB on time, sought compromise legislation that could lead to reauthorizing the Elementary and Secondary Education Act, the basic authorization that housed not only the federal accountability rules but also the fundamental parts of all federal policy toward K–12 education.

The replacement for NCLB was the Every Student Succeeds Act (ESSA), which came into effect in 2016. Again, this was a complicated law, but perhaps its most significant change was to return much of the decision making back to the states. States were still required to have regular student testing, but the states could decide what results were expected and how the results were to be translated into school policy.

At a conceptual level, it is possible to put the accountability aspects of policy into the general federalism framework. By these standards, NCLB was quite backward. It required states to develop their own standards and testing regimes, including defining what was meant by student proficiency. Then, if schools failed to make adequate yearly progress, the federal government set the operational changes in schools that were required. While the federal government may be the more appropriate level of government to decide on goals and performance standards for students, it is quite unprepared to set the operational choices of schools that fail to meet these standards.

On the other hand, ESSA leaves setting of standards and goals at the state level, even though the quality of education has huge cross-state implications. In 2019, 42 percent of the US population lives in a state different from their state of birth, and the quality of the labor force has huge implications for state economic development (Hanushek, Ruhose, and Woessmann 2017). ESSA moves school operational decision making back to the states, which is more in line with the proper level of government for operational decisions.

The implications of this change in the locus of educational decision making is not fully understood. The evaluation of NCLB by Dee and Jacob (2011) suggests that NCLB had a positive effect on US achievement even with its conceptual flaws. It is, however, hard to evaluate the change to ESSA.

One way to evaluate the situation is to look at the policies toward teacher quality. NCLB pushed hard on evaluations of teacher quality that were linked to student outcomes. ESSA completely relaxed these policies.

It is possible to trace the changes over time in these two sets of policies by using the database of the National Council on Teacher Quality (NCTQ).[10] Our measure of the change in accountability is simply how states change their use of input-based and outcome-based teacher evaluation policies times the impact of each on achievement. The results of this exercise are still ongoing, but it is possible to show the adjustments that states made to the change from NCLB to ESSA.

When we code various components of outcome-based teacher policies (figure 7.11) and input-based teacher policies (figure 7.12), we see a distinct policy change. After Race to the Top and NCLB were in effect, states moved to more outcome-based policies (figure 7.11, 2015); but with the advent of ESSA, they started to discard outcome-based policies (figure 7.11, 2019). The movement toward input-based policies—which were not covered systematically by NCLB or ESSA—was much more random (figure 7.12, 2015 and 2019).

Output-based policies cumulative 4-year change, 2015

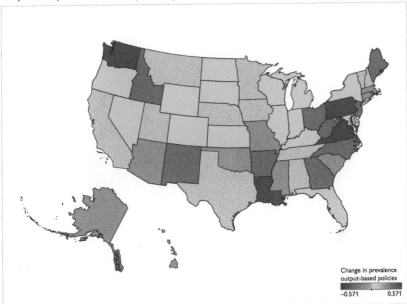

Output-based policies cumulative 4-year change, 2019

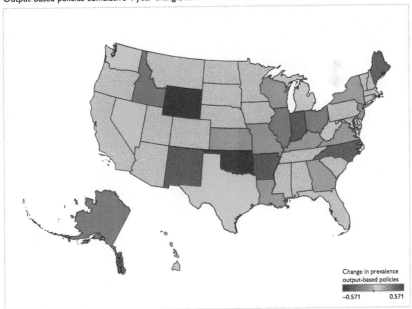

Figure 7.11 Three-year change of adoption of outcome-based teacher policies: 2015 and 2019

Source: Hanushek, Saenz-Armstrong, and Salazar (2023), from data by the National Council on Teacher Quality.

Input-based policies cumulative 4-year change, 2015

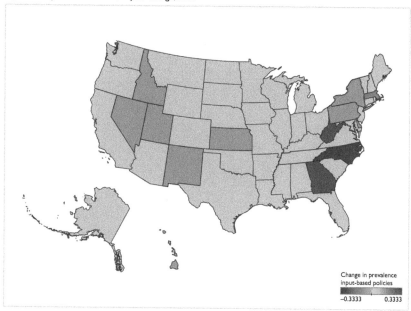

Input-based policies cumulative 4-year change, 2019

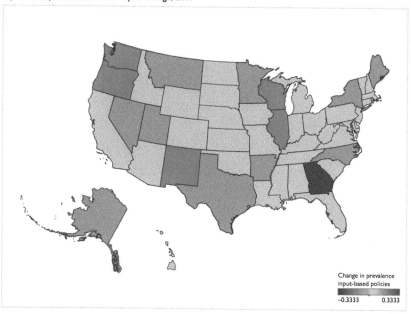

Figure 7.12 Three-year change of adoption of input-based teacher policies: 2015 and 2019

Source: Hanushek, Saenz-Armstrong, and Salazar (2023), from data by the National Council on Teacher Quality.

The impact of these state changes related to two different federal account-ability policies depends on the achievement impact of these teacher policies. This is the subject of ongoing research. There is, however, some hint at the result of the change in the NAEP scores of figure 7.1. Here we see that scores began to decline before the beginning of the pandemic but after the change in accountability laws.

Some Tentative Conclusions

The United States has a very complicated educational system that involves decision making at multiple levels. The primary actor is the states. The states dictate the organization of the schools into districts and the range of school choice options that exist. While the states determine the funding formula, local districts also have a role to play, since they on average generate an equal amount of funding to the state. The details of the state-local split vary dramat-ically across the states. The federal government contributes roughly 10 per-cent of funding, focused on children in poverty and special needs students.

The results of this system have not been good. The United States has performed below the Organisation for Economic Co-operation and Development (OECD) average in terms of achievement. There is also a wide variation in performance across US states. These performance results will have long-term implications for the well-being of society.

In terms of federalism, the federal government has assumed a dispro-portionate role in decision making through the establishment of a national accountability system. But the negative responses to the rules of NCLB have led the federal government to return central elements of school accountabil-ity to the states. The evidence is not entirely in, but it appears that this has led to decreases in student achievement.

Another aspect of federalism has seen conflicting forces. Over time, various types of school choice have expanded, signaling an increased role of parents. At the same time, the number of school districts has declined precipitously, lead-ing to larger school districts that place decision making farther from individual parents. The results of these changes have not been well analyzed, leaving some significant questions about the effectiveness of the overall federal system.

Notes

1. This review relies heavily on the analysis in Hanushek (2023).

2. Main NAEP has much larger samples of students in order to provide state-by-state performance data. It has also tested twelfth-grade reading and math and various

other subjects such as history, civics, and geography on a less regular basis and using significantly smaller samples of students. These additional tests do not provide consistent time series data.

3. The rule of thumb, derived from scores on vertically aligned tests, is that one standard deviation of achievement is equivalent to three to four years of school.

4. For a more complete history and analysis of court actions, see Hanushek and Lindseth (2009).

5. For a discussion of the use of property taxes, see Fischel (2006). See also the discussion about the relationship between equalization suits and referenda to limit school spending (Fischel 2006; Fischel 1989; Silva and Sonstelie 1995).

6. For a review and analysis of different court judgments, see Hanushek and Joyce-Wirtz (2023).

7. There are more dimensions of choice, but they do not interact significantly with overall financing and decision making across schools. Most importantly, while districts with assigned attendance zones for neighborhood schools predominate, many districts have magnet schools with a specialized focus that draw students from the entire district or have open enrollment across all schools in the district (see Abdulkadiroğlu and Andersson 2023). Such choices in general do not affect the total funding for the district, whereas the choices in figure 7.8 will affect funding for traditional districts. They do have impacts on school performance; see Angrist, Hull, and Walters (2023) and CREDO (2023).

8. This overview follows from an ongoing research agenda joint with Avinash Thakker.

9. This section reflects the ongoing analysis in Hanushek, Saenz-Armstrong, and Salazar (2023).

10. Details can be found in Hanushek, Saenz-Armstrong, and Salazar (2023).

References

Abdulkadiroğlu, Atila, and Tommy Andersson. 2023. "School Choice." Chapter 3 in *Handbook of the Economics of Education*, vol. 6, edited by Eric A. Hanushek, Stephen Machin, and Ludger Woessmann, 135–85. Amsterdam: Elsevier.

Angrist, Joshua, Peter Hull, and Christopher R. Walters. 2023. "Methods for Measuring School Effectiveness." Chapter 1 in *Handbook of the Economics of Education*, vol. 7, edited by Eric A. Hanushek, Stephen Machin, and Ludger Woessmann, 1–60. Amsterdam: North-Holland.

Center for Research on Education Outcomes (CREDO). 2023. *National Charter School Study III*. Stanford, CA: CREDO.

Coons, John E., William H. Clune, and Stephen D. Sugarman. 1970. *Private Wealth and Public Education*. Cambridge, MA: Belknap Press of Harvard University Press.

Dee, Thomas S., and Brian A. Jacob. 2011. "The Impact of No Child Left Behind on Student Achievement." *Journal of Policy Analysis and Management* 30, no. 3 (Summer): 418–46.

Fischel, William A. 1989. "Did Serrano Cause Proposition 13?" *National Tax Journal* 42, no. 4 (December): 465–74.

———. 2006. "The Courts and Public School Finance: Judge-Made Centralization and Economic Research." Chapter 21 in *Handbook of the Economics of Education*, vol. 2, edited by Eric A. Hanushek and Finis Welch, 1279–325. Amsterdam: North-Holland.

Handel, Danielle V., and Eric A. Hanushek. 2023. "US School Finance: Resources and Outcomes." Chapter 3 in *Handbook of the Economics of Education*, vol. 7, edited by Eric A. Hanushek, Stephen Machin, and Ludger Woessmann, 143–226. Amsterdam: North-Holland.

———. 2024. "Contexts of Convenience: Generalizing from Published Evaluations of School Finance Policies." *Evaluation Review* 48 (3): 461–94, https://doi-org.stanford.idm.oclc.org/10.1177/0193841X241228335.

Hanushek, Eric A. 2003. "The Failure of Input-Based Schooling Policies." *Economic Journal* 113, no. 485 (February): F64–F98.

———. 2023. "Fixing Schools through Finance." In *A Nation at Risk +40: A Review of Progress in US Public Education*, edited by Stephen L. Bowen and Margaret E. Raymond, 161–80. Stanford, CA: Hoover Institution Press.

Hanushek, Eric A., and Matthew Joyce-Wirtz. 2023. "Incidence and Outcomes of School Finance Litigation: 1968–2021." *Public Finance Review* 51, no. 6 (November): 748–81.

Hanushek, Eric A., Jacob D. Light, Paul E. Peterson, Laura M. Talpey, and Ludger Woessmann. 2022. "Long-Run Trends in the US SES-Achievement Gap." *Education Finance and Policy* 17, no. 4 (Fall): 608–40.

Hanushek, Eric A., and Alfred A. Lindseth. 2009. *Schoolhouses, Courthouses, and Statehouses: Solving the Funding-Achievement Puzzle in America's Public Schools*. Princeton, NJ: Princeton University Press.

Hanushek, Eric A., and Steven G. Rivkin. 1997. "Understanding the Twentieth-Century Growth in US School Spending." *Journal of Human Resources* 32, no. 1 (January): 35–68.

Hanushek, Eric A., Jens Ruhose, and Ludger Woessmann. 2017. "Knowledge Capital and Aggregate Income Differences: Development Accounting for US States." *American Economic Journal: Macroeconomics* 9, no. 4 (October): 184–224.

Hanushek, Eric A., Patricia Saenz-Armstrong, and Alejandra Salazar. 2023. "Balancing Federalism: School Accountability from NCLB to ESSA." Paper presented at the Association for Public Policy Analysis and Management Fall Conference, Atlanta, Georgia, November 9–11 (publication forthcoming).

Hanushek, Eric A., and Ludger Woessmann. 2012. "Do Better Schools Lead to More Growth? Cognitive Skills, Economic Outcomes, and Causation." *Journal of Economic Growth* 17, no. 4 (December): 267–321.

———. 2015. *The Knowledge Capital of Nations: Education and the Economics of Growth*. Cambridge, MA: MIT Press.

Organisation for Economic Co-operation and Development (OECD). 2019. *PISA 2018 Results, vol. 1*. Paris: OECD.

Reardon, Sean F. 2011. "The Widening Academic Achievement Gap between the Rich and the Poor: New Evidence and Possible Explanations." Chapter 5 in *Whither Opportunity? Rising Inequality, Schools, and Children's Life Chances*, edited by Richard J. Murnane and Greg J. Duncan, 91–116. New York: Russell Sage Foundation.

Silva, Fabio, and Jon Sonstelie. 1995. "Did Serrano Cause a Decline in School Spending?" *National Tax Journal* 48, no. 2 (June): 199–215.

US Department of Education. 2022. *Digest of Education Statistics 2022*. Washington, DC: National Center for Education Statistics.

PAUL E. PETERSON: I can't see where you're getting your total for parental choice in [figure 7.8], because the privates are going down. Homeschooling is flat. There's some increase in charter, but there's a steep increase in your top line.

ERIC A. HANUSHEK: Paul, thank you. That observation points out an error [which has been corrected in the final version of the chapter].

What's been happening over time, I think, is parents are given more choice and options in the operations of schools. There's a counteracting—a countervailing—force that I find interesting, that I've been pushed to look at further by writing this paper. And that's the amount of consolidation of school districts. At the beginning of World War II, there were 100,000 to 120,000 school districts in the United States and there are now 13,400 and some. There is this precipitous fall in the number of school districts, which I interpret as saying that school districts are getting larger over time and they're moving further from parental input. Michael [Boskin] can speak to the role of school boards and other things in this, but that there has been this really big drop.

PETERSON: It's the school consolidation movement. The number of school districts declines because of the strong state efforts to consolidate rural school districts together, as people left rural areas for towns and cities. States gave local districts extra state money if they were willing to consolidate. The little red schoolhouse disappeared as districts consolidated. A study by [Martin R.] West and [Christopher R.] Berry shows that this had an adverse effect on student learning, which impacts earnings decades later. Consolidation was promoted in the name of better education, but the impact was quite the opposite.

HANUSHEK: There are a few states that stand out for really quite dramatic changes. Like North Dakota goes from three hundred school districts to two hundred or something in this twenty-five-year period or thirty-five-year period. That's the problem with my graph. I can't do the subtraction.

8

Infrastructure in a Federal System

Michael J. Boskin and Valentin Bolotnyy

The proper goal of restructuring the public sector cannot simply be decentralization. . . . The basic issue is one of aligning responsibilities and fiscal instruments with the proper levels of government.

—Wallace E. Oates, "An Essay on Fiscal Federalism,"
Journal of Economic Literature, 1999

The United States certainly has infrastructure needs. The American Society of Civil Engineers, serious if somewhat self-interested, rates the nation's infrastructure a C– in its 2021 report card (ASCE 2021). Some claim there is a multitrillion-dollar "infrastructure deficit," and others have blamed inadequate public investment in infrastructure for holding back US economic productivity (e.g., Aschauer 1991). In 2021, this point of view was used to justify the trillion-dollar Infrastructure Investment and Jobs Act (IIJA). Yet others argue that a closer analysis shows US infrastructure in much better shape and advocate for improving the allocation of funding over massive new expenditures (Duranton, Nagpal, and Turner 2020). In a similar vein, the World Economic Forum's 2019 Global Competitiveness Report rated the United States thirteenth out of 141 countries on infrastructure—behind top-rated Singapore and Hong Kong but ahead of countries like Sweden and Denmark. While there is clearly ample opportunity to do considerable productive long-run infrastructure investment, how much should be spent, which projects should be prioritized, and what role should government—at the federal, state, or local level—have in these investments remain contentious questions.

In seminal work originating in the 1970s, economist Wallace E. Oates laid out key principles for fiscal federalism (Oates 1972; Oates 2008).

His "decentralization theorem" emphasizes, under several assumptions, that unless there are cost advantages associated with the centralized provision of public goods, decentralized provision, with its ability to more closely align with local needs and preferences, will make more people better off. This argument also makes room for equity considerations, with Oates pointing out that intergovernmental grants to jurisdictions can be warranted if they have a relatively small tax base or relatively high costs of providing essential services. Further, he articulates what he calls a traditional theory of fiscal federalism, with the following policy prescription (Oates 2008): "Where there are spillover benefits associated with the provision of local public goods, the central government should introduce matching intergovernmental grants that serve to internalize the external benefits. The grants will provide the necessary inducement to local officials to extend provision of the local service to the socially efficient level." In other words, public good provision is optimally financed and delivered by local authorities, unless the central authority has cost advantages (i.e., economies of scale) or unless the local public goods also benefit other parts of the country.

Though this theory remains sound decades later, it crucially relies on good data, good research, and good faith assessments of the costs and benefits of public good provision. It says little about the practical realities of the "three C's": competence, capacity, and comparative advantage. While we do not address these here, they are discussed elsewhere in this volume. But surely the absolute or relative competence at different levels of government and the private sector; the capacity, and not just physical capacity and scale economies; and the comparative advantage of different jurisdictions at and within different levels of government should play an important role in the allocation of responsibilities and resources in a federal system in a free society. Current policy debates on infrastructure investment all too often either ignore the theory or work with cost-benefit estimates, explicitly or implicitly, that do not stand up to scrutiny. One such prominent argument, borne out of the Great Depression, is that infrastructure spending by the federal government is especially warranted during recessions, as it can dramatically spur growth and raise employment and incomes. When the Federal Reserve lowers interest rates and government borrowing rates are low, the argument goes, deficit finance becomes a cheap way to increase employment. Existing research, in fact, suggests that this is a misguided conclusion.

First, while infrastructure spending may have made for good short-run stimulus in the 1930s, that is no longer the case (Glaeser 2016; Ramey

2020). Only a small fraction of those unemployed today have the skills and experience for the kind of work required by today's infrastructure challenges, few of which require only a shovel. Tower crane operators, wind turbine technicians, and other skilled tradespeople cannot be trained overnight upon a sudden influx of infrastructure dollars. Additionally, planning and approval hurdles that were absent in the 1930s are omnipresent today, slowing the speed with which funds can be disbursed and infrastructure built. As a result, massive infrastructure spending within a short window of time may lead not to increases in employment but to backlogs that result in higher profits for a relatively small set of contractors and higher wages for the limited supply of skilled workers (Balat 2017). Higher costs in turn mean fewer highway miles repaved, bridges repaired, and electricity lines properly maintained. Worse yet, when federal funding is massive, local political incentives to spend all allocated funds exacerbate the tendency to fund too many low-return projects, along with boondoggles like California's high-speed rail project.

Second, large public infrastructure projects—highways, dams, and the like—are designed to last many decades, and aside from the recent rise in short-term interest rates driven by high inflation and the Federal Reserve's response to it, interest rates on long-term government debt will eventually rise to a more reasonable positive inflation-adjusted level.[1] Rolling over large amounts of debt accumulated in a low interest rate environment will eventually be much more expensive, making the infrastructure spending far from a cheap lunch.

If infrastructure investment policy should not be motivated primarily by short-run economic stimulus or by cheap debt, what guiding principles should policymakers use instead? We lay out and discuss these principles, rooting them in the fundamentals of fiscal federalism and applying them to today's infrastructure challenges, including the impending large influx of federal spending from the IIJA. We stress the importance of establishing capabilities and incentives for rigorous cost-benefit analysis at various levels of government; prioritizing the highest net benefit projects; financing work through user fees wherever possible; making infrastructure adaptive and planning for technological change; and focusing policy on creating the right incentives for the federal, state, local, and private actors. Throughout, we explain how the appropriate federal and local responsibilities are connected to each principle and make recommendations for sound infrastructure policies.

Overview

America's infrastructure, the conduit for our economic activity, is vast and varied by any measure. It connects us to the water and power we need in our homes, offices, factories, and schools. It brings our food to our grocers and products and mail to our doorstep. It enables us to use our computers and smartphones. And, of course, it enables us to travel to work, school, leisure, and tourism destinations. In short, it is an essential part of our lives and plays an important role in their quality. US infrastructure, in its physical nature, consists primarily of the wide-ranging inventory laid out in table 8.1. A more expansive definition would also include cloud data servers, airwave spectrum, IT and traditional infrastructure inside homes and businesses, and other technologies. Trains, cars, buses, trucks, airplanes, ships, cargo containers, and other items crucial to the transportation process could also be included.

Table 8.1 makes clear an often underappreciated fact: infrastructure ownership varies widely across and within types of infrastructure—sometimes ownership is public, sometimes it's private, and sometimes it's something in between. Cell towers and antennas are often owned by private companies, such as Crown Castle, American Tower, and AT&T Towers; bridges can be fully owned by a state, but also by quasi-independent interstate partnerships like the Port Authority of New York and New Jersey; and electricity lines can be owned by publicly regulated private utility companies. Though policy discussions often get simplified in their focus on government-owned and operated infrastructure, the US infrastructure landscape is much more varied and complex—a clear sign that focusing on government spending alone is inadequate infrastructure policy. As crises often reveal, the federal government often does have a crucial role to play in facilitating coordination and collaboration across infrastructure providers, especially across state lines, and in ensuring that responsible levels of safety and condition are maintained. Thus, the regulatory dimension of federal-state-local-private relationships—from standards to coordination practices to the strings attached to financial support—deserves considerable attention as well.

Adhering closely to the principles below has the potential to increase the return on public and private spending on infrastructure. With historic levels of funding recently allocated to infrastructure through Congress's IIJA of November 2021, adherence to the principles today has potential to be especially valuable and consequential.

Table 8.1 Inventory of US infrastructure

Infrastructure type	Quantity
Highways and roads	4.17 million miles
Railroad bridges	100,000
Bridges	More than 617,000
Heavy rail track	140,000 miles
Commuter and light rail track	10,049 miles
Commercial ports	926
Airports	19,853 airports
	14,784 are private use
	5,069 are public use
Dams and resevoirs	91,000
Oil and gas pipelines	3.3 million miles
Electricity lines	160,000 miles of high-voltage; millions of miles of low-voltage power lines
Cell sites (towers and antennas)	417,215
Fiber-optic cable	More than 4 million miles
Solar panels	More than 2 million
Wind turbines	73,352
Satellites	3,432 satellites
	31 civil
	2,992 commercial
	409 government and military

Sources: Data for highways and roads from US Bureau of Transportation Statistics 2023. Data for railroad bridges from ASCE 2017. Data for bridges, commercial ports, and dams and reservoirs from ASCE 2021. Data for heavy rail, commuter rail, and light rail track from US Bureau of Transportation Statistics 2023; in directional route-miles; light rail includes streetcar rail and hybrid rail. Data for airports from FAA 2022. Data for oil and gas pipelines from Pipeline and Hazardous Materials Safety Administration 2023. Data for electricity lines from EPA 2023. Data for cell sites from CTIA 2021. Data for fiber-optic cable from S&P Global Market Intelligence 2019. Data for solar panels from SEIA 2019. Data for wind turbines from USGS 2023. Data for satellites from Union of Concerned Scientists 2023; for comparison, of the satellites currently in space, 177 are Russian and 541 are Chinese; the vast majority of commercial satellites are owned by Starlink; see Witze 2023.

Guiding Principles
Establish Capabilities and Incentives for
Rigorous Cost-Benefit Analysis

As with any decision that requires the appropriation of scare resources, rigorous cost-benefit analysis should be at the core of government infrastructure spending. How rigorously policymakers are able to evaluate competing projects and proposals depends in part on the data they have at their disposal. Infrastructure projects are no exception.

Given how central infrastructure is to our daily lives, the data required for such cost-benefit analyses are wide-ranging. Accurate projections of the benefits of a new bridge require good data on past usage of comparable bridges and projections of future usage, along with elasticities of substitution across routes and modes of transportation. Sensible projections of population distributions, especially of the potential users of the infrastructure, along with user incomes and the availability of relevant technologies, all depend on high-quality data. Data on economic activity in the region are also important to understanding, among other things, the positive and negative externalities of the new construction. Is the benefit likely to be concentrated in the county where the bridge will be located, or will it be shared widely by others in the state or even the country?

Answers to these and other questions of the sort will only be as accurate as the data that go into the analyses, the competence of those conducting it, and the degree of professionalism and independence from political manipulation. In many jurisdictions, however, the data are often narrow, incomplete, and inaccurate. While over forty state departments of transportation (DOTs) use the same software (Bid Express) to run their infrastructure procurement bidding, there is no centralized database that allows for these data to be studied. How can states learn from one another's successes and mistakes, and how can the externalities of each state's procurement practices be understood without such data transparency? As prior work has shown (e.g., Bajari, Houghton, and Tadelis 2014; Bolotnyy and Vasserman 2023), how the procurement process is structured can have significant implications for project effectiveness and efficiency.

Project uncertainty can also drive up costs and may similarly arise from a lack of good data and from the unpredictability of timing, level, and regulatory requirements from own or "higher-level" government funding. The underground mess of infrastructure in New York is a striking example of the high costs of going into projects blind. In a process known colloquially as "peek and shriek," contractors dig into New York roads knowing what they have to fix but having no idea what other infrastructure they will encounter along the way or how difficult their work will ultimately be (Rueb 2016). Poor coordination across utilities, city authorities, contractors, and other actors, along with poor recordkeeping on the location and condition of various infrastructure components, all snowball into painful delays and cost overruns. Investments in and maintenance of the infrastructure behind infrastructure projects—the data, the software, the sensors and robots that assess infrastructure conditions, etc.—can substantially reduce these problems (Vasserman 2020; Mims 2023). With accurate, up-to-date data and systems that allow for detailed cost-benefit analyses, state and federal authorities will be better positioned to take on the most productive projects.

The cost-benefit analysis process must also be well defined and based on assumptions that are both clearly shared with the public and defensible. It is all too easy to manipulate projections of costs and benefits for political or other purposes. Classic examples are assuming far greater population growth—and hence benefits to more people—and low discount rates, which raise the relative value of distant benefits compared to near-term capital costs. The cost-benefit analysis of California's high-speed rail assumed that California's population would grow to sixty million in coming decades—whereas it has been falling in recent years from a peak of forty million—growth that was supposed to lead to dramatically greater congestion that would have justified the huge cost of the project.

It's not just the funding levels but also the rules, restrictions, and requirements, i.e., the regulations that accompany the funding levels, that determine the costs and benefits of infrastructure projects. Cost-benefit analysis should not, for example, focus solely on the costs, as the Trump administration's "Two-for-One" rule—remove two regulations for every new regulation—effectively did, de-emphasizing the benefit side of the equation (Masur 2020). Nor should cost-benefit analysis wade deeply into unquantifiable territory, as in the Obama administration's inclusion of "equity, human dignity, fairness, and distributive impacts" in analyses or the Biden administration's effort to make sure that cost-benefit analysis "fully accounts for regulatory benefits that are difficult or impossible to quantify" (Masur 2020; Biden 2021). If approaches to cost-benefit analysis are politically driven and change with every administration, the federal and the state regulatory apparatus can experience swings in effectiveness that have little to do with actual costs and benefits and only increase regulatory uncertainty and overall costs.

While steps should be taken to ensure rigor and consistency in prospective cost-benefit analysis, retrospective cost-benefit analysis should also become institutionalized. Knowing that spending and regulation will eventually have to be reviewed for effectiveness will incentivize greater care in the budgeting and regulation-creation process, and this review will provide the government with an opportunity to make informed improvements to existing policies. Moreover, retrospective cost-benefit analysis will allow us to see how well our prospective cost-benefit analysis is doing and to improve data collection and forecasting practices. Finally, empowering politically independent analysis and review, perhaps by a separate, independent agency, might also limit the temptation to fund poor projects and to place unnecessary regulatory burdens on the economy. Such an agency could be modeled on the Congressional Budget Office (CBO) and could audit a random selection of infrastructure projects. By putting a spotlight on different project stages, the agency could limit fiscal cross-hauling across states and encourage stakeholders to take rigorous cost-benefit analysis more seriously when selling projects to their constituents.

Prioritize Highest Net Benefit Projects

Rigorous and transparent cost-benefit analysis will be helpful not only in project planning but also in project prioritization and implementation. A clearly articulated and publicly available analysis can make it harder for political actors, at all levels, to prioritize projects that might have low social net benefit but high short-term political net benefit for their favored constituents. Such projects often involve new, salient, and customized construction, with California's high-speed rail project being a prime, misbegotten example. The highest net benefit projects are often regular maintenance projects, because they not only improve infrastructure quality contemporaneously but also prevent exponential, snowballing deterioration. Maintenance that would have prevented the 2007 rush-hour collapse of the I-35W Mississippi River bridge in Minneapolis would have had a high net benefit. Ditto California's Oroville Dam Causeway maintenance, for which an investment of millions of dollars would have prevented the need to evacuate a quarter million people and to spend billions on repairs. Of course, there is the political reality that shiny new projects and ribbon-cutting ceremonies provide better publicity for elected officials than do repairs and maintenance.

Also likely of high net benefit are projects that enable the use of targeted pricing mechanisms that in turn reduce negative externalities like congestion and pollution. License plate–scanning tollbooths and cameras that make congestion pricing possible are some examples of this kind of infrastructure. Integrating these technologies near our seaports and airports, where the confluence of cargo traffic and rush-hour traffic generates large congestion costs and economic losses, deserves especially high prioritization. These projects and others that have high net benefits (due to potentially high "positive externalities"—benefits to society beyond the local area) are the kinds of things that the federal government should prioritize, working actively with the states. For example, with twenty-five US port complexes accepting 85 percent of internationally traded goods and only 4 percent of these goods staying in the local market where they enter the United States, the benefit of having our major ports function effectively is widely diffused across the country and even among our trading partners (Tomer and Kane 2015). While the construction and upkeep of locally used infrastructure should be financed and prioritized locally, infrastructure with large implications for economic activity across the country should be prioritized and partly financed appropriately at the federal level.

Finance through User Fees Wherever Possible

While there are substantial positive social externalities to everyone drinking clean water, driving on smoothly paved roads, and being connected to the internet, the most direct benefits of improved infrastructure are obtained by those who use it. It makes sense, therefore, that we have systems through which we pay individually for the electricity, water, gas, broadband, and other infrastructure that we use. These payment systems, however, could still be more widely deployed across our roads and bridges. Just as utility companies raise electricity pricing when demand would otherwise exceed supply to balance the grid and prevent blackouts, cities should employ the so-called dynamic pricing (fees or tolls varying with congestion) used on some highways and tollbooths to decrease congestion and pollution.[2] In some cases, where the likely benefits of these systems are large and diffuse, it makes sense for the federal government to partner with states to finance these systems.

Once in place, however, the fees collected would both support optimal infrastructure usage and serve as a reliable source of maintenance financing.[3] If usage were to decrease over time as individuals switched to alternative modes or routes of transportation, the piece of infrastructure would take itself out of commission by popular demand instead of by decree. The path of funding maintenance with user fees is not without its pitfalls, however. The case of the Pennsylvania Turnpike has shown that politics has a tendency to distort how money is actually spent. Taking advantage of the fact that the turnpike could take on debt, the state required it to send more money than it had to the Pennsylvania Department of Transportation for a wide range of infrastructure projects, putting the turnpike into a major debt crisis and forcing it to raise user fees to levels that dramatically reduced demand (Hoffman 2022). Policymakers should thus take extra care to make sure that the revenue collected is devoted first and foremost to cover expected maintenance costs, and only then allocate any surplus revenues to other needs.

User fees are a particularly appealing source of financing for new construction, with contractors due to receive the user fees incentivized to build quickly and provide maintenance efficiently. They can also serve as a way to temper the power of interest groups to disrupt construction plans with add-ons and modifications (Brooks and Liscow 2019), since such requests can be saliently tied to an increase in user fees and help future users push back on such lobbying. Relatedly, infrastructure for which demand is low is unlikely to be built if user fees are the main source of financing. The Detroit People Mover monorail and Alaska's Gravina Island Bridge, commonly referred to as the "bridge to nowhere," for example, would likely not exist under a user fee system (Glaeser 2016). In addition to offering up-front savings to taxpayers, preventing the construction of unproductive infrastructure will save our cities and towns decades of urban planning headaches, burdensome maintenance costs, and even environmental damage.

User fee systems can also be adjusted to subsidize usage where necessary. As Ashraf, Glaeser, and Ponzetto (2016) show, for example, subsidizing individual usage of infrastructure such as water and sewage pipes in areas where people are too poor to cover those costs could be desirable due to large and widespread positive benefits. The authors also caution, however, that the optimal usage of subsidies depends not just on the type of infrastructure in question but also on the government's institutional capacity and ability to prevent waste and corruption.

However, introducing user fees for existing, previously zero-fee infrastructure is much harder to achieve politically than having user fees from the get-go. It is hard to sell a new bridge toll, for example, to finance that bridge's maintenance, in part because maintenance is less salient to the public than new construction. It is also difficult to predict maintenance costs, due to uncertainty around the condition of an old bridge, so contractors would likely demand high tolls for commitments to long-term contracts. State and federal officials could, however, work together on transition plans that involve a phased-in user fee approach for existing infrastructure, accompanied by budget-neutral reductions in fees that are less well targeted at the usage of specific infrastructure (e.g., vehicle registration fees, electricity delivery fees, etc.). Major federal infrastructure bills could come with incentives tying the disbursement of additional dollars to a state's commitment to establish stable and adequate sources of maintenance funding. Funding for maintenance is plagued by political wrangling, leading to years of deferred maintenance. A proper division of commitments between federal and local authorities can enable the long-term health of US infrastructure (Fitzsimmons 2017).

Make Infrastructure Adaptive and Plan for Technological Change

Accurate data and infrastructure that allow for the widespread use of user fees will provide authorities with the tools to finance and prioritize the highest net benefit infrastructure projects across the country. The power of these tools is their ability to provide up-to-date information and to allow for more dynamic use of the infrastructure. New technologies develop and both add to the nation's infrastructure and sometimes displace existing modes. Fiber-optic replaces coaxial cable. Cellular telephony decreases the need for additional landline infrastructure. Solar and wind power create a need for connectivity upgrades but may eventually decrease the need to expand traditional transmission lines, when large-scale affordable battery storage that nets out to environmental improvement, accounting for manufacture and disposal, eventually becomes available. Demand also changes as the population both grows and ages, and the shock of the COVID-19 pandemic makes working from home more common (Aksoy et al. 2022; Aksoy et al. 2023).

While so much of the future is hard to forecast, we know, as the Greek philosopher Heraclitus wisely noted, that the only thing that remains constant is change, whether in technology or in population patterns. Infrastructure by its very nature is inclined to be fixed, serving as the foundation and conduit for economic activity. However, knowing what we know now, for example, about the negative unintended consequences of lead, asbestos, and fossil fuel usage, along with a range of threats facing American infrastructure, we would do well to have systems in place that allow us to adapt our infrastructure to new knowledge and evolving challenges.

Winter Storm Uri, which took out power across Texas for days in February 2021, is a prime example. Though the frequency of such storms had been forecasted to grow, the state and its energy producers failed to adapt and properly insulate and winterize their systems (Norton 2021). While other states were hit similarly hard by the storm, their infrastructure and their ability to tap into energy sources across state lines kept them from experiencing the kind of humanitarian crisis that unfolded in Texas. Similar episodes abound, from Hurricane Katrina in New Orleans and lead contamination in Flint, Michigan, to the Oroville Dam crisis in California and the Colonial Pipeline ransomware attack that shut down fuel delivery to the East Coast (Plumer 2017; Sanger and Perlroth 2021).

Local authorities know their needs and vulnerabilities best, but coordination across jurisdictions is often crucial to crisis preparedness and response. This is where federal authorities can play an important role in setting sensible standards for safety and maintenance, incentivizing timely monitoring and reporting of issues, and facilitating collaboration and coordination across authorities. To ensure the resilience and long-term productivity of infrastructure across the country, we need to make sure that our investments in construction and maintenance are forward looking and have the entire country's social welfare in mind.

Focus Federal Policy on Incentives

An important role of the federal government should be to put in place the right incentives for the state, local, and private actors so that returns on taxpayer investments are maximized. In practice, this means incentivizing uniform data collection and rigorous cost-benefit analysis; helping localities move to user fee–based financing systems; encouraging investments in adaptive infrastructure through long-run rather than short-run planning; and realigning cost-sharing and matching grants to reflect local, state, and national benefits far more closely. In cases where infrastructure crosses state lines, has substantial spillovers, or where (reasonably set minimum) uniform standards across the country allow net benefits to be increased, the federal government should serve a coordinating role. While federal financing can serve as a powerful carrot and regulation as a powerful stick, rigorous cost-benefit analysis should be guiding the federal government's use of these tools, as it should at the state and local level (California's high-speed rail boondoggle is a classic example of poor ex ante cost-benefit analysis).

And that analysis must include accurate information on the distribution of (potential) benefits among local, state, and national jurisdictions. To cite a core potential problem, if the federal government is paying for 80 percent of an infrastructure project and the state (or local) government 20 percent, that means the elected representatives at the lower level have an incentive to promote projects with pretty low local benefits, in theory anything over 20 percent of the cost, since their voters will only pay 20 percent. But all have that incentive, so in total there can be lots of poor-return projects unless the spillovers are the large majority of benefits. Since we are all residents of a locality, a state, and the nation, inattention to this issue can result in massive wasteful fiscal cross-hauling. In theory, the reverse could also be true if the federal share is far smaller than the spillover percentage. But in practice, most federal funding comes with large federal shares that likely exceed spillovers, in some cases substantially.

Careful consideration should be given to the incentive structures built into fund disbursements to prevent moral hazard at the local level and a kind of tragedy of the fiscal commons. Increasing competition and transparency in the procurement process (e.g., Lewis-Faupel et al. 2016; Liscow, Nober, and Slattery 2023); encouraging experimentation with auction designs that limit bureaucratic disruptions and take into account time to completion (e.g., Summers and Lipson 2016; Gupta et al. 2015), as was successfully done in California in response to the freeways collapsing from the Northridge earthquake; allowing allocated budgets to roll over instead of expiring at the end of a fiscal year (e.g., Liebman and Mahoney 2017); and discouraging excessive customization in project design (e.g., Goldwyn, Levy, and Ensari 2020) are all areas where federal action can play an important role. Random audits of the use of federal funding for effectiveness, coupled with enhanced transparency, could also help increase accountability and success while decreasing corruption (e.g., Ferraz and Finan 2008; Campos et al. 2021). Finally, incentivizing crisis prevention, in the same way that health insurance companies incentivize healthy behaviors to decrease the probability of expensive future procedures, should help states invest in maintenance and adaptation to emerging threats. In effect, the more the federal government serves as a catalyst rather than a micromanager, the better.

Short-Run Stimulus, Long-Run Investment, or Both?

Many policymakers, interest groups, and constituents alike still view infrastructure spending as shovel-ready work that is both desperately needed and great at creating new jobs. Recent academic evidence on the matter, however, suggests that better allocation of infrastructure spending versus increased spending is more important for long-run productivity (Duranton, Nagpal, and Turner 2020) and casts doubt on whether a large allocation of federal funds for infrastructure will work to effectively reduce unemployment (e.g., Balat 2017; Gallen and Winston 2019; Ramey 2020).

Garin (2019) studies how funding allocated by the federal government for road construction projects through the 2009 American Recovery and Reinvestment Act (ARRA) affected local employment. He finds that every dollar of ARRA spending increased local construction payrolls by thirty cents but had virtually no effect on employment.[4] Balat (2017) analyzes the effect of ARRA spending on highway-related procurement in California, finding that the sudden infusion of cash into an industry that was already working near capacity did not grow the number of construction firms or construction employment but resulted in higher procurement prices. This capacity constraint is directly at odds with a 1930s vision of what infrastructure spending can accomplish. The highly specialized and technologically advanced nature of the work now requires skills, experience, and certifications that make it difficult to quickly expand the number of firms and workers. In California, Balat (2017) finds that the government not only paid 6.2 percent more on ARRA projects, it also paid 4.8 percent more on other projects as a result of ARRA, thereby increasing construction company revenues but forgoing about $335 million that could have been spent on other roadwork.

Additional studies, such as Ramey (2020), demonstrate that infrastructure spending is usually slow to move from appropriation to implementation to actual use, making even the most productive and most shovel-ready projects poor candidates for short-run economic stimulus. In fact, as Gallen and Winston (2019) argue, disruptions that come from a slew of highway infrastructure projects can even result in negative short-run effects on total employment. Studies of the ARRA also provide cautionary tales on the ability of infrastructure spending to create jobs in the short run and on the cost of doing so. Leduc and Wilson (2017), for example, find a "flypaper" effect, whereby federal highway grants under ARRA induce states to spend more of their own funds on highway infrastructure as well. The explanation for this apparent—it may just be spending that would have occurred anyway but was delayed in anticipation of the federal funds—complementary state spending, however, is rent seeking: states with the largest volume of political contributions from public works contractors are the ones that see the largest flypaper effects. Moreover, the study measures the direct effects of federal spending on highway construction-sector employment and finds a cost of $500,000 per job in 2010. This is considerably more costly than the roughly $125,000–$200,000 per job that other papers have attributed to ARRA spending overall (Wilson 2012; Conley and Dupor 2013), and about ten times higher than typical construction worker earnings at that time.

Long-run productivity is a different story, but the devil is in the details. As discussed above, the research literature generally stresses that quality and rigor behind fund allocation is key to large long-run returns, much more so than the sheer volume of spending. Other research also makes clear that infrastructure spending can generate long-run winners and losers. Analyzing the effects of new regional highway construction in China, Baum-Snow et al. (2020) show that such construction can increase population and economic output in major cities at the expense of the hinterlands. Highways that improve connections to major ports, however, appear to make all areas better off. Careful consideration of spillovers and path-dependency during cost-benefit analyses is thus crucial for project selection and prioritization, as well as for state and federal financing decisions.

Reflecting on Past Experiences and Looking Ahead

What can we learn from recent infrastructure policies as we look ahead to future legislation and reforms that define local, state, and federal responsibilities for infrastructure? An abundance of recent experiences has highlighted how crucial effective, reliable, and safe infrastructure is to the well-being of citizens across the country. Whether it's lead contamination in Flint, Michigan, erosion at the Oroville Dam in California, a sewage line failure in Jackson, Mississippi, or the collapse of the I-35W bridge in Minneapolis, Minnesota, communities take a huge human and economic hit when the infrastructure they rely on fails. The May 2021 closure of the I-40 bridge linking Arkansas and Memphis, Tennessee—home to FedEx and the largest cargo airport in the world—also illustrated that infrastructure failures can cause disruptions that reverberate far beyond the immediately affected community. The flip side of these notable failures is the simple, yet often neglected, fact that when the infrastructure we take for granted is working well, it is generating benefits that make our quality of life possible.

Infrastructure failures and successes are often determined by policy, with high stakes for getting it right. Failure by authorities to arrange for adequate incentives and resources for maintenance can result in disruptions or worse, consequences that are possibly costlier than the maintenance would have been in the first place. Negligent cost estimates, unmoored from responsible cost-benefit analysis, can lead to wasteful spending with low returns on investment. Thinking of infrastructure spending as effective short-run economic stimulus and trying to rush spending risks backlogs, higher prices, and hundreds of thousands of taxpayer dollars spent for each job created. On the other hand, setting incentives right after a major disaster, like the $200,000-a-day bonus for contractors to speed up Santa Monica Freeway repairs after the 1994 Northridge earthquake, can spur cost-effective infrastructure repairs and get the economy moving again. Partnerships between states and the federal government to improve forest management on federal lands can reduce wildfire risk and the associated destruction. And having federal authorities serve as arbiters when neighboring states cannot resolve water usage disputes, as the government did in the spring of 2023 with Arizona, California, and Nevada around usage of the Colorado River, can ensure that communities have access to fresh water for the long run. As these and many other past experiences have shown, the relationship between the federal and local governments can either generate pitfalls or prevent them.

The 2021 Infrastructure Investment and Jobs Act (IIJA) is a valuable case study of policy, both good and bad. By allocating $550 billion over five years in *additional* federal funding for roads, bridges, transit, ports, airports, the electric grid, water systems, and broadband—increasing federal funding on infrastructure over this period to $1.2 trillion—the law makes a historically large investment in the nation's infrastructure (Tomer et al. 2021). Table 8.2 breaks down the allocation of *additional* funds by type of infrastructure, in the context of several other recent infrastructure bills. Federal spending on ports, waterways, airports, cybersecurity, and environmental monitoring infrastructure has especial potential to generate positive externalities across the country and appears to follow the principle that projects with positive externalities should be subsidized. Federal spending on broadband in low-income and rural areas also has the potential to be appropriate under the same principle. Some education scholars estimate the social return on such investment for public K–12 education alone to be above 200 percent in states such as Alabama (Goulas, Han, and Raymond 2021); if even a quarter of that return was realizable, these would be outstanding investments. In contrast, it is not clear why the federal government, rather than states and localities, should be paying for school buses and ferries.

Table 8.2 Infrastructure allocations over time, by act (2009–2022)

ARRA (2009)

Infrastructure	Spending allocated
Transportation infrastructure	**48.1**
Highways and bridges	27.5
Transit	8.4
Rail	8
Airports	1.3
Ports	1.5
Other transportation	1.4
Energy infrastructure	**39.3**
Smart grid and transmission	11
Renewable energy	9.4
Energy efficiency	6.3
Fossil energy research	4.6
Carbon capture	3.4
Nuclear energy	2.4
Other energy	2.2
Water and environmental	**18.2**
Clean/drinking water	6
Superfund, brownfields cleanup	1.2
Environmental restoration, preservation	3.4
Other	7.6
Broadband	7.2
Other infrastructure	11.2
Total	**$124 billion**

MAP-21 (2013–2015)

Infrastructure	Spending allocated
Highways	77.2
Transit	21.6
Safety	2.2
Other	4.1
Total	**$105.1 billion**

FAST Act (2016–2021)

Infrastructure	Spending allocated
Highways	225
Transit	61
Rail	20.5
Safety	16
Research	4
Total	**$326.5 billion**

IIJA (2022–2026)

Infrastructure	Additional spending allocated
Roads and bridges	110
Passenger and freight rail	66
Safety	11
Public transit	39.2
Broadband	65
Ports and waterways	16.6
Airports	25
Water infrastructure	55
Power and grid	65
Resiliency	47.2
Clean school buses and ferries	7.5
Electric vehicle charging	7.5
Reconnecting communities	1
Addressing legacy pollution	21
Western water infrastructure	8.3
Total	**$545.3 billion**

Note: (1) MAP-21 was extended through 2015 by the Highway and Transportation Funding Act of 2015. (2) The ARRA was a single-tranche investment in 2009. The infrastructure bill in place was SAFETEA-LU (2005–2009, extended through 2012 until MAP-21 augmented it).

Laudably, the law allocates a significant amount of funding, across infra-structure categories, through a competitive grant process that has the poten-tial to ensure the money goes to projects with high benefit-cost ratios—if and only if the politics that usually seeps into the decision can be kept at bay. Two sections of the legislation also place a commendable, if still limited, empha-sis on user fees. Section 13001, titled "Strategic Innovation for Revenue Collection," extends $75 million over five years to municipalities and state-level DOTs in support of pilot programs that explore "user-based alternative revenue mechanisms . . . to maintain the long-term solvency of the Highway Trust Fund." Section 13002 in turn dedicates $50 million over five years toward a nationwide motor vehicle per-mile (VMT) user fee pilot, with the same objective. While these pilots do not commit Congress to implementing user fees in future legislation, they will result in a report and should provide a basis for a more informed nationwide conversation on sustainable infrastruc-ture financing, one that does not require Highway Trust Fund bailouts with general taxpayer dollars. Moreover, with Utah, Oregon, Virginia, and Hawaii now voluntarily running their own VMT programs, we should soon have additional evidence on the pains and benefits of user fees straight from these laboratories of democracy.

As table 8.2 demonstrates, federal infrastructure spending has come in waves that are heavily influenced by the political process. ARRA directed about $124 billion toward a wide range of infrastructure categories, in response to infrastructure needs but also to an economic and financial crisis. In a similar vein, the IIJA of 2021 was motivated as much by need as by the misguided view that the spending would create many new jobs. The law, as a result, does not fundamentally address pitfalls in the existing structure of federal infrastructure spending. One-off spikes in federal appropriations risk not only backlogs and higher prices but also an unsustainable "build-it-and-forget-it" mindset that perpetuates unfunded and deferred maintenance.

User fees and the creation of sustainable funding mechanisms that sup-port the infrastructure over the long term are notably missing from the law, leaving us with significant incentives for localities to shirk on spending their own dollars on infrastructure, waiting until the infrastructure is in bad shape, and hoping for another windfall from the federal government. Indeed, a study of federal spending through the ARRA found states decreasing their own spending on highways by 81 percent in response to the influx of federal funds (Dupor 2017). A 2021 CBO report of various federal infrastructure spending scenarios projected that states would decrease spending on physical infrastructure by fifteen cents for every federal dollar allocated; the report's 2016 analysis, looking more broadly at federal allocations, projected state and local spending would decrease by thirty-three cents for every federal dollar (CBO 2021).

The IIJA sections that invest in user fee pilots and move us toward more sustainable income streams for the Highway Trust Fund capture the spirit of what is necessary. The roller-coaster nature of the balance of the Highway Trust Fund, shown in figure 8.1, captures well the current unsustainability and inconsistency of federal infrastructure spending. Future legislation should build on the IIJA and do what the IIJA, ARRA, Moving Ahead for Progress in the 21st Century Act (MAP-21), Fixing America's Surface Transportation Act (FAST Act), and other infrastructure legislation have failed to do: combine federal infrastructure spending, especially capital spending, with requirements for minimum maintenance funds for the new infrastructure and incentives for complementary financing through user fees.

In addition to user fees, future legislation should work on reforms that set better incentives in other respects as well. It should revise the 90-10 rule for federal-state spending shares on the Interstate Highway System. As a 2018

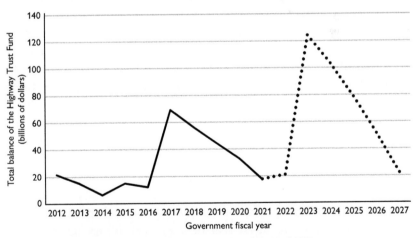

Figure 8.1 Total balance of the Highway Trust Fund (2012–2027)

Note: Highway Trust Fund start-of-year balances from 2012–2021 reflect the actual account balance at the beginning of the year. For the years 2022–2027, the projections are taken from the FY2023 budget. Prior to FY2017, the Highway Trust Fund was referred to as the Transportation Trust Fund in the Income, Outgo, and Balance tables of the Budget.

Source: Analytical Perspectives, Budget of the United States Government, FY2014–23.

CBO analysis showed, in 2017 the federal government covered 41 percent of all capital spending on transportation and water infrastructure and 10 percent of the operation and maintenance costs for that infrastructure, a strong contrast to its coverage of 90 percent of spending on interstate highways (CBO 2018). An improved approach, to interstate highway funding and to funding of other forms of infrastructure, would anchor the spending shares to clear and systematic calculations of national and local costs and benefits. For a start, an update to Ned Gramlich's analyses from the 1990s that found 67 percent of spending on interstate highways benefits the local area and that most interstate highway drivers are from within the same state (Gramlich 1990; Gramlich 1994), would be a helpful foundation for revisions of the 90-10 rule. Indeed, Duranton, Nagpal, and Turner note in a similar spirit that "like public transit, the Interstate system is largely organized around the provision of short trips in urban areas" (2020, 166).

Future legislation should also ground itself in firmer assumptions on returns to investment. The IIJA assumes, for example, a 33 percent return on investment from some of the spending, expecting $56 billion in additional tax revenue to cover over 10 percent of the additional federal spending. Such a return is wildly unrealistic and considerably exceeds CBO estimates (ranging from 6 percent to 9.2 percent) and academic estimates (5 to 12 percent) for returns on infrastructure spending (CBO 2021; Ramey 2020). Although spread out over five years, the law comes at a time of large supply-chain disruptions from the COVID-19 pandemic, worker shortages, backlogs for contractors, and rising inflation—all of which do not bode well for getting a lot of bang for the taxpayers' buck. Further raising alarms are members of the Society for Benefit-Cost Analysis who have recently warned that the Office of Management and Budget is being politicized and building value judgments into calculations of economic efficiency that are distorting decision making (Dudley and Viscusi 2023).

Finally, observers have noted that the allocation of funding through competitive grants, with a cumbersome submission process and the absence of adequate data infrastructure in many localities, can result in winning localities where the returns on investment are not as high as they can be (Tomer et al. 2021). Helping states and localities build out data systems that allow them to run pilots, monitor their infrastructure, and compete for competitive grants on relevant outcomes could thus have also been a valuable feature of the law and should be considered in future legislation.

Conclusion

The Infrastructure Investment and Jobs Act of 2021, historic in its size and scope, will likely not be the last historic federal infrastructure spending bill to wind up being debated in Congress. Leaning, however, on existing research and on the work that will likely come out of evaluations of the IIJA, policymakers would do well to move on from views that large infrastructure spending bills are a good short-run stimulus and a cost-effective way of addressing our country's infrastructure needs. Instead, this chapter encourages work toward a world where our infrastructure is consistently and sustainably funded with incentives for both overall quality and usefulness, and where the allocation of responsibilities among different levels of government avoids wasteful fiscal cross-hauling. The principles we present here—establishing capabilities and incentives for rigorous cost-benefit analysis; prioritizing highest net benefit projects; financing with user fees wherever possible; making infrastructure adaptive and planning for technological change; and making federalism about incentives—are meant to guide policymakers who embark on this task. Using these principles, we believe policymakers at each and all levels of government can better leverage our federal system—making the most of our cities and states as laboratories of democracy—to avoid boondoggles and waste, while increasing the country's long-run growth and productivity.

We are grateful to Marco Scalera for excellent research assistance and Dennis Epple, Thomas Nechyba, Carlos X. Lastra-Anadón, and other participants at the September 2023 Hoover Federalism Conference for helpful comments. This chapter is partly adapted from Michael J. Boskin, Testimony to the House Transportation Committee, September 30, 2021.

Notes

1. Indeed, as they have done as of this writing.

2. London's Congestion Charge has so far been an example of significant success, reducing congestion and increasing property values in affected areas (Leape 2006; Tang 2021).

3. David Pearce is credited with being the first to note the fact that user fees both increase efficiency and generate revenues, calling this the "double dividend" (Pearce 1991).

4. At a June 13, 2011 press conference with the President's Jobs Council, President Obama himself acknowledged that "shovel-ready was not as shovel-ready as we expected."

References

Aksoy, Cevat G., Jose M. Barrero, Nick Bloom, Steven J. Davis, Mathias Dolls, and Pablo Zarate. 2022. "Working from Home around the World." Working Paper No. 30446. National Bureau of Economic Research.

———. 2023. "Time Savings When Working from Home." Working Paper No. 30866. National Bureau of Economic Research.

American Society of Civil Engineers (ASCE). 2017. "2017 Infrastructure Report Card: A Comprehensive Assessment of America's Infrastructure."

———. 2021. "2021 Report Card for America's Infrastructure."

Aschauer, David A. 1991. "Infrastructure: America's Third Deficit," *Challenge* 34, no. 2 (March/April): 39–45.

Ashraf, Nava, Edward L. Glaeser, and Giacomo Ponzetto. 2016. "Infrastructure, Incentives, and Institutions." *American Economic Review* 106, no. 5 (May): 77–82.

Badlam, Justin, Tony D'Emidio, Adi Kumar, Sara O'Rourke, and Rob Dunn. 2021. "The US Bipartisan Infrastructure Law: Breaking It Down." McKinsey & Company. https://www.mckinsey.com/industries/public-sector/our-insights/the-us-bipartisan-infrastructure-law-breaking-it-down.

Bajari, Patrick, Stephanie Houghton, and Steven Tadelis. 2014. "Bidding for Incomplete Contracts: An Empirical Analysis." *American Economic Review* 104, no. 4 (April): 1288–319.

Balat, Jorge. 2017. "Highway Procurement and the Stimulus Package: Identification and Estimation of Dynamic Auctions with Unobserved Heterogeneity." Working Paper.

Baum-Snow, Nathaniel, J. Vernon Henderson, Matthew A. Turner, Qinghua Zhang, and Loren Brandt. 2020. "Does Investment in National Highways Help or Hurt Hinterland City Growth?" *Journal of Urban Economics* 115 (January): 103–24.

Biden, Joseph R. 2021. "Modernizing Regulatory Review: Memorandum for the Heads of Executive Departments and Agencies." White House Briefing Room.

Boadway, Robin, and Anwar Shah. 2009. *Fiscal Federalism: Principles and Practice of Multiorder Governance.* Cambridge: Cambridge University Press.

Bolotnyy, Valentin, and Shoshana Vasserman. 2023. "Scaling Auctions as Insurance: A Case Study in Infrastructure Procurement." *Econometrica* 91 (4): 1205–59.

Brass, Clinton T., Jennifer E. Lake, Carol H. Vincent, Karen Spar, and Pamela J. Jackson. 2009. "American Recovery and Reinvestment Act of 2009 (P.L. 111-5): Summary and Legislative History." Congressional Research Service report R40537.

Brooks, Leah, and Zachary Liscow. 2019. "Infrastructure Costs." Hutchins Center Working Paper No. 54, Brookings Institution.

———. 2020. "Can America Reduce Highway Spending? Evidence from the States." In *Economic Analysis and Infrastructure Investment,* edited by Edward L. Glaeser and James M. Poterba, 107–50. Chicago: University of Chicago Press.

Campos, Nicolás, Eduardo Engel, Ronald D. Fischer, and Alexander Galetovic. 2021. "The Ways of Corruption in Infrastructure: Lessons from the Odebrecht Case." *Journal of Economic Perspectives* 35, no. 2 (Spring): 171–90.

Congressional Budget Office (CBO). 2018. "Public Spending on Transportation and Water Infrastructure, 1956 to 2017."

———. 2021. "Effects of Physical Infrastructure Spending on the Economy and the Budget under Two Illustrative Scenarios."

Conley, Timothy G., and Bill Dupor. 2013. "The American Recovery and Reinvestment Act: Solely a Government Jobs Program?" *Journal of Monetary Economics* 60, no. 5 (July): 535–49.

CTIA. 2021. "2021 Annual Survey Highlights."

Dudley, Susan, and W. Kip Viscusi. 2023. "Biden's OMB Politicizes Cost-Benefit Analysis." *Wall Street Journal*, August 28.

Dupor, Bill. 2017. "So, Why Didn't the 2009 Recovery Act Improve the Nation's Highways and Bridges?" *Federal Reserve Bank of St. Louis Review* 99, no. 2 (Second Quarter): 169–82.

Duranton, Gilles, Geetika Nagpal, and Matthew A. Turner. 2020. "Transportation Infrastructure in the US." In *Economic Analysis and Infrastructure Investment*, edited by Edward L. Glaeser and James M. Poterba, 165–218. Chicago: University of Chicago Press.

Federal Aviation Administration (FAA). 2022. "National Plan of Integrated Airport Systems (NPIAS) 2023–2027." US Department of Transportation.

Ferraz, Claudio, and Frederico Finan. 2008. "Exposing Corrupt Politicians: The Effects of Brazil's Publicly Released Audits on Electoral Outcomes." *Quarterly Journal of Economics* 23, no. 2 (May): 703–45.

Fitzsimmons, Emma G. 2017. "Key to Improving Subway Service in New York? Modern Signals." *New York Times*, May 1.

Gallen, Trevor, and Clifford Winston. 2019. "Transportation and Its Effects on the US Economy: A General Equilibrium Approach." Technical report, Purdue University.

Garin, Andrew. 2019. "Putting America to Work, Where? Evidence on the Effectiveness of Infrastructure Construction as a Locally Targeted Employment Policy." *Journal of Urban Economics* 111 (May): 108–31.

Glaeser, Edward L. 2016. "If You Build It . . . Myths and Realities about America's Infrastructure Spending." *City Journal* (Summer).

Goldszmidt, Ariel, John A. List, Robert D. Metcalfe, Ian Muir, V. Kerry Smith, and Jenny Wang. 2020. "The Value of Time in the United States: Estimates from Nationwide Natural Field Experiments." Working Paper No. w28208. National Bureau of Economic Research.

Goldwyn, Eric, Alon Levy, and Elif Ensari. 2020. "The Boston Case: The Story of the Green Line Extension." Marron Institute of Urban Management Report, New York University.

Goulas, Sofoklis, Chunping Han, and Margaret E. Raymond. 2021. "Alabama Broadband for Education." In *Innovative Alabama: A Report by the Hoover Institution Prepared for the Alabama Innovation Commission*, 111–52. https://www.hoover.org/sites/default/files/research/docs/innovativealabama_ch6.pdf.

Gramlich, Edward M. 1990. *A Guide to Benefit-Cost Analysis.* Englewood Cliffs, NJ: Prentice-Hall.

———. 1994. "Infrastructure Investment: A Review Essay." *Journal of Economic Literature* 32, no. 3 (September): 1176–96.

Gupta, Diwakar, Eli M. Snir, and Yibin Chen. 2015. "Contractors' and Agency Decisions and Policy Implications in A+B Bidding." *Production and Operations Management* 24, no. 1 (January): 159–77.

Hoffman, Chris. 2022. "Audit: Pennsylvania Turnpike Raising Tolls to Pay Debt Is 'Unsustainable.'" CBS News, September 7.

Kirk, Robert S., John Frittelli, Linda Luther, William J. Mallett, and David R. Peterman. 2012. "Surface Transportation Funding and Programs under MAP-21: Moving Ahead for Progress in the 21st Century Act (P.L. 112-141)." Congressional Research Service report R42762.

Kirk, Robert S., John Frittelli, Linda Luther, William J. Mallett, David R. Peterman, and Bill Canis. 2016. "Surface Transportation Funding and Programs under the Fixing America's Surface Transportation Act (FAST Act; P.L. 114-94)." Congressional Research Service report R44388.

Leape, Jonathan. 2006. "The London Congestion Charge." *Journal of Economic Perspectives* 20, no. 4 (Fall): 157–76.

Leduc, Sylvain, and Daniel Wilson. 2017. "Are State Governments Roadblocks to Federal Stimulus? Evidence on the Flypaper Effect of Highway Grants in the 2009 Recovery Act." *American Economic Journal: Economic Policy* 9, no. 2 (May): 253–92.

Lewis-Faupel, Sean, Yusuf Neggers, Benjamin A. Olken, and Rohini Pande. 2016. "Can Electronic Procurement Improve Infrastructure Provision? Evidence from Public Works in India and Indonesia." *American Economic Journal: Economic Policy* 8, no. 3 (August): 258–83.

Liebman, Jeffrey B., and Neale Mahoney. 2017. "Do Expiring Budgets Lead to Wasteful Year-End Spending? Evidence from Federal Procurement." *American Economic Review* 107, no. 11 (November): 3510–49.

Liscow, Zachary D., Willliam Nober, and Cailin Slattery. 2023. "Procurement and Infrastructure Costs." SSRN Working Paper No. 4522676.

Mallela, Jagannath, Suri Sadasivam, and Jerry Ullman. 2014. "Massachusetts Demonstration Project: Reconstruction of Fourteen Bridges on I-93 in Medford Using Accelerated Bridge Construction Techniques." Report of the Transportation Research Board of the US Department of Transportation, Federal Highway Administration.

Masur, Jonathan. 2020. "Cost-Benefit Analysis under Trump: A Comment on Dan Farber's Regulatory Review in Anti-Regulatory Times." *Chicago-Kent Law Review* 94, no. 3 (April): 665–72.

Mehrotra, Neil, Matthew A. Turner, and Juan Pablo Uribe. 2020. "Does the US Have an Infrastructure Cost Problem? Evidence from the Interstate Highway System." Working Paper.

Mims, Christopher. 2023. "America's Bridges, Factories and Highways Are in Dire Need of Repairs. Bring in the Robots." *Wall Street Journal*, August 18.

Norton, Kara. 2021. "Why Texas Was Not Prepared for Winter Storm Uri." *Nova Education*, March 25.

Oates, Wallace E. 1972. *Fiscal Federalism*. New York: Harcourt Brace Jovanovich.

———. 2008. "On the Evolution of Fiscal Federalism: Theory and Institutions." *National Tax Journal* 61, no. 2 (June): 313–34.

Pazzanese, Christina. 2021. "Analysts in Economics, Public Policy Give Biden Infrastructure Plan High Marks." *Harvard Gazette*, May 6.

Pearce, David. 1991. "The Role of Carbon Taxes in Adjusting to Global Warming." *Economic Journal* 101, no. 407 (July): 938–48.

Pipeline and Hazardous Materials Safety Administration. 2023. US Department of Transportation. Website accessed December 1. https://www.phmsa.dot.gov.

Plumer, Brad. 2017. "The Crisis at Oroville Dam, Explained." *Vox*, February 15.

Ramey, Valerie A. 2020. "The Macroeconomic Consequences of Infrastructure Investment." In *Economic Analysis and Infrastructure Investment*, edited by Edward L. Glaeser and James M. Poterba, 219–76. Chicago: University of Chicago Press.

Rueb, Emily S. 2016. "New York 101: Why Are the Streets Always under Construction?" *New York Times*, August 18.

S&P Global Market Intelligence. 2019. "Fiber Route Mile Leaderboard," March 4. https://www.spglobal.com/marketintelligence/en/news-insights/blog/fiber-route-mile-leaderboard.

Sanger, David E., and Nicole Perlroth. 2021. "F.B.I. Identifies Group behind Pipeline Hack." *New York Times*, May 10.

Schotter, Casey J., and Gayle Rhineberger-Dunn. 2013. "The I-35W Bridge Collapse: Crimes of Commission and Omission Resulting from the Confluence of State Processes and Political-Economic Conditions." *Critical Criminology* 21, no. 4 (November): 477–92.

Solar Energy Industries Association (SEIA). 2019. "United States Surpasses 2 Million Solar Installations," May 9.

Summers, Lawrence H., and Rachel Lipson. 2016. "A Lesson on Infrastructure from the Anderson Bridge Fiasco." *Boston Globe*, May 25.

Tang, Cheng Keat. 2021. "The Cost of Traffic: Evidence from the London Congestion Charge." *Journal of Urban Economics* 121 (January): 103302.

Tomer, Adie, Caroline George, Joseph W. Kane, and Andrew Bourne. 2021. "America Has an Infrastructure Bill. What's Happens Next?" Brookings Institution, Commentary, November 9.

Tomer, Adie, and Joseph W. Kane. 2015. "The Great Port Mismatch: US Goods Trade and International Transportation." Global Cities Initiative: A Joint Project of Brookings and JPMorgan Chase.

Union of Concerned Scientists. 2023. UCS Satellite Database, updated May 1.

US Bureau of Transportation Statistics. 2023. "System Mileage within the United States." Dataset accessed December 1.

US Environmental Protection Agency (EPA). 2023. "US Electricity Grid and Markets." Last updated April 18.

US Geological Survey (USGS). 2023. "US Wind Turbine Database," November. https://eerscmap.usgs.gov/uswtdb.

Vasserman, Shoshana. 2020. "Comment on 'Procurement Choices and Infrastructure Costs.'" In *Economic Analysis and Infrastructure Investment*, edited by Edward L. Glaeser and James M. Poterba, 277–332. Chicago: University of Chicago Press.

Weinstock, Lida R. 2021. "Infrastructure and the Economy." Congressional Research Service report R46826.

Wilson, Daniel J. 2012. "Fiscal Spending Jobs Multipliers: Evidence from the 2009 American Recovery and Reinvestment Act." *American Economic Journal: Economic Policy* 4, no. 3 (August): 251–82.

Witze, Alexandra. 2023. "2022 Was a Record Year for Space Launches." *Nature* 613, no. 7944 (January): 426.

9

Federalist System of Healthcare Financing in America

Thomas MaCurdy and Jay Bhattacharya

Introduction

The healthcare sector comprises a prominent segment of the American economy, touching all people's lives and supporting their health and well-being. This sector currently consumes nearly one-fifth of the US GDP, with its share continually rising. In 2019, the healthcare sector employed 11 percent of American workers, and healthcare spending accounted for 8.1 percent of consumer expenditures, one of the largest categories. Healthcare expenditures absorbed over 20 percent of total government spending and over 25 percent of federal government spending; in addition, health insurance constituted 26 percent of nonwage compensation, the largest component (BLS 1980–2019a, 1980–2019b, 2019a, 2019b, 2010–2023; BEA 1987–2019a; CMS 1960–2022; and authors' calculations).

The United States faces serious challenges in maintaining the ever-increasing burden of financing healthcare, which will relentlessly worsen in the upcoming decades. Private funding still makes up the largest financing source of healthcare spending, but this share has been falling steadily and will dip below the 50 percent mark in the next few years. Public funding will soon become the largest financing source, coming from a combination of federal and state coffers. Many commentators have fervently warned about the fiscal unsustainability of current public policies in maintaining the healthcare sector in its existing form with its projected trends.

In seeking policy reforms, all parties balance options in a spectrum demarcated by America's federalist system that allows for varying divisions of responsibilities and authorities between the federal and state governments in operating public programs. Both levels of government play prominent roles in managing and funding healthcare policies, and all policy solutions aimed at circumventing the looming fiscal crisis in healthcare financing involve a rebalancing of the roles.

At one end of the federalism spectrum, advocates call for a more significant federal role in managing and funding healthcare, such as Medicare for All. These advocates point to the success of other countries in operating such health systems, such jurisdictions having central governments without powerful local governments.

At the other end of the spectrum, advocates promote giving states considerable discretion in offering health programs and more responsibility for funding costly special features. These advocates point to the success of welfare reform adopted in the mid-1990s when the federal government turned authority for designing and operating cash support antipoverty programs to the states and provided block funding grants with few qualifying criteria.

This paper presents an overview of America's health sector, focusing on its financing perspective, and explores the need and options for significant policy reforms to prevent a public fiscal crisis that goes well beyond healthcare alone. More specifically, the following discussion addresses five questions:

- What comprises the financing of healthcare spending in the United States, and where do the different types of health insurance fit into the picture?
- How is the landscape of healthcare financing changing over time?
- What roles do federal and state governments play in the design of healthcare programs and the evolution of their financing?
- What is the nature of the perceived fiscal crisis in healthcare funding?
- What prospects exist for restructuring America's federalist health policy system to create sustainable funding in the upcoming decades?

The discussion below consists of four sections. The first describes the sources of funding for healthcare and the relevance of these sources in financing the care of different segments of the US population. The second section outlines the roles public funding plays in healthcare financing, highlighting the federal government's circumstances. Next, there is a summary of the activities of states in healthcare policies, focused on identifying differences in design and operational features, potentially offering insights into cost-saving approaches. The final section assesses the features and prospects of several reforms of health policies advocated to enhance aspects of competition, reduce public spending, and stem the looming fiscal crisis of health financing.

Overview of Healthcare Funding and Insurance

National health accounts (NHAs) provide the framework for measuring the levels and composition of economic activities and spending in the healthcare sector, with these accounts compatible with national income and product accounts. NHA statistics "identify all goods and services that can be characterized as relating to healthcare in the nation, and determine the amount of money used for the purchase of these goods and services" (Rice, Cooper, and Gibson 1982). NHA data provides essential information for understanding the structure of healthcare funding and delivery in the United States and critical factors underpinning international comparisons and formulation of public health policy.

Sources of Healthcare Spending and Consumption

Two perspectives exist for measuring NHA activities and spending: where dollars come from (funding sources) and where dollars go (expenditures on goods and services). Figure 9.1 shows the levels and composition of spending from the funding perspective in 2021. For context, figure 9.2 below presents the second measurement perspective, showing the services and products purchased with this spending. The first of these perspectives provides a vital understanding of federalism's role in healthcare financing.

In figure 9.1, private funds sponsor a large portion of direct payments for healthcare, with 20 percent coming from private insurance and 10 percent from out-of-pocket (OOP) payments. Private insurance in NHA includes premiums paid to traditional managed care, self-insured health plans and indemnity plans, and the net cost of private health insurance (the difference between health premiums earned and benefits incurred). Figure 9.1 categorizes spending by sponsor type, aimed at estimating the individual, business, or tax source ultimately responsible for financing healthcare bills. Thus, while NHA data considers private health insurance as a private source of funding, the sponsor classifications in NHA divide this measure into business, household, and government sponsor categories based on who bears the underlying financial responsibility for the health insurance premiums.

Employer-sponsored insurance (ESI) comprises the largest source of health coverage in the United States and the primary source of private health insurance. ESI covers the majority of the nonelderly population, including over 160 million Americans representing over 60 percent of the nonelderly population. Employers offer ESI to their employees and dependents as a benefit of employment, with the bulk of funding coming from premiums paid for by employers and the remainder paid by employees through premium contributions.

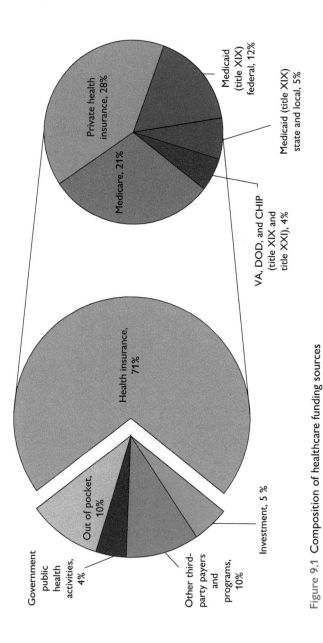

Figure 9.1 Composition of healthcare funding sources

Note: Figures have been rounded, and added sums may not match.

Source: CMS 2023b.

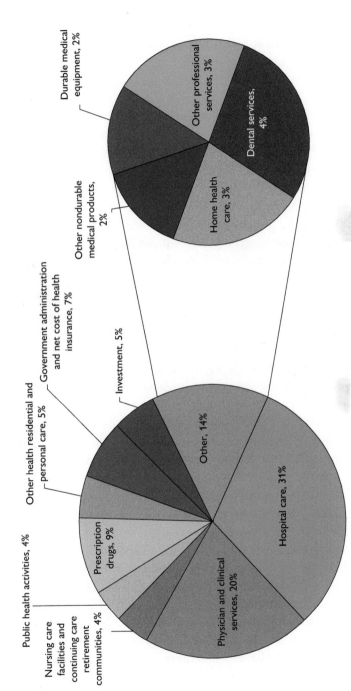

Figure 9.2 Composition of healthcare expenditures on services and products

Note: Figures have been rounded, and added sums may not match.

Source: CMS 2023b.

Out-of-pocket funding sources include direct consumer spending for all healthcare goods and services, including coinsurance, deductibles, and any amounts not covered by insurance.

Enacted in 1965, Medicare pays the largest share of public funding for healthcare, contributing 15 percent to overall spending. Medicare provides nearly universal insurance coverage for the elderly (age sixty-five and over) and disabled nonelderly. The structure of Medicare consists of four programs: Part A pays for enrollees' hospital care; Part B pays for outpatient care and physician services; Part C, modernized in 2003, provides an option for Medicare enrollees to receive their health insurance from a private plan (typically a plan with managed care features) rather than through the government; and Part D, enacted in 2006, pays for prescription drugs for enrollees. Medicare subsidizes premiums for all these programs, with Medicare financing leading to the premiums paid by Medicare enrollees falling below actuarially fair values (the values needed to pay for the healthcare costs incurred by Medicare). Most enrollees pay no premiums for Medicare Part A at all. The shortfall in covering Medicare costs comes from payroll and income taxes paid principally by people still in the workforce.

Medicaid, created alongside Medicare in 1965, pays the second largest share of public funding for healthcare, contributing 12 percent to overall spending. Medicaid provides highly subsidized insurance coverage to low-income families, with enrollees essentially making no payments in either premiums or cost sharing. Unlike Medicare, which is run by the federal government and administered uniformly across the United States, Medicaid is jointly run by the federal and state governments. Both levels of government contribute to its public funding, with the federal government matching state funding and solely covering some program services. State governments have wide latitude to set budgets, determine eligibility rules, and decide the relative generosity of their local Medicaid programs.

The Children's Health Insurance Program (CHIP), enacted in 1997, provides medical coverage for youths age eighteen and under whose parents earn too much to qualify for Medicaid but not enough to gain health insurance coverage for their children through private insurance or ESI. CHIP represents a US federal healthcare program administered and named differently by each state, with responsibility for managing CHIP programs falling to the state's Medicaid administration. CHIP provides many free medical services to its enrollees, but some require a copayment. Some states also require a monthly premium that cannot exceed 5 percent of the annual household income. The bulk of CHIP spending comes from public funding paid by both the federal and state governments. As with Medicaid, the federal government provides matching funds to each state.

The Department of Defense (e.g., TRICARE) and Veterans Affairs (VA) funding sources in figure 9.1 pay for the healthcare services of military personnel and qualified veterans. The federal government solely covers the public funding of this spending.

Not explicitly identified in figure 9.1, the Affordable Care Act (ACA), enacted in 2010, includes premium tax credits and cost-sharing reductions to lower healthcare expenses for lower-income individuals and families and allows states to extend Medicaid coverage to all non-Medicare eligible individuals under age sixty-five (children, pregnant women, parents, and adults without dependent children) with incomes up to 133 percent of the federal poverty level (FPL). The ACA created state-based health benefit exchanges (marketplaces) through which individuals can purchase coverage, with premium and cost-sharing credits available to individuals and families with income between 133 and 400 percent of FPL. It also created separate SHOP (Small Business Health Options Program) exchanges through which small businesses can purchase coverage.

ACA mandated that ACA-compliant health insurance plans cannot deny coverage to anyone, including those with preexisting conditions, and further required employers to pay penalties for employees who received tax credits for health insurance through an exchange, with exceptions for small employers. All ACA-compliant health insurance plans must cover specific "essential health benefits," such as emergency services, family planning, maternity care, hospitalization, prescription medications, mental health services, and pediatric care, and provide preventive services (e.g., checkups, patient counseling, immunizations, and numerous health screenings) to policyholders at no cost.

The federal government covers practically all the spending on ACA, with the cost of marketplace and SHOP subsidies alone reaching about a quarter of the federal spending on Medicaid (CBO 2022, 2023b; and authors' calculations). In figure 9.1, this source of funding principally shows up in the "Other third-party payers and programs" category, with this category accounting for 10 percent of overall healthcare spending in total.

Figure 9.2 shows the allocation of health spending on goods and services. More than half of expenditures go to hospitals and physicians, with hospitals receiving almost a third of all expenditures and physicians earning a fifth. Two expenditure items fall outside conventional notions of healthcare: administrative costs associated with managing payment systems (government and private insurance) and investment costs related to noncommercial research and structures/equipment. In total, these indirect health expenditures account for 12 percent of spending.

Growth in Health Spending

Figure 9.3 shows the growth in health spending as a share of the economy since the turn of the century, with the share steadily increasing from 13.3 percent of GDP in 2000 to 18.3 percent in 2021. Sixty years ago, health accounted for 5 percent of the US economy, growing to 12.1 percent in 1990 and 18.3 percent in 2021 (CMS 1960–2022, National Health Expenditure Accounts, and associated downloadable data tables; and authors' calculations). After relatively slow growth throughout the 1990s, the health spending share of the economy increased by 4 percentage points in the first decade of this century and about 1 percentage point in the second decade.

The increase in healthcare funding over the past two decades comes from public funding, with the share paid by private funds essentially remaining constant. Private funds still comprise the largest funding source of healthcare payments, but just barely in 2021 at 51 percent. In 2000, private funding accounted for over 60 percent (CMS 1960–2022, National Health Expenditure Accounts, and associated downloadable data tables;

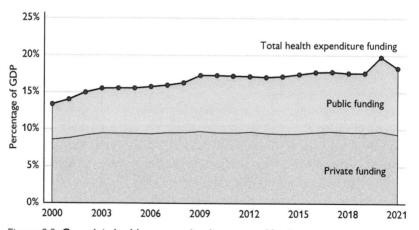

Figure 9.3 Growth in healthcare spending by source of funds

Source: Chantrill 2023, national spending analysis; authors' calculations.

and authors' calculations). The higher share paid by public funding arises from increasing shares of the population enrolled in Medicare, Medicaid, State Children's Health Insurance Programs, and veterans' health benefits. Also, policy changes like the introduction of the Medicare prescription drug benefit (Part D) in 2006 and a significant expansion of Medicaid eligibility in 2014 played important roles.

Composition of Health Financing and Insurance

Figure 9.4 shows the health insurance and sources of funding coverage of the nonelderly (under age sixty-five) in America in 2021. The figure distinguishes coverage according to three family income levels: below 150 percent of FPL, between 150 and 400 percent, and above 400 percent. Not surprisingly, the types of coverage that people enroll in vary substantially depending on their income.

For the lowest-income families, Medicaid and CHIP fund 57 percent of their health insurance coverage, followed by ESI at 15 percent as the second largest funder. Medicare supplies almost 5 percent of insurance (through its disability eligibility) for this population, with ACA (nongroup coverage and basic health program) covering 4 percent. Around 9 percent of low-income families have no insurance, with the bulk of their healthcare spending ultimately covered by supplementary Medicaid and other government programs, discussed further below.

For middle- and high-income families, ESI delivers most health insurance coverage, covering 52 percent of middle-income individuals and a dominating 88 percent of the highest income. Medicaid, CHIP, and ACA insure about 30 percent of the middle-income group and less than 8 percent of the highest-income population. Nearly 10 percent of middle-income families have no insurance, with less than 8 percent without insurance for the high-income group.

Viewed from a funding source perspective, figure 9.4 suggests that public funding conservatively finances two-thirds of health insurance for low-income nonelderly Americans, about one-third for those with middle incomes, and not more than 9 percent for high-income individuals.

Challenges in Public Funding of Healthcare

As documented above, the principal source funding the increasing healthcare burden in the United States comes from the public side of finance, which the following discussion explores in more detail.

Millions of People

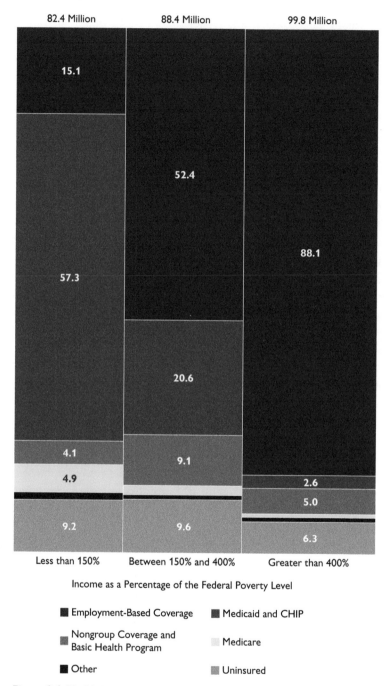

Figure 9.4 Health insurance coverage for nonelderly

Source: CBO 2022.

Composition and Growth of Government Healthcare Financing

Figure 9.5 decomposes the share of GDP spent on healthcare funded by public financing shown in figure 9.3 into its federal, state, and local government components. The curves track the share of GDP allocated by governments to health spending since 2010 and forecasted through 2028. Combined, federal, state, and local governments expended more than 8 percent of GDP on health in 2023, up from 7.5 percent in 2010, and an amount projected to reach 10 percent by 2028. Local government spending remained slightly below 1 percent of GDP from 2010 to 2023; total state funding increased from 3 to 3.5 percent over this period; and federal government direct spending increased from about 3.5 percent to over 4 percent since 2010, with projections taking it to over 5 percent by 2028.

A substantial part of state and local government spending on healthcare represents pass-through transfers paid for by the federal government. Figures 9.6 and 9.7 document the size and growth of these transfers. Figure 9.6 shows the levels and growth of the share of GDP allocated by the federal government to health, with federal total funding in this figure divided into a direct funding component captured by figure 9.5 and the transfer component supporting state and local total funding shares shown in figures 9.6 and 9.7. Figure 9.7 divides state and local total spending into their direct funding paid for by their treasuries and the federal transfer component provided to support state and local total spending.

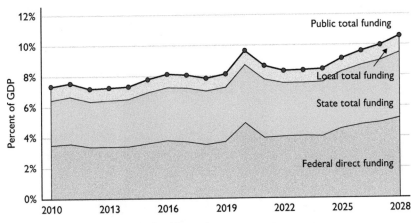

Figure 9.5 Public spending on healthcare by government sources

Source: Chantrill 2023, national spending analysis; authors' calculations.

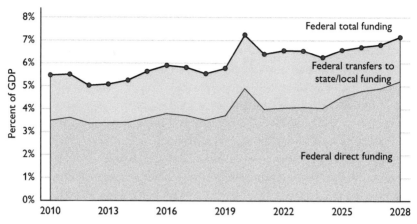

Figure 9.6 Share of federal health spending transferred to state and local governments
Sources: Chantill 2023, national spending analysis; authors' calculations.

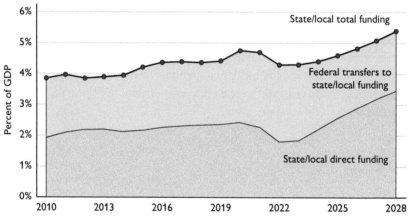

Figure 9.7 Share of state and local health spending paid by the federal government
Source: Chantrill 2023, national spending analysis; authors' calculations.

These figures reveal that federal funding constitutes the primary source of growth in healthcare spending. Federal direct funding has increased by about 0.5 percentage points since 2010, with a projected increase of over 1 percentage point in the next five years. Federal transfers also increased by about 0.5 percentage points since 2010, but current law dictates no growth through 2028. Direct funding by state and local government has fluctuated over the past decade but changed little overall. Federal budget agencies' five-year forecasts of this direct spending expect this share to rise by 1.5 percentage points to compensate for assumed zero growth in federal transfers. Extrapolating from experience about such budget assumptions strongly suggests that federal transfers will grow in the future as in the past to support most of the growth in total state and local funding needed to fund the anticipated overall increase in healthcare spending.

Role of Healthcare Financing in Federal Budgets

With the primary growth in healthcare funding coming from the federal government, understanding the role of healthcare spending in the context of the overall federal budget becomes central to reforming policies in America's federalist system of funding healthcare.

The federal government and many state and local governments face a challenging fiscal outlook in maintaining current policies and trends in public spending, given existing profiles for public revenues. Figures 9.8 and 9.9 illustrate the budget outlook for the federal government through the next decade based on the Congressional Budget Office's analyses.

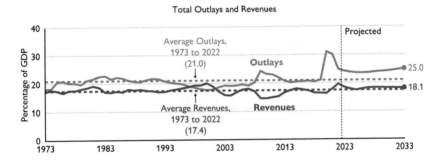

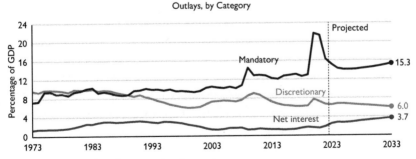

Figure 9.8 Federal outlays growing faster than revenues

Source: CBO 2023a.

Figure 9.8 forecasts federal spending growing from 24 percent of GDP in 2023 to 25 percent in 2033. This trend continues for the following two decades, reaching 29 percent of GDP by 2053. Federal revenues effectively do not increase as a percentage of GDP.

Total spending comprises mandatory and discretionary spending and net outlays for interest. Mandatory spending encompasses outlays governed by statutory criteria and not usually constrained by the annual appropriation process (including most federal benefit programs). Discretionary spending comprises federal activities funded through or controlled by the congressional appropriations process (including most defense spending, infrastructure, education, international affairs, and justice). In the federal budget, net outlays for interest consist of the government's interest payments on federal debt, offset by interest income that the government receives.

Figure 9.8 shows that mandatory spending and interest payments on the debt constitute the primary sources of growth in federal government outlays. After a short recovery from pandemic-related outlays, mandatory spending is projected to grow relentlessly after 2026 from 14 to 15 percent of GDP by 2033 and continuing to 17 percent by 2053. Net outlays for interest will increase significantly during that period—from 2.5 percent of GDP in 2023 to 6.7 percent in 2053.

The projected budget deficits imply that federal debt will reach 120 percent of GDP in the next decade. Forecasts for 2053 indicate a debt of over 180 percent of GDP by 2053 (CBO 2023a, 2023b and associated downloadable data tables; and authors' calculations). The interest payment required to fund this debt would exceed all mandatory spending other than for the major healthcare programs and Social Security by 2027, all discretionary outlays by 2047, and all spending on Social Security by 2051.

Figure 9.9 shows that spending on the major healthcare programs and interest account for the overall growth in federal outlays in the next three decades. Under current policies, budget forecasts estimate that the share of federal outlays allocated to major health programs will grow by 11 percentage points over the next three decades. Estimates place the share of outlays devoted to interest to increase by 13 percentage points.

Medicare spending growth accounts for more than four-fifths of the forecasted increase in spending on the major healthcare programs over the next thirty years, with Medicare spending equaling 3.1 percent of GDP in 2023 and projected to reach 5.5 percent in 2053 (CBO 2023c, figs. 2–4). Spending on Medicaid and CHIP and the spending related to ACA (e.g., subsidies for

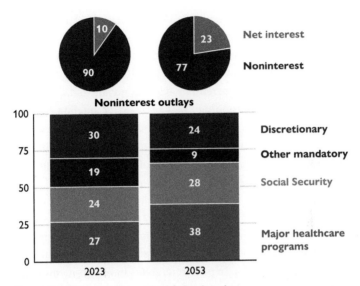

Figure 9.9 Sources of growth in federal outlays

Note: Figures have been rounded, and added sums may not match.

Source: CBO 2023c.

health insurance purchased through the marketplaces) is projected to grow by 0.4 percentage points over the next three decades, starting at 2.7 percent of GDP in 2023 and reaching 3.1 percent in 2053.

Over the past five decades, spending on major healthcare programs has grown faster than the economy, with this trend projected to persist in the foreseeable future. Net federal spending on those programs amounts to 5.8 percent of GDP in 2023 and increases to 8.6 percent in 2053.

Fiscal Need for Major Reforms of Health Policies

Stemming the unsustainable growth in the federal debt and the resulting devouring of federal spending by interest payments requires substantial reforms in federal healthcare funding. While states' total spending on healthcare programs rose over the past decades as a share of GDP, this increase came principally from federal transfers and not from state and local governments' own revenues. Experience suggests that there will be little change in this trend in the upcoming decades. Future increases in states' direct funding might arise in response to federal mandates requiring payments by states for eligibility and services not principally paid for by federal funds—e.g., the federal government could remove its commitment to fully fund the expansion of Medicaid eligibility provided by ACA—but states' balanced budget constraints would effectively prevent such expansions.

The next section summarizes the differences in the health insurance programs and regulations currently in effect in states to provide perspective on the range of options states currently have to innovate and design their own approaches to healthcare funding. This perspective offers a framework for assessing the wisdom of expanding states' role in healthcare financing and regulation in an era when the federal government does not have the fiscal capacity to maintain current policy and is unlikely to have the political capabilities to enact substantial reforms.

Variation across States in Healthcare Funding

While the federal government plays a dominant role in financing and regulating healthcare in the United States, state governments are also important, as seen in previous sections. In principle, states have considerable leeway on healthcare markets, including significant issues such as what services insurance policies are required to cover, who is eligible for public insurance, and other vital topics. However, federal law considerably constrains state power and thus often limits or preempts the range of state authority in these areas.

This section surveys three significant areas of state decision making on healthcare: (1) the administration of the Medicaid and CHIP programs; (2) the administration of the ACA; and (3) the regulation of private insurance and healthcare service organizations. Despite the potentially expansive scope of state activities, the state's role in healthcare—at least regarding healthcare financing—is surprisingly limited relative to the role played by the federal government and the private sector.

Overview of State Differences in Medicaid and CHIP

States have considerable freedom of action in the administration of the Medicaid program in some aspects, less so in others. Medicaid covers a range of healthcare services, such as primary and preventive care, hospital care, prescription drugs, long-term care, and dental and vision care for children. The benefits and costs of Medicaid vary by state and eligibility group, but they must meet certain federal standards of adequacy and affordability. The 2010 expansion of Medicaid under the ACA allowed states to cover adults with incomes up to 138 percent of the federal poverty level (FPL), or about $17,000 for an individual in 2021. However, not every state has opted to expand Medicaid coverage under ACA's provisions.

CHIP is a critical element of the healthcare safety net in the United States. Like Medicaid, CHIP is a federal-state partnership. It provides health insurance coverage to low-income children who are not eligible for Medicaid but whose families cannot afford private insurance. Also, like Medicaid, the CHIP program covers a comprehensive set of services, such as preventive care, immunizations, hospital care, dental care, vision care, and mental health services. While CHIP eligibility, benefits, and costs vary by state, the federal government limits state variation by requiring that each state's CHIP program meets specific federal standards.

The remainder of this section discusses some critical moving parts of the Medicaid and CHIP programs, emphasizing the aspects that vary the most across states. These indicate the range and directions of experimentation with these programs that the federal government permits states to conduct under current law. First is a discussion of different types of healthcare organizations authorized by Medicaid programs—independent physician groups and hospitals paid via a traditional fee-for-service system, managed care organizations paid via a capitation arrangement, and a variation on managed care organizations called primary-care case management. The following section discusses variations in state administration of Medicaid nursing home services for the elderly. The last section discusses state variation in CHIP eligibility.

States' Use of Medicaid Managed Care

Medicaid managed care delivery is a model of providing healthcare services to Medicaid beneficiaries through contracts with private managed care organizations (MCOs) that assume the risk and responsibility of coordinating and paying for the care of their enrollees. Medicaid managed care delivery has grown significantly in the past decades as states have sought to improve access, quality, and efficiency of care for their Medicaid populations while containing costs. The number of states that use Medicaid managed care delivery has increased from twenty-seven in 1999 to forty in 2019. The types of managed care arrangements that states use vary, but the most common are comprehensive risk-based MCOs, which cover a broad range of physical and behavioral health services for a fixed monthly payment per enrollee.

The proportion of Medicaid beneficiaries enrolled in Medicaid managed care delivery increased from 57 percent in 2008 to 69 percent in 2018. The enrollment varies by state, eligibility group, and service type, but most children, adults, and pregnant women are enrolled in comprehensive risk-based

MCOs. At the same time, the elderly and disabled are more likely to be enrolled in fee-for-service (FFS) or other arrangements. The spending on Medicaid managed care delivery has increased from $92 billion in 2008 to $308 billion in 2018. The spending accounts for about half of the total Medicaid spending and varies by state, eligibility group, and service type. The spending growth reflects the expansion of enrollment, benefits, and payment rates for Medicaid managed care delivery.

Table 9.1 displays the proportion of Medicaid enrollees in each state in 2021 who receive care through a comprehensive managed care plan or through a primary-care case management organization (PCCM); the remainder enroll through a more traditional FFS arrangement and may also have coverage through limited benefit plans that cover, for instance, dental care and other ancillary healthcare expenses. A PCCM is a type of managed care

Table 9.1 State variation in Medicaid managed care

State	% in comprehensive MCO	% in PCCM
Alabama	0.0	79.3
Alaska	—	—
Arizona	80.0	—
Arkansas	4.7	42.4
California	82.4	—
Colorado	10.6	84.3
Connecticut	—	—
DC	81.1	—
Delaware	87.1	—
Florida	78.3	—
Georgia	72.1	—
Hawaii	100.0	—
Idaho	5.6	80.8
Illinois	75.4	—
Indiana	78.8	—
Iowa	93.9	—
Kansas	88.1	—
Kentucky	89.4	—
Louisiana	85.3	—

Table 9.1 (continued)

State	% in comprehensive MCO	% in PCCM
Maine	—	68.9
Maryland	85.4	—
Massachusetts	40.5	26.9
Michigan	100.0	—
Minnesota	86.7	—
Mississippi	61.2	—
Missouri	74.2	—
Montana	—	79.2
Nebraska	99.6	—
Nevada	75.6	—
New Hampshire	91.3	—
New Jersey	96.2	—
New Mexico	83.0	—
New York	75.2	—
North Carolina	60.6	20.3
North Dakota	27.0	41.8
Ohio	85.9	—
Oklahoma	0.1	58.4
Oregon	85.8	—
Pennsylvania	93.9	—
Rhode Island	84.6	—
South Carolina	66.6	0.1
South Dakota	—	61.1
Tennessee	92.9	—
Texas	81.7	—
Utah	82.9	—
Vermont	68.5	—
Virginia	91.3	—
Washington	88.3	0.2
West Virginia	81.0	—
Wisconsin	69.1	—
Wyoming	—	—

Source: MACPAC 2023, Exhibit 29, "Percentage of Medicaid Enrollees in Managed Care by State."

arrangement in the Medicaid program that provides coordinated and comprehensive care to Medicaid beneficiaries through a primary-care provider (PCP). A PCP is a physician, nurse practitioner, or other healthcare professional who serves as the main point of contact for the beneficiary's healthcare needs. The PCP is responsible for providing preventive and primary-care services, making referrals to specialists and other providers, and overseeing the quality and utilization of care. The PCP receives a monthly fee from the state for each beneficiary enrolled in their practice, in addition to the fee-for-service payments for the services they provide.

A PCCM differs from a managed care organization, which is a private entity that contracts with the state to provide a full range of healthcare services to Medicaid beneficiaries for a fixed monthly payment per enrollee. A PCCM is usually less restrictive and costly than an MCO but may offer fewer benefits and less care coordination. The availability and features of PCCMs vary by state, depending on their policy goals and operational capacities.

Differences in Medicaid Nursing Home Benefits for the Elderly

While Medicare provides comprehensive financing of healthcare services for the elderly, including doctors, hospitals, and prescription drugs, it does not provide payments for long-term nursing home care. Instead, nursing home benefits are one of the long-term care services that Medicaid covers for elderly people who qualify for the program. States vary in how they provide nursing home benefits, including eligibility criteria, availability of nursing home beds, reimbursement rates, and support for managed care as a vehicle to pay for nursing home benefits.

The eligibility criteria for nursing home benefits   States have different income and asset limits, functional and medical needs assessments, and spousal impoverishment protections for determining who qualifies for nursing home benefits under Medicaid. For example, some states use the federal minimum income limit ($2,382 per month for an individual in 2021), while others use higher or lower limits. Some states also have more or less stringent criteria for assessing the level of care needed for nursing home admission.

The availability and quality of nursing home beds   States have different supply and demand factors that affect the availability and quality of nursing home beds for Medicaid beneficiaries. For example, states vary in the number of nursing home beds per elderly resident and the quality ratings of nursing homes. Some states also have moratoriums or certificate-of-need laws that restrict the expansion or entry of new nursing homes.

The reimbursement rates and policies for nursing homes States have different methods and levels of reimbursing nursing homes for providing care to Medicaid beneficiaries. For example, some states use case-mix systems that adjust payments based on the complexity of residents, while others use flat rates or other systems. States vary in Medicaid daily payments to nursing homes, incentive payments, quality adjustments, and supplemental payments.

The use of managed care or waiver programs for nursing home benefits States have different approaches to delivering and financing nursing home benefits through managed care or waiver programs that aim to improve care coordination, quality, and efficiency. For example, some states contract with managed care organizations that assume the risk and responsibility of providing nursing home benefits to Medicaid beneficiaries, while others use fee-for-service or other arrangements. Some states also apply for waivers from the federal government that allow them to provide home and community-based services as an alternative to nursing home care for eligible beneficiaries.

Differences in CHIP Eligibility

Rules for children to be eligible for the CHIP program vary across states, depending on their income thresholds, enrollment caps, waiting periods, and other criteria. Generally, states can cover children up to age nineteen with family incomes up to 200 percent of the federal poverty level, or about $53,000 for a family of four in 2021. However, some states have higher or lower income limits, ranging from 133 percent to 400 percent of the FPL. Some states also have CHIP programs covering pregnant women, parents, and adults.

The benefits and costs of CHIP also vary across states, but they must meet certain federal standards. CHIP benefits must include a comprehensive set of services, such as preventive care, immunizations, hospital care, dental care, vision care, and mental health services. CHIP costs must be affordable and cannot exceed 5 percent of the family's income. States can charge premiums, copayments, or deductibles for CHIP enrollees, depending on their income and the type of services they use.

Table 9.2 displays the income eligibility levels for families to qualify for the CHIP program in 2021 in each state. These ranges are shown as a proportion of the federal poverty level. For instance, "100–125 percent" means that a family would qualify for CHIP if its income was between 100 percent and 125 percent of the federal poverty level. Under CHIP, states can implement Medicaid expansion, separate CHIP, or a combination program. Ten states (Alaska, Hawaii, Maryland, New Hampshire, New Mexico, North Dakota, Ohio, South Carolina, Vermont, and Wyoming) and the District of Columbia use Medicaid expansion, and two states (Connecticut and Washington) use separate CHIP. Thirty-eight states use combination programs, although some of these are combination programs solely due to the transition of children in families with income less than or equal to 133 percent FPL from separate CHIP to Medicaid. In five states with combination programs (Michigan, Minnesota, Nebraska, Oklahoma, and Rhode Island), separate CHIP coverage is only through the unborn child option. This option makes children eligible for CHIP even while in their mother's womb, and it is especially important for children born to undocumented immigrant mothers who may themselves not qualify for Medicaid.

Under Medicaid-funded coverage, there is no lower threshold for income eligibility. The eligibility levels listed in table 9.2 are the highest income levels under which each age group of children is covered under the Medicaid state plan. The eligibility levels listed under CHIP-funded Medicaid coverage are the income levels to which Medicaid has expanded using CHIP funds, which became available when Congress authorized CHIP in 1997. For states that set different CHIP-funded eligibility levels for children ages six to thirteen and fourteen to eighteen, this table shows only the levels for children ages six to thirteen. In addition, Section 2105(g) of the act permits eleven qualifying states to use CHIP funds to pay the difference between the regular Medicaid matching rate and the enhanced CHIP matching rate for Medicaid-enrolled, Medicaid-financed uninsured children whose family income exceeds 133 percent FPL (not separately noted on this table).

Differences in Affordable Care Act

While the ACA is a federal law, it relies heavily on decisions by states to implement it. As with Medicaid and CHIP, though, the range of options the federal government permits states to make is limited. A significant exception to this statement is that—due to a decision by the US Supreme Court—states have the option not to implement ACA's expansion of Medicaid eligibility for

Table 9.2 CHIP eligibility thresholds as a percentage of the federal poverty level

| State | CHIP program type | M-CHIP (Medicaid expansion CHIP) | | | Separate CHIP for uninsured children age 0–18 | |
		Infants under age 1	Age 1–5	Age 6–18	Birth through age 18	Unborn children
Alabama	Combination	—	—	107–141	312	—
Alaska	Medicaid expansion	159–203	159–203	124–203	—	—
Arizona	Combination	—	—	104–133	200	—
Arkansas	Combination	—	—	107–142	211	209
California	Combination	208–261	142–261	108–261	—	317
Colorado	Combination	—	—	108–142	260	—
Connecticut	Separate	—	—	—	318	—
DC	Combination	194–212	—	110–133	212	—
Delaware	Medicaid expansion	206–319	146–319	112–319	—	—
Florida	Combination	192–206	—	112–133	—	—
Georgia	Combination	—	—	113–133	247	—
Hawaii	Medicaid expansion	191–308	139–308	105–308	—	—
Idaho	Combination	—	—	107–133	185	—
Illinois	Combination	—	—	108–142	313	208
Indiana	Combination	157–208	141–158	106–158	250	—
Iowa	Combination	240–375	—	122–167	302	—
Kansas	Combination	—	—	113–133	225	—

(continued)

Table 9.2 (continued)

State	CHIP program type	M-CHIP (Medicaid expansion CHIP)			Separate CHIP for uninsured children age 0–18	
		Infants under age 1	Age 1–5	Age 6–18	Birth through age 18	Unborn children
Kentucky	Combination	—	142–159	109–159	213	—
Louisiana	Combination	142–212	142–212	108–212	250	209
Maine	Combination	—	140–157	132–157	208	—
Maryland	Medicaid expansion	194–317	138–317	109–317	—	—
Massachusetts	Combination	185–200	133–150	114–150	300	200
Michigan	Combination	195–212	143–212	109–212	—	195
Minnesota	Combination	275–283	—	—	—	278
Mississippi	Combination	—	—	107–133	209	—
Missouri	Combination	—	148–150	110–150	300	300
Montana	Combination	—	—	109–143	261	—
Nebraska	Combination	162–213	145–213	109–213	—	197
Nevada	Combination	—	—	122–133	200	—
New Hampshire	Medicaid expansion	196–318	196–318	196–318	—	—
New Jersey	Combination	—	—	107–142	350	—
New Mexico	Medicaid expansion	200–300	200–300	138–240	—	—
New York	Combination	—	—	110–149	400	—

Table 9.2 (continued)

State	CHIP program type	M-CHIP (Medicaid expansion CHIP)			Separate CHIP for uninsured children age 0–18	
		Infants under age 1	Age 1–5	Age 6–18	Birth through age 18	Unborn children
North Carolina	Combination	194–210	141–210	107–133	211	—
North Dakota	Medicaid expansion	147–170	147–170	111–170	—	—
Ohio	Medicaid expansion	141–206	141–206	107–206	—	—
Oklahoma	Combination	169–205	151–205	115–205	—	205
Oregon	Combination	133–185	—	100–133	300	185
Pennsylvania	Combination	—	—	119–133	314	—
Rhode Island	Combination	190–261	142–261	109–261	—	253
South Carolina	Medicaid expansion	194–208	143–208	107–208	—	—
South Dakota	Combination	147–182	147–182	111–182	204	133
Tennessee	Combination	—	—	109–133	250	250
Texas	Combination	—	—	109–133	201	202
Utah	Combination	—	—	105–133	200	—
Vermont	Medicaid expansion	237–312	237–312	237–312	—	—
Virginia	Combination	—	—	109–143	200	—
Washington	Separate	—	—	—	312	193
West Virginia	Combination	—	—	108–133	300	—
Wisconsin	Combination	—	—	101–151	301	301
Wyoming	Medicaid expansion	154–200	154–200	119–200	—	—

Source: MACPAC 2023, Exhibit 35, "Medicaid and CHIP Income Eligibility Levels as a Percentage of the FPL for Children and Pregnant Women by State."

certain low-income individuals. This section discusses four additional aspects with important state inputs: Section 1332 waivers under ACA, which gives states some options for the administration of ACA; the state operation of ACA insurance exchange markets; state-sponsored "public option" insurance plans offered on these markets; and state actions to increase the availability of ACA health insurance plans for rural residents.

States' Use of Section 1332 Waivers under ACA

A Section 1332 waiver is a provision of ACA that allows states to apply for a waiver of certain requirements of the law and implement alternative strategies for providing health insurance coverage to their residents. These waivers aim to enable states to pursue innovative and flexible approaches that are at least as comprehensive, affordable, and accessible as ACA and do not increase the federal deficit. Some examples of policies that states have implemented or proposed under Section 1332 waivers are reinsurance programs, state-based subsidies, basic health programs, and waivers of the small business health options program.

Some limitations exist on what policies states can implement under Section 1332 waivers. According to ACA, states can only request waivers of certain provisions of the law, such as the individual and employer mandates, the essential health benefits, the premium tax credits and cost-sharing reductions, the marketplaces, and the metal tiers of coverage (bronze, silver, gold, and platinum). States cannot waive other consumer protections, such as the guarantee issue, rating rules, and the prohibition on preexisting condition exclusions. States must also enact a law authorizing actions under the waiver before applying for federal approval. Additionally, states must demonstrate that their waiver proposals meet the following four criteria, known as the guardrails:

- *Coverage must be comprehensive.* States must provide coverage at least as comprehensive as the essential health benefits required under ACA.
- *Coverage must be affordable.* States must provide coverage that is at least as affordable as what would be provided under ACA, considering premiums, deductibles, copayments, and other out-of-pocket costs.
- *A comparable number of people must have coverage.* States must ensure that at least an equivalent number of residents have health insurance coverage under the waiver as would have coverage without it.

- *The waiver must not increase the federal deficit.* States must show that their waiver will not increase the federal deficit over the waiver period (which can be up to five years) or over the ten-year budget plan submitted by the state.

Examples of policies that states have implemented under Section 1332 waivers include the following programs.

Reinsurance programs Several states have established reinsurance programs to help lower premiums and stabilize the individual health insurance market. Table 9.3 provides a list of states with such programs. Reinsurance programs provide payments to insurers for high-cost enrollees, reducing the risk and uncertainty that insurers face. These states have received federal approval to use a portion of the savings from lower marketplace subsidies (due to lower premiums) to help fund their reinsurance programs, a system known as pass-through funding.

Table 9.3 State reinsurance programs, as of July 2022

State	Effective years	Notes
Alaska	2018–22	On March 17, 2022, Alaska submitted a Section 1332 waiver extension application to extend its currently approved waiver. The Departments are reviewing the extension application and the public comment period ended on May 18, 2022.
Colorado	2023–27	On June 23, 2022, CMS approved Colorado's request to amend its State Innovation Waiver under Section 1332 of ACA. This approval is effective from January 1, 2023, through December 31, 2027.
Delaware	2020–24	
Georgia	2022–26	On April 29, 2022, the Departments sent a letter to Georgia informing the State that the departments were suspending Part II of Georgia's Section 1332 waiver, the Georgia Access Model, until certain requirements are met.

(continued)

Table 9.3 (continued)

State	Effective years	Notes
Idaho		On May 5, 2022, Idaho submitted a Section 1332 waiver application. The Departments are reviewing the waiver application, and the public comment period ended on July 3, 2022.
Maine	2019–23	On February 10, 2022, Maine submitted a Section 1332 waiver amendment application to amend its currently approved waiver. The amendment would extend its current reinsurance program to a pooled individual and small group market and transition to a retrospective claims cost-based reinsurance program. The Departments are reviewing the waiver. The public comment period ended on April 26, 2022.
Maryland	2019–23	
Minnesota	2018–22	On May 12, 2022, Minnesota submitted a Section 1332 waiver extension application to extend its currently approved waiver. CMS is reviewing the extension application, and the public comment period ended on July 3, 2022.
Montana	2020–24	
New Hampshire	2021–25	
New Jersey	2019–23	
North Dakota	2020–24	
Oregon	2018–22	On March 31, 2022, Oregon submitted a Section 1332 waiver extension application to its currently approved waiver. The Departments are reviewing the extension application and the public comment period ended on June 4, 2022.
Pennsylvania	2021–25	
Rhode Island	2020–24	
Virginia	2023–27	The Departments approved Virginia's waiver application on May 18, 2022.
Wisconsin	2019–23	

Note: The "Departments" are the US Department of Health and Human Services and the Department of the Treasury.

Source: CMS 2022.

State-based subsidies   A few states, such as California and Vermont, have created state-based subsidies to supplement the federal marketplace subsidies and make coverage more affordable for low- and moderate-income consumers. These states have also received pass-through funding to offset some of the costs of their state-based subsidies.

Basic Health Program (BHP)   Minnesota and New York have established BHPs to provide coverage to low-income residents who are not eligible for Medicaid but would otherwise qualify for marketplace subsidies. BHPs offer standardized plans with lower premiums and cost sharing than marketplace plans. These states have also received pass-through funding equal to 95 percent of the federal marketplace subsidies that BHP enrollees would have received if they had enrolled in marketplace plans.

Waiver of Small Business Health Options Program (SHOP)   Hawaii has waived the requirement to establish a SHOP, the marketplace for small businesses, because it has a long-standing state law requiring employers to offer their employees health insurance. Hawaii has also received pass-through funding equal to the amount of small business tax credits that would have been available under ACA.

State-Run ACA Insurance Exchange Marketplaces

A federally facilitated marketplace (FFM) is a health insurance marketplace operated by the federal government through the website HealthCare.gov. A state-based marketplace (SBM) is a health insurance marketplace operated by a state through its own website. Both types of marketplaces are created under ACA to provide consumers with access to affordable and comprehensive health insurance plans. Table 9.4 provides a list of which states have federally run exchanges and which states have state-run exchanges. The table also lists the average number of insurance providers in rural areas in 2020; many states have only a single plan available. For every plan sold in the ACA health insurance exchanges, the ACA requires that the medical loss ratio of plans be at least 80 percent. This means that, at most, 20 percent of health plan premiums are permitted to be spent on nonmedical reimbursement items such as administrative costs, profits, etc.

The main difference between an FFM and an SBM is each state's level of control and flexibility over its marketplace. States that choose to operate their own SBMs can tailor their marketplaces to meet their specific needs and

Table 9.4 Exchange features by state

State	Exchange type	Average number of issuers in rural areas, PY2020
Alabama	Federally facilitated marketplace	1
Alaska	Federally facilitated marketplace	1
Arizona	Federally facilitated marketplace	2
Arkansas	State-based marketplace, federal platform	4
California	State-based marketplace	2
Colorado	State-based marketplace	4
Connecticut	State-based marketplace	4
DC	State-based marketplace	N/A
Delaware	Federally facilitated marketplace	N/A
Florida	Federally facilitated marketplace	3
Georgia	Federally facilitated marketplace	2
Hawaii	Federally facilitated marketplace	2
Idaho	State-based marketplace	5
Illinois	Federally facilitated marketplace	2
Indiana	Federally facilitated marketplace	2
Iowa	Federally facilitated marketplace	2
Kansas	Federally facilitated marketplace	3
Kentucky	State-based marketplace	2
Louisiana	Federally facilitated marketplace	3
Maine	State-based marketplace	3
Maryland	State-based marketplace	2
Massachusetts	State-based marketplace	8
Michigan	Federally facilitated marketplace	4
Minnesota	State-based marketplace	4
Mississippi	Federally facilitated marketplace	3
Missouri	Federally facilitated marketplace	3
Montana	Federally facilitated marketplace	3
Nebraska	Federally facilitated marketplace	2
Nevada	State-based marketplace	3
New Hampshire	Federally facilitated marketplace	3
New Jersey	State-based marketplace	N/A

Table 9.4 *(continued)*

State	Exchange type	Average number of issuers in rural areas, PY2020
New Mexico	State-based marketplace	5
New York	State-based marketplace	7
North Carolina	Federally facilitated marketplace	2
North Dakota	Federally facilitated marketplace	3
Ohio	Federally facilitated marketplace	5
Oklahoma	Federally facilitated marketplace	2
Oregon	State-based marketplace, federal platform	6
Pennsylvania	State-based marketplace	6
Rhode Island	State-based marketplace	N/A
South Carolina	Federally facilitated marketplace	4
South Dakota	Federally facilitated marketplace	2
Tennessee	Federally facilitated marketplace	3
Texas	Federally facilitated marketplace	2
Utah	Federally facilitated marketplace	3
Vermont	State-based marketplace	2
Virginia	State-based marketplace, federal platform	2
Washington	State-based marketplace	3
West Virginia	Federally facilitated marketplace	3
Wisconsin	Federally facilitated marketplace	4
Wyoming	Federally facilitated marketplace	1

Sources: (Column 2) KFF 2024; (column 3) CMS 2023a.

preferences, such as setting their own open enrollment periods, establishing their own eligibility and enrollment systems, certifying their own qualified health plans, conducting their own consumer outreach and assistance, and implementing their own policies and innovations to improve access and affordability. States that use the FFM rely on the federal government to perform most of these functions, although they can still regulate their insurance markets and assist consumers with enrollment.

One example of an option that the federal government has left open to states that operate their own ACA marketplace is that they are permitted flexibility over open enrollment periods. These are the time frames when individuals can enroll in or change their health insurance plans through the marketplaces created by ACA. The federal open enrollment period for 2022 coverage ran from November 1, 2021, to January 15, 2022. However, states that operate their own marketplaces have the flexibility to extend their open enrollment periods beyond the federal deadline. States differ in how long and when they extend their open enrollment periods, depending on their policy goals and operational capacities.

State-Run "Public Option" Insurance Plan Offered on ACA Exchange

A public option is a health insurance plan offered by the government, alongside private plans, on the health insurance marketplaces created by ACA. The public option aims to give consumers more choice, competition, and affordability in the health insurance market. ACA legislation itself does not provide financing or authorization for a federal public option, but several states have passed legislation to offer one. As of 2022, three states provide a public option on their ACA health insurance markets:

- *Colorado*: The state's public option, known as the Colorado Option, is a standardized plan offered by private insurers but regulated by the state. The plan has lower premiums and cost sharing than other plans on the marketplace and covers essential health benefits, preventive services, and primary care. The state also sets reimbursement rates for providers and hospitals participating in the plan.
- *Nevada*: The state's public option, known as the Nevada Public Option, is a plan offered by private insurers that contract with the state's Medicaid managed care organizations. The plan has lower premiums and cost sharing than other plans on the marketplace and covers essential health benefits, preventive services, and behavioral health. The state also sets reimbursement rates for providers and hospitals participating in the plan.
- *Washington*: The state's public option, known as Cascade Care, is a set of standardized plans offered by private insurers but administered by the state. The plans have lower premiums and cost sharing than other plans on the marketplace and cover essential health benefits, preventive services, and dental and vision care for children. The state also sets reimbursement rates for providers and hospitals participating in the plans.

Challenges with Rural Provider Networks

A major structural problem for the states in implementing ACA is the thinness of rural markets for health insurance. It is often difficult for states to guarantee that at least one insurer offers a plan on ACA exchanges for rural areas. One of the main challenges for insurers to compete in rural areas is the lack of provider networks, which are essential for negotiating lower prices and ensuring access to care. Rural areas often have fewer providers, higher costs, and lower quality care than urban areas, making it hard for insurers to attract and retain customers. Additionally, rural areas have lower population density and higher rates of poverty, chronic conditions, and uninsurance, increasing insurers' risk and uncertainty.

As a result, some rural areas have experienced insurer exits or limited choices on ACA exchanges, especially in states that have not expanded Medicaid. To address this challenge, some states have encouraged insurer participation and competition in rural areas through measures such as providing reinsurance programs, expanding Medicaid, creating regional or statewide rating areas, and facilitating provider collaboration. Table 9.4 lists the average number of insurers in rural areas by state as of 2020.

State Insurance Adequacy Regulation

Beyond Medicaid and ACA, states nominally have regulatory authority over healthcare provision. For instance, states are responsible for oversight over the licensing of physicians, the malpractice system, hospital quality, and a vast array of other topics. Most of these options, though, have only a marginal or indirect effect on macro trends in healthcare financing. While regulation of private insurance market products, in principle, could provide an avenue for states to have an appreciable impact on state-level macro health spending, in fact, a federal law—the Employee Retirement Income Security Act (ERISA) of 1974—preempts the ability of states to pass laws or regulations that impact employer-provided health insurance. This section describes some states' experiments with mandating health insurance coverage and how ERISA constrains state actions in insurance markets.

States' Mandated Insurance Coverage

Five states (California, Massachusetts, New Jersey, Rhode Island, and Vermont) and Washington, DC, mandate insurance coverage for individuals and families. Except for Vermont, all of them financially penalize residents who do not have coverage for at least part of the year. The amount of the penalty in the states depends on a family's size and income, and it is typically capped at the price of bronze plans available for purchase in the ACA exchanges in the state. The idea is that the penalty will push families to buy insurance, rather than pay the equivalent amount in penalties. Table 9.5 lists the states that mandate that individuals be covered by health insurance.

Table 9.5 States mandating health insurance coverage

State	Effective date	Penalty structure
California	January 1, 2020	CA residents without coverage or an exemption will pay a penalty when filing state tax returns. The penalty will be the higher of either: • A flat amount based on the number of people in the tax household ($900 per adult and $450 per dependent child under 18), or • 2.5% of the amount of gross income that exceeds the filing threshold requirements based on the tax filing status and number of dependents.
DC	January 1, 2019	Citizens and legal residents are required to have health insurance, with exceptions for individuals experiencing financial hardship. The penalty will be the higher of either: • A flat dollar amount ($745 per person and $375.50 per child under the age of 18), or • 2.5% of household income that is over the federal tax filing threshold. *There is a maximum tax penalty for not having coverage in DC: in 2024, this amount is $2,235/year per person; for households with more than one person without coverage, it is multiplied by the number of people in the household without coverage up to a maximum of 5.
Massachusetts	January 1, 2019	Residents must have minimum creditable coverage or pay the penalty, with exceptions for individuals experiencing hardship.

Table 9.5 (continued)

State	Effective date	Penalty structure
Massachusetts (continued)		The penalty will be: • 150% to 300% FPL: half of the lowest-priced enrollee premium that could be charged to an individual at the corresponding income level for the tax year. • Above 300% FPL: half of the lowest-priced individual bronze premium. • For married couples, the amount will equal the sum of individual penalties. *Penalty applies only to adults. No penalty if income is at or below 150% FLP.
New Jersey	January 1, 2019	Unless exempt, residents must have health insurance coverage throughout the year. Residents who do not have coverage must pay a penalty, which depends on the family size and income and is "capped at the statewide average annual premium for Bronze Health Plans in New Jersey." In 2024, for an individual taxpayer, the minimum penalty was $695 and the maximum penalty $3,960. For a family with two adults and three dependents earning $200,000 per year or less, the minimum penalty was $2,351 and the maximum penalty $4,500. *The penalty amount is capped at the cost of the statewide average annual premium for bronze plans per person.
Rhode Island	January 1, 2020	All residents are required to have qualifying health coverage unless exempt. The penalty will be the higher of either: • A flat dollar amount ($695 per person and $347.50 per child under the age of 18), or • 2.5% of modified adjusted gross income that is over the federal tax filing threshold *The maximum penalty can be no more than the average bronze plan amount as determined by HealthSource RI. For those with partial-year coverage, the fee is one-twelfth of the annual amount for each month without coverage. There is no penalty for people who are uninsured for less than three consecutive months.

(continued)

Table 9.5 (continued)

State	Effective date	Penalty structure
Vermont	January 1, 2020	Residents must report if they had health insurance (including Medicaid and Medicare) for each month of the year when filing a state tax return.
		*There is no cash penalty for not having health insurance.

Sources: (California) Franchise Tax Board 2024; DC Health Link 2024; Commonwealth of Massachusetts 2024; State of New Jersey 2023; (Rhode Island) HealthSource RI 2024; Vermont Health Connect 2024.

ERISA and State Regulation of Private Health Insurance

ERISA stands for the Employee Retirement Income Security Act of 1974, a federal law that regulates employee benefit plans, including health insurance plans, sponsored by private employers. ERISA preempts state laws relating to employee benefit plans, meaning states cannot impose additional or conflicting requirements on these plans.

One of the implications of ERISA preemption is that states cannot mandate healthcare benefits provided by employer-sponsored health insurance plans within the state. For example, suppose a state requires health insurance plans to cover a specific service, such as infertility treatment or mental health counseling. In that case, this requirement does not apply to employer-sponsored plans that ERISA governs. This preemption limits the ability of states to regulate the quality and scope of healthcare coverage for millions of workers and their dependents enrolled in these plans.

However, some exceptions and limitations exist in ERISA preemption. For instance, ERISA does not preempt state laws that regulate insurance companies, such as licensing, solvency, and consumer protection laws. Therefore, states can still impose benefit mandates on health insurance policies sold by insurers to employers or individuals, as long as these policies are not self-funded by the employers. Self-funded plans are those where the employer assumes the financial risk of paying for the healthcare claims of its employees rather than purchasing an insurance policy from an insurer. Self-funded plans are more common among large employers who can spread the risk among a large pool of employees.

Another exception to ERISA preemption is ACA's essential health benefits (EHB) requirement, which applies to all non-grandfathered health insurance plans in the individual and small group markets, regardless of whether they are sold on or off the exchanges. The EHB requirement establishes a minimum set of ten categories of benefits that these plans must cover, such as ambulatory care, hospitalization, prescription drugs, maternity and newborn care, and preventive services. States can also choose to define their own EHB benchmarks within these categories as long as they are at least as comprehensive as the federal default benchmark. However, the EHB requirement does not apply to employer-sponsored plans in the large group market or self-funded plans in any market.

Limited Innovation by States in the Design of Healthcare Policies

While the range of authority that states have over healthcare markets may seem expansive, in fact, from a fiscal perspective the federal government sharply limits the range of policy discretion granted to states. States have most power over the set of people to be covered by public insurance sources and over what sets of services are to be provided to people on public insurance. They have regulatory authority over some aspects of medical practice by physicians and hospitals. But federal law greatly restricts state governments' ability to control private and public healthcare expenditures within their states.

First, federal matching and waiver requirements for Medicaid and CHIP limit states' authority. Medicaid and CHIP are joint federal-state programs. The federal government matches a certain percentage of each state's spending on these programs, depending on the state's per capita income and the eligibility group. The federal government also grants waivers to states that allow them to implement alternative or innovative approaches to provide Medicaid and CHIP services. However, these matching and waiver requirements also constrain the ability of states to design and finance their own Medicaid and CHIP programs, as they have to comply with federal rules and standards.

Relevant to this point is the well-known "flypaper effect." The flypaper effect suggests that a government grant to a recipient state increases local public spending more than an increase in local income of an equivalent size. In other words, money sticks where it hits. For traditional Medicaid, the federal government matches a certain percentage of each state's Medicaid spending, depending on the state's per capita income. The matching rate ranges from 50 percent to 83 percent, averaging 61 percent in 2020. With such high matching rates, states pay a heavy cost for restricting Medicaid eligibility and will be loath to do so unless there is tremendous political pressure (such as faced by some Republican-led states regarding Obamacare's Medicaid expansion—more on that below). And, of course, it may not be wise policy to restrict the set of poor, elderly, disabled, or children who are eligible for public health insurance in the first place.

Second, as discussed previously, federal law limits the ability of states to regulate most employer-provided health insurance plans. ERISA preempts state laws that impose additional or conflicting requirements on these plans, such as benefit mandates, premium taxes, or consumer protections. This limits the ability of states to regulate the quality and scope of healthcare coverage for millions of workers and their dependents enrolled in these plans. It prevents, for instance, states from passing regulations to evaluate the quality and efficiency of care provided in these plans in a bid to reduce expenditures on low-value healthcare.

Finally, while state and federal governments can regulate, fundamental market forces and competition in the healthcare sector play a primary role in healthcare spending outcomes. Healthcare is a market; therefore, the sector is influenced by various market forces and competition factors that affect the supply and demand of healthcare services and products, such as providers, insurers, consumers, employers, pharmaceuticals, medical devices, and technology. The demand for services is affected by demographic realities like the aging of the workforce, the growing number of elderly in the United States, and the high rates of chronic conditions like obesity, diabetes, and heart disease in the population. These factors can affect the prices, quality, utilization, and innovation of healthcare in different ways, depending on each actor's market structure and behavior. States have limited control over these market forces and competition factors, as they may face legal, political, or economic barriers to intervene or influence them.

Policy Options for Addressing the Fiscal Crisis in Public Financing of Healthcare

With the current policies of the public financing of healthcare widely deemed fiscally unsustainable in the next decades, governments must undertake major reforms to resolve the imminent insolvency problems. Reform proposals generally fall into three basic categories: (1) for Medicare, modify payment approaches to stem its excessive growth in federal spending; (2) for health programs with shared federal and state funding, delegate more responsibilities and authorities to states; and (3) for private insurance, relax federal restrictions on health insurance allowing states greater freedom in enabling private insurance to substitute for public funding. The latter two categories involve restructuring the federalist system of health policy toward reducing the federal role. The following discussion summarizes and evaluates features of these three categories of health reform policies.

Policy Approaches for Enhancing Competitiveness in Medicare

As discussed above, the federal government must sharply mitigate the growth in Medicare spending to prevent interest payments on its debt from crowding out considerable shares of spending on all other programs and services. The 2022 *Medicare Trustees Report* posits two principal factors explaining the excessive growth of Medicare healthcare costs in the upcoming decades: (1) increasing enrollment and (2) rising per capita costs. Increasing enrollment reflects an aging population, with no viable policy options available for limiting Medicare eligibility in the near future. Rising per capita costs consist of two components: volume/intensity (i.e., quantity) and price (i.e., per service). Projections attribute the higher per capita costs predominately to greater volume/intensity of services and not to price changes.

A principal motivation underlying proposed Medicare reforms by policymakers is to slow the growth of per capita costs by engaging competitive forces to reshape care delivery. Such policy approaches fall into three main categories: (1) consumer-directed healthcare, (2) competitive bidding of Medicare services, and (3) value-based purchasing (VBP) (i.e., pay for performance). Consumer-directed policies operate on the patient side of the equation, with beneficiaries induced to share in Medicare spending through their decisions to select lower-cost healthcare options. Competitive bidding and VBP policies operate on the provider side, both intended to reduce the per capita Medicare costs. Whereas competitive bidding focuses on introducing market-style competitive forces to lower the price component of per capita costs, VBP targets engaging these forces to lower the volume/intensity component. The following discussion briefly summarizes these three policy reform approaches and their prospects for achieving savings in Medicare spending.

Potential Roles of Consumer-Directed Healthcare

The basic idea motivating greater integration of consumer-directed healthcare policies in Medicare revolves around the vision that patients, faced with exposure to the financial consequences of their decisions, would reduce Medicare spending through diminished use of low-value services and cost-ineffective innovations in healthcare delivery. When beneficiaries have substantial insurance coverage of deductibles and copayments, many experts believe they seek excessive nonemergency and discretionary medical services, driving up Medicare spending.

Advocates of this approach for reducing Medicare spending point to the coverage provisions of Medigap insurance policies in traditional (i.e., FFS) Medicare as a primary culprit in shielding patients from the financial implications of their treatment decisions. The Medicare Payment Advisory Commission (MedPAC) recommended restricting Medigap coverage, citing MedPAC reports (Hogan 2009, 2014) that argued that eliminating first-dollar coverage in secondary insurance would yield savings in Medicare spending. Legislation implemented these recommendations in 2015, and starting in 2020, Medigap plans sold to new Medicare enrollees no longer covered the deductible in Medicare for physician and outpatient services.

Critics of the effectiveness of this approach point out that most Medicare spending occurs for beneficiaries with costs far beyond the maximum out-of-pocket (MOOP) thresholds currently mandated by the Centers for Medicare & Medicaid Services (CMS) for Medigap plans. The highest-cost users in Medicare FFS—constituting less than 10 percent of beneficiaries, with total annual per capita medical costs exceeding $37,400 in 2019—accounted for more than two-thirds of total Medicare costs and even a larger share of Medicare outlays covering the federally insured share of these costs. The lowest-cost two-thirds of beneficiaries—with total annual per capita medical costs below $3,500 in 2023—accounted for only 5 percent of total Medicare FFS medical costs and even a smaller share of Medicare outlays.

Medigap plans offer ten standard packages of benefits, with the highest MOOP falling below $7,000 in 2023. High-deductible Medigap plans, with monthly premiums of about $150, offer annual deductibles falling below $3,500. With these levels of MOOPs, the Medicare beneficiaries who account for nearly all Medicare spending face little cost exposure and incentives to save costs.

The same challenges exist in effectuating consumer-directed healthcare forces to save spending in those parts of Medicare associated with managed care. MOOP in Medicare Advantage (MA) could not exceed $8,300 for individuals in 2023. In practically all regions of the country, MA plans exist with MOOPs below $5,000, with no monthly premium beyond that paid to Medicare for discounted cost shares for physician and outpatient services.

Medicare beneficiaries also eligible for Medicaid face no cost sharing in any form. Medicaid pays both the premiums and any cost share not covered by Medicare.

An avenue available in Medigap and MA plans for exposing beneficiaries to the financial costs of their decisions involves offering lower premiums to those enrollees willing to forgo some high-cost delivery selections. However, current CMS regulations rule out such options. Medigap premiums can only depend on beneficiaries' age and not on their prospective health risk (preexisting conditions). While MA premiums can vary to incorporate services supplemental to those in traditional Medicare, MA plans must cover the same range of services available in traditional Medicare, including all varieties of high-cost services. MA premiums paid by individuals do not depend on their age or health circumstances.

Consequently, policy opportunities for adapting Medigap and MA plans to generate savings in Medicare spending through patient financial incentives would necessitate allowing for either (1) considerable increases in MOOPs; or (2) some dependence of premiums on the health risk (preexisting conditions) of insurance enrollees. Given the unlikely prospects of such changes, no effective opportunities exist for exposing high-cost insurance enrollees to the costs of their decision making. Moreover, Medigap plans in traditional Medicare cover less than a third of the Medicare beneficiary population, and much of the remainder faces even less exposure to costs (e.g., beneficiaries with supplementary coverage through Medicaid [duals], VA, or TRICARE).

Potential Roles of Competitive Bidding in Medicare

Advocates for introducing competitive bidding features into Medicare aim to reduce the price-per-service component of per capita Medicare costs. Under current policy, price determination in Medicare's FFS payment systems essentially involves calculating the cost of production and setting prices to cover these imputed costs. Competitive bidding introduces market forces intended to lower prices below these administrative calculations. Establishing competitive bidding in a market requires two essential conditions: (1) products must be well-defined and understood by suppliers and consumers; and (2) the market must embody a competitive environment to achieve lower costs.

Individual Medicare "products" do exist that satisfy the first condition, which policymakers have or could consider for competitive bidding. Medicare already competitively bids such items as durable medical equipment and generic pharmaceuticals (in Part D), which readily satisfy the first criterion cited above. Policymakers might also entertain introducing competitive bidding for such products as lab tests and imaging.

Other potential categories of Medicare "products" include some forms of bundled services representing relatively distinguishable and complete care components. Medicare managed care represents a prominent example, with the bundling constituting the full range of services covered under traditional Medicare. MA plans competitively bid premiums and cost-sharing regimes subject to CMS regulations. Other potential service bundles in traditional Medicare include diagnosis-related groups used by Medicare to pay for the services of acute hospitals. A similar possibility exists in the case of reimbursements to skilled nursing homes, which receive payments depending on the delivery composition of six service bundles (e.g., physical therapy and nursing services).

Serious challenges, however, arise in satisfying the second condition required to establish competitive markets in Medicare. Effective bidding requires a sufficient number of firms (bidders) to avoid collusion and monopolies. Economics describes such a market as having a low concentration ratio of firms—meaning that no firm possesses a high concentration or share of the market.

This condition fails in many Medicare instances for two reasons. First, many of the most expensive medical products and services (e.g., new brand-name drugs) operate under patents, giving innovating firms monopoly rights. Second, in many medical care markets there are few providers offering services. Rural markets typically have one hospital available, and many others have just two or three covering a large service area. Plus, effective competitive bidding implies that one hospital wins and the others lose, which would mean the allocation of all Medicare services for the bid "product" to a single hospital. This winning hospital would need to expand capacities substantially, and losers would essentially no longer serve Medicare beneficiaries for that service and would likely go out of business.

Another factor limiting the promise of competitive bidding in reducing Medicare costs is the fact that Medicare administrative pricing already incorporates a form of competitive bidding in healthcare markets through the commercial insurance side of the market. Statutes and regulations keep Medicare prices for services and products below these unconstrained healthcare prices. Commercial in-network prices already reflect health-organization competition and physician-hospital integration. Studies show that these commercial prices vary considerably across regions, with typical prices far exceeding Medicare FFS prices for many distinct medical procedures. Consequently, such evidence does not support the view that competitive bidding in Medicare would yield lower prices for many medical services.

The Promise of Value-Based Purchasing Policies

Much of the policy reforms in Medicare over the last decade focused on transforming reimbursement in FFS programs to reward healthcare providers for achieving outcomes rather than for the quantities of services (inputs). Broadly labeled value-based purchasing (VBP)—or pay for performance (P4P)—these new reimbursement frameworks aim to pay for "value," defined as the health outcomes and quality achieved relative to the costs of the care. Cost efficiency of care constitutes a significant component of value, with other measures included to track nonmonetary aspects of the quality of care (e.g., mortality, measures of activities of daily living). Currently, VBP payment systems cover all major provider types in Medicare (e.g., hospitals, physicians, nursing homes).

The new design of cost measures conforms to providers' self-view of what constitutes efficient practice, with clear benchmarks guiding clinicians on the steps needed to improve performance and raise their incomes. The cost constructions accumulate claims-based expenses of treatments delivered by providers who are assigned accountability for episodes of care and the costs of services delivered by other providers for care directly clinically related to the accountable providers' treatments. Cost includes treatments directly delivered by the evaluated provider and the cost of care downstream deemed preventable with high-quality original treatment (e.g., hospital readmissions). Providers receive performance scores benchmarked against peer groups performing the same type of care. Achieving high performance requires providers to balance the benefits of their delivered services against the systematic cost savings attained by mitigating costly poor health outcomes in the episode and by coordinating care with other involved providers to keep costs low.

With such cost measures sufficiently weighted in scoring performance, accountable providers can secure higher personal incomes through VBP rewards by generating cost savings across the entire episode of care. Cost savings come from the forgone revenues of other providers who no longer deliver unnecessary services or services arising from poor outcomes (e.g., hospitalizations). Such VBP designs emulate competitive markets for providers treating similar illnesses, with VBP rewards and penalties acting to incentivize the changes in healthcare delivery needed to optimize scores (i.e., achieve lower total costs).

Finally, whereas our exploration of policy opportunities suggests dim prospects for implementing reforms in the consumer-directed and competitive bidding areas to produce impactful savings in Medicare spending, advances and expansions of VBP programs offer a rich set of prospects for supporting significant redesigns of care delivery, promising to save considerable costs. Medicare's VBP programs aim to lower the volume/intensity component of per capita Medicare costs. When tailored appropriately, VBP programs introduce market-style forces in healthcare delivery that penalize waste and encourage care coordination in Medicare, thus saving money. Whereas Medicare payment systems cover service costs, VBP programs value outcomes and can act as pricing systems. Operating like prices, rewards and penalties incentivize healthcare providers to make those changes in practice needed to optimize performance scores. With scoring metrics properly specified, VBP programs can emulate competitive market structures in the healthcare industry.

Delegating More Authority to States for Shared Healthcare Financing

Drawing on the discussion in the previous section, the following subsections explore several reforms in health policies that states might pursue if given an expanded role in financing and regulating their healthcare programs. The existing federal regulatory and funding environment sharply constrains the opportunities for states to innovate and devise policies limiting spending on healthcare. However, commentary in the literature points to a range of reforms that some states would implement if given the opportunity.

The first section discusses options for states to reform their Medicaid offerings, given the constraints and opportunities provided by ACA. Next is a discussion of options states have to restructure and reform ACA health insurance exchange marketplaces, then a discussion of options for states to expand the provider networks available to Medicaid patients, which are quite limited at present in most states. The last section discusses options for states to regulate pharmaceutical offerings and pricing in state Medicaid programs.

Opportunities for States to Reform Medicaid under ACA

One of the most controversial aspects of the ACA was its provision requiring states to expand Medicaid programs to cover low-income adults with incomes up to 138 percent of the federal poverty level, or about $17,000 for an individual in 2021. Unlike the traditional Medicaid program, where eligibility for coverage depends on income, assets, and other criteria, such as family structure, ACA's Medicaid expansion depends only on income relative to the federal poverty level. Under ACA, the federal government covers 90 percent of the cost of expansion, while states cover the remaining

10 percent. However, a 2012 Supreme Court decision made Medicaid expansion optional for states, and as of 2023, twelve states have not adopted it. States can adopt ACA's Medicaid expansion or not as they see fit, though the movement has been in the direction of adoption.

According to the flypaper-effect hypothesis (discussed above), state governments would increase their healthcare spending more when they receive more federal grants than when they have more state income. However, in the case of ACA's Medicaid expansion, some states are reluctant to embrace expansion nearly a full decade after the federal funds became available to do so. Why have some states decided against expanding Medicaid coverage under ACA? Some considerations include:

- *The fiscal impact of expansion*: Some states are concerned about the long-term cost and sustainability of expanding Medicaid, especially in times of economic downturn or uncertainty. Opponents of expansion have expressed worry that even a 10 percent share of expansion costs could strain their budgets and crowd out other spending priorities, such as education, transportation, or public safety. They also worry that the federal government could reduce or eliminate its funding for expansion in the future, leaving them with an unfunded mandate.
- *The political opposition to expansion*: Some states face strong resistance to expanding Medicaid from their governors, legislators, or voters, who are ideologically opposed to ACA or the role of the federal government in healthcare. They view expansion as an endorsement of ACA or a dependency on federal handouts and prefer to pursue their own solutions for healthcare reform. They also distrust the federal government's promises and regulations regarding expansion and fear losing their autonomy and flexibility in managing their Medicaid programs.
- *The alternative approaches to expansion*: Some states are exploring or pursuing other ways to provide healthcare coverage to their low-income populations without fully expanding Medicaid under ACA. For example, some states have applied for or received waivers from the federal government to implement modified versions of expansion, such as imposing premiums, copayments, or work requirements on Medicaid enrollees or using federal funds to purchase private insurance plans for them. Other states have proposed

or enacted state-funded programs offering limited benefits or subsidies toward the purchase of private insurance to certain low-income individuals.

Options for Reforming ACA Marketplace Exchanges

Healthcare exchange marketplaces are online platforms where consumers can compare and purchase health insurance plans that meet the standards and requirements of the ACA. The ACA gives states the option to create and operate their own marketplaces. However, as seen in the third section of this paper, the range of choices available to states to customize marketplaces to local needs is limited under the ACA. Some of the aspects that states can customize include:

- *The design and features of the marketplace website*: States can decide how to present and display information about health plans, such as premiums, benefits, quality ratings, provider networks, and consumer reviews. States can also add tools and resources to help consumers compare and choose plans, such as calculators, decision support tools, chatbots, or videos. States can also integrate their marketplace websites with other state programs or services, such as Medicaid, CHIP, or social services.
- *The outreach and enrollment strategies*: States can decide how to market and promote their marketplace to consumers, such as through advertising, media campaigns, social media, or events. States can also choose how to provide consumer assistance and education, such as through navigators, brokers, agents, call centers, or community organizations. States can also tailor their outreach and enrollment efforts to specific populations or regions, such as rural areas, minority groups, or young adults.
- *The plan management and oversight policies*: States can decide how to certify and regulate health plans that participate in their marketplace, such as by setting standards for network adequacy, benefit design, quality improvement, or consumer protection. States can also decide how to monitor and evaluate health plan performance and compliance, such as by collecting data, conducting audits, imposing sanctions, or resolving disputes.
- *The innovation and experimentation opportunities*: States can apply for waivers from the federal government to implement alternative

or innovative approaches to provide health insurance coverage to their residents through their marketplace. For example, states can use waivers to modify the eligibility criteria, benefit requirements, subsidy structure, or marketplace enrollment periods. States can also use waivers to create public options, reinsurance programs, or other initiatives that aim to improve access, affordability, and quality of health insurance coverage, as discussed above.

While these options may have a considerable impact on the experience of people in accessing and signing up for a health insurance plan in a state's ACA health insurance exchange and may have some marginal impact on the types of plans available, none of these options are likely to make a significant dent on the macro-level fiscal challenges of financing health spending in the United States. None of the alternatives fundamentally change the underlying supply and demand forces determining American health spending.

Options to Expand Provider Networks for Medicaid Enrollees
One of the challenges that Medicaid enrollees face is finding physicians willing to see them and provide them with adequate and timely care. This is partly due to the inadequate provider networks that often exist for Medicaid patients, which limit their access and choice of healthcare providers. Provider networks can vary in size, composition, quality, and geographic distribution, depending on the plan's policies and the market conditions, and many of these depend on state Medicaid policies. The fiscal consequences of inadequate networks are challenging to quantify because inadequate healthcare in the early stages of managing a health condition can sometimes lead to the need for much larger expenditures as the disease progresses.

The primary reason for inadequate provider networks for Medicaid patients is that providers receive lower reimbursement for equivalent services provided to Medicaid patients than they do for other patients with Medicare or private insurance, so physicians are reluctant to participate in Medicaid. Low rates can affect the profitability and sustainability of providers, especially those who serve a large share of Medicaid patients. They can also affect the quality and availability of care, as providers may reduce their services, staff, or equipment.

Another reason physicians are deterred from participating in Medicaid is the administrative burden associated with the program, such as complex billing procedures, extensive documentation requirements, frequent audits, or delayed payments. Administrative burdens can increase the financial and time costs of providing care and reduce the satisfaction and morale of providers.

A third reason provider networks are inadequate for Medicaid patients is the limited supply and uneven distribution of providers across states and regions, especially in rural areas or underserved specialties. Provider shortages can affect the access and quality of care for Medicaid enrollees, as they may face longer wait times, longer travel distances, or referral delays. Provider shortages can also affect health plans' competition and negotiation power, as they may have fewer options or incentives to contract with providers.

States have the flexibility to design and administer their own Medicaid programs within federal guidelines, and they can also apply for waivers to implement innovative or alternative approaches to providing Medicaid services.

Some options that states have to expand the network of doctors and hospitals available to enrollees under the Medicaid program include the following:

Increasing the reimbursement rates for providers who participate in Medicaid One of the main barriers to provider participation in Medicaid is the low payment rates compared to Medicare or private insurance. States can use federal or state funds to raise the rates for certain services, specialties, or regions and incentivize more providers to join or stay in the Medicaid network. For example, some states have increased the rates for primary care, behavioral health, or rural health services.

Implementing alternative payment models for providers who participate in Medicaid Another way to improve provider participation and performance in Medicaid is to change how Medicaid reimburses providers from fee-for-service to value-based payment models. These models reward providers for delivering high-quality, cost-effective, and coordinated care rather than for the volume of services. Some examples of value-based payment models are capitation, shared savings, pay for performance, or bundled payments. These options are discussed in more detail above.

Expanding the scope of practice and roles of nonphysician providers who participate in Medicaid A third option to expand the network of providers in Medicaid is to allow nonphysician providers—such as nurse practitioners, physician assistants, pharmacists, or community health workers—to provide more services and functions within their scope of practice and training. These providers can help increase access, quality, and efficiency of care for Medicaid enrollees, especially in underserved areas or populations. Some examples of expanding the scope of practice and roles of nonphysician providers are allowing them to prescribe medications, order tests, refer patients, or manage chronic conditions.

Altering Regulations of Pharmaceutical Benefits in Medicaid

Medicaid patients sometimes have problems accessing prescription drug medications due to several factors. Perhaps the most important of these is Medicaid's reimbursement rates and policies for pharmacies and drug manufacturers. Payments may be lower than what they receive from other payers, such as Medicare or private insurance. This may affect the availability and affordability of drugs for Medicaid patients, even if their OOP payments for prescription drugs are low, as pharmacies and drug manufacturers may limit their participation.

State Medicaid programs sometimes impose specific rules or restrictions on the use of certain drugs, such as requiring clinical criteria, step therapy, quantity limits, or prior approval before dispensing or covering them. These requirements may delay or deny Medicaid patients' access to needed drugs or create administrative burdens and confusion for them and their providers. Finally, Medicaid patients may have difficulty finding or accessing pharmaceutical providers who will accept their coverage and dispense drugs to them, especially in rural areas or underserved specialties.

Some options where states can regulate Medicaid payments and coverage of prescription drugs include the following:

Setting reimbursement rates for pharmacies that dispense drugs to Medicaid beneficiaries   States can use different methods and levels of payment, such as the actual acquisition cost, the national average drug acquisition cost, or the federal upper limit for generic drugs. States can also adjust the rates based on the type, quantity, or quality of drugs dispensed. All three methods are variations on a theme aimed at setting the prices that Medicaid pays pharmacies based on actual or average costs of drug acquisition by pharmacies themselves.

Negotiating supplemental rebates with drug manufacturers   In addition to the mandatory rebates required by the federal government, states can leverage their purchasing power and formulary management to obtain additional discounts or concessions from drug manufacturers, such as price freezes, volume discounts, or performance-based agreements.

Implementing preferred drug lists or prior authorization policies for specific drugs or classes of drugs   States can use these tools to encourage the use of lower-cost or more effective drugs and to limit the usage of higher-cost or less effective drugs. States can also use these tools to manage the utilization and quality of medications, such as by requiring clinical criteria, step therapy, or quantity limits. Depending on implementation details, these changes may improve policy by focusing limited resources on high-value drugs or they may prevent patients from obtaining medically necessary drugs in a timely way. Sometimes both are true of such programs.

Participating in multistate purchasing pools or arrangements for prescription drugs   States can join forces with other states or entities, such as Medicaid managed care organizations, to increase their bargaining power and achieve economies of scale in purchasing drugs. States can also share information and best practices with other states or entities to improve their drug management strategies.

Allowing States Greater Flexibility in Regulating Private Health Insurance Options

The Employee Retirement Income Security Act (ERISA) is a federal law that sets minimum standards for most retirement and health plans in the private sector. It aims to protect the rights and benefits of employees and their beneficiaries participating in these plans. It also regulates the fiduciaries who manage and control the plan assets and requires them to act in the best interest of the plan participants. ERISA covers various types of plans, such as pensions, 401(k)s, health insurance, disability insurance, and life insurance. ERISA does not apply to plans sponsored by governmental entities, churches, or plans outside the United States. With regard to the topic of our paper, the critical thing to know about ERISA is that it limits the extent to which states can regulate employer-provided health insurance.

ERISA considerably constrains states in serving as laboratories of experimentation to address healthcare financing issues. However, if ERISA provisions governing employer-provided health insurance were relaxed, states could implement various reforms to health insurance markets that are currently preempted or challenged by federal law. Some examples of such reforms that states would likely implement include the following:

State-level employer mandates   States could require employers to offer health insurance coverage to their employees or pay a penalty or a fee to the state. This could increase the coverage and affordability of health insurance for workers and their dependents and reduce the uncompensated care costs for the state, though likely at the cost of higher state taxes. For example, despite the possibility that ERISA might preempt its ability to do so, Massachusetts enacted an employer mandate as part of its 2006 health reform. This reform served as a model for the national ACA, which is not subject to ERISA preemption.

State-level public options   States could create public health insurance plans that compete with private plans offered by employers to employees. Several states offer a publicly administered health insurance product on the state-based ACA marketplaces, as described previously. For example, Washington, Colorado, and Nevada have enacted or proposed public option plans offered by private insurers but regulated by the state.

State-level single-payer systems   States could create universal healthcare systems that provide comprehensive health insurance coverage to all residents through a single public payer that collects taxes and pays providers. For example, Vermont passed single-payer legislation in 2011 but later abandoned it due to fiscal and political challenges.

In addition to policies like these focused on expanded insurance coverage, a relaxation of ERISA would permit states to regulate the quality and pricing of privately provided healthcare services by promulgating standards for the measurement of quality of health services provided by physicians and hospitals, like the episode-based care cost and quality assessment described in the previous discussion.

Consequential Changes Required in the Direction of America's Health Policies

The contemplated reforms in health policies discussed above will not solve the looming fiscal insolvency of public funding confronting America in the coming decades. The necessary reforms will involve substantial alterations in healthcare delivery and a decrease in the per capita consumption of healthcare relative to the paths anticipated, assuming current policies continue to apply. Significant reductions must occur in the growth rate of public spending on healthcare.

A popular set of proposals for reforming health policy in the United States involves restructuring the federalist system to delegate more program design and funding responsibilities to state and local governments. These proposals embody combinations of two essential elements: (1) decoupling states from federal regulations that restrict reform options; and (2) providing federal funding that minimally distorts states' decisions relating to health program designs and operations.

Regarding the decoupling of federal regulations, the federal government invariably imposes restrictions on federal healthcare funding to states—restrictions that rigorously constrain states' range of actions in designing and managing their programs. Federal authorities mandate state aid programs to operate according to federal preferences and force states to increase spending on activities that federal policymakers deem important. Federal aid programs tend to be poorly managed by federal and state governments, with state policymakers unable to manage programs effectively in the complex federal regulatory environment. In many cases, these federal regulations result in spending that states would otherwise not pursue.

Relaxing the federal regulatory environment and giving states more flexibility in tailoring their healthcare programs would likely lead to reduced spending on healthcare programs while meeting population needs. Residents of each state have different preferences for health policies and different views on taxes and spending. In America's federal system, state and local governments can maximize value by designing policies to suit the preferences of their residents. At the same time, individuals can freely move to jurisdictions that suit them best.

Turning to the funding element of restructuring the federalist system, the use of "block grants" represents the centerpiece of most proposals to assist states in financing local health insurance programs. In its most basic form, the federal government pays annual lump sums (block grants) to states designated to support the provision of health insurance and care to their residents. Proposed calculations of block grant values depend on a variety of factors. Grant amounts can (1) depend on per capita amounts and states' population and composition; (2) impose per capita caps and vary according to enrollment; (3) redistribute resources across states and populations to finance activities deemed high-value by the federal government; and (4) increase in times of economic downturns, natural disasters, or higher-than-expected costs (such as when a new drug or procedure increases healthcare costs). Block grants often come with maintenance of effort (MOE) rules, ensuring minimal state funding levels and health insurance coverage for particular populations. The critical feature of block grants is that states are made to pay for incremental provisions of healthcare beyond some basic care levels used in determining block grant values.

Block grants mitigate many of the public finance shortcomings of the existing federal funding mechanisms. Under current law, the federal government deems health insurance as an entitlement, with coverage ensured to everyone who qualifies, paid for by a combination of state and federal government funds. Such combined funding allows both federal and state policymakers to claim credit for the spending and be responsible for portions of the tax costs. Such circumstances raise the ratio of the political benefits of spending to the tax costs, thus inducing excess spending. Additionally, the ability of the federal government to finance spending through debt produces the impression of deep pockets. States respond by expanding those programs highly subsidized by federal sources and by taking advantage of federal funding matching provisions to increase spending on programs beyond levels of marginal benefits. Many federally funded programs include MOE rules that restrict states from reducing state funding of a program when they take federal aid. MOE rules can discourage states from finding program efficiencies and saving taxpayer money. Together, these features of the existing funding system encourage imprudent deficit financing.

Shifting federal funding to block grants forces state policymakers to balance the benefit of healthcare spending with the cost of raising taxes to pay for it. Moreover, whereas the federal government's debt finances much of its spending, state governments must generally balance their budgets and limit their debt issuance. The federal government could reduce its debt accumulation by controlling the size of its block grants.

America faces significant challenges in restructuring its federalist system of healthcare funding necessary to achieve sustainable financing profiles in the upcoming decades. The longer the current system remains in place, the more dramatic will be the reforms needed to avoid a fiscal crisis in the public financing of all programs supported by federal and state governments.

References

Bureau of Economic Analysis (BEA). 1987–2019a. "National Accounts Government Current Expenditures." US Department of Commerce.

———. 1987–2019b. "Gross Domestic Product: Chain Price Index (2012=100)." US Department of Commerce.

Bureau of Labor Statistics (BLS). 1980–2019a. "Annual Social and Economic Supplement, Current Population Survey." US Department of Labor.

———. 1980–2019b. "Labor Force Statistics from the Current Population Survey." US Department of Labor.

———. 2010–2023. "Industries at a Glance: Health Care and Social Assistance—NAICS 62." US Department of Labor.

———. 2019a. "Consumer Expenditures in 2018." Report 1086. US Department of Labor.

———. 2019b. "Employer Costs for Employee Compensation." News release, US Department of Labor, December 18.

Centers for Medicare & Medicaid Services (CMS). 1960–2022. "National Health Expenditure Accounts." Data set (National Health Expenditure Data: Historical). CMS.gov.

———. 2022. "Data Brief on Section 1332 Waivers: State-Based Reinsurance Programs." CCIIO Data Brief Series, December 8.

———. 2023a. "Health Insurance Exchange Coverage Map." CMS.gov.

———. 2023b. "Nation's Health Dollar, Calendar Year 2021." National Health Statistics Group, Office of the Actuary, US Department of Health and Human Services.

Chantrill, Christopher. 2023. USgovernmentspending.com (federal, state, and local government budgets). Accessed February 1. https://www.usgovernmentspending.com.

Commonwealth of Massachusetts. 2024. "Individual Mandate Penalties for Tax Year 2021." Mass.gov. Published January 22, 2021; updated February 5, 2024.

Congressional Budget Office (CBO). 2022. "Federal Subsidies for Health Insurance Coverage for People under 65: 2022 to 2032."

———. 2023a. "An Update to the Budget Outlook: 2023 to 2033."

———. 2023b. "Federal Subsidies for Health Insurance Coverage for People under Age 65: CBO and JCT's May 2023 Baseline Projections."

———. 2023c. "The 2023 Long-Term Budget Outlook."

DC Health Link. 2024. "DC's Individual Responsibility Requirement." Online, accessed February 1.

Franchise Tax Board (California). 2024. "Personal Health Care Mandate." Last updated February 2.

HealthSource RI (Rhode Island). 2024. "RI Health Insurance Mandate." Online, accessed February 1.

Hogan, Christopher. 2009. "Exploring the Effects of Secondary Coverage on Medicare Spending for the Elderly." A study conducted by staff from Direct Research LLC for the Medicare Payment Advisory Commission (June).

————. 2014. "Exploring the Effects of Secondary Coverage on Medicare Spending for the Elderly." A report by Direct Research LLC for the Medicare Payment Advisory Commission (August).

Kaiser Family Foundation (KFF). 2024. "State Health Insurance Marketplace Types, 2024." Online, accessed February 1.

Medicaid and CHIP Payment and Access Commission (MACPAC). 2023. Most Current MACStats Compiled (December).

Rice, D., B. Cooper, and R. Gibson. 1982. "US National Health Accounts: Historical Perspectives, Current Issues, and Future Projections." In *La santé fait ses comptes* (*Accounting for Health*), edited by Emile Levy. Paris: Economica.

State of New Jersey. 2023. "NJ Shared Responsibility Requirement." NJ.gov. Updated November 1.

Vermont Health Connect. 2024. "Individual Mandate FAQ." Department of Vermont Health Access. Online, accessed February 1.

THOMAS MACURDY: Medicare is undergoing major reforms right now. The program is moving to a pay-for-performance sort of system, with fee for service vanishing. Irrespective, the reason why America's healthcare is so costly is we spend a lot of money on sick people. Other countries don't.

JOSHUA RAUH: Hasn't the profession for the last ten years been trying to run away from the results of the Oregon Health [Insurance] Experiment, where putting people on Medicaid in a quasi-exogenous way didn't improve health outcomes?

MACURDY: Yes, but that was already known.

JAY BHATTACHARYA: It was the RAND Health Insurance Experiment that first failed to show a causal link between health insurance coverage and mortality. For most of the population, health insurance likely doesn't save lives.

MACURDY: Yes, it doesn't do very much of that. Medicaid coverage sends beneficiaries to the emergency rooms, because they can't get care otherwise.

BHATTACHARYA: For most of the population, it doesn't matter that much. But for a small fraction on whom a lot of money is spent, it matters a ton.

MACURDY: You can obtain drug plans in Medicare, at this point, where the program spends a hundred thousand dollars a year for a life expectancy extension of two months. Such cases are not uncommon.

RAUH: And that was added by Medicare Part D, right? The middle of the first decade of the 2000s, that was when they—

MaCurdy: Yes, Part D. The criteria for including high-cost drugs on Part D formulas relies primarily on whether the drug is effective. No cost-benefit analysis is performed.

Dennis Epple: So, Tom, is this $28 million because the cost to whoever is manufacturing this medication is really $28 million?

MaCurdy: These drugs can be expensive to produce. For drugs produced at low marginal costs, we do have the problem you just described related to encouraging drug innovation. This is also a challenging policy issue in the medical device area.

Bhattacharya: Other countries, for the same medication, it'll be half that cost.

MaCurdy: Yes. But the thing is, that's not really fair to the US.

Eric A. Hanushek: But they're using our technology.

MaCurdy: Exactly. They are. Germany, France will come along and say to pharmaceutical manufacturers, "If you don't give us a discount on this drug, we're going to take all your drugs off our formulary." The manufacturers cave in negotiations and give price discounts, recognizing that these markets are small relative to overall sales.

Bhattacharya: This is something that the Bush administration tried: to allow the reimportation of drugs from foreign countries. In the Bush administration, what happened was that there was a pushback saying, "Well look, we don't know that Canada is regulating drugs appropriately. We'll get bad, unsafe drugs from Canada." During the Trump administration, some folks said, "Okay, let's not actually get the drugs. We'll just import the lower drug prices from Canada." But given the political influence of pharmaceutical companies, it's very difficult politically to put any of that through into policy.

MaCurdy: If we were able to do that, it would put some elasticity in the demand, because that means when the drug companies came along and gave France a good deal, they realized, "Oh, the US is going to take advantage of this." We must move to something of that nature creating an open competitive market. Other countries take advantage of our research. We pay for it. They don't.

JOHN B. TAYLOR: Do you guys have a reform?

BHATTACHARYA: We suggest a few things like block grants to states to encourage experimentation. Our paper proposes several of these kinds of ideas. But I don't think they meet the scope of the problem we're facing of excessively high health spending and inadequate medical coverage for millions. Dennis, you asked the right question. How do we reform the healthcare system so it spends money more wisely? There are some easier things like, for instance, there was this drug called Aduhelm [aducanumab], which was aimed at slowing the progress of Alzheimer's disease, and it was shown in clinical trials to be very effective at reducing lab values of proteins that correlate with the progress of Alzheimer's.

But unfortunately, the clinical trial showed no ability of the drug to prevent Alzheimer's disease. And it was a tremendously expensive drug. That's the first time I've seen Medicare actually say no to a drug, and I believe its expense was a major factor. At first Medicare approved the drug for use, but there was a lot of political pressure about its lack of clinical efficacy and high expenditures, and so Medicare ultimately said no. But the way that the FDA is now set up, you can basically, with a drug, show an effect on a biomarker that has no clinical benefit—just the biomarker—and the FDA basically will approve it.

MACURDY: And then, once it's approved, it's difficult for Medicare not to allow it. Advocates argue that it's available and effective. The most recent law passed declaring that it lowered the price of drugs only lowered the cost covered by beneficiaries, not the total cost paid to drug plans. The government increased its share of costs.

Moreover, this legislation decreased the max out of pocket. Previous law imposed no max out of pocket for drugs when patients reached the catastrophic payment portion of Part D plans' schedules, with beneficiaries paying only 5 percent in this portion. But 5 percent of a hundred thousand is noticeable; 5 percent of a million's noticeable. The new legislation caps the annual maximum out of pocket at about $2,000.

HANUSHEK: So, the traditional argument with the FDA was that they were too slow. Now, you're saying they're too fast?

BHATTACHARYA: They're too fast. Yes.

HANUSHEK: Or is it they don't take into account anything about cost-benefit analysis?

RAUH: Well, there's in theory a difference between approving something for private use, like any private agent who has the money for it can pay for and use it, versus for government programs. The problem is, when the FDA approves it, it means that Medicare is going to pay for anybody who needs it. It seems like there's no way out of this without some kind of rationing of who's actually going to get access to the technology through the government program.

BHATTACHARYA: This is the reason we include suggestions for pay-for-performance reforms in our paper. The idea is that, say a doctor describes some drug to you or gives you surgery or a recommendation for some surgery, there's a law called MACRA [Medicare Access and CHIP Reauthorization Act], which requires every doctor in the country who accepts Medicare dollars to be evaluated. Basically, Medicare will provide a report card on nearly every doctor in the country. Actually, Tom and I worked helping CMS [Centers for Medicare and Medicaid Services] develop this system. Suppose there are two drugs—one's really expensive, one's cheap—and then you follow the patients along and there's no difference in the outcomes between patients who receive one drug versus the other. In the report card, the doctor who prescribed the high-cost drug will get dinged. Maybe they'll get a C on their report card instead of an A. And the grade matters, because it's closely tied to physician payments. It's tied to a lot of money, actually. There is an 18 percent swing in Part B payments for each doctor based on the grade they get on these evaluations for MACRA. So in principle you could move doctors to start prescribing the cheaper drugs as long as they have no big effect on outcomes. I mean, that is a tool you can use for reform. The big question is: Is it enough to solve the cost and access problems?

HANUSHEK: Do doctors know which are effective when they're prescribing?

MACURDY: They do when they get dinged.

BHATTACHARYA: I'll tell you a story about this. So to create this system of grading, we held panels of experts to provide input. And one of the panels was about cataract surgery. In these surgeries, doctors have choices over what lens to use to replace the cloudy ones in cataract patients. During one of these panels, the question came up: "Well, a patient goes blind shortly after the surgery, should the surgeon be be held responsible in their report card for this bad outcome?" One of the physicians on this expert panel actually said out loud that if the patient goes blind after the cataract surgery, it's an act of God and thus the doctor should not be held responsible. The rest of the room of physician experts was very dismissive of this comment, and ultimately, physicians are dinged in their report card if their cataract surgery patient goes blind after the surgery.

MICHAEL J. BOSKIN: I have to make just a couple of quick comments. One is, clearly, this will reverberate throughout the federal system, because if the federal government starts curtailing, there'll be pressures on state and local governments to spend. They'll start reducing payments to hospitals and so on. County hospitals will be bearing more of a burden. So all that's, I think, really important. In any event, fingers crossed that we'll implement many of the things you've recommended and that'll get us at least a leg up.

10

When Are State Liabilities Federal Liabilities? Social Insurance and Federalism

Joshua Rauh and Jillian Ludwig

Introduction

In recent decades, the United States has seen a trend toward increasing federalization of the financing of government programs, even as states continue to control the administration of those programs. This can be seen in the most basic fact that federal spending as a share of total government spending has increased from 65 percent to 71 percent between 1993 and 2021 (see figure 10.1). In keeping with the theory of cyclical ratcheting, which states that spending increases during recessions and remains high during the expansions that follow (Hercowitz and Strawczynski 2004), central government spending has accelerated during major crises such as the global financial crisis of 2008 and the COVID-19 pandemic and has not returned to pre-recession levels in the years that followed.

Programs that are to a large extent administered by the federal government but funded by states are numerous. In this essay, we examine the increasing federal financing of state-run programs via two examples—unemployment insurance (UI) and Medicaid. We then consider the extent to which there has been greater implicit centralization of state and local government debt and unfunded pension liabilities. We conclude that many state liabilities have become de facto federal liabilities, despite states' status as sovereign entities with taxation and debt issuance authority.

Much of the discussion around federalism traces back to Oates (1972), who argued the optimal degree of centralization versus decentralization in a federal system depends on a trade-off between the benefits of tailored service provision and the costs of providing public goods and services at a local level. On one hand, Oates suggested that decentralization can lead to improved public-sector efficiency, because local governments are closer to the people and thus have a better understanding of their needs and preferences. This proximity allows local governments to provide goods and services that are better tailored to local conditions and preferences, which Oates referred to as the "decentralization theorem." On the other hand, Oates notes that centralization can result in cost savings due to economies of scale and the ability to manage spillover effects across jurisdictions. The optimal degree of centralization or decentralization, therefore, depends on balancing these competing considerations.

The level at which public goods should be financed is a separate question. The footloose nature of tax bases offers a justification for raising some revenues at a more centralized level than the level of service provision, especially for non-benefit taxes, which are taxes that are not directly related to the benefits that the taxpayer receives (McLure et al. 1983; Gordon 1983; Gamkhar and Oates 1996). The programs we look at in this paper often involve conditional grants, in which the federal government picks up some share of a program administered by state governments. The rationale for such grants is usually that the local services have some spillover benefits for residents of other jurisdictions (Oates 1999). Unconditional grants, or programs that involve an unconditional component, are generally viewed as serving a purpose of fiscal equalization based on differing fiscal needs or fiscal capacity.

Economic justifications of the increased centralization would therefore have to fall under one of three categories: (1) tax bases have become more responsive to taxation for a given level of positive spillover effects across jurisdictions; (2) spillover effects of the public programs have become stronger for a given level of behavioral response to taxation; or (3) there is a greater need for fiscal equalization, perhaps due to increased inequality across jurisdictions. While it is beyond the scope of this paper to assess whether these conditions are met, it is also difficult to see strong evidence of any of these trends in practice. Furthermore, as we show when we consider pensions and unfunded debts, implicit guarantees by the federal government on the liabilities of the most indebted jurisdictions do not translate into implicit guarantees for the poorest regions or those with the least fiscal capacity.

This essay proceeds as follows. The first section considers spending shares of federal versus state governments over time, as well as the evolution of the federal funding share of state expenditures. The following sections address unemployment insurance and Medicaid specifically as examples of programs where the federal role has ratcheted up during times of crisis and does not recede afterward. The fourth section considers the evolution and distribution of pension liabilities and debt, and it is followed by a concluding summary of the trends described.

Role of the Federal vs. State Governments over Time

As shown in figure 10.1, the federal share of total government expenditures tends to rise in crises and not subside to pre-crisis levels thereafter over the last thirty years. Measurement of the federal share of total government spending is possible using the National Income and Product Accounts (NIPA) of the US Bureau of Economic Analysis (BEA). The graph shows three local peaks: first after the national security buildup following the 2001 terrorist attacks, second following federal government expansions in the wake of the global financial crisis of 2008–9, and third as a result of the federal government's response to the COVID-19 virus. Importantly, in these data series, programs with rules-based shared financing such as UI and Medicaid are apportioned to the federal or state government based on the source of financing. Direct transfers from the federal government to states without an expectation of specific services that states then spend are counted as state spending. This includes transfers for programs financed by federal government block grants, such as the federal funding of the Temporary Assistance for Needy Families program.

The increase in the federal share of expenditures in figure 10.1 therefore could reflect both increases in federal spending on federal programs (that are larger than increases in state spending on state programs) or increases in federal financing of state-administered programs such as UI and Medicaid. Increases in federal transfers to states without specific strings attached would, in contrast, tend to depress this line.

Figure 10.2 shows that federal payments to US state and local governments have in fact increased dramatically as a share of total expenditures by those states, rising from 16 percent in 1993 to 25 percent in 2021. So, while figure 10.1 shows that federal expenditures as a share of total expenditures have increased, figure 10.2 shows that states are increasingly relying on federal transfers to finance their own spending. In sum, the federal government is controlling more of the spending, as well as financing more of the expenditures, of the state and local governments.

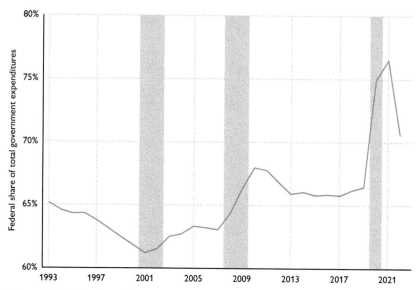

Figure 10.1 Federal spending as a share of total government spending

Note: Total Government Spending is measured as the sum of federal and state and local government expenditures less the sum of current and capital grants-in-aid. Shading indicates recessions as defined by the NBER.

Source: US Bureau of Economic Analysis NIPA Tables 3.1 and 3.2.

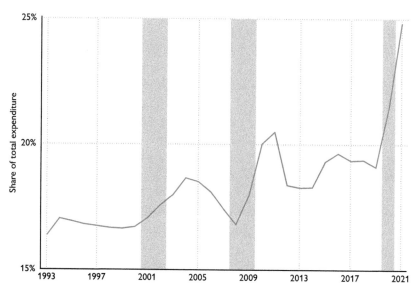

Figure 10.2 Intergovernmental revenue from the federal government as a share of total state and local expenditures, US total

Note: Shading indicates recessions as defined by the NBER.

Source: US Census Bureau's State and Local Government Finance Historical Datasets.

Figure 10.3 shows the heterogeneity across states in the federal government's support of state-level expenditures by highlighting the three states that as of 2021 had the largest federal intergovernmental revenue to state expenditure ratio and the three that had the smallest. States with high ratios may devote a larger share of their expenditures to jointly financed programs such as Medicaid and UI while also generally having relatively lower revenue from own-sources compared to what they are receiving from the federal government. While states experience different intergovernmental revenue-to-expenditure ratios over time, these ratios have broadly trended upward in recent years across states.

A separate but related question is the extent to which residents of different states benefit on net from federal programs of taxing and spending. Schultz and Holland (2023) consider this "balance of payments" question by considering total federal direct payments, grants, contracts, and other transfers on a per capita basis by state. States with relatively more low-income residents pay lower federal taxes per capita and receive more in federal benefits per capita,

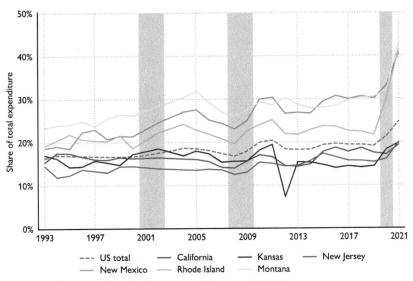

Figure 10.3 Intergovernmental revenue from the federal government as a share of total state and local expenditures, highest and lowest states

Note: Displays states with highest and lowest federal intergovernmental revenue-to-expenditure ratio as of 2021. Shading indicates recessions as defined by the NBER.

Source: US Census Bureau's State and Local Government Finance Historical Datasets.

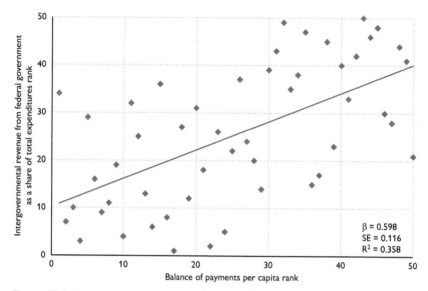

Figure 10.4 Intergovernmental revenue from the federal government as a share of total state and local expenditures rank vs. balance of payments per capita rank, 2021

Note: States are ranked based on federal intergovernmental revenue-to-expenditure ratio and balance of payments per capita in order from largest to smallest.

Sources: Revenue and expenditure data from US Census Bureau's State and Local Government Finance Historical Datasets; balance of payments data from Rockefeller Institute of Government.

giving them large net benefits. However, some higher income states also have a substantially favorable balance of payments with the federal government due to state businesses' receipts of federal contracts. As a result, as shown in figure 10.4, there is an imperfect mapping between the level at which a given state benefits from redistribution, as measured by the balance of payments per capita, and the extent to which state expenditures are financed by the federal government.

Unemployment Insurance

The unemployment insurance (UI) program in the US, which provides benefits for eligible workers during involuntary spells of unemployment, is one example of a program that is jointly administered by states and the federal government yet has become increasingly federalized over time. The entitlement program is designed to pay benefits to covered workers based on their earnings over a fifty-two-week period, up to a limit set by states, for as long as twenty-six weeks in most states.[1] In general, UI eligibility is determined by labor search efforts, reason for job separation, and previous earnings. Weekly benefit amounts are determined by the state but typically replace up to half of an individual's previous wages. Beyond the regular UI program, there is a permanent extended benefits (EB) program offering an additional thirteen to twenty weeks of benefits. States are required to provide EB coverage during periods of elevated unemployment. Individuals then become eligible to receive EB after exhausting regular UI benefits. While the federal government provides a broad framework for UI, state officials have some amount of autonomy in designing programs in their states.[2]

The UI program is funded by both federal and state employer payroll taxes (FUTA and SUTA, respectively), which are levied on most businesses.[3] While FUTA revenues mainly cover the administrative costs of UI and a 50 percent share of EB costs, SUTA revenues are much larger, funding the payment of regular benefits in each state and the remaining half of EB costs.

The gross FUTA rate for all taxable businesses is 6 percent on the first $7,000 of wages paid to each employee, but the net FUTA rate is just 0.6 percent, since employers in states that are fully compliant with federal guidelines receive a 5.4 percentage point tax credit.[4] SUTA is a variable-rate tax, and states select both the rates and bases of the tax.[5] States are induced to use an experience rating system whereby employers are charged differing SUTA rates based on the amount of UI benefits paid to previous employees, or otherwise face FUTA credit reductions and increased SUTA rates for all employers in the state (Anderson and Meyer 2000).[6] Under this structure, firms that have undergone layoffs or have experienced downturns face higher SUTA payroll taxes, meaning that state UI taxes are in effect pro-cyclical (Johnston 2021).

Unemployment Trust Funds and Solvency

Revenues generated by states' UI payroll taxes are held in separate accounts within the Unemployment Trust Fund (UTF), housed at the US Treasury. The solvency of a state's trust fund is measured by comparing a state's reserve ratio (trust fund balance divided by total wages) to its benefit cost rate (benefits paid divided by total wages). This ratio is called the average high cost multiple (AHCM). According to the US Department of Labor (DOL), a state's UTF is adequately solvent and prepared for a recession when its AHCM is at least 1.0.[7]

Some states, however, consistently fail to achieve UTF solvency, let alone adequate solvency levels for recession. In these cases, the federal government provides loans called Title XII advancements so insolvent states can continue to pay out UI entitlement benefits. Figure 10.5 displays the Title XII loan balances per eligible employee of select states over time. Intuitively, loan balances typically increase during economic downturns when the incidence and duration of claims are likely to rise, trust funds are depleted, and state revenues may be lower. States are required to pay regular benefit payments as well as the balance and interest on the loan, which accrues daily, once a Title XII advancement has been taken out. States are incentivized to do this in a timely manner or face a 0.3 percentage point reduction in the standard FUTA payroll tax credit for each additional year there is an outstanding balance.[8] For example, employers in a state with an outstanding Title XII loan balance for five consecutive years would be subject to a FUTA tax rate of at least 1.8 percent compared to the usual 0.6 percent net rate with the full tax credit. To avoid this, states often choose to broadly raise SUTA payroll tax rates or charge employers special assessments in order to make principal and interest payments on Title XII loans and replenish their UTFs following an

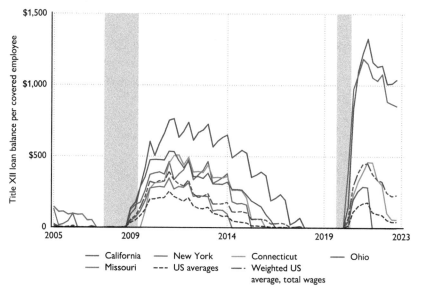

Figure 10.5 Title XII loan balance per covered employee (quarterly)

Note: US averages are calculated yearly. Shading indicates recessions as defined by the NBER.

Source: US Department of Labor.

economic downturn. This payroll tax increase, however, may slow economic recovery and cool employers' hiring efforts, especially for distressed firms who face mechanically increased SUTA rates due to layoffs (Weiner et al. 2012; Johnston 2021).

Regardless of the incentive to maintain adequate reserves in the UTF to prepare for a future rise in UI claims, recent recessions have revealed that many states have been unprepared for crisis. Figure 10.6 displays the solvency levels of a selection of states from 2005 to the end of 2022. In the quarter preceding the start of the global financial crisis, thirty-one states did not meet the threshold for adequate solvency of their UTF account (AHCM of at least 1.0). Prior to the recession sparked by COVID-19 lockdowns, twenty-two states did not reach 100 percent solvency based on their AHCM levels.[9] California, for example, has maintained a solvency level well below 100 percent for over twenty years and has frequently been completely insolvent during that period. In fact, the Golden State's AHCM never went above

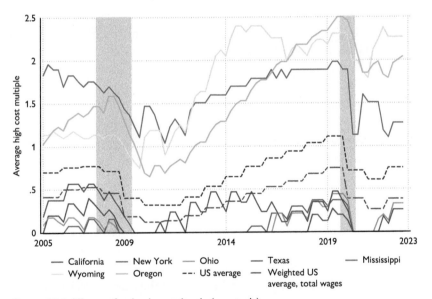

Figure 10.6 UI trust fund solvency levels (quarterly)

Note: Average High Cost Multiple compares a state's quarter reserve ratio (trust fund balance as a percent of total wages) to the average of the state's three highest calendar year benefit cost rates (total benefits paid as a percent of total wages) in the past twenty years or a period including three recessions, whichever is longer. US Averages are calculated yearly. Shading indicates recessions as defined by the NBER.

Source: US Department of Labor.

40 percent between 2000 and 2023. By contrast, Wyoming had an average solvency level of nearly 170 percent over the same time period—even their lowest AHCM during this period was 35 percentage points higher than California's highest solvency level.

UI in Times of Crisis

Despite the fact that many states consistently underfund their UTF, the federal government often steps in to bolster UI programs during financial crises in an effort to stabilize the economy. In both the global financial crisis and the COVID-19 recession, unemployment rose significantly, and the incidence of UI claims increased substantially across the country. During the COVID-19 crisis, the volume of initial claims peaked at over six million claims in one week in April 2020 compared to a weekly average of just 218,000 during 2019, according to US DOL data. Likewise, continuing claims reached over twenty-three million in May 2020, nearly fourteen times higher than the weekly average level of continuing claims in the previous year. Given the high volumes of claims, increasingly long spells of unemployment for workers, and underprepared state UI trust funds, the federal government opted to substantially expand its role in the UI program, enacting large-scale changes to its operation in both recent recessions.

Global Financial Crisis

In response to the global financial crisis, the federal government enacted the Emergency Unemployment Compensation (EUC08) program in June 2008 and subsequently amended the law with various other legislation, producing the largest ever extension of UI benefits at the time of its passage. After several expansions, EUC08 allowed eligible workers to claim UI benefits for up to fifty-three additional weeks following exhaustion of twenty-six weeks of regular UI and twenty weeks of EB, for a total of ninety-nine weeks of benefits as of late 2009.[10] The emergency program persisted at this level through late 2012 and tapered off through the end of 2013. The federal government bore the full cost of both the EUC08 extension and the permanent EB program throughout this time, and interest on Title XII advances was waived in 2009 and 2010.

From mid-2008 to the end of 2013, the federal government paid a total of $230.1 billion of EUC08 benefits based on DOL data, more than 8.5 times the amount of benefits paid through emergency programs during the dotcom recession of the early 2000s (Nicholson and Needels 2011). At the same time, thirty-six states depleted their trust funds from 2007 to 2009 and accumulated over $50 billion in debt to the federal government in aggregate. By the end of 2014, twenty-three states still had $15 billion in outstanding federal debt and $10 billion in private debt due to UI.[11]

COVID-19

While the EUC08 extension of benefits was historically significant, the policy was similar in nature to federal UI interventions in previous recessions (Simon 2021). The UI provisions included in the federal response to COVID-19, and especially in the Coronavirus Aid, Relief, and Economic Security (CARES) Act, however, dwarfed previous policies in terms of outlays and were largely unprecedented in form.

The Families First Coronavirus Response Act (FFCRA), signed into law on March 18, 2020, was the first federal COVID-19 response to include UI provisions. The law suspended cost sharing for EB and shifted 100 percent of costs to the federal government, offered additional administrative funding for states, and waived interest on Title XII loans to insolvent states throughout 2020.[12]

That same month, the CARES Act expanded on FFCRA policies and created three new UI programs: Pandemic Emergency Unemployment Compensation (PEUC), Pandemic Unemployment Assistance (PUA), and Federal Pandemic Unemployment Compensation (FPUC). PEUC, like previous federal interventions during recessions, extended the duration of benefits for those who had exhausted regular UI benefits. Initially, PEUC offered thirteen additional weeks of benefits, but after subsequent extensions, claimants could receive an additional fifty-three weeks of UI.

PUA, a novel federal intervention, expanded UI coverage to traditionally ineligible workers, substantially increasing the pool of claimants during the pandemic. Newly eligible workers included gig economy workers, self-employed individuals, and recent entrants into the labor market who were previously unable to receive UI due to lack of employment history. PUA-eligible workers were able to claim regular, PEUC, and EB benefits. By mid-May 2020, initial PUA claims rose to over 2.2 million, nearly matching the number of seasonally adjusted regular initial claims in that same week.

Another unprecedented policy, FPUC, provided an extra $600 per week in benefits for all claimants. The program was designed to replace 100 percent of the US mean wage when combined with the average state UI benefit, yet due to wage heterogeneity across states and sectors, the additional benefit often resulted in significantly higher replacement rates. According to Ganong et al. (2020), 76 percent of workers nationally saw replacement rates above 100 percent, and the median national replacement rate was 145 percent between April and July 2020. Some states with lower pre-pandemic wage levels such as Georgia and Oklahoma saw rates over 160 percent. This high replacement rate prompted serious distributional concerns, given that workers who claimed UI benefits during the pandemic were likely to receive a raise compared to previous earnings, yet those who maintained employment likely did not see similar increases in weekly wages.

CARES Act provisions were extended multiple times during and after the height of the COVID-19 crisis. The Lost Wages Assistance program, the Continued Assistance Act, and finally, the American Rescue Plan Act extended PEUC, PUA, and FPUC through September 2021. As of mid-2023, the US DOL estimates that the federal government spent over $675 billion on COVID-19-related UI programs. At the same time, states paid out $175 billion in UI benefits from the start of the pandemic through September 2021, leaving state UTFs with a negative aggregate balance of –$11 billion due to accrued Title XII loan debt (Walczak and Funkhouser 2021).

UI and Federalism

The federal government's efforts to stabilize the economy during recent crises have accelerated the financial and administrative centralization of the UI program and brought to light structural issues that affect states' labor market dynamics as well as UTF funding behavior and program administration.

Experience Rating

Unlike in any other country, the UI program in the United States relies on revenue from payroll taxes with variable individualized rates, as discussed above (Guo and Johnston 2021). Whereas most countries use a uniform payroll tax to fund unemployment compensation, states in the US are essentially required to use an experience rating system based on unemployment risk or otherwise tax all employers at a 5.4 percent rate (Anderson and Meyer 2000; Guo and Johnston 2021). Though this structure is intended to deter employers from engaging in layoffs and reward firms that avoid them, the payroll tax in practice functions as a tax on employment by raising the cost of an additional employee for a firm. Because rates are linked to layoff activity, taxes are likely to be higher for firms following economic downturns and especially high for the most distressed firms, effectively discouraging hiring when unemployment is already elevated.

In fact, Johnston (2021) estimates that the reduction in hiring resulting from increased unemployment tax rates accounted for 12 percent of unemployment following the global financial crisis. Likewise, Guo (2023b) estimates a labor demand elasticity of −2.4 to UI tax rates, with more pronounced employment effects for younger, low-earning workers. While there is evidence that experience rating is effective at reducing downsizing behavior (Duggan, Guo, and Johnston 2023), the impact of reduced hiring in the face of increased state UI tax rates may lead to so-called jobless recoveries, as experienced during the global financial crisis (Johnston 2021).

The experience rating system also affects the role of employers in claims decisions. Firms are acutely impacted when previous employees make unemployment claims, producing an incentive for firms to appeal UI claims of former employees and to "police the system" (Anderson and Meyer 2000). Anderson and Meyer (2000) and Lachowska, Sorkin, and Woodbury (2022) find that experience rating systems reduce the number of claims made while increasing the number of appeals and claim denials. This may lessen the positive effects of UI if eligible workers are not able to make claims or receive benefits, and may produce a cost for employers who have to contest invalid claims to ensure they are not charged higher payroll tax rates.

Despite the fact that states are, in essence, required by the federal government to use experience rating systems for UI taxes, it remains an open question whether this is an optimal design for every state, given the policy's trade-offs (Guo and Johnston 2021).

UTFs and Moral Hazard

As seen during both the global financial crisis and the COVID-19 pandemic, states are frequently unprepared for economic downturns and the associated rise in unemployment claims. Though there are ex post disincentives for states that accrue Title XII loan balances due to insufficient reserves, they evidently do not deter states from underfunding their UTFs during stable economic periods. Rather, shortsighted policymaking and federal bailouts produce an incentive for states to keep reserve levels low (Galle 2018).

To build up trust funds in the long term, states must choose between raising unemployment payroll tax rates and cutting UI benefits in the short term, both economically and politically undesirable options (Galle 2018). On one hand, high SUTA rates, like high corporate tax rates, increase the likelihood that footloose firms will relocate to states with more preferential payroll tax regimes (Giroud and Rauh 2019). Multi-establishment firms are shown to be significantly more likely to close locations in high-unemployment tax states in the face of economic downturns (Guo 2023a). In the event that firms do not relocate to states with lower rates or close establishments altogether, increased rates dampen hiring efforts and impact employment levels, particularly when job growth is needed most. On the other hand, states can limit duration or amount of benefits in an effort to shore up reserves (Smith and Wenger 2013). Reducing benefits during slumps, however, may weaken the countercyclicality of the UI program, hurt state economies during downturns, and constitute an unpopular policy decision for state officials. Rather than enact these policies, shortsighted policymakers choose to underinvest in their state's unemployment reserves.

This decision is made easier because states know that the federal government will step in and supply Title XII advances to cover benefits in the event that claims surpass reserves, thus lowering the perceived risk of trust fund insolvency. While interest may be accrued on some federal advances, loans taken out and repaid between January and September of a given year, called cash-flow advances, are interest-free. Furthermore, as was the case during both the global financial crisis and the COVID-19 pandemic, interest is often waived on loans altogether during recessions. Ultimately, these bailouts to states with insolvent trust funds produce significant moral hazard, effectively encouraging imprudent policy when it comes to building UTF reserves (Galle 2018).

Labor Disincentives and Income Dynamics

Moral hazard associated with the UI program exists not only at the state level but also at the individual level. Perhaps the most common debate surrounding the optimal design of UI is about the potential labor disincentives that excessively generous benefits may produce. The primary concern is that the provision of unemployment benefits may discourage individuals from working or may lessen search efforts. While states generally have the ability to set benefit levels as they see fit, we have seen that the federal government greatly expands benefits during recessionary periods, and this may impact local labor markets.

For example, the CARES Act provisions discussed previously were authorized to continue through September 2021, however, by that time, twenty-six states had already opted to withdraw from the federal programs. Some states noted that a tighter labor market and increased hiring efforts made the extended UI benefits unnecessary.[13] Others specifically highlighted that work disincentives caused by pandemic UI programs hindered economic recovery in their state.[14]

Research on the distortionary effect of UI, however, is somewhat mixed. Chetty (2008) argues that UI is not as distortionary as many perceive it to be, given that unemployment durations caused by UI benefits are largely produced by a liquidity effect rather than a substitution effect or distortions on job search incentives. Dube (2021) similarly finds that reductions in benefit amounts after the expiration of the $600 weekly FPUC payments did not produce large changes in employment, suggesting that the generous benefits did not have significant distortionary effects during that period. Conversely, Meyer and Mok (2014) show that an increase in weekly benefit amounts in New York resulted in a significant increase in UI claims as well as an increase in the duration of claims. Studying a reduction in maximum benefit duration in Missouri following the global financial crisis, Johnston and Mas (2018) find that a cut in potential duration resulted in a reduction of time spent unemployed, suggesting that the benefit cut produced increased job search efforts.

While there is not a consensus on the work incentives associated with unemployment benefits, the universal approach used by the federal government when enacting UI interventions during the pandemic resulted in unprecedentedly high average replacement rates, affecting income dynamics in all states (Ganong et al. 2020). The additional FPUC payment more than doubled the normal maximum weekly benefit amounts in forty-five states. For example, Mississippi's maximum weekly benefit amount grew from $235 to $835 per week with FPUC. This extra benefit likely stretches much further in a state with a low cost of living like Mississippi, where the average home cost is $128,000, than it does in Hawaii, where the average home cost is five times that.[15] Because it ignored the crucial state-by-state variation in normal weekly benefit amounts, cost of living, and other economic conditions, the federal government's COVID-19 UI response likely resulted in large-scale inefficiencies and changes to state income dynamics.

Medicaid

The Medicaid program, like UI, is a joint federal and state program that administers medical services to certain low-income populations. While state participation in the program is voluntary, every state participates and therefore follows certain federal guidelines to receive the federal share of Medicaid funding. Similar to UI, the federal framework for Medicaid offers some design flexibility, resulting in different programs across the country.

Since its creation in the 1960s, Medicaid expenditures, especially federal Medicaid expenditures, have grown every year with few exceptions, as displayed in figure 10.7.[16] Much of this increase can be attributed to eligibility expansions and subsequently higher rates of enrollment. As Medicaid is a means-tested program, eligibility is determined by financial need; however, there are also categorical criteria that affect eligibility. Prior to the passage of the Affordable Care Act (ACA), only certain groups, such as low-income families with children, pregnant women, and individuals with disabilities were required by federal law to be eligible for a state's Medicaid program. After ACA was implemented in 2014, though, states could opt into a Medicaid expansion that made adults with income up to 138 percent of the federal poverty level eligible, regardless of other categorical criteria. This expansion alone resulted in an estimated 8.8 percent rise in enrollment nationally in fiscal year 2014, significantly increasing Medicaid expenditures ever since, especially for the federal government.[17] According to the Centers for Medicare and Medicaid

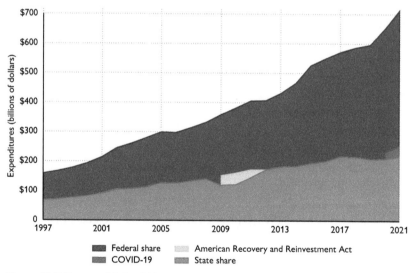

Figure 10.7 State and federal Medicaid expenditures

Note: Medicaid expenditures based on total net expenditures for the Medical Assistance Program reported in Medicaid Financial Management Reports.

Source: Centers for Medicare and Medicaid Services.

Services, as of 2021, the federal government spent more than $498 billion on the Medical Assistance Program while state governments spent $219 billion.

The federal government finances a majority of Medicaid spending through reimbursements to states, who pay service providers directly. Each state's reimbursement rate is determined by its federal medical assistance percentage (FMAP) rate, which is calculated annually. By statute, FMAP rates must fall between 50 percent and 83 percent, but the exact percentage is based on the state's per capita income in relation to the overall US per capita income. States with lower income levels receive a higher rate of federal reimbursement. In 2019 (the last year before COVID-19-related measures were enacted), fourteen states received the minimum 50 percent reimbursement rate, while Mississippi had the highest reimbursement rate at 76.39 percent.[18] The state share of the Medical Assistance Program then is at most 50 percent of the total cost of the program. States have some discretion in terms of funding sources for their shares of Medicaid expenditures, but most state funding comes from state general funds.

Medicaid in Times of Crisis

Medicaid is countercyclical in nature—enrollment typically rises during recessions, when unemployment rates increase and wages decline, making more people eligible for coverage. Indeed, in both the global financial crisis and the COVID-19 pandemic, Medicaid enrollment expanded significantly. Between 2007 and 2009, enrollment grew by 9.7 percent while unemployment rose to 9.5 percent and state tax collections fell by 10.2 percent.[19] Similarly, from February 2020 to September 2020 alone, enrollment increased by 10.3 percent, coinciding with a dramatic increase in unemployment in April 2020, resulting in a significant increase in Medicaid expenditures. To account for greater demand during times when state governments are also likely to see a decline in revenues, the federal government often assists states during recessions by raising FMAP rates.

Global Financial Crisis

During the global financial crisis, the federal government made an effort to stabilize the economy and ensure continued service despite depleted state revenues through the American Recovery and Reinvestment Act (ARRA). The legislation included $103 billion in federal aid to states, primarily in the form of increased FMAP rates for all states from October 2008 through June 2011. During that period, every state received a 6.2 percentage point increase in their federal matching rates, and states experiencing particularly high levels of unemployment received further increases. Rate increases were phased down in the final two quarters of the program. A hold-harmless provision was also included in ARRA, meaning that a state's FMAP rate could not decrease below its 2008 level for the duration of the relief program. To be eligible for enhanced FMAP rates through ARRA, states needed to comply with "maintenance of effort" requirements, which ensured that states did not restrict their Medicaid eligibility standards or procedures while receiving federal aid. The law also instituted requirements for states to expedite claim payments to providers.

By the first quarter of fiscal year 2011, state ARRA-increased FMAP rates ranged from 61.59 percent in states that would have received 50 percent match rates regularly to 84.86 percent in Mississippi. In 2011, twenty-seven states benefited from the hold-harmless provision, meaning ARRA allowed states to avoid drops in their FMAP rates that would have come about using the regular rate formula due to increased per capita income levels (KFF 2011).

COVID-19

The COVID-19 pandemic led to a surge in Medicaid enrollment that resulted in a significant increase in expenditures. Through the FFCRA, enacted in 2020, the federal government again increased FMAP rates by 6.2 percentage points and required maintenance of effort standards and continuous coverage for the duration of the pandemic public health emergency (PHE). The continuous coverage requirement prohibited states from disenrolling individuals from Medicaid unless it was requested, regardless of any Medicaid eligibility reviews. This allowed people to remain covered without interruption for the duration of the pandemic emergency. In December 2022, Congress enacted legislation that delinked continuous coverage provisions from the PHE, and states were allowed to end coverage beginning in April 2023, prior to the formal end of the PHE in May 2023. The act also allowed for sunset provisions that would gradually phase out the FFCRA FMAP increases by the end of 2023 to avoid significant losses in coverage and large increases in state Medicaid spending.[20]

Over the course of the continuous coverage period, it is estimated that states received over $117 billion in enhanced federal funding. At the same time, state expenditures on Medicaid remained stable and even dipped below pre-pandemic levels despite the fact that enrollment was considerably larger during the continuous coverage period (Williams, Burns, and

Rudowitz 2023). According to the Congressional Budget Office (CBO), of the 73.6 million people it estimated to be enrolled in Medicaid in 2022, 12.9 million were enrolled because of the continuous coverage provisions, suggesting nearly a fifth of enrollees would have been otherwise ineligible for coverage (CBO 2022a).

Medicaid and Federalism

Through both economic downturns and legislative reforms, the role of the federal government in the provision of Medicaid has grown substantially in recent decades. Concretely, federal Medicaid expenditures increased nearly 450 percent between 1997 and 2021, while state expenditures have grown by about half as much. Medicaid expenditures account for a significant portion of state general funds—18 percent nationally as of state fiscal year 2021.[21] Decisions made by the federal government regarding Medicaid, therefore, have substantial budget implications for state governments.

Medicaid Expansion and the Affordable Care Act

The Affordable Care Act (ACA), signed into law in 2010, constitutes the largest federal healthcare reform law since Medicare and Medicaid were created in 1965. While the ACA includes a number of other healthcare provisions, perhaps the most significant change made to Medicaid through the ACA was the expansion of eligibility to include all adults with incomes up to 138 percent of the federal poverty level regardless of other categorical criteria. Although expansion was originally set forth as a requirement, a 2012 Supreme Court decision made Medicaid expansion optional for states. Beginning in 2014, twenty-five states opted in to expand eligibility, resulting in an 8.8 percent increase in enrollment in 2014 and a 7.2 percent increase in 2015 (MACPAC 2022). As of 2023, just ten states have not opted to expand.[22]

To fund the expansion, the federal government initially offered a 100 percent matching rate for newly eligible enrollees through the ACA until 2017. In the following years, the matching rate declined slightly each year until it reached 90 percent in 2020, where it remains currently for all states that have opted into Medicaid expansion. Accordingly, the federal share of Medicaid expenditures grew significantly following expansion, while the state share remained relatively stable even for states that opted in. In 2015, total federal Medicaid spending grew by 18 percent to $331 billion, with ACA expansion funding accounting for about one-fifth of the total expenditures (Clemens and Ippolito 2018). Meanwhile, the state share of spending grew by 5 percent in 2015, according to Centers for Medicare and Medicaid Services (CMS) data.

The impact of ACA funding on states that have opted into expansion is significant, although heterogeneous. In 2021, ACA funding as a percent of total federal Medicaid spending in expansion states ranged from 4 percent in Oklahoma (opted in to expansion in 2021) to 54 percent in Washington (opted in to expansion in 2014) with a median of 32 percent according to CMS data. While research suggests that Medicaid expansion has not significantly impacted state budgets, expansion does make states highly reliant on the federal government, as evidenced by analysis of potential reform efforts at the federal level (Gruber and Sommers 2020).

In a report on options to reduce the federal deficit, the CBO concluded that reducing the federal matching rate for ACA enrollees to the standard FMAP rate would likely cause states to discontinue coverage for those enrollees because of the strain expanded coverage would put on state budgets (CBO 2022b). In fact, many states included provisions in their expansion legislation to unwind expansion if federal matching falls below certain thresholds (Clemens and Ippolito 2018).

Targeting and Timing of Federal Aid

As discussed above, the federal government frequently provides aid to states during economic downturns to ensure that countercyclical programs like Medicaid can continue in the face of state budget constraints. Similar to emergency programs for UI, federal Medicaid assistance offered to states during recessions is often one-size-fits-all in the form of enhanced FMAP rates for all states, yet this misses crucial variation in state economic conditions. For example, between February 2020 and September 2020, the increase in Medicaid enrollment per state resident ranged from 0.009 to 0.054 people. States like New York and Nevada experienced greater increases in enrollment per resident, while Alabama and Wyoming saw smaller increases in enrollment per resident (Clemens, Ippolito, and Veuger 2021).

Despite this heterogeneity, each state received a blanket 6.2 percent increase in FMAP rates through FFCRA. Indeed, Clemens, Ippolito, and Veuger (2021) find that FFCRA Medicaid relief funds were not strongly correlated to enrollment shocks during the COVID-19 pandemic. This suggests that rather than providing aid to states that likely needed it most, the enhanced FMAP reimbursements actually benefited states with higher baseline expenditures instead. In contrast, Clemens, Ippolito, and Veuger (2021) also assess the state aid delivered through the American Rescue Plan Act (ARPA) during the pandemic and find that because this assistance was tied to state unemployment rates, the aid was somewhat better targeted to states in need.

As pandemic-era Medicaid rules wind down, it is unclear how states will be impacted. The end of the continuous coverage period is likely to result in a decrease in enrollment in many states. Williams, Burns, and Rudowitz (2023) estimate that enrollment will fall by 18 percent nationally between March 2023 and March 2024, yet disenrollment rates will vary by state. Once enhanced FMAP rates are also phased down, it is likely that states will see a sharp increase in their own Medicaid spending, as was the case when the enhanced FMAP rates provided during the great recession concluded. In fact, state Medicaid spending grew by 19.8 percent in fiscal year 2012 compared to the previous year, following the end of ARRA FMAP rate increases (Williams 2022). States similarly expect that a decrease in federal Medicaid spending post-FFCRA will impact their own budgets greatly, particularly if enrollment remains high.

Pensions and Debt

The previous sections have shown how the increased costs of state-administered programs have been accompanied by an increase in the federal share of the financial burden of those programs. While it would require substantial political will, such programs could be reformed. Less flexible are the debts and unfunded liabilities that state and local governments have acquired over time. Concerns during the COVID-19 panic about state and local government finances drove over $900 billion of federal "relief" for state and local governments (Clemens and Veuger 2023). States accepting such aid were under no requirement to renegotiate any debts or outstanding obligations or reform any programs. The unconditional nature of these transfers raises the question of the extent to which state and local debts and liabilities are also implicitly federal liabilities.

The stable nature of state and local debts may be attributable to balanced budget requirements and other fiscal rules, such as state controls on local debt, which vary across states but overall limit the extent of the growth of municipal bond debt (Epple and Spatt 1986). In addition, over 60 percent of municipal bond debt is in the form of revenue bonds that are backed by a specific revenue stream and hence have a dedicated source of funding for repayment. With that said, there are significant differences in indebtedness across states.

As shown in figure 10.8, state and local government bonds and loans outstanding rose in the first decade of the 2000s and have remained largely stable at around $3.2 trillion since 2010, yet declined as a share of GDP from 20 percent to 12 percent during the same period.

Figures 10.9a and 10.9b show on a logarithmic scale the relationship between the share of total municipal debt outstanding and the size of the states' populations and economies as measured by gross state product. Over 90 percent of the variation in the debt share is captured by state size, leaving 6 percent to 10 percent unexplained and thus reflecting differences in relative debt burdens. The slopes of the lines of best fit are 1.091 and 1.063, respectively, suggesting that larger states have somewhat more debt than would be predicted by a perfect linear relationship between debt and population with a slope of 1.

More significant than the evolution of bond indebtedness has been the growth of unfunded pension liabilities, which according to Federal Reserve statistics, reached $4.4 trillion in the first quarter of 2023. Figure 10.10 shows this evolution over time, with data from the Federal Reserve's Financial Accounts of the United States (Table L.120.b).

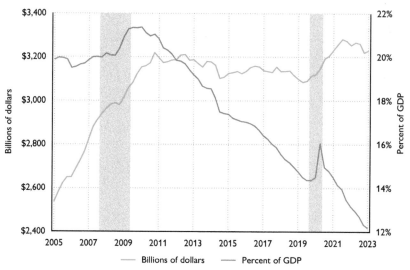

Figure 10.8 State and local governments' debt securities and loan liabilities

Note: Shading indicates recessions as defined by the NBER.

Sources: Liability from St. Louis Fed FRED Economic Data; GDP data from US Bureau of Economic Analysis.

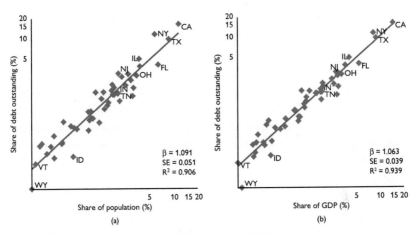

Figure 10.9 State share of total debt outstanding, 2021

Note: Displays line of best fit. Log scales.

Sources: Debt data from US Census Bureau's State and Local Government Finance Historical Datasets; population data from US Census Bureau; GDP data from US Bureau of Economic Analysis.

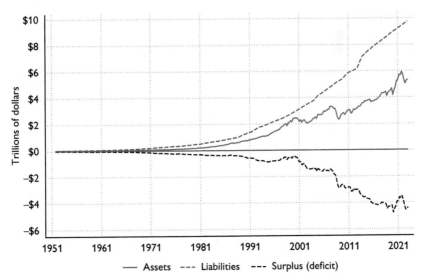

Figure 10.10 Federal reserve state and local pension assets and liabilities

Source: Federal Reserve Flow of Funds Z.1 (L.120.b).

As discussed in Giesecke and Rauh (2023), these official figures from the Federal Reserve are larger than the liabilities that state and local governments disclose in their annual financial reports, due largely to the use of lower discount rates. The Federal Reserve figures, however, do not represent a true value of the liability as a guaranteed payment, which would require discounting using a default-free yield curve. Default-free market value pension valuation treats pension promises as similar in their default characteristics to low-risk government bonds, as opposed to either the Federal Reserve's approach (fixed discount rates periodically updated based on corporate bond yields) or the approach of the systems themselves (fixed discount rates based on expected returns on plan assets). Nonetheless, despite increases in the value of plan assets from around $2 trillion in the year 2000 to over $5 trillion in 2022, unfunded liabilities grew from less than $1 trillion to the current $4.4 trillion in this period, as the rate of growth of liabilities substantially outpaced the rate of growth of assets. This is remarkable given that pension fund assets tend to have heavy risk loadings on the US stock market, which increased in value by a factor of over three times over this time period based on the S&P 500 index level.

To a somewhat greater extent than the overall level of debt, unfunded pension liabilities are unequally distributed across states. As shown in figures 10.11a and 10.11b, the coefficients on lines of best fit are below 1, in the range of 0.90–0.95, and the fit as measured by R-squared is 0.84–0.85. There is thus significantly more variation in unfunded liabilities not explained by state size. Among medium- to large-size states, California, Illinois, New Jersey, and Ohio sit above the lines of best fit, while Texas, New York, Florida, Indiana, and Tennessee sit below it.

In aggregate, the underlying risk factors involve the evolution of benefits on the liability side, the exposure of assets to market risk on the asset side, and the extent to which pension funding will be increased. These risk factors also have cross-sectional components, although to some extent the federal government may view unfunded pension liabilities as a common problem. Given the reaction of the federal government to shocks such as COVID-19, as well as dynamics surrounding union pension rescue packages, it would not be unreasonable to think that state and local government pension liabilities will be rescued as well. Such a possibility raises moral hazard on the part of states, removing incentives to address their own fiscal challenges.

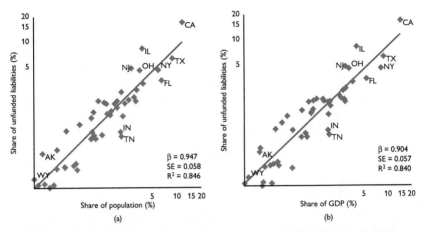

Figure 10.11 State share of total unfunded pension liabilities (market value), 2021

Note: Displays line of best fit. Log scales.

Sources: Pension data from publicpension.stanford.edu; population data from US Census Bureau; GDP data from US Bureau of Economic Analysis.

The political dynamics of pension bailouts from the recent rescue of union pension plans foreshadow what might occur if a state or local government seeks federal government support. In 2022, the Biden administration applied $36 billion in federal funds to cover the deficit in the Teamsters' Central States Pension Fund. This follows a $10 billion 2019 rescue of coal miners' pensions, all part of a system of multiemployer pensions covering unionized workers in the private sector (Rauh 2018).

Conclusion

The optimal extent to which services are provided at a federal versus local level and funded at a state versus local level is a long-standing research question. This essay has explored the increasing federalization of government programs and the implications for state and federal liabilities. Despite states' status as sovereign entities with taxation and debt issuance authority, many state liabilities appear to have become de facto federal liabilities, since the federal government's support role expands dramatically when state and local systems come under pressure. Thus, programs that may ex ante have appeared to be largely state-funded have increasingly proven to be federally funded. This will be even more so the case if the unfunded liabilities that have financed an expansion in state and local government expenditures also prove to be federal liabilities.

Notes

1. While Montana offers more than twenty-six weeks of benefit payments, thirteen states offer fewer than twenty-six weeks. For more information, see *Policy Basics: How Many Weeks of Unemployment Compensation Are Available?*, updated December 18, 2023. Washington, DC: Center on Budget and Policy Priorities.

2. See Congressional Research Service (hereafter CRS), *Unemployment Insurance: Programs and Benefits* (RL3362), October 18, 2019.

3. Employers with at least one employee for at least twenty weeks of the year or who have paid at least $1,500 to employees in any quarter of that year pay FUTA and SUTA.

4. See CRS, *The Unemployment Trust Fund (UTF): State Insolvency and Federal Loans to States* (RS22954), updated January 13, 2023.

5. SUTA rates range from 0 to over 14 percent, with bases ranging from $7,000 to $62,500 as of tax year 2022.

6. For an explanation of SUTA experience rating requirements, see Conformity Requirements for State UC Laws on the US Department of Labor website (n.d.), https://oui.doleta.gov/unemploy/pdf/uilaws_exper_rating.pdf.

7. The latest Department of Labor solvency report can be found at the US Department of Labor website (March 2023), https://oui.doleta.gov/unemploy/docs/trustFundSolvReport2023.pdf.

8. A full explanation of FUTA rates and credits can be found on the Congressional Research Service (CRS) website: https://crsreports.congress.gov/product/pdf/RS/RS22954.

9. States below 100 percent solvency in quarter three of 2019 include Arizona, California, Colorado, Connecticut, Delaware, Illinois, Indiana, Kentucky, Maryland, Massachusetts, Minnesota, Missouri, New Hampshire, New Jersey, New York, Ohio, Pennsylvania, Rhode Island, Tennessee, Texas, West Virginia, and Wisconsin.

10. See Katelin P. Isaacs and Julie M. Whittaker, *Emergency Unemployment Compensation (EUC08): Status of Benefits Prior to Expiration* (R42444), Congressional Research Service, August 11, 2014.

11. See US DOL's 2014 State Unemployment Insurance Trust Fund Solvency Report.

12. CRS, *Unemployment Trust Fund.*

13. See Iowa Workforce Development memorandum, May 10, 2021, https://governor.iowa.gov/sites/default/files/documents/2021-05-10--MEMORANDUM.pdf.

14. See South Carolina governor Henry McMaster to Daniel Ellzey, May 6, 2021, https://governor.sc.gov/sites/default/files/Documents/5-6-21 Gov McMaster to Dir Ellzey re Federal UI benefit termination.pdf.

15. See World Population Review, "Cost of Living Index by State 2023," https://worldpopulationreview.com/state-rankings/cost-of-living-index-by-state.

16. See CRS, *Medicaid Financing and Expenditures* (R42640), updated November 10, 2020.

17. CRS, *Medicaid Financing and Expenditures*. See also CRS, *Medicaid: An Overview* (R43357), updated February 8, 2023.

18. A full list of FMAP rates can be found at Kaiser Family Foundation (hereafter KFF), https://www.kff.org/medicaid/state-indicator/federal-matching-rate-and -multiplier.

19. See CRS, *Medicaid Recession-Related FMAP Increases* (R46346), May 7, 2020.

20. For details on unwinding FFCRA Medicaid provisions, see Suzanne Wikle and Jennifer Wagner, *Unwinding the Medicaid Continuous Coverage Requirement*, Center for Law and Social Policy, updated April 28, 2023.

21. For state-by-state breakdowns, see KFF, *Medicaid Expenditures as a Percent of Total State Expenditures by Fund*, SFY 2021.

22. Nonexpansion states include Alabama, Florida, Georgia, Kansas, Mississippi, South Carolina, Tennessee, Texas, Wisconsin, and Wyoming. For information on Medicaid expansion, see KFF, *Status of State Medicaid Expansion Decisions*, October 4, 2023.

References

Anderson, Patricia M., and Bruce D. Meyer. 2000. "The Effects of the Unemployment Insurance Payroll Tax on Wages, Employment, Claims and Denials." *Journal of Public Economics* 78, nos. 1–2 (October): 81–106.

Chetty, Raj. 2008. "Moral Hazard versus Liquidity and Optimal Unemployment Insurance." *Journal of Political Economy* 116, no. 2 (April): 173–234.

Clemens, Jeffrey, and Benedic Ippolito. 2018. "Implications of Medicaid Financing Reform for State Government Budgets." *Tax Policy and the Economy* 32:135–72.

Clemens, Jeffrey, Benedic Ippolito, and Stan Veuger. 2021. "Medicaid and Fiscal Federalism during the COVID-19 Pandemic." *Public Budgeting & Finance* 41, no. 4 (Winter): 94–109.

Clemens, Jeffrey, and Stan Veuger. 2023. "Lessons from COVID-19 Aid to State and Local Governments for the Design of Federal Automatic Stabilizers." Aspen Economic Strategy Group, January 11. Washington, DC: American Enterprise Institute.

Congressional Budget Office (CBO). 2022a. "Federal Subsidies for Health Insurance Coverage for People under 65: 2022 to 2032." Pub. no. 57962 (June 30).

———. 2022b. "Options for Reducing the Deficit, 2023 to 2032, Volume I: Larger Reductions." Pub. no. 58164 (December 7).

Dube, Arindrajit. 2021. "Aggregate Employment Effects of Unemployment Benefits during Deep Downturns: Evidence from the Expiration of the Federal

Pandemic Unemployment Compensation." National Bureau of Economic Research (NBER) Working Paper Series w28470 (February). Cambridge, MA: National Bureau of Economic Research.

Duggan, Mark, Audrey Guo, and Andrew C. Johnston. 2023. "Experience Rating as an Automatic Stabilizer." *Tax Policy and the Economy* 37:109–33.

Epple, Dennis, and Chester Spatt. 1986. "State Restrictions on Local Debt: Their Role in Preventing Default." *Journal of Public Economics* 29, no. 2 (March): 199–221.

Galle, Brian. 2018. "How to Save Unemployment Insurance." *Arizona State Law Journal* 50, no. 4 (Winter): 1009.

Gamkhar, Shama, and Wallace Oates. 1996. "Asymmetries in the Response to Increases and Decreases in Intergovernmental Grants: Some Empirical Findings." *National Tax Journal* 49, no. 4 (December): 501–12.

Ganong, Peter, Pascal Noel, and Joseph Vavra. 2020. "US Unemployment Insurance Replacement Rates during the Pandemic." *Journal of Public Economics* 191 (November): 104273.

Giesecke, Oliver, and Joshua Rauh. 2023. "Trends in State and Local Pension Funds." *Annual Review of Financial Economics* 15:221–38.

Giroud, Xavier, and Joshua Rauh. 2019. "State Taxation and the Reallocation of Business Activity: Evidence from Establishment-Level Data." *Journal of Political Economy* 127, no. 3 (June): 1262–316.

Gordon, Roger H. 1983. "An Optimal Taxation Approach to Fiscal Federalism." *Quarterly Journal of Economics* 98, no. 4 (November): 567–86.

Gruber, Jonathan, and Benjamin D. Sommers. 2020. "Fiscal Federalism and the Budget Impacts of the Affordable Care Act's Medicaid Expansion." National Bureau of Economic Research (NBER) Working Paper Series w26862 (March). Cambridge, MA: National Bureau of Economic Research.

Guo, Audrey. 2023a. "The Effects of State Business Taxes on Plant Closures: Evidence from Unemployment Insurance Taxation and Multi-establishment Firms." *Review of Economics and Statistics* 105, no. 3 (May): 580–95.

———. 2023b. "Payroll Tax Incidence: Evidence from Unemployment Insurance." Discussion paper, Santa Clara University. arXiv preprint arXiv:2304.05605.

Guo, Audrey, and Andrew C. Johnston. 2021. "The Finance of Unemployment Compensation and Its Consequences." *Public Finance Review* 49, no. 3 (May): 392–434.

Hercowitz, Zvi, and Michel Strawczynski. 2004. "Cyclical Ratcheting in Government Spending: Evidence from the OECD." *Review of Economics and Statistics* 86, no. 1 (February): 353–61.

Johnston, Andrew C. 2021. "Unemployment Insurance Taxes and Labor Demand: Quasi-experimental Evidence from Administrative Data." *American Economic Journal: Economic Policy* 13, no. 1 (February): 266–93.

Johnston, Andrew C., and Alexandre Mas. 2018. "Potential Unemployment Insurance Duration and Labor Supply: The Individual and Market-Level

Response to a Benefit Cut." *Journal of Political Economy* 126, no. 6 (December): 2480–522.

Kaiser Commission on Medicaid and the Uninsured. 2011. "Impact of the Medicaid Fiscal Relief Provisions in the American Recovery and Reinvestment Act (ARRA)." Kaiser Family Foundation (KFF), October 1. https://www.kff.org/medicaid/issue-brief/impact-of-the-medicaid-fiscal-relief-provisions/.

Lachowska, Marta, Isaac Sorkin, and Stephen A. Woodbury. 2022. "Firms and Unemployment Insurance Take-Up." National Bureau of Economic Research (NBER) Working Paper Series 30266 (July). Cambridge, MA: National Bureau of Economic Research.

McLure, Charles E. 1983. *Tax Assignment in Federal Countries.* Canberra, Australia: Centre for Research on Federal Financial Relations, Australian National University, in association with the International Seminar in Public Economics.

Medicaid and CHIP Payment and Access Commission (MACPAC). 2022. *MACStats: Medicaid and CHIP Data Book.*

Meyer, Bruce D., and Wallace K. C. Mok. 2014. "A Short Review of Recent Evidence on the Disincentive Effects of Unemployment Insurance and New Evidence from New York State." *National Tax Journal* 67, no. 1 (March): 219–51.

Nicholson, Walter, and Karen Needels. 2011. "The EUC08 Program in Theoretical and Historical Perspective." *Mathematica Policy Research.* Washington, DC: US Department of Labor.

Oates, Wallace E. 1972. *Fiscal Federalism.* New York: Harcourt Brace Jovanovich.

———. 1999. "An Essay on Fiscal Federalism." *Journal of Economic Literature* 37, no. 3 (September): 1120–149.

Rauh, Joshua D. 2018. *How the Multiemployer Pension System Affects Stakeholders: Hearing before the Joint Select Committee on Solvency of Multiemployer Pension Plans of the United States Congress,* 115th Congress, July 25 (testimony of Joshua D. Rauh, Senior Fellow and Director of Research, Hoover Institution).

Schultz, Laura, and Lynn Holland. 2023. *Giving or Getting? New York's Balance of Payments with the Federal Government.* Rockefeller Institute of Government, March 23.

Simon, Amy. 2021. *Unemployment Insurance at a Crossroads: Tracing Program Design during and beyond COVID-19.* American Enterprise Institute, October 20.

Smith, Daniel L., and Jeffrey B. Wenger. 2013. "State Unemployment Insurance Trust Solvency and Benefit Generosity." *Journal of Policy Analysis and Management* 32, no. 3 (June): 536–53.

Walczak, Jared, and Savannah Funkhouser. 2021. "States Have $95 Billion to Restore Their Unemployment Trust Funds—Why Aren't They Using It?" Tax Foundation, September 22.

Weiner, Jennifer, and New England Public Policy Center. 2012. *When the Tide Goes Out: Unemployment Insurance Trust Funds and the Great Recession, Lessons for and from New England.* New England Public Policy Center Research Report 12-1, April. Federal Reserve Bank of Boston.

Williams, Elizabeth. 2022. "Medicaid Enrollment & Spending Growth: FY 2022 & 2023." Kaiser Family Foundation (KFF), October 25. https://www.kff.org/medicaid/issue-brief/medicaid-enrollment-spending-growth-fy-2022-2023.

Williams, Elizabeth, Alice Burns, and Robin Rudowitz. 2023. "Fiscal Implications for Medicaid of Enhanced Federal Funding and Continuous Enrollment." Kaiser Family Foundation (KFF), June 16. https://www.kff.org/medicaid/issue-brief/fiscal-implications-for-medicaid-of-enhanced-federal-funding-and-continuous-enrollment.

11

Is the United States Still a Competitive Federal System?

Paul E. Peterson and Carlos X. Lastra-Anadón

In democratic societies, competitive federalism exists when elected officials at lower tiers of government have independent authority to determine a broad range of tax, expenditure, and regulatory policies (Feld et al. 2004). Within such a system, the higher and lower tiers each have a specific domestic policy function to perform (Peterson 1995). The central government executes the redistributive function, the reallocation of resources from the productive to the dependent segments of society.[1] The lower tiers of government carry out the developmental function by establishing a regulatory framework and providing services that foster community prosperity and growth. Their focus on development is a byproduct of constraints imposed by their structural position within a competitive federal system. States, provinces, municipalities, and special districts compete with one another for human, material, and financial capital. To enjoy prosperity, states and municipalities need to offer services and establish regulatory frameworks that attract productive residents and business without imposing overly burdensome taxes (Peterson 1981, 1995; Tiebout 1956). Winners typically enjoy higher property values, increased economic activity, population growth, and enhanced fiscal strength. Losers struggle with property devaluation, capital flight, out-migration, and fiscal stress. If losses are extreme, the state or municipality risks bankruptcy.

Competitive federalism is an unusual form of government. Although 40 percent of the world's population is said to live within a federal system (Forum of Federations 2021), it is the large countries that select this form of government. Only 23 to 25 of the world's 193 countries have any form of federalism, competitive or not (Rodden 2006, 23; Forum of Federations 2021). In noncompetitive federal systems, the national government places sharp limits on lower tiers of government, either by appointing its officers or by financing and closely regulating their expenditure. Only in the United States,

Canada, and Switzerland do independently elected officials exercise broad authority over tax, expenditure, and regulatory policies (Feld et al. 2004; Lauden and Smith 2000, 634, 636, 653–54; Rodden 2006; see also Olowu 2002, 19; Republic of India 2006, 8).[2] Among these three, the United States seems to provide the clearest contemporary example of competitive federalism, as in the other two countries the number of lower-tier governments is fewer, making it easier for them to coordinate action.

Tocqueville noticed the exceptional aspects of federalism in the United States as early as 1835 when he wrote "Americans love their towns for much the same reasons that highlanders love their mountains. In both cases the native land has emphatic and peculiar features; it has a more pronounced physiognomy than is found elsewhere" (quoted in Winthrop 1976, 96). He regarded its federal institutions as foundational for both political liberty and economic prosperity (Hancock 1990; Winthrop 1976).

Developmental vs. Redistributive Functions

Differences between higher and lower tiers of government are propensities, not inevitabilities. Political struggles within a democratic society may generate outcomes inconsistent with the broad propositions outlined above. The national government can and does undertake developmental projects, especially large-scale ones (space exploration, basic scientific research) beyond the capacity of lower-tier governments. State and local tiers of government experiment in redistribution. They are more likely to do so if they enjoy a monopoly over valued resources or are well situated in a highly desirable location, in a scenic setting or adjacent to a harbor, waterway, or transportation hub. For example, the politics and policies of San Francisco differ from those in most other cities in part because its setting is unparalleled (DeLeon 1992).

Despite these exceptions, throughout the twentieth century, national and subnational tiers of government usually focused on their distinctive functions (Peterson 1995). However, recent changes in US politics have had the potential to alter those foci. To see whether the structure of federalism in the United States has shifted in response to political developments, we look at types of public expenditures and sources of revenue by central and local governments between fiscal years 1993 and 2021.

To describe recent political changes, following V. O. Key (1949), we divide society into two broad categories, the "haves" and "have-nots." The group of haves consists of households who are self-sufficient enough that their outputs spill over to the benefit of others. The have-nots are those who are not productive enough to be self-sufficient, but who remain partially or wholly dependent on charity or government assistance.

The relative power of the haves and have-nots has shifted back and forth over the three-quarters of a century since the end of World War II. The close balance of forces is evident from the shifting back and forth in partisan control of the presidency and the regularity with which the party controlling the executive lacks control of one or both houses of the legislative branch. Only in a few instances has one party been so dominant that it controls both branches, the most recent cases in point being short periods within the Johnson, Obama, Trump, and Biden administrations. Still, in the postwar era, the "arc of history," to borrow a phrase from President Obama, bends toward the have-nots (Obama 2016). As this segment has gained greater political weight and become more politically sophisticated, it has enlarged the size of the public sector, broadened the range of services provided to have-nots, and tightened regulations on the productive segment of society, or the haves.

But has politics altered the structure of the federal system? Has political change shifted the focus of lower-tier governments? To address that question we trace trends at both the national and lower governmental tiers in (1) the share of expenditures allocated for developmental and redistributive purposes; and (2) the progressivity of revenue streams received by each level of government. If the structure of competitive federalism has remained essentially intact, we expect to see little change in the percentage of state and local expenditures paid from their own fiscal resources that is allocated to developmental rather than redistributive purposes. We also expect to observe little change in sources of revenue. But if political trends have been powerful enough to alter the structure of the federal system, we expect to see an increasing share of state and local expenditure allocated for redistributive purposes and an increasing use of progressive taxes by state and local governments.

Lower Tiers of Government in a Federal System

The traditional role of the lower tiers of government is to provide a set of services that sustain the community's economic development. As James Bryce (1921, 132) phrased it a century ago:

It is the business of a local authority to mend the roads, to clean out the village well or provide a new pump, to see that there is a place where straying beasts may be kept till the owner reclaims them, to fix the number of cattle each villager may turn out on the common pasture, to give each his share of timber cut in the common woodland.

The role played by lower tiers of government remains no less significant today than when Bryce penned these words. Admittedly, the size of government has risen steeply in the intervening period. Between 1962 and 1993, outlays for redistributive and developmental purposes by the central government rose from 5 percent to 11 percent of the GDP (table 11.1; Peterson 1995, 54, table 3-1). Outlays by state and local governments rose nearly as rapidly. In 1962, they were at 7 percent of GDP (Peterson 1995, 54, table 3-1), higher than the outlays by the central government. By 2018, they had increased steeply to 10.3 percent of GDP, a somewhat lower rate of increase than that of the central government (table 11.2). Yet state and local tiers of government still accounted for nearly half of US government domestic spending allocated toward redistributive and developmental purposes.[3]

Table 11.1 National expenditure, 1993–2021 (2018 US $billions)

Items	1993	Share	2018	Share	2021	Share	Annual growth rate 1993–2018	Annual growth rate 2018–2021
Developmental								
Transportation	56	0.05	93	0.04	154	0.03	2.0%	18.5%
Utilities	7	0.01	2	0.00	6	0.00	-4.5%	40.2%
Safety	24	0.02	60	0.02	71	0.01	3.7%	5.7%
Education	76	0.06	96	0.04	298	0.05	0.9%	46.2%
Natural resources	69	0.06	76	0.03	443	0.08	0.4%	79.8%
Science and tech	27	0.02	32	0.01	36	0.01	0.6%	4.1%
Post office	3	0.00	-1	0.00	-3			23.9%
Subtotal Developmental	**262**	**0.22**	**357**	**0.15**	**1,006**	**0.18**	**1.2%**	**41.2%**
GDP share	2.4%		1.8%		4.7%			
Redistributive								
Welfare	743	0.61	1,466	0.60	2764	0.49	2.8%	23.6%
Health and hospitals	159	0.13	551	0.22	796	0.14	5.1%	13.1%
Housing and development	52	0.04	84	0.03	103	0.02	2.0%	6.8%
Subtotal Redistributive	**954**	**0.78**	**2,101**	**0.85**	**4,670**	**0.82**	**3.2%**	**30.5%**
GDP share	8.8%		10.3%		21.6%			
Total Developmental and Redistributive	**1,216**	**1.00**	**2,458**	**1.00**	**5,675**	**1.00**	**2.9%**	**32.2%**
GDP share	11.2%		12.1%		26.3%			
Other expenditure								
Pensions/medical insurance	103		147		162		1.4%	3.4%
Administration	21		24		274		0.6%	125.5%
Defense	466		631		754		1.2%	6.1%
International affairs	28		49		47		2.3%	-1.4%
Interest	318		325		352		0.1%	2.7%
Subtotal Other expenditure	**935**		**1,176**		**1,590**		**0.9%**	**10.6%**
GDP share	8.6%		5.8%		7.4%			
Total National expenditure	**2,151**		**3,634**		**7,265**		**2.1%**	**26.0%**

Note: Share is over total developmental and redistributive expenditure.

Source: Budget of the United States (2021), Table 3.2, Outlays by Function and Subfunction: 1962–2025.

Table 11.2 State and local direct expenditure, 1993–2021 (2018 US $billions)

Items	1993	Share	2018	Share	2021	Share	Annual growth rate 1993–2018	Annual growth rate 2018–2021
Developmental								
Transportation	94	0.08	159	0.08	154	0.06	2.1%	-1.0%
Natural resources	41	0.03	72	0.03	74	0.03	2.3%	1.0%
Safety	140	0.12	27	0.01	286	0.12	-6.4%	120.4%
Education	511	0.42	986	0.47	1,003	0.42	2.7%	0.6%
Utilities	187	0.15	323	0.15	337	0.14	2.2%	1.4%
Miscellaneous	(1)	0.00	7	0.00	15	0.01		28.8%
Subtotal Developmental	**972**	**0.80**	**1,574**	**0.75**	**1,870**	**0.78**	**1.9%**	**5.9%**
GDP share	9.0%		7.7%		8.7%			
Redistributive								
Welfare	194	0.16	607	0.29	650	0.27	4.7%	2.3%
Health and hospitals	24	0.02	(120)	-0.06	(186)	-0.08		15.7%
Housing	21	0.02	33	0.02	62	0.03	1.8%	23.4%
Subtotal Redistributive	**239**	**0.20**	**520**	**0.25**	**526**	**0.22**	**3.2%**	**0.4%**
GDP share	2.2%		2.6%		2.4%			
Total Developmental and Redistributive	**1,211**	**1.00**	**2,093**	**1.00**	**2,397**	**1.00**	**2.2%**	**4.6%**
GDP share	11.2%		10.3%		11.1%			
Other expenditure								
Pensions/medical insurance	158		365		530		3.4%	13.3%
Administration	148		293		106		2.8%	-28.8%
Interest on debt	88		111		107		0.9%	-1.2%
Subtotal Other expenditure	**394**		**769**		**743**		**2.7%**	**-1.1%**
GDP share	3.6%		3.8%		3.4%			
Total State and local expenditure	**1,605**		**2,862**		**3,140**		**2.3%**	**3.1%**

Note: Share is over total developmental and redistributive expenditure.

Source: US Census Bureau, Annual Surveys of State and Local Government Finances (multiple years).

When the lower tiers of government play such a major role in the provision of public services, they can adapt services to local needs and tastes. They can learn desired levels of service provision and estimate price levels by observing choices made by neighbors (Berry and Berry 1990; Walker 1969). Local governments can also explore new policy options without forcing wholesale change nationwide. As Justice Louis Brandeis observed: "A single courageous State may, if its citizens choose, serve as a laboratory; and try novel social and economic experiments without risk to the rest of the country" (New State Ice Co. v. Liebmann 1932, 262; but see Tarr 2001). If the experiment seems successful, others will try it out; if it fails or proves controversial, others will modify or ignore it.

Within a competitive system, state and local governments resist taking responsibility for large-scale redistributive programs. If states and localities attempt to tax the rich unduly and give generously to the poor, they become perverse magnets that attract dependent households but repel productive ones. For example, states that pay high welfare benefits to needy families are more likely to attract dependent households (Peterson and Rom 1990). More generally, residents of local communities "vote with their feet" by choosing to live in a locality where government services and regulatory practices suit their preferences and needs (Hirschman 1970; Hoxby 2000; Tiebout 1956). Between 2015 and 2020, about 13 percent of the population moved to a new place of residence annually (Frost 2020). If the prosperous are taxed unduly, they will search for alternative residences (Rauh and Shyu 2021). Locational responsiveness of high-income residents to state and local tax differentials increased with the passage of federal tax legislation in 2017 limiting federal income tax deductions for taxes paid to lower tiers of government. Population shifts from high-tax states (California, New York, and Illinois) to low-tax states (Florida, Texas, Montana, and Colorado) have been so substantial that the former lost seats in the House of Representatives as part of the reapportionment that followed the 2020 population census (Ax 2021). Other shifts from large central cities to suburbs, towns, exurbs, and more remote locations have accelerated since the onset of the COVID pandemic (Roberts 2020; Whyte 2020). All such moves affect property values at both the departure and destination points. Local policymakers have strong incentives to choose options likely to benefit a community's economic and social development. Perhaps that is why Bryce thought local officials exhibited a "narrowness of mind and the spirit of parsimony." If it were otherwise, Bryce added, "there would be less of that shrewdness which the practice of local government forms" (Bryce 1921, 132–33).

Throughout the twentieth century, the "spirit of parsimony" at the state and local levels remained well entrenched. Local expenditure focused on activities designed to enhance local prosperity, not interfere with it. Admittedly, state and local governments in the United States were not immune from the growth-in-government syndrome characteristic of the postwar era. However, the level of redistributive expenditure of state and local governments from own fiscal sources continued at a relatively modest level even after political changes in the aftermath of the Vietnam War. Self-financed expenditure for redistributive purposes by local governments budged upward from only 0.76 percent of GNP in 1962 to just 0.94 percent of GNP in 1990. Self-financed state redistributive expenditures expanded from 1.4 percent to only 2.5 percent of GNP during this period (Peterson 1995, 54, tables 3-2, 3-3).

In sum, the tiers of government in the United States in 1990 continued to fulfill their historic functions. Government expanded in size, but lower tiers remained faithful to modern versions of traditional responsibilities: to repair trails, upgrade wells, mend fences, police streets, and school the community's children. They executed government's development function.

Political Pressures for Redistribution

Political changes in the late twentieth century nonetheless threatened to alter the developmental focus of lower tiers of the federal system. Congress added free medical services, free and subsidized food services, housing subsidies, enlarged welfare benefits, compensatory education, and other programs for low-income households to its redistributive portfolio. To implement these policies, it provided intergovernmental grants to state and local governments. To administer these programs, state and local governments hired many more employees and recruited policy specialists whose perspectives were not always consistent with the traditional role of the lower tiers of government. As the number of employees increased, they became a fertile field for union organizers.

Intergovernmental Programs

Federal grants for redistributive programs (largely for payments to individuals) increased fiftyfold from $11.4 billion to $630.3 billion in constant 2012 dollars between 1955 and 2021, a shift from 0.4 percent to 3.3 percent of GDP over the period (figure 11.1). The grants generally came at little cost to lower tiers of government. Yet the clear redistributive purposes of these activities carried an implicit message that state and local governments can—and should—execute redistributive policy.

Policy Professionals

Federal grants initially generated intergovernmental conflict between national and lower tiers of government (Pressman and Wildavsky 1973). Housing for the poor was resisted locally by those who insisted it not be placed in "my backyard." When it was built, it was concentrated in dangerous high-rise silos or designed to serve an elderly, middle-class clientele. Grants directed toward the education of children from low-income households ended up funding traditional school operations. However, policy professionals

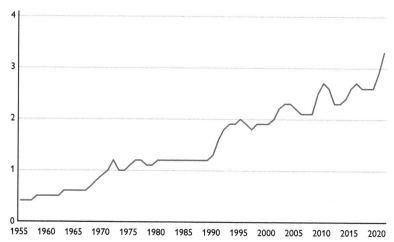

Figure 11.1 Transfers from national to state and local governments as a share of GDP, 1955–2021

Source: Budget of the United States (2021), Table 6.1, Composition of Outlays: 1955–2028.

sympathetic to the needs of program recipients were eventually hired to grease the intergovernmental machinery. They proved more loyal to their programs and their professional mission than to any tier of government for which they worked (Grodzins 1966). Gradually, they acquired the power to shape the broad range of public services (public health, mental health, special education, compensatory education, low-income housing, and welfare) in ways that adapted to nationally designed programs (Peterson, Rabe, and Wong 1986).[4] The new system acquired the moniker "cooperative federalism" (Grodzins 1966).

Collective Bargaining

As state and local government took on more responsibilities, the number of local government employees jumped upward—from 3.6 million in 1955 to 13.9 million in 2020 (figure 11.2). The number of those working for state governments shifted upward from about 1.2 million in 1955 to 5.2 million in 2020.[5] With a tripling of the size of the public-sector workforce, trade unions perceived an opportunity to broaden their constituency at a time when the manufacturing sector was in decline and trade unions in the private sector were suffering steady enrollment losses. But to capitalize on the opportunity, public-sector unions needed to overturn long-standing laws prohibiting collective bargaining and union strikes in the public sector.[6]

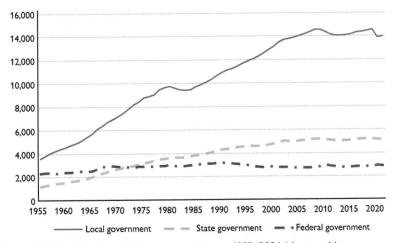

Figure 11.2 **Number of public-sector employees, 1955–2021 (thousands)**

Source: US Bureau of Labor Statistics, All Employees, Federal (CES9091000001), retrieved from FRED, Federal Reserve Bank of St. Louis.

In the 1950s, northern Democrats introduced bills in Congress that would allow federal employees to select unions to bargain collectively on their behalf. A stout Republican–Southern Democratic coalition blocked their passage, but in 1963, President John F. Kennedy issued an executive order granting federal employees the right to bargain on matters related to their working conditions, though not on wages and benefits that have direct impacts on governmental expenditure.

The presidential order opened the floodgates at state and local tiers of government. Over the next decade and a half, thirty-three states passed laws that imposed upon municipalities, school boards, and other lower tiers of government the duty-to-bargain collectively with their employees (Lovenheim and Willén 2019). The topics subject to bargaining included salaries, benefits, working conditions, and general school policy, such as the number of charter schools that could open within a district (Sowell 2020) and school openings during the COVID pandemic (Hartney and Finger 2022).

These changes in the intergovernmental system—enlarged grant programs, recruitment of policy professionals sympathetic to have-nots, and public-sector collective bargaining—posed a challenge to the structure of competitive federalism. It is plausible that together they were potent enough to alter the propensity of state and local tiers of government to concentrate their focus on development policy.

Data

To explore this topic, we track changes in domestic expenditure as well as changes in sources of revenue for both the national tier and the lower tiers of government between 1993 and 2021, the latest year for which relevant information is available.

Domestic Expenditure

We present domestic expenditure at selected intervals for this twenty-eight-year period as reported by the *Annual Survey of State and Local Government Finances* (hereinafter *AS*) issued yearly by the US Census Bureau.[7] We classify most expenditure as either developmental or redistributive.[8] We classify as developmental the following categories of domestic expenditure: transportation, natural resources (parks and recreation), safety (police and fire), education, utilities, and miscellaneous. We assume that the primary purpose of these expenditures is to sustain the well-being of the community as a whole, though some redistribution may occur. For example, there may be lower utility rates for low-income groups and more intensive safety protection in communities with high concentrations of poverty. We classify education as a developmental expenditure, because a primary purpose of educational institutions is to enhance human capital. It may also contribute to equal educational opportunity, but most research suggests that disparities in student performance between those from higher and lower socioeconomic backgrounds increase as students age and move to higher grades in school (Jencks and Phillips 1998; Shakeel and Peterson 2022). We classify the welfare, housing, and health and hospital categories in the *AS* data set as redistributive expenditure.

We place employee pensions and medical insurance in a separate category because it is part of the compensation package offered to public-sector employees. We are unable to distinguish between benefits received by employees whose activities are developmental from those whose activities are redistributive.[9]

We allocate expenditure to the tier of government that is the source of revenue used to cover its cost. For example, medical services paid out of grants from the national government are identified as expenditures by the highest tier but medical services paid from state and local sources of revenue are classified as expenditures by the lower tiers.[10] Classification error may occur when placing government-reported data into these analytical categories. Any government program may be in service of both developmental and redistributive purposes, and the function of a program may vary with the setting in which it is provided.

Sources of Revenue

The way in which a government obtains its revenues also fosters either developmental or redistributive objectives. If residents generally receive benefits from services commensurate with the amount of taxes paid, then revenue policy fosters a developmental objective. If have-nots receive more benefits from services than taxes paid, and haves do not, the tax system fosters a redistributive objective. Consistent with these propositions, we assume that the greater the progressivity with which governments access revenue, the greater the redistribution. Conversely, the less progressive the system of revenue collection, the more government is pursuing developmental objectives. We rank order tax sources by conventional notions of progressivity.

Our rank order from most to least progressive is as follows:

1. Individual income tax. The federal individual income tax and most state income taxes levy higher rates on households of higher income.
2. Corporate income tax. Corporate taxes are at least in part a tax on earnings of stockholders who are usually members of households of higher income.
3. Property tax. Taxes on property are generally proportional to property values.
4. Excise and sales taxes. Sales and excise taxes are consumption taxes that fall on households roughly in proportion with their expenditures except they generally fall more heavily on luxury items than necessities.
5. Federal payroll tax (social insurance trust). The tax is set at a constant level on wages and then it is capped; it falls more heavily on lower-income to middle-income workers than on higher-income ones.
6. Utility and liquor store revenue; charges, fees, and miscellaneous taxes. These sources of revenue usually capture a larger share of the income of lower-income households.

We exclude from own local revenues any amounts received from the central government through intergovernmental grants. We also exclude revenues received from state and local insurance trusts to cover pension and medical insurance costs, as state and local governments withdraw those sums from funds they have invested for this purpose.

Trends in Domestic Expenditure, Revenue Sources, and Debt

In this section, we trace trends in expenditure and revenue sources over the twenty-eight years 1993–2021. All calculations are percentages of GDP or in constant dollars.

Domestic Expenditure

Redistributive expenditure by the national government grew almost fivefold, from $0.95 trillion in 1993 to $4.7 trillion in 2021 (table 11.1 and figure 11.3). Up until 2018, the average annual rate of increase was 3.2 percent, though the rate of increase fluctuated within that period. Redistributive expenditure declined from 8.8 percent to 7.8 percent of GDP between 1993 and 2000, but Congress then added prescription drug benefits to Medicare and Medicaid during the Bush administration and passed the Affordable Care Act during the first years of the Obama administration. Redistributive spending rose to 11.7 percent of GDP by 2010, with most of the increase driven by expenditures for hospitals and healthcare. Between 2010 and 2018, economic growth and reduced expenditure for housing and community development facilitated a decline in redistributive spending to 10.3 percent of GDP, but this was followed by a sharp increase to 21.5 percent of GDP in 2020 and 21.6 percent of GDP in 2021. This was fueled by increases in welfare payments, which almost doubled after 2018, and health spending, which went up by 44 percent.

Developmental expenditure by the central government increased from $262 billion in 1992 to $357 billion in 2018, a 1.2 percent annual rate of increase (table 11.1). That increase was concentrated in the safety budget, perhaps as a function of increased concern about terrorists and illegal immigration. National development expenditure as a share of GDP declined from 2.4 percent to 1.8 percent. In the period between 2018 and 2021, developmental expenditure grew sharply, at an annual rate of 41 percent, driven by natural resources and education. However, the developmental share of total expenditures by the national government declined from 85 percent in 2018 to 82 percent in 2021, as redistributive expenditures grew at a much faster rate.

At the state and local level, expenditure from own sources climbed from $1.6 trillion in 1993 to $2.9 trillion in 2018, an annual rate of increase of

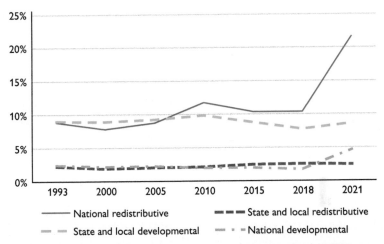

Figure 11.3 Expenditure by level of government and type as a share of GDP, 1993–2021

Note: We exclude pensions and medical insurance, administration, defense, international affairs, and debt interest.

Sources: US Census Bureau, Annual Surveys of State and Local Government Finances (multiple years); Budget of the United States (2022), Table 3.2, Outlays by Function and Subfunction, 1993–2028.

2.5 percent (table 11.2 and figure 11.3).[11] The amount spent for redistributive purposes rose from $239 billion to $520 billion in 2018, an annual growth rate of 3.2 percent. As a percentage of GDP, redistributive expenditure went from 2.2 in 1993 to 2.6 in 2018 but then slipped to 2.4 in 2021.

Welfare (public assistance and other cash transfer programs) constitutes the largest item within state and local redistributive spending category. It also is the one that grew the most, at an annualized 4.7 percent between 1993 and 2018 and by 2.3 percent annually between 2018 and 2021. Offsetting these increases, the category defined as "health and hospitals" paid for from state and local sources shows a decline in expenditure in the period before 2018 (when expenditures from federal grants are excluded), while housing expenditure grew modestly at 1.8 percent between 1993 and 2018.

Developmental expenditure by state and local governments shows a broadly similar pattern. It rose from about $1.0 trillion in 1993 to $1.7 trillion in 2010, or from 9.0 percent to 9.8 percent of GDP, probably due in part to a contracting economy. It then retreated to 7.7 percent by 2018, as expenditures plateaued and the economy expanded. By 2021, it was $1.9 trillion, or again 8.7 percent of GDP. Overall, the increase in 1993–2021 was 2.4 percent annually, rather less than the 2.9 percent increase for redistributive expenditure. As of 2021, education, the largest single category, constitutes the largest of development expenditures, with about $1 trillion (and 42 percent of total developmental and redistributive expenditure). This compares to the $650 billion in welfare, the largest redistributive expenditure.

As mentioned, the amount spent by state and local governments on pensions and medical insurance for government employees is not classified as either redistributive or developmental. These expenditures climbed steadily from $158 billion in 1993 to $365 billion in 2018, a steep annual rate of increase of 3.4 percent. The introduction of collective bargaining seems to have encouraged state and local governments to greatly increase employee benefits (Biggs and Richwine 2014; Costrell and Dean 2013; Koedel, Ni, and Podgursky 2014; Koedel and Podgursky 2016).

Between 2018 and 2021, welfare expenditures jumped to $530 billion. This increase was driven by increases in unemployment compensation, which increased by 511 percent between 2018 and 2021 due to rapid expansion of unemployment benefits during the COVID pandemic.

In sum, both redistributive and developmental expenditures had increased steeply over the twenty-five-year period 1993–2018. But redistributive expenditure as a share of total expenditure by the lower tiers of government did not change materially between 1993 and 2018. In 2021, redistribution is 22 percent of state and local redistributive and developmental spending, as compared to 20 percent in 2018 and 22 percent in 1993. Although shifts occur within this period, no secular trend is evident. The structure of competitive federalism appears to have remained substantially unchanged. However, expenditures devoted to pensions and health insurance increased by an annual rate of 3.4 percent, the largest rate of increase for any large category of expenditure. Collective bargaining is driving up employee costs. It is the most dynamic element in state and local finance.

Revenues

In 1993, the individual income tax levied by the central government generated 70 percent of the revenue received by the national government (table 11.3 and figure 11.4). That percentage ebbed and flowed over the next twenty-five years, becoming 78 percent of total national government revenue in 2018. By 2021, it slipped to 75 percent. As a source of revenue for the national government, the corporate income tax reached a high of 20 percent in 2005 but fell to 9 percent in 2018, very likely due both to changes in tax law and to

Table 11.3 National revenue, 1993–2021 (2018 US $billions)

Items	1993	Share	2018	Share	2021	Share	Annual growth rate 1993–2018	Annual growth rate 2018–2021
Individual income tax	816	0.70	1,684	0.78	1,947	0.75	2.9%	5.0%
Corporate income tax	188	0.16	205	0.09	354	0.14	0.3%	20.0%
Subtotal income taxes	**1,004**	**0.86**	**1,888**	**0.87**	**2,302**	**0.88**	**2.6%**	**6.8%**
GDP share	9.3%		9.3%		10.7%			
Insurance (Social Security and other)	186	0.16	316	0.15	345	0.13	2.1%	2.9%
Excise taxes	77	0.07	95	0.04	72	0.03	0.8%	-8.9%
Charges, fees, and other	81	0.07	176	0.08	230	0.09	3.1%	9.4%
Subtotal consumption, payroll taxes, and other	**158**	**0.14**	**271**	**0.13**	**302**	**0.12**	**2.2%**	**3.7%**
GDP share	1.5%		1.3%		1.4%			
Total National revenue	**1,162**	**1.00**	**2,159**	**1.00**	**2,603**	**1.00**	**2.5%**	**6.4%**

Source: Budget of the United States (2021), Table 2.1, Receipts by Source.

international shifts in capital. By 2021, it was 14 percent. Revenue from the payroll tax fluctuated between 12 percent and 15 percent between 1993 and 2021 but no strong secular trend takes place. Revenue from the excise tax plunged from 7 percent in 1993 to 4 percent of the total in 2018, and it slipped further to 3 percent by 2021, as government tariffs were lowered as part of efforts to enhance international trade. With 87 percent of revenue coming from individual and corporate income taxes in 2018, it seems clear the US national government tax system remains decidedly progressive.

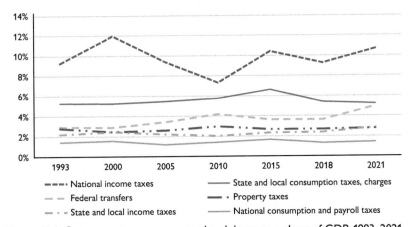

Figure 11.4 Government revenue source breakdown, as a share of GDP, 1993–2021

Sources: US Census Bureau, Annual Surveys of State and Local Government Finances (multiple years); Budget of the United States (2021), Table 2.1, Receipts by Source, 1934–2028.

Redistributive forms of taxation account for a much smaller share of all revenue received by state and local governments from their own sources (table 11.4 and figure 11.4). The amount generated by the individual and corporate income taxes as a portion of total revenues varies between 16 percent and 19 percent during the twenty-five years, but it is only slightly greater in 2018 than in 1993, at 18 percent. In 2021, it is, at 20 percent, only a bit higher. The share generated by the property tax slips modestly from 21 percent in 1993 to 18 percent in 2018, rising to 20 percent in 2021. The trend for the sales tax drifts downward from 23 percent to 20 percent in 2018 and then turns upward to 22 percent in 2021. Meanwhile, the share of revenue from the most regressive sources—utility and liquor store sales, charges, and miscellaneous items—increases from 39 percent to 45 percent, but then subsides to 38 percent in 2021. Altogether, the share of revenues from taxes on consumption (sales and other consumption-based revenues) imposed at the state and local level increases from 63 percent in 1993 to 65 percent in 2018. It then falls to 60 percent in 2021. We may add to that figure the revenue from the

Table 11.4 State and local revenue, 1993–2021 (2018 US $billions)

Items	1993	Share	2018	Share	2021	Share	Annual growth rate 1993–2018	Annual growth rate 2018–2021
Individual and corporate income tax	239	0.16	482	0.18	613	0.20	2.8%	8.4%
GDP share	2.2%		2.4%		2.8%			
Property taxes	304	0.21	547	0.20	600	0.20	2.4%	3.1%
GDP share	2.8%		2.7%		2.8%			
Sales taxes	335	0.23	611	0.22	657	0.22	2.4%	2.4%
GDP share	3.1%		3.0%		3.0%			
Subtotal taxes	**879**	**0.60**	**1,640**	**0.60**	**1,871**	**0.62**	**2.5%**	**4.5%**
Utility and liquor store revenue	104	0.07	184	0.07	181	0.06	2.3%	-0.6%
Charges	239	0.16	548	0.20	543	0.18	3.4%	-0.3%
Other taxes	72	0.05	121	0.04	133	0.04	2.1%	3.1%
Miscellaneous	159	0.11	241	0.09	270	0.09	1.7%	3.8%
Subtotal other consumption-based revenues	**575**	**0.40**	**1,094**	**0.40**	**1,126**	**0.38**	**2.6%**	**1.0%**
GDP share	5.3%		5.4%		5.2%			
Intergovernmental revenue	318		740		1,067		3.4%	13.0%
GDP share	2.9%		3.6%		4.9%			
Total State and local revenue	**1,771**		**3,474**		**4,064**		**2.7%**	**5.4%**

Note: Share is over taxes and other consumption-based revenues.

Source: US Census Bureau, Annual Surveys of State and Local Government Finances (multiple years).

property tax if it is assumed that benefits from expenditures are commensurate with property taxes paid. Once that assumption is made, the share of taxes from less redistributive sources rises to 80 percent. The more redistributive sources—individual and corporate income taxes—account for no more than 20 percent of total revenues in 2021. In other words, there is little sign that sources of revenue upon which state and local governments depend became substantially more redistributive over the entire period.

Debt

The structure of competitive federalism can be threatened by steep increases in liabilities incurred by lower-tier governments. If the debts of lower-tier governments expand rapidly, they can reach a point at which they become unsustainable (Boskin 2020). In the case of state and local governments, excessive debt at the lower tiers could force bailouts by the central government, putting the equilibrium of competitive federalism at risk. We find, however, that in aggregate, the ratio of state and local government debt to revenue did not expand between 1993 and 2021 (figure 11.5).[12] The cost of servicing state and local debt had also not increased as of 2021, as interest rates remained low. However, this is likely to change with the subsequent steep increase in interest rates.

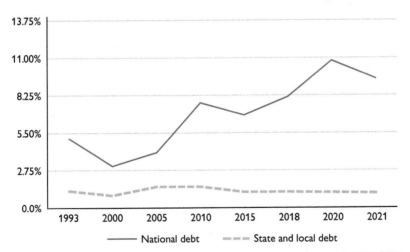

Figure 11.5 Debt levels over total own source yearly revenues (percent), 1993–2021

Source: Board of Governors of the Federal Reserve System (US), Federal Government and State and Local Governments, Debt Securities and Loans, Liabilities Level (FGSDODNS and SLGSDODNS), retrieved from FRED, Federal Reserve Bank of St. Louis.

Equally worrisome, state and local governments may be asked to address imbalances in pension assets and liabilities in the coming decades. Between 1993 and 2021, pension expenses rose by 3.4 percent annually, faster than state and local expenditures classified as either developmental or redistributive (table 11.2).[13] The rapid expansion of pension liabilities is viewed as posing "the threat of default" for numerous state and local governments, which are thought to be burdened by liabilities that are becoming "unaffordable" (Biggs 2014; Farrell and Shoag 2017). The increase in these obligations is a direct consequence of past increases in the responsibilities and, consequently, the employment levels of state and local governments. Though currently a matter of growing concern, the challenges would be mitigated if current inflationary trends continue, as inflation reduces the value of the obligations state and local governments have incurred.

Discussion

The structure of competitive federalism in the United States has remained essentially intact over the past thirty years, despite strong redistributive pressures amid a fluctuating political climate. Revenue and expenditure trends have not decisively shifted the responsibilities or the resources of the lower tiers in government. Although total state and local expenditure shifted upward throughout this period, little secular change in the portion allocated to redistributive purposes took place. Nor has the tax system become more progressive. The major fiscal change has been the share of GDP allocated for employee pensions and medical insurance and the increasing risks from increased liability-to-asset ratios in pension funds. Collective bargaining appears to have had a detectable effect on the way employees are being compensated and on the risks facing pension funds, though this could change if inflation reduces the value of current state and local obligations. Overall, the resources of the lower tiers of government remain directed toward development purposes.

That does not mean that this system of competitive federalism in the United States will remain unaltered in coming decades. The threat of public-sector bankruptcies, especially if pension and medical insurance liabilities escalate, together with an increasing tendency on the part of the national government to relieve institutions in distress, could alter competitive federalism if debts of state and local tiers are routinely covered by the central government. Several municipal governments have declared bankruptcy in recent years—Bridgeport, CO; Harrisburg and Westfall, PA; Central Falls, RI; Moffett, OK; and in California, Stockton, Vallejo, Desert Hot Springs, and San Bernardino. The Detroit school district also declared bankruptcy, with assets divided between pension recipients and bond holders. A new debt-free district was formed. The state of Illinois has teetered on the verge of bankruptcy for much of the twenty-first century (Peterson and Nadler 2014).

Bankruptcy does not by itself alter the structure of a federal system. Eight states defaulted on their debt during an economic crisis between 1841 and 1843, and only half ever compensated investors in full (Peterson and Nadler 2014, 26). Bankruptcies occurred during the deep depression of the 1930s, and the State of New York bailed out New York City when it veered out of fiscal control during the 1960s (Peterson 1981). Although these distressed municipalities and states asked for assistance from the national government, Congress refused to bail them out.[14] Senators and representatives from states and districts that were not facing similar levels of distress saw little reason to pay the debt of jurisdictions they viewed as less prudent. State and local governments cannot be sure the national government will provide substantial assistance in times of fiscal challenge. Nonetheless, calls for federal intervention have become ever more insistent. The dean of the law school at the University of California (Berkeley) urged federal loans to states troubled during the 2008–9 recession, and the famed investor Warren Buffett said it would be hard for the federal government to deny help to states when it had rescued large corporations such as General Motors (Peterson and Nadler 2014, 32).

When the COVID-19 pandemic swept across the country, the federal government did, indeed, respond to similar calls for fiscal relief. In addition to providing moneys to individuals and businesses, Congress enacted four fiscal relief measures that funded state and local governments at levels not previously reached: Families First Coronavirus Response Act (FFCRA); Coronavirus Aid, Relief, and Economic Security (CARES) Act; Consolidated Appropriations Act (CAA); and American Rescue Plan Act (ARPA).

The four pieces of legislation together authorized more than $1.3 trillion in federal grants to state and local governments (table 11.5). The grants were spread out over a multi-year period, but the expected distribution of funds was heavily concentrated on the first three fiscal years, with $125 billion expended in 2020, $738 billion in 2021, and $291 billion in 2022.

Table 11.5 Distribution of federal stimulus funds for state and local governments, by type of expenditure (2020 US $billions)

Type	Act	Total package
Developmental	CAA	69
	CARES	44
	ARPA	284
	Total	397
Redistributive	CAA	38
	CARES	26
	FFCRA	1
	ARPA	107
	Total	172
General purpose	CARES	340
	ARPA	402
	Total	742
	Grand total	1,319

Note: Funds appropriated by state and local governments, including the State and Local Fiscal Recovery Funds of the American Rescue Plan Act (ARPA); Families First Coronavirus Response Act (FFCRA); Coronavirus Aid, Relief, and Economic Security (CARES) Act; and Consolidated Appropriations Act (CAA).

Sources: Congressional Budget Office (CBO), "Estimated Budgetary Effects of H.R. 1319, American Rescue Plan Act of 2021," March 10, 2021; CBO, "H.R. 6201, Families First Coronavirus Response Act," April 2, 2020; White House, "President Biden Announces American Rescue Plan," January 20, 2021.

With the enactment of these fiscally expansionary pieces of legislation, the recent subsidization of lower-tier governments by the central government rose to an unprecedented level. The share of state and local revenues coming from federal transfers climbed to over 26 percent in 2021 (figure 11.6), raising concern that the delicate balance may have been permanently altered. Such a shift could undermine the self-reliance of state and local governments that is necessary to preserve a system of competitive federalism. Two-thirds of the authorized relief funds are designated for general purposes, giving lower tiers of government wide latitude in their use of the funds. California used it to give rebates of $1,100 to households with one dependent and $600 to other taxpayers. Illinois, the country's most fiscally distressed state, anticipated a budget deficit of nearly $4 billion in November 2020, but with large, mostly unrestricted grants from the federal government, it was able to balance its budget without a tax increase. The

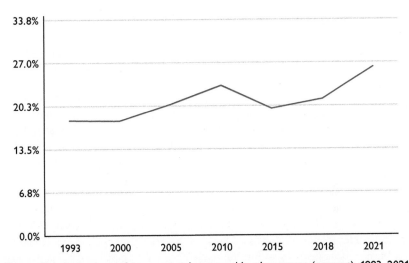

Figure 11.6 Federal transfers over total state and local revenues (percent), 1993–2021

Sources: US Census Bureau, Annual Surveys of State and Local Government Finances (multiple years); Budget of the United States (2021), Table 2.1, Receipts by Source: 1993–2028; authors' estimation.

national government may be setting new expectations for lower-tier governments in fiscal distress. If Congress can be expected to react to economic downturns with sufficient fiscal revenues to cover state and local deficits, then states and localities can be expected to take greater fiscal risks in more prosperous times. To preclude reckless behavior, the central government will begin to impose tighter controls. The autonomy that has been at the heart of competitive federalism will erode.

The structure of competitive federalism in the United States stands as one of the least understood pillars undergirding centuries of economic prosperity. Further, it sustains the liberties of those who may who lack access to power at the national level. Like our republic, it shall endure, as Benjamin Franklin said to Elizabeth Willing Powel, "if you can keep it."[15]

Notes

1. To avoid confusion, we refer to the highest tier of government in the United States as the "central" or "national" government, not the "federal" government. We save "federal" for references to systems of government.

2. The European Community may have been a system of competitive federalism until recently, but the peaceful departure of the United Kingdom from the Community suggests that it is more accurately classified as a confederation of autonomous states, much like the United States under the Articles of Confederation.

3. The figures discussed in this paragraph exclude interest on debt and general administrative expenses but include pensions and medical insurance.

4. In response to the COVID pandemic, for example, public health professionals at all tiers of government exercised extensive influence over economic and social policy.

5. By contrast, the number of employees working for the national government did not change significantly throughout this period. The size of the military sector declined substantially after the end of the Vietnam War. The number of nonmilitary federal employees remained relatively constant at about two million throughout the postwar period. Only 2.8 million people worked for the federal government in 2020, but more than the 2.2 million in 1955.

6. Even pro-union political figures opposed the practice. In 1935, Franklin Delano Roosevelt signed the National Labor Relations Act (NLRA), which established the legal framework that gave a union the authority to negotiate on behalf of private-sector employees when selected as the agent by a majority of them. Yet Roosevelt said similar arrangements within the public sector were unconstitutional because only a democratically elected legislature could commit the public purse. As late as 1960, New York City mayor Robert Wagner Jr., son of the Senator who had sponsored the NLRA in Congress, expressed the view that public-sector bargaining was unconstitutional in the State of New York, though he subsequently altered his position when teachers went on strike (Peterson 2010, 110–15).

7. Peterson (1995) used the decennial *Compendium of Government Finances*, but the Census Bureau no longer releases that document. The two sources use similar if not identical principles of classification.

8. General administration and the interest paid to service general governmental debt are excluded from this analysis.

9. We do not assume that the share of employees is roughly the same as the share of expenditure for each category, because some activities (education) require more personnel than others (welfare). Nor do we assume that employee pensions and medical insurance expenditure may be classified as redistributive on the grounds that benefits are considerably more generous in the public than the private sector (Biggs and Richwine 2014; Costrell and Dean 2013; Koedel, Ni, and Podgursky 2014; Koedel and Podgursky 2016), suggesting they have become an inefficient form of compensation. Benefits substitute for salary, even if they do so inefficiently. The category by itself is of interest, as it shows substantial secular change over the period.

10. We are unable to distinguish between state and local expenditures, because the *Annual Survey of State and Local Government Finances* does not separate federal grants given to local governments from those given to states.

11. We consider state and local expenditures from own sources only. In calculating them, they are therefore netted of federal transfers.

12. The trajectory of state and local debt is similarly flat in this period when we compare it with GDP levels.

13. This is not the case for the national government's pension expenditures (table 11.1), which have been growing less (1.4 percent) than total national development expenditure (2.9 percent), and about the same as national redistributive expenditure (1.2 percent).

14. The national government assumed the debts of states incurred during the Revolutionary War. It was argued that state indebtedness was on behalf of a national cause.

15. The quote was related by James McHenry, Maryland delegate to the Constitutional Convention, in a journal entry dated September 18, 1787.

References

Allison, Graham, and Philip Zelikow. 1999. *Essence of Decision: Explaining the Cuban Missile Crisis*, 2nd ed. New York: Longman.

Ax, Joseph. 2021. "US Census Hands More House Seats to Republican Strongholds Florida and Texas." Reuters. April 26.

Berry, Francis Stokes, and William D. Berry. 1990. "State Lottery Adoptions as Policy Innovations: An Event History Analysis." *American Political Science Review* 84, no. 2 (June): 395–415.

Biggs, Andrew G. 2014. "The Public Pension Quadrilemma: The Intersection of Investment Risk and Contribution Risk." *Journal of Retirement* 2, no. 1 (Summer): 115–27.

Biggs, Andrew, and Jason Richwine. 2014. "Putting a Price on Teacher Pensions." In *The Global Debt Crisis*, edited by Paul E. Peterson and Daniel Nadler, 62–79. Washington, DC: Brookings Institution Press.

Boskin, Michael J. 2020. "Are Large Deficits and Debt Dangerous?" *AEA Papers and Proceedings* 110 (May): 145–48. Nashville, TN: American Economic Association.

Bryce, James. 1921. *Modern Democracies*. New York: Macmillan.

Costrell, R. M., and Jeffrey Dean. 2013. "The Rising Cost of Teachers' Health Care." *Education Next* 13, no. 2 (Spring): 66–73.

DeLeon, Richard E. 1992. *Left Coast City: Progressive Politics in San Francisco, 1975–1991*. Lawrence: University Press of Kansas.

Farrell, James, and Daniel Shoag. 2017. "Risky Choices: Simulating Public Pension Funding Stress with Realistic Shocks." *Brookings* (blog), November 30.

Feld, Lars P., Horst Zimmermann, and Thomas Döring. 2004. "Federalism, Decentralization and Economic Growth." Marburg Working Papers on Economics No. 200430, Philipps-Universität Marburg, Faculty of Business Administration and Economics, Department of Economics (Volkswirtschaftliche Abteilung).

Forum of Federations. 2021. "Federalism by Country." http://www.forumfed.org/countries.

Friedman, Brandis. 2020. "Dr. Anthony Fauci on Current COVID-19 Situation, Vaccine Prospects." WTTW News (website), October 29.

Frost, Riordan. 2020. "Who Is Moving and Why? Seven Questions about Residential Mobility." *Housing Perspectives* (blog), May 4.

Grodzins, Morton. 1966. *The American System: A New View of Government in the United States.* Chicago: Rand McNally.

Hancock, Ralph C. 1990. "Tocqueville on the Good of American Federalism." *Publius: The Journal of Federalism* 20, no. 2 (Spring): 89–108.

Hartney, Michael T., and Leslie K. Finger. 2022. "Politics, Markets, and Pandemics: Public Education's Response to COVID-19." *Perspectives on Politics* 20, no. 2 (June): 457–73.

Henderson, Michael B., Paul E. Peterson, and Martin R. West. 2021. "Pandemic Parent Survey Finds Perverse Pattern: Students Are More Likely to Be Attending School in Person Where Covid Is Spreading More Rapidly." *Education Next* 21, no. 2 (Spring): 34–48.

Hirschman, A. O. 1970. *Exit, Voice, and Loyalty: Responses to Decline in Firms, Organizations, and States.* Cambridge, MA: Harvard University Press.

Hoxby, Caroline. 2000. "Does Competition among Public Schools Benefit Students and Taxpayers?" *American Economic Review* 90, no. 5 (December): 1209–38.

Jencks, Christopher, and Meredith Phillips, eds. 1998. *The Black-White Test Score Gap.* Washington, DC: Brookings Institution Press.

Key, V. O., Jr. 1949. *Southern Politics in State and Nation.* New York: Knopf.

Koedel, Cory, Shawn Ni, and Michael Podgursky. 2014. "Structural Flaws in the Design of Public Pension Plans." In *The Global Debt Crisis*, edited by Paul E. Peterson and Daniel Nadler, 80–93. Washington, DC: Brookings Institution Press.

Koedel, Cory, and Michael Podgursky. 2016. "Teacher Pensions." In *Handbook of the Economics of Education*, vol. 5, edited by Eric A. Hanushek, Stephen Machin, and Ludger Woessmann, 281–303. Amsterdam: Elsevier.

Lauden, Stuart, and Constance E. Smith. 2000. "Government Debt Spillovers and Creditworthiness in a Federation." *Canadian Journal of Economics* 33, no. 3 (August): 634–61.

Lovenheim, Michael F., and Alexander Willén. 2019. "The Long-Run Effects of Teacher Collective Bargaining." *American Economic Journal: Economic Policy* 11, no. 3 (August): 292–324.

Moorhead, Molly. 2012. "Mitt Romney Says 47 Percent of Americans Pay No Income Tax." *Politifact*, September 18.

Obama, Barack. 2016. "It's Not Often You Can Move the Arc of History." CNN, filmed November 2 in Chapel Hill, NC. YouTube video.

Olowu, Dele. 2002. "Property Taxation and Democratic Decentralization in Developing Countries." Institute of Development Studies Seminar Paper. https://archive.ids.ac.uk/gdr/cfs/pdfs/Olowu2.pdf.

New State Ice Co. v. Liebmann, 285 U.S. 262 (1932).

Peterson, Paul E. 1981. *City Limits.* Chicago: University of Chicago Press.

———. 1995. *The Price of Federalism.* Washington, DC: Brookings Institution Press.

———. 2010. *Saving Schools: From Horace Mann to Virtual Learning.* Cambridge, MA: Harvard University Press.

Peterson, Paul E., and Daniel Nadler. 2014. "Competitive Federalism under Pressure." In *The Global Debt Crisis*, edited by Paul E. Peterson and Daniel Nadler, 15–37. Washington, DC: Brookings Institution Press.

Peterson, Paul E., Barry Rabe, and Kenneth Wong. 1986. *Making Federalism Work*. Washington, DC: Brookings Institution Press.

Peterson, Paul E., and Mark C. Rom. 1990. *Welfare Magnets: A New Case for a National Standard*. Washington, DC: Brookings Institution Press.

Pressman, Jeffrey L., and Aaron Wildavsky. 1973. *Implementation*, 3rd ed. Berkeley: University of California Press.

Rauh, Joshua, and Ryan J. Shyu. 2021. "Behavioral Responses to State Income Taxation of High Earners: Evidence from California." National Bureau of Economic Research (NBER) Working Paper Series 26349 (May). Cambridge, MA: National Bureau of Economic Research.

Republic of India. 2006. "Public Administration Country Profile." United Nations Division for Public Administration and Development Management (January). https://recruitmentindia.in/wp-content/uploads/2018/10/UNPAN023311.pdf.

Roberts, Jeff John. 2020. "Are People Really Fleeing Cities because of COVID? Here's What the Data Shows." *Fortune Quarterly Investment Guide*, July 17.

Rodden, Jonathan A. 2006. *Hamilton's Paradox: The Promise and Peril of Fiscal Federalism*. Cambridge: Cambridge University Press.

Rodden, Jonathan, and Susan Rose-Ackerman. 1997. "Does Federalism Preserve Markets?" *Virginia Law Review* 83, no. 7, Symposium: The Allocation of Government Authority (October): 1521–72.

Shakeel, M. Danish, and Paul E. Peterson. 2022. "A Half Century of Student Progress in US Student Achievement: Agency and Flynn Effects, Ethnic and SES Differences." *Educational Psychology Review* 34:1255–342.

Sowell, Thomas. 2020. *Charter Schools and their Enemies*. New York: Basic Books.

Tarr, G. Alan. 2001. "Laboratories of Democracy? Brandeis, Federalism, and Scientific Management." *Publius: The Journal of Federalism* 31, no. 1 (Winter): 37–46.

Tiebout, Charles. 1956. "A Pure Theory of Local Expenditures." *Journal of Political Economy* 64, no. 5 (October): 416–24.

Tocqueville, Alexis de. 1969. *Democracy in America*. Edited by M. P. Mayer. Garden City, NY: Doubleday.

Walker, Jack L. 1969. "The Diffusion of Innovation among the American States." *American Political Science Review* 63, no. 3 (November): 880–99.

Weingast, Barry R. 1995. "The Economic Role of Political Institutions: Market-Preserving Federalism and Economic Development." *Journal of Law, Economics, and Organization* 11, no. 1 (April): 1–31.

White, Martha C. 2020. "Families Fleeing the City Are Pushing Up Home Prices amid Tight Supply." NBC News, June 24.

Whyte, Liz Essley. 2020. "White House Warns 10 Local Areas about Coronavirus Numbers in Private Call." Center for Public Integrity, August 6.

Winthrop, Delba. 1976. "Tocqueville on Federalism." *Publius: The Journal of Federalism* 6, no. 3 (Summer): 93–115.

12

Monetary Aspects of, and
Implications for, Federalism

John B. Taylor

While it might not seem important to focus on fiscal and monetary issues in a volume on federalism, nothing could be further from the truth. The macroeconomic environment—growth, stability, inflation—has large effects on state and local spending, taxes, and interest costs on debt through several channels. Fiscal and monetary policy have been stretched far beyond their usual norms and require considerable adjustment, which is likely to have sizable effects on state and local governments and their relationship with the federal government.[1]

The discussion here begins with the federal budget, and this leads naturally to an overview of monetary policy issues. I then examine the important implications of national fiscal and monetary policy for federalism.

The State of the Federal Budget

Consider two tables drawn directly from the Budget of the US Government for Fiscal Year 2024 as submitted in March 2023. Table 12.1 shows the projected growth rate of real GDP from 2021 through 2031 in both year over year and fourth quarter to fourth quarter percentages. Note the rebound from the pandemic in 2021. However, there is very little growth after that for the next ten years by either measure. The average is only about 2 percent per year.

Table 12.2 shows the total federal budget for the same period, both in billions of dollars and as a percent of GDP. Outlays and receipts continue to grow, as does the deficit in billions of dollars. As a percent of GDP, receipts, outlays, and the deficit remain high. Receipts and outlays show virtually no decline. Thus, the fiscal state of the union is not good. Efforts need to focus on reducing budget totals with the ultimate aim of a balanced budget.

Basic economic theory and empirical models imply that high federal government debt has a cost: it reduces real GDP and real income per household

Table 12.1 Growth rate of real gross domestic product (real GDP)

	2021	2022	2023	2024	2025	2026	2027	2028	2029	2030	2031
% change, year/year	5.9	1.8	0.6	1.5	2.3	2.1	2.0	2.0	2.1	2.2	2.2
% change, Q4/Q4	5.7	0.2	0.4	2.1	2.4	2.0	2.0	2.0	2.1	2.2	2.2

Source: Data from Office of Management and Budget (2023), Table S-9, Economic Assumptions, 167.

Table 12.2 Budget totals in billions of dollars and percent of GDP

	2022	2023	2024	2025	2026	2027	2028	2029	2030	2031
Receipts	4,897	4,802	5,036	5,419	5,773	6,080	6,400	6,669	6,953	7,264
Outlays	6,273	6,372	6,883	7,091	7,294	7,589	8,003	8,205	8,639	9,040
Deficit	1,376	1,569	1,846	1,671	1,521	1,509	1,604	1,536	1,686	1,776
Budget totals as a percent of GDP:										
Receipts	19.6%	18.2%	18.5%	19.1%	19.5%	19.7%	19.9%	19.9%	19.9%	19.9%
Outlays	25.1%	24.2%	25.3%	24.9%	24.6%	24.6%	24.9%	24.5%	24.7%	24.8%
Deficit	5.5%	6.0%	6.8%	5.9%	5.1%	4.9%	5.0%	4.6%	4.8%	4.9%

Source: Data from Office of Management and Budget (2023), Table S-1, Budget Totals, 135.

compared to what these would be with lower debt levels. A reexamination of the issues yields the same results. Hence, there is a need for a fiscal consolidation strategy in which government spending grows more slowly than GDP, and government spending is thus reduced as a percentage of GDP.

Formal model simulations with such a fiscal consolidation show that the impact on real GDP would be positive in both the short run and the long run. Real GDP increases throughout the model simulation, with the benefits rising over time. Even in the short run, the consolidation of government finances is found to boost economic activity in the private sector sufficiently to overcome the reduction in government spending. Consumption and output increase at the start, with further increases later on. Investment rises by only a little in the short run, but by more in the longer run.

The economic rationale for these positive results is straightforward: With a gradually phased in and credible budget plan, households can take into account future reductions in government spending and higher expected future incomes. Businesses will also be able to adjust.

Given a reduction in tax rates in later years, they would also face more favorable conditions for production, investment, and work effort. To reap these positive benefits, it is essential that the tax and budget plan be credible.

There is another possible policy response, one that would work better in the future.[2] The response is based on certain established economic principles: that fiscal policy should be *permanent, pervasive, and predictable,* and thereby effect incentives throughout the economy. There are many good fiscal packages that are consistent with these three principles. One would consist of: (1) Committing to keep income tax rates where they are, effectively making current income tax rates permanent; (2) Making the tax credits permanent rather than temporary; (3) Enacting responsible government spending plans that meet reasonable long-term objectives and that put the US economy on a credible path to budget balance; and (4) Recognizing that the "automatic stabilizers" will help stabilize the economy, and therefore make them part of the overall fiscal package, even if they do not require legislation.

This is not the kind of economic policy that has recently been proposed. Rather than being predictable, the policy response has created uncertainty about the debt, growing federal spending, future tax rate increases, and new regulations. Rather than being permanent, it is temporary, and thereby has not created a lasting economic approach. And rather than being pervasive, it targets certain sectors or groups. It is not surprising, therefore, that the policy has resulted in lower growth forecasts.

The good news is that we can get back to a strong recovery by following an economic policy based on these clear economic principles. As argued in a *Wall Street Journal* article "A Better Strategy for Faster Growth" (Shultz et al. 2013), recent experience makes the case for doing so stronger than ever.

Guidelines for Fiscal Policy: Permanent, Pervasive, and Predictable

The mantra often heard during debates about stimulus proposals is that it should be temporary, targeted, and timely (see Elmendorf and Furman 2008, for example). Going forward, we need a renewed set of principles and a new mantra. Based on the arguments presented above, as well as experience and basic economic theory, I recommend this alternative mantra for fiscal policy: permanent, pervasive, and predictable.

> **Permanent**   The most obvious lesson learned from the recent stimulus program is that one should have strong misgivings about a temporary stimulus program. Such a program is not likely to have much impact, and any impact it has will be short lived. Temporary is not a principle we want to follow if we want to get the economy moving again. Rather we should be looking for more lasting or permanent fiscal changes. More lasting or permanent tax changes will be more effective in helping to turn the economy around in a lasting way. We need to worry about the next few years, not just the next few months.
>
> **Pervasive**   One of the arguments in favor of targeting the stimulus package is that by focusing on people who were "liquidity constrained" the program would be more cost effective. But such targeting does not prevent the stimulus from being ineffective. Moreover, targeting implies letting tax rates increase. But increasing tax rates on businesses or on investments would increase unemployment and further weaken the economy. Better to seek an across-the-board approach where both employers and employees benefit. When people are losing their jobs and their life savings, the last thing they want government to do is increase tax rates on the firms who hire them or on the asset markets where their money is invested.
>
> **Predictable**   While timeliness is an admirable attribute, it is only one temporal property that a good fiscal policy should have in a large, dynamic economy. Even more important is that policy actions be clear and understandable—that is, predictable—so that individuals and firms know what to expect as they make decisions that depend

on future government actions. One of the most widely heard complaints about government interventions is that they have been too erratic or ad hoc. In my view, financial markets are clamoring for clarity. Economic policy—not only fiscal policy and monetary policy discussed here, but also regulatory policy and international policy—works best when it is as predictable as possible.

Monetary Policy Issues

With these fiscal policy principles in mind, we turn to a discussion of monetary policy. Starting around 2017, the Federal Reserve began to move to a more rules-based monetary policy of the type that had worked well in the United States in the 1980s and 1990s. Many papers written at the Fed and elsewhere reflected this revival, and they showed the benefits of rules-based policies. In July 2017, when Janet Yellen was Chair of the Federal Reserve Board, the Fed began to include a whole section on rules-based monetary policy in its *Monetary Policy Report.*

Many central bank leaders and monetary policy experts made favorable comments about the rules-based policy, and central bankers were supportive. Jerome Powell, who followed Janet Yellen as chair of the Federal Reserve Board, said: "I find these rule prescriptions helpful." Mario Draghi, then president of the European Central Bank, said, "We would all clearly benefit from . . . improving communication over our reaction functions." Raghu Rajan, former governor of the Reserve Bank of India, said, "What we need are monetary rules." The evidence was that the move toward rules-based policy was beneficial and economic performance improved.

This move toward monetary policy rules was interrupted when the pandemic hit in 2020. Rules were removed from the Fed's *Monetary Policy Report* in July 2020. In February 2021, rules were put back, only to be taken out again in the February 25, 2022, edition of the report. But on March 3, 2022, Chair Powell said that rules would be back in. And in the *Monetary Policy Report* released on June 17, 2022, policy rules were back in, including the Taylor rule, which was back as the first on the list.

This approach has continued through the Fed's *Monetary Policy Report* released on March 3, 2023. As stated in the report, "Throughout 2021 and 2022, the target range for the federal funds rate was below the prescriptions of most of the simple rules, though that gap has narrowed considerably as the FOMC [Federal Open Market Committee] has expeditiously tightened the stance of monetary policy and inflation has begun to moderate" (FRB 2023).

Table 12.3 **Rules included in the March 2023** *Monetary Policy Report*

A. Monetary policy rules	
Taylor (1993) rule	$R_t^{T93} = r_t^{LR} + \pi_t + 0.5(\pi_t - \pi^{LR}) + (u_t^{LR} - u_t)$
Balanced-approach rule	$R_t^{BA} = r_t^{LR} + \pi_t + 0.5(\pi_t - \pi^{LR}) + 2(u_t^{LR} - u_t)$
Balanced-approach (shortfalls) rule	$R_t^{BAS} = r_t^{LR} + \pi_t + 0.5(\pi_t - \pi^{LR}) + 2min\{(u_t^{LR} - u_t), 0\}$
Adjusted Taylor (1993) rule	$R_t^{T93adj} = max\{R_t^{T93} - Z_t, ELB\}$
First-difference rule	$R_t^{FD} = R_{t-1} + 0.5(\pi_t - \pi^{LR}) + (u_t^{LR} - u_t) - (u_{t-4}^{LR} - u_{t-4})$

Note: R_t^{T93}, R_t^{BA}, R_t^{BAS}, R_t^{T93adj}, and R_t^{FD} represent the values of the nominal federal funds rate prescribed by the Taylor (1993), balanced-approach, balanced-approach (shortfalls), adjusted Taylor (1993), and first-difference rules, respectively.

R_{t-1} denotes the midpoint of the target range for the federal funds rate for quarter t–1, u_t is the unemployment rate in quarter t, and r_t^{LR} is the level of the neutral real federal funds rate in the longer run that is expected to be consistent with sustaining maximum employment and inflation at the FOMC's 2 percent longer-run objective, represented by π^{LR}. π_t denotes the realized four-quarter price inflation for quarter t. In addition, u_t^{LR} is the rate of unemployment expected in the longer run. Z_t is the cumulative sum of past deviations of the federal funds rate from the prescriptions of the Taylor (1993) rule when that rule prescribes setting the federal funds rate below an effective lower bound of 12.5 basis points.

The Taylor (1993) rule and other policy rules generally respond to the deviation of real output from its full capacity level. In these equations, the output gap has been replaced with the gap between the rate of unemployment in the longer run and its actual level (using a relationship known as Okun's law) to represent the rules in terms of the unemployment rate. The rules are implemented as responding to core PCE inflation rather than to headline PCE inflation because current and near-term core inflation rates tend to outperform headline inflation rates as predictors of the medium-term behavior of headline inflation.

Source: Federal Reserve Board, *Monetary Policy Report*, March 3, 2023, 43.

Table 12.3 shows the rules included in the March 3, 2023 Report. The notation is standard, and is given in the footnote to the table. The symbol r is the interest rate, π is the inflation rate, u is the unemployment rate, and the superscript *LR* means the long run. The results are similar to what one finds by looking at the Taylor rule, which is listed first. The results can be compared by looking at the average gap in percentage points between the FOMC interest rate and the settings of each of the other rules.

Getting Back on Track

It is good that rules are now back in the Fed's *Monetary Policy Report*, and it is good that they might continue in future monetary policy reports. It would be more helpful if the Fed incorporated more aspects of these rules or strategy ideas into its actual decisions. Apparently, this has recently begun to happen, as I show by comparing the interest rate path and policy rules for the interest rate. But at first, only small changes were seen in actual monetary policy.

So a gap existed between rules-based policy and policy actions. This was the case at the Fed and also at other central banks. Thus, high inflation will continue unless monetary policy actions—including monetary actions in other countries—are taken. Events in Ukraine and the Russian response recently raised reported inflation, but not the basic story.

Figure 12.1 shows the effective federal funds rate from late 1960 through late 2023. While the gap between the rules and the effective funds rate has narrowed, it still exists.

To illustrate this, the equation in figure 12.2 shows the Taylor rule as it appeared over thirty years ago in Taylor (1993). The variables are defined below the equation. Note that y shown in the equation is the percentage deviation of real GDP from its potential, which is closely related to the deviation of the unemployment rate from the natural rate.

Now let us use the equation to see when and by how much the Fed was—and continues to be—behind the curve. Using this policy rule, we can see that if the inflation rate is 2 percent and the target for the interest rate is 2 percent, then the interest rate should be 4 percent. That is $2 + 2 = 4$. If the equilibrium interest rate is 1 percent, then the funds rate should be 3 percent.

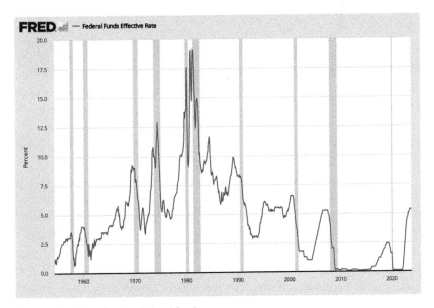

Figure 12.1 The effective federal funds rate

Source: Board of Governors of the Federal Reserve System (US), retrieved from FRED, Federal Reserve Bank of St. Louis.

$$r = p + .5y + .5(p - 2) + 2$$

where

   r   is the federal funds rate,
   p   is the rate of inflation over the previous four quarters
   y   is the percent deviation of real GDP from a target.

Figure 12.2 Taylor rule

Source: Taylor (1993), 202.

During much of 2022 the actual rate was thus well behind the curve. If the inflation rate rises to 3 percent, then the funds rate should be 4.5 percent $(1 + 3 + .5(3 - 2) = 4.5)$, which is about where it is now. If the inflation rate is 4 percent, then the funds rate should be 6 percent $(1 + 4 + .5(4 - 2))$.

Thus, if we use the Taylor rule in the most recent *Monetary Policy Report,* and plug in an inflation rate over the past four quarters of 4 percent, a target inflation rate of 2 percent, an equilibrium interest of 1 percent, and the gap between real GDP and its potential level of 0 percent, then you get a federal funds rate of 6 percent. So even with these inflation numbers, the Fed is still behind the curve, though as Chair Powell has indicated, the Fed may be still catching up. Note that these calculations assume that the equilibrium interest rate is 1 percent.

Federalism and the Impact on State and Local Government Fiscal Policy

It is important to emphasize that this type of fiscal and monetary policy at the federal level, especially the fiscal consolidation, will have important impacts on state and local fiscal issues. This effect may seem obvious to those who are not focused on the relationship between federal and state issues, but it is essential to understanding the importance of the federalism environment and how it operates in the United States.

First, slower growth of federal spending will induce slower growth of expenditures that the federal government will pass on to the state and local sector. This will tend to reduce the total size of state and local expenditures.

Second, stronger long-run national economic growth from the improved fiscal consolidation would improve the revenue side of the state and local finances as income tax receipts grow with a stronger economy. This impact will be amplified with higher sales taxes, due to stronger economic growth and the resulting higher consumer spending.

Third, a steadier and more predictable future path of the economy and federal finances would enable better planning by state and local governments, and thereby reduce the general tendency to increase spending at the state and local level during recessions.

All this provides an incentive at the state and local level to wait to receive the federal funds rather than make commitments for future spending, and this puts less stress on natural capacity issues, which may then imply less real output. These are the key benefits at the state and local level of more predictable and permanent aspects at the federal level.

Conclusion

There are many fiscal packages that are consistent with the three principles that good policy should be predictable, permanent, and pervasive, and these would put the economy on the road to an improved fiscal and monetary state, and therefore faster and more inclusive economic growth.

One example fiscal package would consist of the following:

- A commitment to keep income tax rates where they are now, effectively making current income tax rates permanent. This would be a significant stimulus to the economy and to the financial markets.
- Responsible government spending plans that meet reasonable long-term objectives, put the US economy on a credible path to budget balance, and are expedited to the degree possible without causing waste and inefficiency.
- An explicit recognition that the "automatic stabilizers" are likely to help stabilize the economy and should be viewed as part of the overall fiscal package, even though they may not require legislation.

Regarding monetary policy, clearly the Fed got behind the curve on rules-based monetary policy in the United States, but it appears to have outlined a method to get back on track. By reviewing the years leading up to the present monetary situation, this paper provides the background needed for analyzing current and future monetary policy decisions.

The answer to the key question, Are we entering a new era of high inflation? is clearly *yes*, unless monetary and fiscal policymakers move toward a more rules-based monetary and fiscal policy, and do not revert to the policy that led to high inflation. An approach based on sensible rules would lead to an appropriate mix between fiscal policy and monetary policy.

There are now more reasons than ever for the fiscal policymakers and central bankers to use a more rules-based fiscal and monetary policy. Central banks should begin to establish rules that markets understand. The policy interest rate would increase as inflation rises, as has already happened. It would of course be a contingency plan, as are all rules, but it would greatly reduce chances of a large, damaging change later.

Notes

1. This paper touches on some of the ideas that I presented at Committees of the House of Representatives in March 2023 (see Taylor 2023a and Taylor 2023b).

2. In testimony entitled "The State of the Economy and Principles for Fiscal Stimulus," which I gave before the Senate Budget Committee in November 2008 (Taylor 2008), I recommended this type of fiscal policy, and followed up in Taylor 2010a, 2010b, 2015, and 2019.

References

Board of Governors of the Federal Reserve Board (FRB). 2023. *Monetary Policy Report*, March 3. https://www.federalreserve.gov/monetarypolicy/files /20230303_mprfullreport.pdf.

Elmendorf, Douglas, and Jason Furman. 2008. "If, When, How: A Primer on Fiscal Stimulus." Strategy Paper, The Hamilton Project, January. Washington, DC: Brookings Institution.

Office of Management and Budget. 2023. *Budget of the US Government, Fiscal Year 2024*. Executive Office of the President.

Shultz, George P., Gary S. Becker, Michael J. Boskin, John F. Cogan, Allan H. Meltzer, and John B. Taylor. 2013. "A Better Strategy for Faster Growth." *Wall Street Journal*, March 24.

Taylor, John B. 1993. "Discretion versus Policy Rules in Practice." *Carnegie-Rochester Series on Public Policy* 39 (December): 195–214. Amsterdam: North-Holland.

———. 2008. "The State of the Economy and Principles for Fiscal Stimulus." Testimony before the Committee on the Budget, US Senate, November 19.

———. 2010a. "Perspectives on the US Economy: Fiscal Policy Issues." Testimony before the Committee on the Budget. US House of Representatives, July 1.

———. 2010b. "Assessing the Federal Policy Response to the Economic Crisis." Testimony before the Committee on the Budget, US Senate, September 22.

———. 2015. "The Economic Effects of a Fiscal Consolidation Strategy." Testimony before the Committee on the Budget, US House of Representatives, June 17.

———. 2019. "The Economic Costs of Rapidly Growing Federal Government Debt." Testimony before the Committee on the Budget, US House of Representatives, November 20.

———. 2023a. "There's Still Time to Get Back to Rules-Based Monetary Policy." Testimony before the Subcommittee on Health Care and Financial Services, Committee on Oversight and Accountability, US House of Representatives, March 9.

———. 2023b. "The Fiscal State of the Union." Testimony before the Committee on the Budget, US House of Representatives, March 29.

Federalism in Key Areas of Policy

Discussants: Thomas Nechyba and Dennis Epple

THOMAS MACURDY: John, do you think these rules should be modified now that the interest rate has such a big impact on the fiscal side? Given the large size of national debt, a single 1 percentage point in interest significantly increases government spending.

JOHN B. TAYLOR: Actually, the rules are fine. What's wrong with the rules?

MACURDY: Well, before, the rules didn't have such a fiscal impact on the interest payments.

TAYLOR: Well, that's a disadvantage. That's a disadvantage. They have a higher interest rate.

MACURDY: It's definitely a disadvantage. These rules were established thirty years ago, and I understand the rules better in that context. Now, do you think there should be any compensation for the fact that when the Federal Reserve raises the interest rate, a large increase in spending occurs? We will have soon more than a trillion dollars spent on interest in upcoming budgets.

TAYLOR: So you're asking should the high interest rates be discouraged because it affects spending? I say no. You have a monetary policy to focus on peak inflation of 2 percent. And let me just mention that this is also an international issue. It's not just the Fed, it's Europe, it's Russia, it's China, it's Japan. And by the way, they all know these things. We talk about it all the time. So there's a possibility that they will move in that direction.

MACURDY: So your position would be no, even though the circumstances are different now, there should be no difference in the rule for what we had, say, twenty years ago.

TAYLOR: Well, think about it. Should we change the 2 percent target for inflation? No, I don't think so. It used to be 1.5; 2 is a reasonable number. Some people say it should be 3 or 4. Let's stick with 2.

Can you go back faster to these fiscal and monetary targets? No, I think this is the right speed. Should you have other things? Maybe the exchange rate should matter. The exchange rate is a factor more for some countries than for others.

MICHAEL J. BOSKIN: Let me make a couple of quick comments. Tom, I think part of the response to your question is that market interest rates will go up if we let inflation stay high. So getting inflation back down is a way to get them back down.

MACURDY: You're saying there's much more of a balancing act than we used to have, that it's more complicated than it was.

BOSKIN: That's a fair point. But I think some of the implications John's drawing out are, number one, if we have a more stable macro environment, that will also mean potential for a more stable fiscally federal system, where we don't have these massive, gigantic splurges of spending during recessions.

MACURDY: Those numbers you're citing are CBO [Congressional Budget Office] budget scoring numbers. If you read CBO reports now, they have this whole block in them stating, "Don't believe our numbers, they're too optimistic."

JOSHUA RAUH: Also, they don't assume these deficits are going to have any real impact on interest rates themselves, either directly or through a Fed attempt to fight inflation?

MACURDY: For scoring purposes, CBO is required to produce forecasts assuming continuation of current law. CBO reports used to have a little footnote discussing qualifications. Its reports now include large text boxes essentially saying these numbers are not real, we have to do this.

BOSKIN: I think we could all conclude that the inflation and the fiscal and monetary mess we're in—hopefully on the latter, we're starting to come out of it a little bit—have dramatic implications for what the federal government's going to be able to do. What responsibilities lie with the state and local level? If the economy's growing more rapidly, it's a lot more revenue for state and local governments. If the economy's growing more slowly, it's a more challenged fiscal environment. If we can get the denominator growing more rapidly, it's much less so.

MACURDY: That is really a big deal because the fiscal obligations are primarily in absolute levels, not in terms of GDP.

BOSKIN: Absolutely. The single most important thing is that we get the economy growing more rapidly, whereas the policies now all seem to be loading weight on growth.

TAYLOR: You mean low growth?

BOSKIN: Low growth. Loading weight to grow, getting harder to grow, more weight is being placed on the scales of trying to grow. Making it harder to grow, more fiscal policy weight on a scale.

MACURDY: I'd probably say right now the problem is we can't get our growth rates up enough.

BOSKIN: That's a fair point. But every bit helps.

THOMAS NECHYBA: Let me get started. When Dennis [Epple] and I sat down and we calculated how much time we have for six papers, we calculated we have about two and a half minutes per paper, which we can't possibly do. So we're only going to say some things and I'll start so Dennis can fill in all the rest. And I'll start by just setting a stage, and I'm going to try to be provocative towards the end, particularly for this audience, but I'll work my way up to it. And I'll start with Paul [Peterson] and Carlos's [Lastra-Anadón] paper on competitive federalism, because they set up what we call fiscal federalism, where you've allocated responsibilities to state and local [and] national governments based on sensible criteria. They articulate some of the real advantages of local provision, but then there are real reasons why you actually need to have some extra funding coming in from the higher levels of government.

One of those reasons that has become more important is that tax bases have become more mobile, and so it's easier for federal governments to raise money. If everything that is best spent locally has to be raised locally, we would get too little funded, opening a strong argument for fiscal interaction between more central and more local governments. It's not the only reason for fiscal interaction but an important one. That's a space we want to talk about, that interaction between the high-level and the lower-level governments. And what Paul warns us of is as this interaction increases, this dependence of lower-level governments on revenues from higher-level governments, there may come a point where we run into the danger that in fact the competitive federal system isn't what it is supposed to be. And the key ingredient that Paul points to, which I agree with completely—and there's a literature on this—is that really the key is for lower-level government budgets to remain hard. If those budgets become soft budget constraints, where local and state governments can essentially view the federal government, in our case, as the piggy bank, then you're distorting decisions in a way that goes exactly counter to a healthy competitive federalism, as Paul calls it.

So the trick is to do this in a way where you don't get to that point, and where you—as we've talked about before—don't impose excessive regulations and kill all the advantages of actually providing things at the more local level that we've talked about that I won't review here. So the question is, at what point does the fiscal interaction between central and local governments erode healthy federalism, and Paul and Carlos do a lot of work on trying to classify different kinds of expenditures. They have to make lots of decisions about what to call "developmental" and what to call "redistributive." And we could probably sit for an hour and quarrel with different aspects of that, but you have to make some decisions in any analysis like this. The same is true with the tax incidence assumptions in their paper, but in the end you make some decisions and you hold those constant and see where your assumptions take you. And Paul and Carlos's analysis comes up with this conclusion: we're not in trouble yet, but we may be getting in trouble soon.

And I think that's a very sensible place to end. I'll quibble slightly with your adopting Mitt Romney's language about productive and dependent people. I don't think you actually needed to make that a point in the paper, and I think it has the potential to rub people the wrong way and then miss the large point you are trying to make. It didn't work out for Mitt Romney very well. So I would suggest changing that. But let me step back a little bit and say, okay, we understand all the advantages of local provision, of local provision of goods and services, even if the financing comes in part from somewhere else. But if that was all there is, we'd just have local governments. We'd just have local governments do everything. So I want to focus a little bit on just creating a simple lens through which to think about fiscal federalism. And I'm going to boil it down to something very simple and oversimplify and say, well, there are basically two reasons why we look to central governments to be involved in this relationship within this fiscal federalism system.

One of them is spillovers. If what you're producing has benefits elsewhere, then the local government doesn't have the right incentives to produce the right quantity. And so there's a role for the higher-level government to realign those incentives. And then the other is, I'm going to call it equity. There are certain categories of goods where we simply think that there ought to be at least a minimum level of access to those public goods and services for everybody. And for that category of goods, we worry that if we have purely decentralized provision, then there are going to be people left behind. There'll be pockets where that's just not done, in particular poor areas and so forth. So spillovers and equity are the two parts of the lens I want to use. When I then think about the papers we've heard about infrastructure, healthcare, and education, I want to take that lens to those places.

I'll try to wrap up quickly, but I was basically trying to say: Let's take a simple lens and cast it on three of the papers that talked about specific categories of fiscal federalism. Let's think about spillovers and equity concerns as really being the reason we're drawing central governments into the fray while trying to preserve the benefits of local provision. I won't talk much about the infrastructure paper, but infrastructure, if you think about the two parts of my simple lens, is an area where we go to central financing or central involvement because of spillovers. It is all about spillovers. It's really not about equity at all—it's not about some communities having more potholes than others and us thinking that's not fair. And what emerges from that spillover focus in the fiscal federalism literature is the recommendation that you have the central government pay for the portion that spills over. If it's 30 percent, then that's 30 percent the central government would cover to get the incentives aligned. And it has to come in the form of a matching grant so that the local government bears only 70 percent of the cost. And of course you have to pay attention to all the other things that were mentioned in the infrastructure paper.

Then let me turn to the fifteen most depressing minutes that we've had today, which is the healthcare paper. If you haven't looked at the paper, you need to. I mean, the level of detail and richness in that paper is extraordinary. You are going to learn stuff by reading that paper, just about what there is, to begin with. It's sort of a tour de force of the healthcare system, but then the paper takes you down a bunch of alleys of possible solutions that end up being dead ends. Much of what people think about, they argue, won't solve the fundamental crisis we are facing in terms of the cost of the healthcare system. One thing we could do, however, and what we should do, they argue, is to block-grant healthcare to the states and allow innovation and cost savings and things like that to happen there.

When we think about why are we looking in healthcare to the government—the central government—in my lens, it's really much less about spillovers and it's all about equity. We care about the fact that we want some basic level of access to healthcare for everyone. And yes, there are some spillover issues, but I think that's just not the primary motivation as it is for infrastructure. And if equity is the primary motivation for fiscal federalism in healthcare, then block granting is actually exactly the right tool that you'd want to use. In that case, unlike the case of spillovers, you don't want to distort incentives through matching grants to cause local governments to want to spend more. Matching grants lower the price for local governments, but block grants don't. They just make funds available at the more local level to insure the equity concerns are met in places with fewer resources.

In other words, with healthcare, you're not trying to internalize spillovers; you're trying to make enough resources available for state and local governments to then be able to run programs innovatively and so forth. And so I'm not sure the paper actually talks about the second part that you mentioned in the talk, that yes, we should do block grants and then we should start cutting them to bring costs down. I'm not sure that I saw that part in the paper, but that is a way to curb the overall expenditures on healthcare while hoping that local innovations will fill in the gaps. But how much we can do that, and how far we can get to addressing the cost problem without decimating healthcare, by simply block granting, is anybody's guess. But it certainly seems like a very sensible way of moving in a direction that's consistent with the theory of fiscal federalism that we have.

Which brings me to the last topic, which is education. And I'm going to ask you for a second to forget everything that you know about how education works in the US. We've learned from Rick's [Eric A. Hanushek] paper that it's the most complicated system in the world, and it's not producing the results we want. It is not working very well at all. And we've learned that there are big disparities across states. And when I now put my lens on and ask why we would ask higher-level governments to become involved—spillovers or equity—I find myself concluding that, well, it's actually both with education. It's certainly equity. Kids need to have access to some basic opportunities. And it's human infrastructure of a kind, and it has the kind of spillovers that physical infrastructure has. Not all the spending that you do investing in kids is going to stay within your jurisdiction—it will have large benefits that transcend local and state boundaries, just like interstate roads.

So if infrastructure is all about spillovers and healthcare is all about equity, education has both elements. And if you imagine coming down from Mars and knowing the basic principles of fiscal federalism and seeing how we are thinking about healthcare and infrastructure, and then you compare that to what we do in education, you would be puzzled, because you would say, wait a second. It seems like the argument is even stronger for federal funding in education—not only for equity as in healthcare but also for spillover reasons as in physical infrastructure. And yet we have almost no federal involvement on the fiscal side in education. We have some other kinds of federal involvement, some of which—as Rick goes through in his paper and argues—is kind of backward, but almost all the money for education comes from local and state governments.

And that's the provocative element of my comments, which is to say: if you knew nothing about the history of how we got to this point, you'd expect education to be largely financed at the central level but provided at the state and local level. I mean, we obviously know the history of how we got here, and so we understand why that is not the case. Education emerged from the bottom up, and that's how the system kind of emerged and that's how we got to where we are. And there were big healthcare initiatives in the sixties, and since then, from the federal government. So that started from the top down. But if you're simply looking at the basic principles, you would be wondering why on earth we're doing this in education. Why are we doing it this way? And I understand that probably the big concerns about, well, if the federal government were really to block-grant big money to states and say, go and implement a good education policy, that the fear is, of course, that all the restrictions would come along with it and they'd start running schools.

But that's the same problem in other areas—like healthcare and infrastructure—where we think we can use block grants or matching grants to harness the power of local control and local decision making while at the same time addressing spillovers and equity concerns. So I'll conclude with that and have us ponder whether we shouldn't just go move to a very different system, especially in light of the evidence Rick presents that we are not doing very well in education under the current way of doing things. I'm curious to see what people think.

DENNIS EPPLE: As Tom [Nechyba] explained, he and I agreed we would each comment on papers in both sessions but with each taking primary responsibility for a subset of papers. My primary focus is on three papers, those by Rick, Michael [McConnell] and Valentin [Bolotnyy], and Josh [Rauh] and Jillian [Ludwig].

I think Rick's is a superb paper. It was educational to me to read it. The only part of the education system that you hadn't touched on much in your paper, Rick, was local delivery of education. However, you did take on that topic in your talk today. In addition to charter schools and private schools, a long-standing form of school choice in the US is parents voting with their feet. Regarding this form of school choice, Boston is very interesting from a research perspective, because school districts and municipality boundaries are coterminous. By contrast, in most places in the US, the boundaries crisscross, complicating the task of analyzing the combined effect of local public services provided by municipalities and school districts.

When I was a graduate student a "few" years ago, the prevailing theory was that wealthy people would move into a suburb; poor people would then move into the suburb to share the benefits provided by the wealthy; the wealthy would then move on to another suburb; and so on. In short, there would be an endless game of musical suburbs. What we see is nothing of the sort. The graph on the screen shows median incomes of Boston municipalities in 2010 on the vertical axis and median incomes in 1970 on the horizontal axis. The 1970 incomes are inflation adjusted to 2010 dollars for comparability. What is most striking about this graph is that the hierarchy of municipalities by income in 2010 is remarkably similar to the income hierarchy in 1970. We do not see musical suburbs. Households do vote with their feet, but residential choice is typically followed by long-term occupancy, not frequent relocation.

A household's preferred suburb is very much dependent on the household's income and the associated ability of the household to afford housing in the suburb. Over time, communities tend to maintain their place in the income hierarchy. The sorting by income observed in the Boston metropolitan area is prevalent in all US metropolitan areas.

School choice plays a significant role in this sorting of households across local jurisdictions. In the data we have for school districts, showing the fraction of kids that are on free or reduced-price lunch, you can see how much the achievement scores go upward as you move up the income hierarchy in these jurisdictions. So, Tom MaCurdy, I completely agree with you on the equity issues; we still face the major challenge of finding a way to bring up the bottom part of the educational performance distribution. Great paper, Rick. I really liked it.

I will next turn to the infrastructure paper. I think it's also an excellent paper. Michael and Valentin make a strong case for user fees for funding infrastructure. And I am largely in agreement with their view. Those of you who are older members of this group will know about what may be the most famous user fee ever imposed; it was celebrated in "Charlie on the MTA" [a popular song from 1949]. At that time, the Boston Metropolitan Transit Authority, MTA, proposed a fare increase from ten to fifteen cents. The turnstiles for entering the subway could only accept one coin. Hence, the fifteen-cent fare would be implemented by requiring a dime for a passenger to go through the turnstile on entry and a nickel to exit the turnstile when a passenger reached their destination. Mayoral candidate Walter O'Brien opposed the fare increase. The Kingston Trio popularized the song "Charlie on the MTA," which was a campaign song for O'Brien. Charlie, the protagonist of the song, paid a dime to enter but did not have a nickel to pay the exit fare, stranding him on the train for eternity.

One important form of user fee is the congestion toll. Congestion tolls have caught on elsewhere in the world more than they have here in the US. That would be worth discussing in the paper. It would also be of interest to discuss what happens to the revenues from user fees. David Pearce in 1991 coined the term "double dividend" to capture the idea that congestion fees create more efficient use of the infrastructure and also generate revenues. This was further explored in some subsequent literature.

Turning to another form of user fee, Larry Goulder here at Stanford was one of the most prominent contributors to the literature discussing Pigouvian taxes for environmental externalities. Based on information on the Transport for London web page, the congestion charge for London is £15 if you drive within the congestion charge zone between 7 a.m. and 6 p.m. on a weekday. On Sundays and bank holidays and Saturdays, the toll applies from noon to 6 p.m. Also, if your vehicle does not meet the Ultra Low Emission Zone standards, you must also pay the Ultra Low Emission Zone charge. So they're really addressing two externalities at once, congestion and pollution. The London toll appears to be a relatively successful application of user fees. The London transport authority, Transport for London, reported in April 2005 that two years on, congestion within the charging zone has reduced by 30 percent, and the volume of traffic in the charging zone has reduced by 15 percent.

An example much closer to where I reside is the Pennsylvania Turnpike. As you probably know, the Pennsylvania Turnpike was the first limited-access highway in the US, and it's financed by user fees. Your entry point to the turnpike and your exit point are electronically recorded. The fee you pay depends on how far you have traveled. In 2007, the state legislature required the Pennsylvania Turnpike to transfer the following amounts in millions of dollars annually to the Commonwealth—the state calls itself the *Commonwealth*— to support transportation projects statewide: $750 in 2008, $850 in 2009, $900 in 2010, and $450 annually from 2011 through 2057. So, basically, user fees on the turnpike are now turned into fees to finance transportation elsewhere in the state. In the fifteen years since then, since 2007, the Turnpike Commission has transferred nearly $8 billion in funding to the Pennsylvania Department of Transportation. The vast majority of that was borrowing by the Turnpike Commission to hand over the money to the state government. So the Turnpike Commission now has a larger outstanding debt than the state of Pennsylvania, and they have to pay it off in the next thirty years.

When I found out about the use of turnpike fees, my first reaction was, "Wow, this is just outlandish." But then it also raises an interesting issue. The turnpike is in some respects close to a monopoly. If you want to get across southern Pennsylvania, the turnpike is the only practical way to go. So, from an efficiency standpoint, maybe it's not a bad way to fund other state projects, because not very many vehicles are going to be deterred from using the turnpike. So I feel a little less strongly about use of funds from the turnpike than I first did, but I am still dubious about it.

Another example of user fees run with unintended consequences is the National Flood Insurance Program. I learned about aspects of this program from two research projects, one from having a doctoral student, Caroline Hopkins, who did research on this topic. The other is my niece, Jennifer Argote, who completed a doctoral degree from LSU [Louisiana State

University] recently and gathered a gold mine of data to study this topic. The National Flood Insurance Program [NFIP] is designed to incentivize local communities to harden protection against prospective floods and to prevent location in zones at high risk of flooding. The quid pro quo from the federal government is subsidized insurance. You can probably predict what's happened with this. Local developers and local governments are all for development. My niece shows that with the subsidized premiums, homeowners in high-risk zones do not pay the price that reflects the flood risk. Therefore, people can continue to live in high-risk areas, some of which are repetitively damaged, costing the taxpayer-funded program billions of dollars. In 2022, the NFIP was $20.5 billion in debt. So this is another example of a fee for service, but way too heavily subsidized. I would say there are two issues here. There's a moral hazard issue, that we're subsidizing so much that there is overinvesting in flood zones. There's also a time inconsistency issue, because when there are severe floods, the federal government jumps in and bails out those who have lost their homes even if they are not insured.

My comments note some challenges in keeping user fees from being distorted to serve purposes for which the fees are not well suited. That said, I want to reiterate that I am in broad agreement with Michael and Valentin about the value of user fees. I think they have written an excellent paper.

Let me next turn to the paper by Joshua and Jillian, which is another fine paper. One of the issues that they discuss is unfunded, or underfunded, pension liabilities. My colleague Chester Spatt and I wrote a paper in 1986 on why we have state restrictions on local debt. The background is that prior to state restrictions [being placed] on local debt, municipal defaults were commonplace. In the late 1870s, 20 percent of municipal debt was in default. That made it devilishly difficult for other municipalities to borrow. Defaults often occurred when an undertaking by a local community failed. For example, some communities borrowed to make investments to try to lure the railroad to come through their town. If the effort failed, default often followed. The problem of defaults prompted states to place restrictions on local debt, and that largely ended defaults on local government debt. State governments adopted similar restrictions on state borrowing, and for the same reason.

The nearest to default since adoption of such debt restrictions was New York City in 1975. The city was $150 million in debt and called on then president Gerald Ford to bail them out. And everybody my age or thereabouts knows what the *Daily News* headline said: "Ford to City: Drop Dead." There's a beautiful article, by the way, in the *New Yorker* in 2015, telling the story.

The article conjectures that Jerry Ford probably lost the subsequent presidential election because that headline became such a prominent nationwide news item.

So, what happened when local governments faced binding debt restrictions? Many turned to underfunding of pension liabilities to current and former public employees. Pittsburgh was out in front on this; well, actually, not in front of Philadelphia. Philadelphia was even worse. Instead of raising taxes to raise contemporaneous wages, cities promised generous pension benefits and kicked the can down the road. Eventually the state stepped in, because this problem was getting so severe and public employees were pressuring the state government to fix the problem. The state mandated, with threat of receivership, that the cities had to deal with their unfunded liabilities. The Pittsburgh city government owned all the parking garages in the city. The city paid its unfunded pension liabilities by selling the revenue stream from their parking garages. They didn't sell the garages, presumably because then the private owners would have to pay property tax. So they continue to own them, but they sold the revenue stream.

It was a pleasure to read these excellent papers. Tom [MaCurdy] mentioned the equity issue, and I meant to bring this up in the context of the last paper. The most depressing economics graph I've ever seen was published in the *Journal of Political Economy* by Chinhui Juhn, Kevin Murphy, and Brooks Pierce in 1993. The graph shows real wages. What it shows is from roughly 1960 to 1970, regardless of what percentile of the earnings distribution you were in, you were in a rising tide raising all boats. And then the median went flat, the lower plummeted and the upper took off, and we had this huge increase in income inequality.

MICHAEL W. McCONNELL: Is that pre-tax?

EPPLE: Yes. I think these growing public federal program expenditures are in part because of the growing income inequality. There is a graph from a paper by Florian Hoffmann, David Lee, and Tom Lemieux in the *Journal of Economic Perspectives* in 2020 that shows income percentiles from 1975 to 2020. It shows that what's happened is that the increase in income inequality that started in the 1970s has continued. And I think this increasing inequality has been a major driver of why we're seeing more federal spending.

Another factor affecting federal spending is the proportion of the population over sixty-five—this came up in Tom's presentation. That proportion has gone from 12.5 percent in 1990 to 17 percent today. The forecast by 2050 is that 22 percent of the US population will be over the age of sixty-five. And so contemplating what that's going to do to government expenditures and deficits is very unsettling indeed.

BOSKIN: We've seen inequality reverse considerably from 2017 to 2019, for example. Not a lot, but even the trend toward increased inequality had reversed for a bit.

EPPLE: Yes, there has been some reversal.

BOSKIN: It actually had reversed. It actually had reversed prior to COVID. Traditional measures.

NECHYBA: But consumption inequality is much less.

BOSKIN: Exactly.

EPPLE: Yes, I absolutely agree with that.

BOSKIN: Taxes and transfers have made a huge difference. And the inequality in consumption is far less than inequality in market income.

I would just make two quick comments. One is on demography. It's not just over sixty-five, but within the elderly population, the elderly are growing much more rapidly. So the fraction of the population over eighty-five is the most rapid, from a lower base, is the most rapidly growing part of the population. Gets back to Jay's point about . . .

I was also going to say, we started with legal issues and what the framers were thinking about when they thought about a federal structure. And we've hit on that a fair amount on and off. For example, the California rule on pensions. There's no state bankruptcy law. So it's maybe somewhat less ambiguous than—maybe more ambiguous than you indicated, Josh, about what would happen, whether Jerry Ford would say, "Clean up your own act, we're not going to do anything." But for a locality, that isn't the case. And we've seen states come in and bail out school districts and towns and cities, etc. But it seems to me, we get back again to this confluence of the legal system and politics and the economics being deeply intertwined maybe in David Kennedy's marble cake formulation. Do I have . . . anybody make any additional comments?

ERIC A. HANUSHEK: Clarifying question, I didn't understand why it mattered how you spent the user piece.

EPPLE: First of all, if I wasn't clear, let me say that I think Jerry Ford did exactly the right thing by not bailing out New York City. I think it matters what you do with the user fees, again, from a potential moral hazard perspective.

HANUSHEK: But you can do bad things with it and you can also have bad incentives.

EPPLE: As I said at the outset, I'm very, very, very strongly in agreement with you about user fees. But then I was thinking about a couple of examples, and I'm not even sure it was misguided what the Turnpike [Commission] did, but it really strikes me as a bit of an issue. The National Flood Insurance Program is more problematic. But my general concern when you're generating a surplus with a user fee is—

HANUSHEK: It encourages you to do bad things.

EPPLE: Yes, I think that is a significant risk. I don't mean to be too much of a pessimist. As I said, I am very much in accord with the view that user fees are the way to go.

RAUH: Well, your example, the fact that the Turnpike Authority's ability to issue bonds to borrow was much greater than that of the state government. And so it becomes then a vehicle for borrowing and for circumventing balanced budget requirements.

HANUSHEK: That's what New York State did, they sold the turnpike because they had a zero-debt requirement and they couldn't go into debt, so they sold the turnpike.

MACURDY: Actually, Tom [Nechyba], I have a concern about your analysis examining this spillover and equity program by program. In the area of healthcare, there's clearly a trade-off and balancing across multiple programs. For example, most services for mental health are paid through state funds. The federal government deems such services as part of its responsibilities, and to assist states in paying for these services, [it] overcompensates states in covering healthcare programs jointly paid for by the feds and states. So the state has more funding in mental health. The feds typically impose regulations governing what states must abide by to receive extra funding in shared programs. I would suspect this phenomenon also happens in school funding. The federal government doesn't look at it program by program. But it's surprising how much influence they have, given how low their contribution is, through regulations.

BOSKIN: That's a pretty fundamental point we all teach in public economics, that there's a permeable membrane between spending and mandates and rules and regulations. And we saw a horrible example of that in the housing markets and rules and regulations leading into the financial crisis.

Val's done some important work on this and I think some pieces of it were overstated, but basically it came clear: if Congress can't spend more money, they'll try to find other ways to accomplish its objectives. We're all human, and that may be creative funding via turnpikes or whatever it happens to be. I do want to end on one deep insight, but more of a fun quip, is that George Schultz, who started his cabinet position (actually it wasn't yet a cabinet position) as director of the budget, was fond of saying that from his observation over a long span of time, both Democrats and Republicans want to spend more, but Democrats enjoy it more.

Part 4

Practitioners' Perspectives

Governor Mitch Daniels

Introduced by Paul E. Peterson

PAUL E. PETERSON: Governor, it's really great to see you. I know we've talked a lot about education policy over the years, and I've admired your work at Purdue and of course all the work you did on school choice and in Indiana when you were governor. But this is a conference on federalism, and so what I would really like to hear you comment on is where were the biggest challenges you faced when you were governing Indiana and you had to operate within a federal system, you had to worry about local governments out there, but you also had to worry about the federal government where it gave you some opportunities. You can mention them, but also we really want to know what were the problems that you encountered because you were working within the federal system?

GOV. MITCH DANIELS: Well, they were frequent, Paul. I am happy to say, I don't think I can cite an example where we were completely thwarted, but I can give you some "for instances" that I don't think will surprise anyone in the audience. Maybe one of the more important arguments we had with them had to do with a program we devised to provide health insurance to the near-poor. And the argument boiled down to my insistence, I guess I'll say, what we really wanted was a program of more or less HSAs [health savings accounts] for poor people that empowered them. First of all, it required of the beneficiary some very, very modest skin in the game, almost a token amount. But the data told us that even a small contribution into a self-managed account would have beneficial effects. And this was a matter of apparently theological objection at the federal level. They really were very, very resistant to anything that wasn't free.

And we prevailed, but only after a long and difficult struggle. And my successor, when he agreed to expand Medicaid, ran into the very same argument, and the Obama administration more or less bludgeoned them out of that requirement. But it was, I think, prototypical in their (the federal administration's) hostility to our view of personal autonomy, our empowerment, our trust that people could make wise decisions. And by the way, the data bore that out, that they could make the same intelligent choices about healthcare utilization and shopping medical bargains and so forth as their wealthier neighbors—[this] was borne out, but that didn't prevent a very long and drawn-out argument.

We had in education, Paul, if you remember, a program called Race to the Top. And we were in, I would say, close alignment—me, our very reform-minded superintendent of instruction at the time—pretty close in alignment with Secretary [Arne] Duncan about the objectives. I mean the plan was supposed to be built around teacher quality, which we knew was the most important single variable around assessment, which common sense told you was essential to improved outcomes around doing something very direct about the worst performing schools. And then the fourth, I think they called it a pillar, was aggressive use of data in every case. So we had no general misalignment there. However, the department insisted on what I think they termed buy-in from, guess who—the teachers' unions. And whatever Arne Duncan thought, the teachers' unions weren't nearly so enthusiastic about things like teacher quality since they primarily are there to protect bad teachers.

So we finally walked away from that program and the money that it might've provided, passed—when we had achieved the political position to do so—passed very sweeping reforms that Arne Duncan happened to think were great, most of them. But we had to do it without the federal government. So those are a couple, I could cite others, but those are a couple of the examples we had. We had lots of arguments environmentally. I was thrilled this year by so many court decisions, and the ones that I was most interested in and that bear most directly here, of course, were around the "major questions" decisions. And I was very pleased at the "waters of the US" decision [*Sackett v. EPA*] also because we were frequently obstructed on those fronts. It just adds cost, adds time to what an activist state otherwise intends to do and otherwise would.

PETERSON: Well, Governor, one of the things you mentioned, the teachers' unions, does come up. Republicans always like local government. They want the local government to do as much as possible, but right now teachers' unions have an enormous influence over local government. They're sitting at both sides of the bargaining table. They play a major role in local elections because nobody else votes in them or very few people vote in them. So, is local government really able to do things given the power that vested interest can exercise in the local arena?

DANIELS: It's uneven, of course. There are plenty of school districts and school boards which have been successful in maintaining quality and standards and some degree of efficiency. One of the reforms that we passed in 2011 narrowed collective bargaining to wages and benefits, essentially. And, at least in our state, so many of the contracts the teachers' unions had extracted went on for scores of pages about decision making. I remember one that offended me particularly was finding clauses that said a principal could not come observe a teacher in a classroom without seven days' notice. Arguably the most important thing a principal could do is to ensure the quality of the teacher in front of those students. So in local government, we at least created the conditions whereby a school administration, school board, can do their duty. One thing I learned was that this is not simply a matter of the unions. People in administrative positions have been socialized to this system. Too many of them came up out of teaching. Sometimes the only way to make more money in a school district is to become the third vice superintendent for buses or something.

PETERSON: We've had a large increase in those administrators. That's a growth sector.

DANIELS: Yeah, it has been. I do think that if you're looking for reasons for optimism, the way in which parents have become concerned about their own rights to raise their own children—the overreach that has led to that, I think, has been a positive thing. You and I have seen, for decades, parent-led reform movements. The problem is parents age out, their kids grow up, but the system doesn't go away, and so there's been a long history of aborted reform efforts.

PETERSON: Well, we've seen dramatic intervention in the local-state system by the federal government with COVID and all the funding of new programs and so forth. So we have a vast amount of money coming into our state and local government system in the last few years. Do you think this is changing the nature of our federal system? Or is this just something that's going to come and go?

DANIELS: Well, federal spending comes and never goes. And that's one of our problems. The day is coming—and I think arithmetically, it's certain—when we're going to have a very, very serious crash, and that—by which I mean an inability to meet our safety net obligations—and that's going to force all kinds of reexaminations. And one can hope that some of that might involve a long overdue transfer or reassignment of authority in various areas to the states. I certainly, for one, hope that's the case. But for the moment, yeah, with the money comes all the strings and demands that we all see in context after context, then states have to try to be resolute about defending their own rights as we did. For instance, in the health insurance example I gave you.

PETERSON: Well, Michael Boskin earlier mentioned all kinds of proposals that have been put out there to clarify the responsibilities between the national, the state, and the local governments. Do you think they need to be clarified? Or are we going to always be sort of stumbling around with a mix such as we've experienced?

DANIELS: Well, I think we've seen that for a long, long time. I mean, I was there when President Reagan talked about a new federalism. Federalism is a matter of convenience, really, on both sides of the aisle. I think I heard some of your previous speakers give examples of this. People like it when it produces a result congenial to them. So no, I think we need that and I actually think there are reasons to hope for that. One, as I say, the federal government's going to run out of fiscal room possibly very suddenly and abruptly. Secondly, in this sadly divided time that we have, you do have Democratic governors, many of whom are proceeding aggressively to advance the interest of their states and will potentially, I think, be allies in this. When governors get together, the subject almost immediately turns to how dysfunctional and inept Washington is, and [it's] maybe one of the few points of political agreement left in our country. And so, one can hope that Democratic governors, who by nature and by nature of the jobs they hold, are almost compelled—not all, but most—are compelled to be practical and realistic and cost-efficient to the extent they can be. And so I'm hoping that both circumstances and the growing contrast between what's done federally and what's done at state levels will eventually produce that possibility. I think I heard it mentioned, but the data has been clear now for well over a decade. People could hardly rate Washington lower than they do, but tend to have a much greater confidence and respect for the job that their states and usually local governments are doing. And this is so important right now. I've argued many, many places and times that skepticism about big government is healthy and all-American, but you can't let it turn into contempt for all government. And we're bordering on that when we look at the national scene. The one place where I think we still have some confidence in institutions tends to be at the state level.

MICHAEL J. BOSKIN: Dan Rubinfeld raised this issue of special districts, regional cooperation, etc. So we have a bunch of those; here we have the Association of Bay Area Governments, we use them for transportation, water, variety of other things. So I'm just wondering if you have any reflections on the kinds of things that Indiana did in cooperation with its neighboring states.

DANIELS: Well, first of all, I think we ought to take a skeptical look at all these special districts. They typically have been ways to tax people more heavily than the elective process would permit. And so I'm not saying they never have a value, but we discouraged them. I don't remember agreeing to authorize a single one during the eight years that I served in our state. Now, state cooperation is a tough thing, but we had some highly successful examples. I will cite the fact that in the course of a massive infrastructure building program that we had for my years there, we were able to build two long-overdue, long-desired bridges over the Ohio River. They have triggered, by the way, a tremendous economic boom, just as well-chosen infrastructure has the potential to do.

But, it was interesting, it was very complicated to do that, and until we made it simple, I think one of the first rules that I learned the hard way is there's a premium on simplicity, and if you're trying to make something significant happen in the public sector at scale, and the breakthrough there was, after a bunch of arguments between the bureaucrats about, in our case we wanted to toll a bridge as opposed to the old-fashioned gas tax financing. We wanted to build it with a P3 partner [public-private partnership] as opposed to, again, the traditional state-run procurement. And the breakthrough was: I finally said to the Democratic governor of Kentucky, I said, "Look, let's make this easy. These bridges are about the same cost, they're about the same timeframe. You build one and we'll build one." Trying to do this fifty-fifty in joint commissions and we're going to have to create something specialized, I said, How about that? So we did. It turned out to be sort of an interesting clinical trial. Our bridge came in substantially cheaper and got done sooner. But anyway, everybody went home happy. I guess I cite that just to say that when two states try to do things cooperatively, it's not twice as complicated, usually it's four times or more. And at least on that occasion, we got by in the way I described. Now, I could also cite all sorts of arguments we had, as particularly with Illinois. It's a blessing to be next to Illinois, in many ways. But they did get in the way, or tried to, and they involved the federal government. There was a huge investment we happily were able to finally secure in growing a refinery up on Lake Michigan. But a lot of specious arguments were made by Illinois and they tried to get the EPA, they did get the EPA to help them obstruct that for a while. But if you're stubborn enough, you can usually prevail.

DENNIS EPPLE: Really found your remarks very interesting. I'm a graduate of Purdue. Hail, Purdue! You're uniquely qualified to comment on the state relationship to higher education and in particular public universities. I wanted to ask you your views about the appropriate state role in funding and so forth.

DANIELS: Well, you can read in today's *Wall Street Journal* the travails of my friend Gordon Gee over in West Virginia, and a prediction that this will be more and more common. It probably will. I believe it's been at least exaggerated, if not a canard, that the problems of public higher ed trace to lower state appropriations. I don't find that persuasive at all. And with declining enrollments, this is both for demographic and, frankly, value choice reasons. This is likely to—the pressure—likely to get more severe. As to the federal government, we probably had more difficulty with the federal government's intrusion at a public university than even at the state administration level. We innovated, for instance, income share agreements as an alternative to some of the more expensive debt. Perfectly good and sound idea. The federal government has basically, the Department of Education has through indirection, has at least for the moment, made it impossible for that market to operate, which is a shame.

We moved into adult education, an online education through the acquisition, we converted a proprietary online university into a public one. You would think that the ideologues who worry that someone might be making some money, you'd think they'd be happy about that. But they weren't and continue really to harass what is now Purdue Global and some of those who've tried to follow what we did there. And then there's Title IX, for instance, which makes it both more expensive and very, very difficult to try to bring justice, but fair-minded justice, to both sides of these sometimes difficult and complicated cases of sexual harassment and so forth. So, I probably encountered more of those problems in the most recent job than the previous one.

EPPLE: Sorry to hear about the intervention with your income sharing, which struck me as really just a tremendous innovation.

JOSHUA RAUH: Thanks, Governor. One of the many things you said that was music to my ears was aggressive use of data, and I was hoping that you might just add a couple comments on some other things that Indiana has done with aggressive use of data, some potential opportunities and maybe some potential challenges. In my group, we do a lot of analysis of state-level economic data. And in my observation, there are two challenges. One is often just getting past the maybe some political obstacles to actually get the data produced and released. And another is actually translating the conclusions that arise when the data come out into action. I actually saw recently there was, not to pick on Indiana because I think actually Indiana is a model on this [and] many things, and this stat would be much worse for other states.

But the Indiana Department of Transportation released a report pointing to total ridership of seventeen million and total expenditures of about $283 million in 2021, which is about $16.50 per ride. And so one would hope that there'd be somebody who's going to look at that and say, "Let's try to reoptimize here. Is that really a price we want to pay per ride? Or is there a way to . . ." So just interested in your thoughts about getting data released and translating data into action.

DANIELS: Well, "What other way makes sense?" is a commonsense rule violated all over the place in public administration. Thinking about transportation, since you brought it up, I'll always remember in trying to figure out how to address Indiana's infrastructure needs, which were at the time estimated at $2 billion to $3 billion, that was real money in 2005. I started with the simplest form of data, piece of data that I knew. I had traveled our toll road many, many times and the last tollbooth before Chicago cost fifteen cents, one-five. Which even then was a challenge. Like who's got a nickel in their pocket? And when I got to the office, I asked somebody: "Fifteen cents," I said. "What does it cost us to collect the toll?" Well, it's government, they don't know. So I said, "Go figure it out." And they came back in two or three weeks and they said, "We think it's about thirty-nine cents."

We were armed with that piece of data and many more we collected. I remember saying at the time, I said, "Well, that's a great business model." I mean, I said, "Look, close this whole—close the tollbooth, fire the ward chairman's nephew or whoever's sitting there. We're twenty-four cents ahead, and just put out a cigar box. Occasionally a motorist will chuck some in just to be a good citizen." But then I'm being only partly facetious. When we put that under the microscope, it became very clear there was enormous trapped value in that toll road. And we went out, we were lucky about the timing, the markets were right, and there was great interest.

It remains a paradox that this country, which is so innovative in many ways, lags the world in terms of privatization of infrastructure. But anyway, we hit the jackpot, got paid $4 billion, cold hard cash, got a better toll road out of it, wound up repaving half the state roads, mileage, rebuilding a third of the state bridges, and we built a host of new projects, like those bridges I mentioned, that had been promised to our citizens for, in some cases, decades. But it all started with an examination of the basic facts that told you that there had to be a better answer there.

I have to just tell you quickly, and it is to a current governor: we all know that in addition to the defense of individual freedom, the other most powerful argument for the federal system is its self-correcting character.

That is to say, when states do things that are stupid, other states take notice. And if states do things that work well, then plagiarism is encouraged. And so I still get phone calls, and I've got one to return in a few minutes, from people who are wrestling with these issues, people from both parties. And again, that's just increasingly valuable and unusual, I think. So I'm just never surprised when Hoover delves into one of the most important subjects around.

But thank you for doing this and for including me. I'll exit with expressing the fantasy that the series of cases we saw this year that reined in federal authority where it had gotten beyond either its statutory or constitutional bounds . . . permit me to fantasize that someday, before too long, somebody brings a successful Tenth Amendment case. And then we get that restoration and reclarification that was mentioned a minute ago. So sorry for the peroration here, but I'm so happy, excited, to see you dealing with this subject as you are.

Governor Jeb Bush

Introduced by Condoleezza Rice

SECRETARY CONDOLEEZZA RICE: I have the honor of introducing—although, as people often say, he really needs no introduction—my good friend and colleague Jeb Bush, the two-term, highly successful governor of the state of Florida. What I'd like to say about Jeb and his time in Florida is that one of the things that made you successful is that there's an enduring character to the issues that you undertook that are still characteristic of the state of Florida today. I'm going to focus on one in particular, because we worked together quite a bit on it, and that's the state of education in the United States. As you know, the federal government has really a minimal role in education. But in fact, the education system is highly decentralized in the United States. Many of the most important decisions—Paul Peterson could tell you about many of the most important decisions—might even be taken at the level of the Board of Education.

And yet our states have been innovators. They have been laboratories for improving education, particularly for underserved kids. One of the vehicles for doing that has been to be very aggressive about parental choice and the opportunity for parents to have a say, particularly parents who don't have the means, in how their kids are going to be educated. Jeb and his team at Excel in Education, which I cochaired for a little while for Jeb, continue to do that hard work. They've come to Hoover conferences about this topic, and they continue to do that hard work with the states, helping states to propose legislation, helping states to actually get legislation through. Jeb started that by leading as the governor of Florida. And Florida is, to this day, still one of the most successful states when it comes to education. Jeb, it's great to have you here to talk about whatever you'd like, but you're the embodiment of successful federalism. And so I'm delighted to have a chance to introduce you.

GOV. JEB BUSH: Thank you, Condi. One quick question since Condi's here. One quick point I didn't realize—behind me is a picture of me painted by my brother. I'm not bragging about me, I'm bragging about my brother. He actually painted a picture that looks a hell of a lot better than me, just for the record.

MICHAEL J. BOSKIN: Rick [Eric] Hanushek, one of our true leaders in the economics of education, has done a tremendous amount of work and probably is the leader in thinking and generating estimates of the harm done by the school lockdowns during COVID. He's going to ask you a couple of questions and then we'll throw it open for the general audience. So, Rick, over to you.

ERIC A. HANUSHEK: Governor, it's wonderful to have you here. I thought it'd be useful to start more generally than Condi did, and talk outside of education because I always view the governor as caught in between the federal government, working with the federal government and with the local government. And I suspect that the challenges of working with the federal government first differ by particular areas, and your opinions on what worked and what was possible and what wasn't. And then, turning the other way, you have to work with all the local people on a variety of areas. And so leaving out education for the minute—we'll get to education—but could you talk more broadly about federalism from the governor who's caught in between these two layers of government?

BUSH: Sure. First of all, one of those charts warmed my heart where Florida was at the lowest per capita state employees. That was the best news I've heard so far. Probably, if you added state and local government public employees, it might've been a little bit higher. But I think we've proven here you don't have to have a large bureaucracy to implement policies. You have to advocate policy first. And so I would say where the federal government didn't intervene was where we had the most success, education probably being the primary place that was the case. And where they either through regulation—principally through regulation—and also through spending where the money was attached to a lot of rules, it was harder. So we don't have a department of labor anymore. We have a workforce board. They modernized the name, but basically we have a Bureaucracy for Workforce Development.

It gets most of its money from the federal government. There are a myriad of rules related to how they operate. And I can remember when I was governor, I went into the Department of Labor because they were kind of angry that I got elected, I think, and started walking around the halls and asking people what they did and actually did more work than that. And more than half of the people working there were complying with rules imposed by Washington. And interestingly, probably the other half, a significant part of the other half were imposing rules on local and state government as well as the not-for-profit groups that were getting the money. And similarly, Department of Education, even though we got 10 percent of our money, or no more than that. Half the building, the tallest building when I got elected in Tallahassee, Florida, the Department of Education building, was there to comply with all the rules. So across the spectrum of government, states love the fact they can get the money, but it's very frustrating to accept the rules when you're trying to innovate. You're taking the money and you're not trying to change how you deliver the services. I guess it's okay. You fill out the forms, you get the money, there's not any accountability, and off you go.

We went to a community-based care model for our child welfare system. We were the first state to do that. That was pretty complicated for Washington because you had to combine federal fundings, pockets of money had to be merged together. And we said, "Look. Give us that flexibility and hold us to account. Give us the accountability measures and we'll meet them." It took a long while to get that done.

Emergency response is another place where, particularly when things go bad, Washington feels compelled to be in the forefront and they're really not set up to lead. Disaster response is set up at the local and state level to respond, and Washington writes a big check. But they want to get much more engaged when there's big public pressure. I mean, gosh, I mean almost every area of government there was a conflict. And then as it relates to how we dealt with local governments, if the mayor of Miami-Dade County was here instead of me, they would probably complain similarly to how I'm complaining about Washington. There is this natural tendency. What's happening more now, I don't know if it's in other states, is preempting local governments' discretion, particularly in the big urban areas with more liberal attitudes.

The preemption model is becoming really prevalent where you say, "You can't do this because we don't like what you're trying to do," as it relates to ordinances. But other than that, there's a pretty good relationship. Frankly, we have the benefit of both having balanced budgets requirements, which separates us from Washington. I think Condi's right, and others that mentioned this.

You almost by nature, because at the end of the fiscal year have to balance a budget, there is more consensus. It's required or you don't get out of town, and then the pressures mount. We're going through this in Washington today. Even with a trillion-and-a-half budget deficit they can't even do their budget, or they don't do a budget. They just wait, and then they threaten to close the system down. No state has that problem. No state has that issue. We have to do it.

HANUSHEK: Thanks very much. Let's talk a little bit about what Condi mentioned. I think when you were governor, the education in Florida really jumped forward. And you can still see it in the data, but not as strongly. You see that things have slipped. And the question is, how do you try to institutionalize things as opposed to having Jeb Bush make sure it happens?

BUSH: Well, first, I don't think we've slipped. We haven't shown progress. We've kind of flatlined, which I'm not happy about. Success is never final, reform's never complete. You have to constantly be pushing. Leadership matters in all this, and our reforms have eroded a bit. I think the main thing is the slight erosion of our accountability system. When we had a chance to raise "cut scores" on our end-of-year tests, we either lowered them or they remained the same.

One of the measurements—Eric, you know so well—is the difference between what is considered proficiency for the NAEP [National Assessment of Educational Progress] test and what states have as proficiency for their reading and math tests. We used to be closer to the NAEP tests and now we're not. And I think that's one place where, if Governor DeSantis wanted to see progress in reading gains and math gains, raising the bar up and having accountability around that would really matter. But I'm proud of what Florida's done.

I mean, we still lead the way as it relates to early literacy. We've got a lot of work to do as it relates to raising standards and raising expectations. We were fiftieth out of fifty for high school graduation. Now we're above the national average. But frankly, getting a high school degree, a diploma right now, is not a really good measurement. It should be college and career readiness. And there we're probably in the middle of the pack or maybe lower. So there's a lot of work that could be done for sure.

HANUSHEK: One of the arguments that's traditionally made about federalism is that states are sort of laboratories for experimentation. And I think that this argument has largely come out of welfare reform, where we had a federal welfare policy and we allowed Wisconsin and other states to do something different, and then we learned from them and so forth.

But that's not what the situation is in education. And the question is, I know that your foundation has worked very hard, and when you meet again in November it's going to continue this, of trying to push ideas across states. But do you see in various areas where states learn from each other and actually progress, and are there mechanisms that promote learning across states?

BUSH: Absolutely. And I'm proud of the work the foundation is doing. We have working groups for ESAs [education savings accounts], working groups for early childhood literacy, working groups for the digital divide and the moneys that are coming down to make sure that the underserved areas have access to high-speed broadband. And on the workforce issue, we are advocating the idea of moving high schools toward career *and* college readiness. States are eager to pass laws. The challenge is, how do you implement these laws? ESAs are particularly incredibly complex, and so we've become the subject matter experts on how to implement these things.

We have many partners that are advocating for these policies, but I think we disproportionately do the implementation work. So one of the things that I think makes federalism so successful is, this is kind of an informal compact. States want to learn from each other, and we're one of the forums in which they do that. But there are also all sorts of compacts as it relates to environmental policy, water policy, etc. Apparently there's a compact that Secretary of State Rice signed for Montana and North Dakota. Transportation compacts. The federalist system works if there is a lot of cooperation.

A hurricane hits Florida, and we have probably fifty different utility companies coordinated by the states in which they operate to come down and it's reimbursed. That compact is incredibly effective. Our country wouldn't get back on track if we didn't have it. So we're seeing—I'll give you the best example that's garnered attention. Even the *New York Times* is writing about it, and ABC News, the so-called Mississippi Miracle.

They took the Florida example of training teachers on the science of reading, eliminating three cueing, focusing on phonics, eliminating social promotion in third grade, starting the strategies at kindergarten, not at the beginning of third grade, and they had dramatic progress. They went from fifty out of fifty to twenty-first in the NAEP test, I think, in five years. And they continue to show that progress.

And during COVID, I think they were the only state or one of two or three states that didn't have the big drops. So there's an example. So what's happening now? The team that implemented the Mississippi work is now working for ExcelinEd [the Foundation for Excellence in Education] and goes to places like Oregon, California, and other states to learn from Mississippi.

We probably have fifteen states that now have seen what Florida did, what Mississippi did, and what other states are beginning to do, and realized that there is a strategy. East Palo Alto, I just read, without the state's involvement or messing with them, implemented a similar kind of strategy. They saw significant gains in reading for low-income kids right here in your neighborhood.

HANUSHEK: Yes, I think everybody recognizes now, "Thank God we're not Mississippi." But they in fact have done quite well. The question is whether it continues when [former state superintendent of education] Carey Wright has retired and—

BUSH: It will. They're proud. They're proud of it. She got her replacement in place, and we work with them, continue to work with them. The previous governor was the leader of this and the lieutenant governor is now the governor. Nothing like success to ensure continued progress.

HANUSHEK: Let me, before we open it up to other people, push you a little in a slightly different direction. Florida's right in the center of immigration issues and getting streams of immigrants coming in, while the federal government is having different policies and inability to make any national policies. Could you speak a little bit about how federalism works in that area?

BUSH: It's possible. I wrote a book with Clint Bolick, I think he's the head of the supreme court in Arizona still, called *Immigration Wars*. One of our ideas was to have states create their own immigration policies, which there is constitutional leeway in that regard. So if a state wants to be restrictionist, they could do that. If a state saw a real need to be able to have workers come in legally and maybe go back as a guest worker program or come legally and work, they should have that right to do. That's not done as much. And immigration, here's another place where federalism hasn't worked.

I suggested to Janet Reno when I was governor and she was attorney general that she should deputize state law enforcement officers to extend the reach of what was then called the Border Patrol. There were two border control officers north of Miami, Fort Lauderdale and Fort Pierce. It's about a 150-, 120-mile coastline. There was a ton of people coming in. I said, "Look. When we apprehend someone who's here illegally and has committed a crime, we have to give them to the federal agents and they have to be released if they're not adjudicated. And you don't have the capability of doing that. Why don't you train our folks and in effect deputize them?" That would be the ultimate positive federalist system.

She rejected it out of hand. I'm not sure what the legal reason is because I believe that this could have been done. Our lawyers said it could have been done. It's this question of not being able to cooperate, not being able to share power, not being able to give up power. So one of the places I think if states were interested in enforcing immigration laws, they should have the right I think with a well-trained law enforcement team to be able to do it. So it's both the enforcement side as well as creating an economic strategy where I see this happening. It is so depressing to me.

This is one of our incredible strengths as a country to be able to have a diverse dynamic country where people come in legally, and they pursue their dreams with a vengeance, and they create opportunities for everybody. We can't get past this hyperventilated, hyperpartisan approach to immigration because we can't enforce our borders. And then it becomes a question of who wins politically rather than how the country could win. So you hit a sore spot for me. I'm really so disappointed. This has been going on for way too long for us to . . . We should get to a consensus on this as quick as we can.

BOSKIN: Jeb, I have a couple of questions. One is just more or less informational. One of the interesting things that's been going on lately has been reciprocity agreements for occupational licensure for a wide range of occupations across states that enhance labor mobility. And it's especially important for low-middle-income workers in a variety of occupations. It's really not talking about cardiac surgeons. So I'm just wondering where Florida stands in that regard, and are you aware of that? Have they been moving in that direction too? Did you do any of that?

BUSH: We did some. In fact, we created universal reciprocity for teachers. If you were licensed in Idaho and you wanted to move to Florida, you would get a license. And we lessened all of the input-driven certifications to get a permanent certification. That was quite helpful because we were growing, sixty thousand students a year, and we had teacher shortages, and our schools of education weren't working as well as they could have to deliver teachers. So that's a place where we did it.

The occupational license areas in a state like Florida, it makes all the sense in the world to do it. Where you come into the challenge is the hairdressers' commission or whatever. They get a license and they think that's the most important thing to defend, and so you have all these special interests that fight against it. We've had some success, but it's not been universal.

I've seen other states have been more aggressive in this and I think that's more than appropriate. I mean, I can't tell if an interior designer that gets certified in Utah, I'm not sure that the variation would be significant enough to be unable to work in Florida. I just think this is kind of a stupid way to create protectionism. Actually, it's not a stupid way, it's an effective way to create protectionism.

BOSKIN: Let me just ask another question. So thinking about political parties and their views about federalism, there was a movement some years ago—Paul Ryan was very influential in this—which was to block-grant a lot more authority to states with far fewer restrictions, which of course is something like the welfare reform model.

And he in particular was going to want to lead with Medicaid. We've moved in the other direction a little bit. So I'm just wondering what your views are and if you have any suggestions for those of us who would like to see some clarity and some improvement in that regard, whether there's anything you might propose.

BUSH: We did have a Medicaid reform idea that fit what you're describing. We got a waiver from the forty-three administration [of President George W. Bush]. It was a waiver for just Jacksonville and Fort Lauderdale. But in return for creating flexibility on how we went about implementing our Medicaid program—part of which was to say that Medicaid beneficiaries would have a choice, they wouldn't be assigned a managed care plan or fee-for-service Medicaid, they would have choices—we said, in return for flexibility in structuring the reform plan, we would accept a version of a defined contribution plan. We accepted a run rate of spending growth that was probably one-third of what the historical run rate was. So I think one of the things that people talk about for block grants—and I'm all for them—is the flexibility to try different things. But sometimes they forget about the part of some degree of accountability. In the case of Medicaid it's to make sure that you have better healthcare outcomes and you do it at a lower cost.

Because if you can prove that, then the beauty of federalism is that that idea then can be replicated in other parts of the country. If you don't have any accountability and you're getting your money without proving that it creates a better result, that's just getting more money.

A place where this would be a home run would be early childhood work. I think, as I recall, there's like fifteen different early childhood literacy, early childhood programs. Four or five years ago the amount of money spent was $24 billion. My guess is probably $80 billion now. Who knows?

I mean the amount of money spent in Washington is incredible. But assume it's $50 billion, and you have all these different programs, have all these different rules, and the money goes down to the states for implementation. The states create a bureaucracy around that money and it finally gets into the sector that's dealing with this. Wouldn't it be better to have a block grant in return for having better outcomes where you measure it to assure the kids come to kindergarten basically ready to take on the K–3 work? The savings are enormous because you have all the bureaucrats that no longer are really necessary.

And in return for eliminating those jobs, you're creating real-world accountability. That kind of approach I think in a world that was less static and more dynamic, you would see that more often than not. The final thing I'd say is, Democrats like federalism when Republicans are in charge of DC. Republicans like federalism when anybody's in charge of DC. So one of the things that I think would be really kind of interesting would be to liberate Gavin Newsom and the California legislature to do whatever they want. Sorry about that, guys. And then compare that to states like Florida, or Texas, or you name your favorite state, and see what works. I'm pretty sure I know what will work, and I think we need to politically at least have that conversation. But the federal government needs to step back and allow that to happen.

Final thing I'd say about this whole issue of shifting power: it's not just money, it's the rulemaking process as well. States need more delegated authority as it relates to water, air quality, environmental policy across the board, transportation policy. We have a very thorough bottom-up transportation program that's thoroughly vetted from the local level, to the regional, to the state level. Those plans should be funded rather than have earmarks come down because a DC politician thinks it's cool to cut a ribbon.

The federal money should be matching these ideas, and I would trust fifty work plans like that over one imposed from up above. Ask [Secretary of Energy] Jennifer Granholm about her transportation policy where she's got a suburban gasoline advance person holding her battery charge spot so when she shows up with her NPR reporter, there's a space for her. These things, they don't work as well. I just promise you, local and state governments across the country aren't perfect, but they seem to be better than Washington.

BOSKIN: What a great idea.

HANUSHEK: Let me just pick up for a second on when you were talking about accountability with grant programs. There seems to be a question in education of what are the standards for accountability? And that's been something that's been discussed from NCLB [No Child Left Behind] through ESSA [Every Student Succeeds Act]. And as I remember, if I'm not mistaken, you had some disagreements with NCLB when that came into effect.

This was sort of an awkward disagreement at that time, I guess. Can you talk a little bit more about how you established the accountability standards in something like education where people don't live in Mississippi all their lives, half of them move to California?

BUSH: Yeah. So my disagreement with No Child Left Behind wasn't the idea of accountability. It's that our accountability system I thought was deeper and better in effect. The problem with No Child Left Behind's accountability system was, at the end of whatever the reauthorization time was, every child in every subgroup had to be proficient, which meant that every school failed. And if you want to have accountability, [former Florida governor] LeRoy Collins said that if you're leading a state and you're going out the port on your ship, you don't want to go past the horizon because no one will follow you.

And that's exactly what happened. The accountability system wasn't as robust because it became irrelevant in some ways. So my critique was that we had a system that worked better. So the answer might be [to] create minimum expectations, because many states had no accountability. The beauty of No Child Left Behind is that it forced states that didn't want to have accountability to create their own, which I thought was a good thing.

But don't impose a single standard. Treat it like: I'm in business now. When you're investing in and looking at helping businesses, you create a vision, you create a strategy, and as you implement the strategy, you hold everybody to account. It's not detailed, top-down accountability. There are transparent, broad expectations, and Washington's not really good at that.

RICE: Jeb, this is not a political question, I promise you. But I'm going to frame it in the following way. If you were asking people on a debate stage who want to be president of the United States, and let's exclude governors from this because they would know the answer, what would you ask them about, "If you are president of the United States, how should you think about federalism? How should you promote federalism?"

Because the tendency is, particularly if you are a lifetime Washington politician, which a lot of the people on that stage are, to fundamentally not understand the states. Would you just tell them to go back and read the Constitution or what would you say?

BUSH: Well, that would be healthy for all of us, I think, in this stage of life. But I think you have to frame it in a positive way. I mean, I don't know what the question would be. But the benefits of federalism are there for people to see. There are states that are doing really interesting things. They should be allowed to do it.

It's become a cliché that power that is closer to home is more respected. We have a real disengagement right now. People don't believe our institutions work. I think some of the polling you saw, you guys in the papers saw that people believe that the local government and state government response to COVID was better.

You try to find intersections of good policy and good politics, and this is one of them. Shifting power back to the states if you're a progressive and you live in a state that would implement progressive policies, you got to like it. And similarly, if you're a reform-minded conservative and you're in a state where you can implement it, you're going to like that a lot more than what goes on in Washington.

I would say the question would have to be, you probably would say, "Why don't you support that," rather than . . . Everybody says they support it, but then specifically, what would you do? This is how I'd do it: "Give me three examples of how you would shift power back to the states as it relates to rule-making and spending."

RICE: That'd be good. We'll pass that one on to the moderators.

BUSH: Yeah, you're right. I don't know who's moderating, but that would be a good one. Vivek [Ramaswamy] will say he wants to eliminate the FBI. He'll do it by executive order. That dude ought to be reading the Constitution.

THOMAS NECHYBA: Governor, we spoke with Mitch Daniels a few hours ago, and he indicated that he saw what a lot of our papers are dealing with—that there's a fiscal cliff coming up at the federal level, and at some point the dam's going to break and something's going to have to happen.

He said one of his hopes was that at that point we would get a chance to revisit federalism and who is responsible for what and things would be handed to the states. My question has two parts. One is, do you agree, do you see that opportunity in this impending potential crisis? Secondly, how would the states, if this truly became a way to hand back responsibilities to states, how would states actually go about funding additional responsibilities if those were handed to them by the federal government?

BUSH: Well, I would hope that if Washington was going to get out of the spending business, it would be phased out over time to give the states the time necessary to adjust.

My experience was, we ended up with a AAA bond rating and cash reserves equaled 25 percent of general revenue. We cut the state government employee base by thirteen thousand out of a number of maybe one hundred thousand. We had these cuts over an eight-year period, and we still increased funding for the most vulnerable.

I think if Washington said we have a crisis, we can no longer provide support for Medicaid or block grants for transportation, that would create a huge problem for states. Because similarly, this is going to create an economic problem. And at least in the states that I'm aware of, growing economies create growing resources, growing revenue. So if you have a declining economy and a shrinking Washington, that'd be a huge problem. And I'm not as optimistic that the natural impulse would be, "Okay, let the states do it." But if they did, a lot of states would have to change their behaviors and become massively reform minded. They'd have to say, "Can I do this for 25 percent less and have a better outcome?"

To me, that would be a great reason to get back in the governor's business, but I'm not sure if everybody else would jump for joy on that.

Can I make one more point? The focus, it seems, is principally on spending. I think where the federal government's encroachment has gotten pretty insidious is on rulemaking and regulations. And for the United States to grow again, we need to build again.

I see a really dangerous situation where we're indebting ourselves massively for these top-down programs as it relates to the infrastructure program and other things that have been appropriated over the last couple of years. And we're not going to be able to get a permit to mine lithium or to refine. We're creating this agenda and then we don't have the ability to be dynamically creating the solution or taking advantage of the opportunity.

So part of federalism, I think, has to be shifting rulemaking powers back to the states. It used to be they're almost completely the jurisdiction of the states and now the states are just small partners. And that would be, to me, one of the most important things to do because we've got to start building things. In order to build things, you've got to get permits. In order to get permits, you've got to streamline this process that is mind-numbing. You can't build a bridge, you can't build a refinery. There're serious problems that can be fixed with federalism at its core.

Governor Jerry Brown

Introduced by Michael J. Boskin

MICHAEL J. BOSKIN: Welcome, Governor Brown. Thank you so much for joining us. We've been debating on and off all day long with various aspects of fiscal federalism, the roles of states and localities and the federal government, how they vary for different types of responsibilities and resources, how they've changed over time, how COVID created some additional fissures, etc. So we'd like to get your perspective on that. I think everybody here knows you or knows of you. Not everybody here's a Californian, but Governor Brown has the unique distinction of having served four terms as governor. A pair of two terms. And he also was mayor of Oakland, and also California attorney general.

So, the governor's had a long history of public service and has helped govern California through lots of ups and downs and contention and political realignment and things of that sort. So I thought we might kick things off with a couple of questions, let you ruminate on them.

GOV. JERRY BROWN: I'm looking forward to this. It is important. And it is also timely that we discuss and hopefully elucidate our unusual system of government.

BOSKIN: Thank you so much, Governor. I'm going to start with a couple of questions and then we'll throw it open for general discussion. But you have many unique perspectives, but during your time in office, what did you see as the biggest opportunities for strengthening, realigning, improving the relationship among different levels of government, perhaps particularly between the state and localities, but also with respect to the federal government?

Brown: Well, that's a broad question. And we've been here before—in 1982—under the Reagan administration, when the president proposed to swap welfare and Medicaid and change the respective responsibilities of the states and the federal government. As it turned out, little of that "swap" actually happened. The forces of the status quo were too strong. Anytime you try to move government structures out of their habituated slot, you encounter enormous resistance.

Unquestionably, it would be very good if we had a clear delineation of federal and state functions. Unfortunately, these functions are intricately entangled, and I don't know that you can untangle them any better than we have, except in the face of a crisis or a very strong president coming into office with that as a major promise. Yes, it is theoretically possible to restructure our federal system, but in practice we're not going to tear up the evolved complex relationships of the federal and the state governments and, analogously, not those of the states and their local governments. I could compare our income tax system to our system of federalism. It's completely crazy, mind-numbingly complex, and not understood by 99 percent of the people. And yet, that's the tax system we have. You can tinker with it, but not modify it in any fundamental way. Same with our system of federalism.

The problem at a very basic level is that the members of Congress want to advance their goals—conservative or liberal—and they do so by passing laws or tax measures with regulatory hooks that compel behavioral change in states and localities. So federal officials, carrying out the mandates of Congress, meddle in state and local affairs. It is very hard to stop that meddling, because if there's local crime or big problems with homelessness or housing, the environment, or toxic waste dumps, then the Congress wants to jump in. The federal agencies are there, and they are there to take regulatory and enforcement actions. And so I think the real task is not so much trying to change the federal structure, however theoretically good that sounds, but rather to bring some common sense and clarity to the functioning of our government.

Boskin: That's great. We've emphasized clarity a little bit here and stability, for sure. Looking back at your time in office, and perhaps more importantly as an observer of what's going on since you left office, where it appears relations among different levels of government are becoming more frayed, we've become more polarized politically, obviously, but every time a Democrat's in the White House, Republican attorneys general are suing them on everything;

and when Republicans are in the White House, we have Democrats suing them on everything. So do you see any opportunities to take advantage of improving that in a way that makes it easier to operate, and reduces the cost and the instability of these kinds of actions and activities, where we have states and the federal government arguing about who has the right to deal with the border, who has the right to do this or anything else? Are there some areas you would single out as perhaps more ripe than others as a way to proceed in improving federalism?

BROWN: We do make progress. There are cases where the federal government overreached and then pulled back. For example, Congress passed the No Child Left Behind Act and then Senator Lamar Alexander, the chairman of the Senate Education Committee, won passage of legislation that modified No Child Left Behind by reducing its complex and overly intrusive mandates—rightfully so. Congress didn't get that far, but they made some progress. President Obama then came along with Race to the Top, and that was another coercive federal intervention. I was the only governor, and California was the only state, that refused to participate in Race to the Top. I didn't participate because I thought the program interfered with the work of locally elected school boards. I might just say on that score, it's very hard to exercise restraint when you have superior power, as the federal government clearly does.

We also saw overreach in the Obama administration's interpretations of Title IX, when federal administrators issued detailed mandates to hundreds of colleges across the country, ordering them in effect to adopt specific codes of student conduct. Here in California, I went in a different direction. When the state legislature passed a bill to codify the federal Title IX regulations—which Trump had rescinded—I vetoed the bill and created a committee consisting of a former Supreme Court justice and two outstanding academic leaders to find a better solution. They crafted an outstanding report with solid but voluntary and flexible guidelines. This approach embodied the principles of federalism in that key decisions were left to individual colleges, not centralized in state mandates. A few years later, the legislature passed a bill on a party-line vote, similar to the one I vetoed. Governor Newsom signed it into law—again demonstrating the power not of federalism but of standardization and distant state authority.

I also supported and signed into law the Local Control Funding Formula. This measure eliminated dozens of state categorical educational programs and returned substantial authority to local school boards, while providing extra funding for low-income schools. Though recent research shows positive results, there are still persistent legislative efforts to reestablish state mandates on how local schools should operate and structure their budgets.

Even when you shift power to local authorities, the political pressure to restore centralized authority never ceases. I'm the chair of the Oakland Military Institute College Preparatory Academy, a charter school that I started in 2001. So I experience very directly the efforts by the legislature to curtail the flexibility and innovative capacity of charter schools. It is a problem that shows no signs of going away.

Legislators—both conservative and liberal—increasingly see the world in polarized terms. This makes for unstable governing, as basic rules shift depending on which party or ideology is in charge. As California attorney general, I sued the federal government under the Clean Air Act to exercise its waiver provisions allowing the State of California to establish its own vehicle emission standards. With Bush in the White House, I lost. But when Obama came into office, we prevailed. And, of course, when Trump came in, things went the other way, only to be reversed when Biden was elected. The only answer is for more centrist politicians of both parties to realize the country is in a crisis and find ways to work together. If we constantly jack up everybody on the Right and on the Left and then they mutually jack each other up, the country is really going to weaken itself, as I think it is doing.

So the only hope is for people who hold different ideological positions to accept that not everything is an absolute value, and therefore they can compromise and find common pathways to settle these very emotional arguments. I've never seen such emotion and belief in so many different areas as I do today. I think we have to just de-escalate the "beliefs" and the emotions and find a greater American calling. Whatever you believe or don't believe, there's always a middle position available. Maybe as things get really bad, we'll get more politicians who will want to rise above the partisanship and find common ground. I do think as things get worse, reasonable people rise to the occasion. In the end, it depends on the capacity of leaders, their ability to communicate with the people, and their maturity to realize we're in profoundly deep trouble in America.

BOSKIN: Well, I think many of us would agree with that. When I look back, as I mentioned in the beginning, at your pair of two terms in office, they included some situations that were either not so common in other states or a more extreme situation in California. I remember when George Shultz and I first came to see you in the '70s to talk about the budget. We had a big budget surplus in California then. In your second time around, you inherited a very large budget deficit. In addition, California's become a one-party state. Now, there are red and blue one-party states, but that doesn't promote the compromise you're talking about or the competition you're talking about too much.

And of course, we have the initiative process, which is taken to its logical or its extreme conclusion in California relative to a variety of other places, that complicates governance and makes a lot of the budget, especially, very inflexible. So I'm wondering how any of those things strike you as being important in thinking about ways forward, either in California, in its relationship to local governments, or more generally, and how overwhelming dealing with the budget deficit, for example, was, relative to your ability to get other things accomplished.

BROWN: Well, just on the budget, when I took over from Arnold Schwarzenegger, I inherited a $27 billion deficit. So I cut several billion dollars and got a tax increase by way of a successful ballot measure, and lo and behold, the deficits turned into massive surpluses. Now, I have to recognize, and I'm sure most of you people do, that a lot of that was the very fast-growing economy, probably the beginnings of inflation. In California, we have very high income tax rates that bring in huge amounts of money when capital gains grow, but the money disappears when the stock market declines and capital gains go down in a recession. This has happened with almost every governor.

I was lucky in my last two terms as governor, we never had a recession. That was unusual. From the time of Governor Earl Warren, every governor except George Deukmejian experienced a recession during their time in office. And when that happens, you have a big deficit. But after the deficit, and especially if you raise taxes, then as the economy comes back, you get more money and then you invest in a lot more programs; then you get a recession and you have to cut back. So it's a roller coaster.

We need a more stable tax system. But the problem is that when we pursue more stable and less volatile revenue sources—like taxing property or services so that money comes in good times and bad—that doesn't feel very fair. Inevitably, when we flatten out the tax we are giving more money to higher-income people, while then increasing broad-based taxes will be quite burdensome to those with less income. And in California, that's not going to be acceptable. So we muddle along.

Another feature in California governance is the use of ballot measures to change state laws, including the constitution itself. If you can spend enough money, you can put almost any initiative on the ballot. For example, Uber and its allies spent $200 million on a ballot measure campaign and were able to repeal a labor law they didn't like. Now, many times ballot measure proponents are unsuccessful, but as long as there's an ability to hire signature gatherers—which there always will be—we will have endless initiative and referendum campaigns to change the law in California.

So I don't know what we can do with the initiative, because anybody who says they are going to curtail the people's right to vote on a ballot measure will fail. Voters are unlikely to vote for a measure that would take away their own power. So the initiative is not going away, and it is not going to be radically changed.

Now, one party in charge for too long, that's another problem. It's a problem because when you have one party, you'll have activist groups that relentlessly push the direction of the ideology of that particular party. Now, the governor can counteract this with the veto, but the governor himself or herself depends on some of the same interest groups. So it does take very creative governing to overcome the pressures when one party dominates government. Resisting the pressure is possible—I've vetoed a lot of bills. If I were governor now, I'd be vetoing a lot more. But there it is.

There's no magic formula for improving our federal system of governing. It's a matter of taking what you have, where you are, and following the least-damaging alternative. I think what's needed is some caution, some humility, and reaching across the political divide. The trouble isn't California. Discontent and dysfunction are more general. We see it in many parts of the country and even in many countries of the world. So that's where we are.

BOSKIN: Okay, let me throw it open to other people for questions. Who'd like to add anything?

THAD KOUSSER: Governor Brown, you came into office [talking] about the wall of debt, right? You have this poster behind you of the wall of debt, not just deficit, but also the bonds. And by the time you left, as you said, it was retired, but it's opened back up again. So what are the prospects? A lot of this conversation in the last hour has been about debt at the national level, debt at the state level. Is this just built into the nature of politicians? Is it because states have limited resources and are always going to need to borrow some during a recession? Or is it something about the federal-state relationship where a state feels like the federal government will bail them out if it's too bad?

BROWN: The state of California by constitutional provision doesn't "borrow," but it has a number of budgetary devices, which you would call "gimmicks," that allow it to get through periods of budget deficit by temporarily taking funds from state special funds, deferring payments, and using funds belonging to local governments. That happened in the Depression and under Arnold Schwarzenegger and in various forms under several other governors. So, in the face of fluctuating state revenues, why does state spending keep growing faster than the economy as a whole? To my mind, the fundamental driver of state spending is that we're in a society with great need and tremendous inequality, with millions of people that are in very disadvantaged situations. So, that calls out to people who want to remedy that—hence the desire for programs and plans, all of which cost money. So if you look around at those who are the most well-off and the people who are in the middle, that's one thing. But if you look at people in the lower 10 percent or 20 percent of the income scale, you find lacking what the average American takes for granted and expects out of life, and that provides a plausible reason for the state, for example, to create a medical program, a school program, or an income subsidy or some type of welfare program.

From a moral point of view, from just a sense of being human, these programs look good. They feel right. The problem is there's no limit to the demand or even the need, but there is a limit to spending, because there's a limit to what the people are willing to provide by way of taxes. In California, unlike the federal government, the state is required to balance the budget every year. It can't go too far into debt unless it is through bonds, and bonds require voter approval and can be voted down. From the way I see the world, I want the state to help people who are struggling, but I don't want fiscal instability. That makes me dubious of state programs if they appear to be expanding too quickly or growing beyond an appropriate size. Of course, what is an appropriate size is a political as well as a fiscal judgment.

That gets us back to federalism. There's a concept in the Catholic Church called "subsidiarity," which I learned about early in life and then came to apply it when I became governor. It holds that those closest to the problems are best positioned to address them. That means giving local authorities the power and money to get things done—and that's what we did. I find that at the local level, that's where people know one another in a more direct way and can exhibit a little more common sense.

So that's one thing, getting the cities and the counties more authority, but in reality, they are still very dependent on state government. And there will always be pressure from advocates for more and more intervention from the state and federal government if they can't get what they want from the local authorities. I would like to think there's some legal structures that could strengthen federalism, but at the end of the day, I see the trajectory as more standardization and more power flowing to higher levels of government and therefore more centralization of decisions.

JOSHUA RAUH: Governor Brown, toward the end of your time in office, you took an attempt at trying to address some of the unfunded pension liability issues, which I think is one of the more destabilizing forces on public finances in California, the unfunded pension liabilities of CalPERS [California Public Employees' Retirement System] and CalSTRS [California State Teachers' Retirement System] and so on. And since then, things got a little better for a time, but now this seems to be getting worse again. Can you provide us with any hope for addressing that issue?

BROWN: Well, I'm not in the hope business, but I can tell you that both California pension systems are funded at about 70 percent, which, barring major catastrophes, will enable them to pay their obligations for a long time. Despite strong opposition, I was able to get substantial pension reforms enacted in my third term as governor. This probably couldn't be done today. It was only successful because we had a real crisis and a huge budget deficit. The result was legislation cutting back public pensions over time—you can't adversely affect the benefits of existing pension holders. And these reforms were much more significant than the critics claimed.

But I didn't stop with these reforms. I joined in a lawsuit challenging the principle of vested rights enshrined in the so-called California rule. I asked the California Supreme Court to find a way to make the rule more flexible, allowing the state to modify pension benefits for those who hadn't yet actually earned them. For example, if employees worked for five years and are going to work another twenty, pension benefits could be modified downward before they start their sixth year. Under the current system, benefits can only be ratcheted upward, never reduced. Benefits can never be changed from the moment you're hired, except to be increased. Unfortunately, the justices refused to reexamine the California rule. They did get rid of certain kinds of pension spiking and gimmicks, but they didn't bite into the big bullet.

That said, I think the next time we have another crisis, the pressure will mount and I think people will be more inclined to tackle the question of vested rights. Yes, there are basic vested rights, but there should be some limits. It should be possible, when there is severe fiscal strain or when governments can't meet their obligations, to modify those benefits that have not actually yet been earned. And when things get a little worse—hopefully not too much worse—I would predict that cases will come before the court, particularly from local governments, because they're going to be hurt far more than the state government. State government only devotes about 20 percent of its funds for salaries and benefits. The bulk of state spending goes to counties, cities, special districts, and school districts, which spend 80 percent of their funds on employees. So local governments are going to feel a much greater pension burden than the state.

Even though all of this may leave you with an ironic view of the governing process, you should know that reform and recovery are always possible. The fact is, our federal system of governance has worked for a very long time—in good times and bad. And yes, things generally have to get worse before political reform becomes plausible. That's just the way it is. Habits die hard, and the government, like each one of us, has habits that don't give way without a counteracting force. Hopefully, the force that brings change won't also cause breakdown.

BOSKIN: You tried to be innovative in a variety of situations, variety of areas, in the relations with local governments. I know you wanted to change school funding formulas that would get more resources to school districts with a lot of disadvantaged students. How much resistance did you have to that? How do you think that's gone?

BROWN: Well, we enacted the Local Control Funding Formula and eliminated a host of categorical programs, which created a plethora of rules, specialized funding streams, and endless audits—all a nightmare for local schools. But the pressures to control from afar are still pervasive. Schools are still spending way too much time on compliance and dealing with prescriptive outside interventions, rules, and reports.

At its core, education and learning are about the knowledge, the skills, and the inspiration of the teacher interacting in a human way with students. And that central reality is too often crowded out by incredibly complex compliance measures—"do this, don't do that"—to make sure that no student is disadvantaged. But when you add up all of the rules, you find a bloated education code between ten and thirteen volumes, depending how big the print is and how many annotations are included. That's thousands and thousands of prescriptions requiring huge amounts of time and money devoted to lawyering and administering, not teaching and learning.

Contemporary education is very much a game of complexity. We really need simplification.

BOSKIN: Governor, thank you, it's been very illuminating.

BROWN: Thank you.

BOSKIN: I think we got a lot of ideas from our three governors and a lot of understanding of some practical realities they confront, which we probably oversimplify with our political economy models. And that's become a much more common thing now in academic research, to have political economy built into models, and that's a step forward.

About the Editor

Michael J. Boskin is the Wohlford Family Senior Fellow at the Hoover Institution and the Tully M. Friedman Professor of Economics, both at Stanford University, and a research associate at the National Bureau of Economic Research. He is the author or editor of more than 150 articles and eighteen books, most recently *Defense Budgeting for a Safer World*. Boskin was the fifteenth chair of the President's Council of Economic Advisers, where he helped resolve the Third World debt and savings and loan crises, expand global trade, introduce emissions trading in environmental regulation, and place the first effective controls on government spending while protecting the defense budget. On presidential candidate Ronald Reagan's tax policy task force, he helped develop the policies that lowered marginal tax rates, indexed tax brackets for inflation, accelerated depreciation, and introduced IRAs and 401(k)s. In 1995–96, he chaired the US Senate's Advisory Commission to Study the Consumer Price Index, whose report has transformed the way government statistical agencies around the world measure inflation, productivity, and real GDP. His research continues to focus on important policy issues in public economics and macroeconomics.

About the
Conference Participants

Dr. Jay Bhattacharya is a professor of health policy at Stanford University, a research associate at the National Bureau of Economic Research, and a senior fellow, by courtesy, at the Hoover Institution. He directs Stanford's Center on the Demography and Economics of Health and Aging. Bhattacharya's recent research has focused on the epidemiology of COVID-19 and policy responses to the epidemic. He is a coauthor of the 2020 Great Barrington Declaration, a proposed alternative to COVID-19 lockdowns, and has published more than 165 articles in peer-reviewed scientific journals. He holds an MD and a PhD in economics from Stanford University.

Valentin Bolotnyy is a Kleinheinz Fellow at the Hoover Institution, a research affiliate at the Institute of Labor Economics (IZA), and an affiliated scholar at Stanford's Deliberative Democracy Lab. His research, often done in partnership with state and local governments, aims to generate and inform innovative policies that improve economic and health outcomes. The objective of all of his work is to strengthen democracy by helping policymakers deliver good outcomes for their constituents. Bolotnyy holds a BA in economics and international relations from Stanford University and a PhD in economics from Harvard University.

David Brady is the Davies Family Senior Fellow, Emeritus, at the Hoover Institution and the Morris Doyle Professor of Public Policy, Emeritus, at Stanford University, and was the Bowen H. and Janice Arthur McCoy Professor of Political Science at Stanford's Graduate School of Business. He has published eight books and more than one hundred academic papers. He has also published essays and articles in the *American Interest*, *Commentary*, *Policy Review*, *RealClearPolitics*, and the *Wall Street Journal*. His study on the electoral basis of gridlock is forthcoming (2024). Brady was elected to the American Academy of Arts and Sciences in 1987.

Jerry Brown was the thirty-fourth (1975–83) and the thirty-ninth (2011–19) governor of California, the longest-serving governor in state history. He has also served as California secretary of state and attorney general, mayor of Oakland, and chair of the state Democratic Party, as well as practicing law. Brown currently serves as chair of the California-China Climate Institute at the University of California–Berkeley; executive chair of the *Bulletin of the Atomic Scientists*; chair of the Oakland Military Institute College Preparatory Academy, a public charter school he founded; and board member of the Nuclear Threat Initiative and Council on Criminal Justice.

Jeb Bush was the forty-third governor of the state of Florida (1999–2007). During his two terms, Bush championed major reform of government pro-grams and led Florida to the forefront of consumer healthcare advances, job growth, and academic standards. Bush maintains his passion for improv-ing the quality of education as the chair of the Foundation for Excellence in Education, a national nonprofit organization he founded to develop and implement reforms that lead to rising student achievement. Governor Bush has written three books, *Profiles in Character, Immigration Wars: Forging an American Solution,* and *Reply All: A Governor's Story 1999–2007.*

Bruce E. Cain is a professor of political science at Stanford's School of Humanities and Sciences and the Spence and Cleone Eccles Family Director of the Bill Lane Center for the American West. He was previously director of the Institute of Governmental Studies at the University of California–Berkeley and executive director of the UC Washington Center. His areas of expertise include political regulation, applied democratic theory, representa-tion, and state politics. He is the author of *Democracy More or Less: America's Political Reform Quandary* and has been published in the *Yale Law Journal,* the *Election Law Journal,* and the *UC Irvine Law Review.* Cain holds a PhD from Harvard University and was elected to the American Academy of Arts and Sciences in 2000.

Brandice Canes-Wrone is the Maurice R. Greenberg Senior Fellow at the Hoover Institution and professor of political science, Stanford University. Currently, she is the director of Hoover's Center for Revitalizing American

Institutions. Throughout her career, Canes-Wrone has published numerous articles and books in the areas of political institutions, mass political behavior, and political economy. Recent publications examine how changes in the local media are related to developments in congressional electoral accountability, and the role of campaign donors in congressional representation. She is an elected member of the American Academy of Arts and Sciences.

John F. Cogan is the Leonard and Shirley Ely Senior Fellow at the Hoover Institution. He was previously a faculty member in the Stanford Public Policy Program (1994–2019) and a senior fellow at the Stanford Institute for Economic Policy Research (2000–22). Cogan served in several positions during President Ronald Reagan's administration, including as deputy director of the Office of Management and Budget (1988–89). He has published widely in professional journals in economics and political science. Among his books is *The High Cost of Good Intentions*, recipient of the 2018 Hayek Prize.

Mitchell E. Daniels Jr. served as a two-term governor of the state of Indiana (2005–13) and as the twelfth president of Purdue University (2013–22), where he prioritized student affordability. In recognition of his leadership, Daniels was named among the World's 50 Greatest Leaders by *Fortune* in 2015 and was elected to the American Academy of Arts and Sciences in 2019. In 2023, Purdue University named its business school for him. Daniels currently serves as a distinguished scholar and senior advisor at the Liberty Fund. He is the author of three books and a contributing columnist for the *Washington Post*.

Steven J. Davis is the director of research and the Thomas W. and Susan B. Ford Senior Fellow at the Hoover Institution and senior fellow at the Stanford Institute for Economic Policy Research. He is a research associate of the National Bureau of Economic Research, economic adviser to the US Congressional Budget Office, and senior adviser to the Brookings Papers on Economic Activity. Davis is also cofounder of the Economic Policy Uncertainty project, the Survey of Working Arrangements and Attitudes, the WFH Map project, the Survey of Business Uncertainty, and the Stock Market Jumps project.

Dennis Epple is the Thomas Lord University Professor of Economics in the Tepper School of Business at Carnegie Mellon University. His current research focuses on public economics, with an emphasis on federalism, the economics of education, and urban economics. He is a fellow of the Econometric Society, a research associate of the National Bureau of Economic Research, a member of the CESifo research network, and a member of the Human Capital and Economic Opportunity Global Working Group. His research has appeared in leading journals in economics and management, and he is a former coeditor of the *American Economic Review* and the *Journal of Public Economics.*

David Fedor is the Stephenson Policy Fellow at the Hoover Institution, where he supports fellowship research within the George P. Shultz Energy Policy Working Group as well as for Hoover's Global Policy and Strategy Initiative. Fedor has worked in economic and security policy analysis across the Indo-Pacific, and for nearly a decade he served on the Hoover team of former US secretary of state George Shultz. He holds BS and MS degrees in Earth systems from Stanford University.

Morris P. Fiorina is the Wendt Family Professor of Political Science at Stanford University and a senior fellow of the Hoover Institution. He has published numerous articles and written or edited fourteen books, most recently *Who Governs? Emergency Powers in the Time of COVID.* Fiorina has served as chair of the American National Election Studies (1986–90) and on the editorial boards of a dozen journals in political science, political economy, law, and public policy. He is an elected member of the American Academy of Arts and Sciences, the American Academy of Political and Social Science, and the National Academy of Sciences.

Eric A. Hanushek, the Paul and Jean Hanna Senior Fellow at the Hoover Institution, is internationally recognized for his economic analysis of educational issues, and his research has had broad influence on education policy. In 2021, he received the Yidan Prize for Education Research. His widely cited studies span the effects of class size reduction, school accountability, teacher effectiveness, and the economic returns to school quality. He has authored or edited twenty-six books and more than three hundred articles.

Michael T. Hartney is a Hoover Fellow at the Hoover Institution and an associate professor of political science at Boston College. His research focuses on state and local government, interest groups, and education policy. Hartney's first book, *How Policies Make Interest Groups: Governments, Unions,* *and American Education*, was published by the University of Chicago Press in 2022. The monograph helps explain the origins, power, and activities of America's teachers' unions, showing how government helped these unions gain influence in education. Hartney earned his PhD from the University of Notre Dame and his bachelor's degree from Vanderbilt University.

Jacob Jaffe is a postdoctoral fellow in the Department of Political Science, Stanford University. He studies American politics, exploring trust in government and how public opinion changes over time and focusing on how Americans experience elections. His research uses novel experimental and computational techniques to study understudied topics in the administration of American elections. He earned his PhD in political science from MIT.

David M. Kennedy is the Donald J. McLachlan Professor of History, Emeritus, at Stanford University. He has long taught courses in twentieth-century US history, US foreign policy, American literature, and the American West. His Pulitzer Prize–winning book, *Freedom from Fear: The American People in Depression and War, 1929–1945*, recounts the history of the American people in two great crises. Kennedy is also the coauthor of the US history textbook *The American Pageant*, now in its eighteenth edition. Kennedy has taught and lectured about American history in many countries overseas and has been featured in several historical documentary films, including *American Creed*.

Thad Kousser is a professor of political science and codirector of the Yankelovich Center at the University of California, San Diego, where he studies American state and national politics. His work and commentary have been published in many political journals and media outlets, and he is the author or editor of several books, including *The Power of American Governors* and *Term Limits and the Dismantling of State Legislative Professionalism*. He has been a visiting professor at Stanford University and a Flinders Fulbright Distinguished Chair at Flinders University (Adelaide, Australia), and has worked as a staff assistant in the California and New Mexico state senates and the US Senate.

Carlos X. Lastra-Anadón is an assistant professor of public policy at IE University (Madrid, Spain) and the research director at its Center for the Governance of Change. His research interests lie at the intersection of politics, education, and innovation policy and examine the potential of federalism for improving outcomes. His research has received funding from the IBM Foundation, the British Academy, the Ramón Areces Foundation, and Harvard's Weatherhead Center, and has been published in outlets such as *Political Science Research and Methods, Publius: The Journal of Federalism,* and the *Journal of Comparative Economics.* Prior to starting his academic career, he worked as a consultant with McKinsey and Company.

Jillian Ludwig is the research program manager for the State and Local Governance Initiative at the Hoover Institution. She previously worked as a research analyst on the team, covering a variety of policy topics, including tax and budget issues and homelessness. She also assists with the Public Policy Lab at the Stanford Graduate School of Business. She received her MSc in political science and political economy from the London School of Economics and her BS in economics and a certificate in French language from the University of Wisconsin–Madison.

Thomas MaCurdy is a senior fellow at the Hoover Institution and at the Stanford Institute for Economic Policy Research and professor of economics at Stanford University. His expertise encompasses domestic policy related to government health, income support, and entitlement programs. MaCurdy has published numerous articles and reports and has served in an editorial capacity for several professional journals. He has directed and participated in projects supporting many federal and state agencies, through which he has accumulated in-depth knowledge and experience in designing, evaluating, and implementing a broad spectrum of programs in the Medicare, Medicaid, and Affordable Care Act (ACA) Marketplace systems.

Michael W. McConnell is the Richard and Frances Mallery Professor at Stanford Law School and director of the school's Constitutional Law Center, and is a senior fellow at the Hoover Institution. He has held chaired professorships at the University of Chicago and the University of Utah and visiting professorships at Harvard and New York University, and has published widely in the fields of constitutional law and theory. From 2002 to 2009, he served as circuit judge on the US Court of Appeals for the Tenth Circuit. His most recent book (coauthored with Nathan Chapman) is *Agreeing to Disagree: How the Establishment Clause Protects Religious Diversity and Freedom of Conscience.*

Thomas Nechyba is professor of economics and public policy studies at Duke University, where he founded the EcoTeach Center and directed the Social

Science Research Institute. He was previously on the faculty at Stanford University and was a national fellow at the Hoover Institution. His research in local public finance, fiscal federalism, urban economics, and the economics of education has been funded by the National Science Foundation and the Spencer Foundation. He is the author of a major textbook in microeconomics, and his work has been published in journals such as the *American Economic Review*, the *Journal of Political Economy*, and the *International Economic Review*.

Paul E. Peterson is a senior fellow at the Hoover Institution and the Henry Lee Shattuck Professor of Government at Harvard University, where he is also director of the Program on Education Policy and Governance. Peterson's research interests include educational policy, federalism, social capital, and charter schools. Peterson is a member of the American Academy of Arts and Sciences and the National Academy of Education. Recent books include *Saving Schools: From Horace Mann to Virtual Learning* and, with Eric A. Hanushek and Ludger Woessmann, *Endangering Prosperity: A Global View of the American School*.

Joshua Rauh is the Ormond Family Professor of Finance at Stanford's Graduate School of Business and a senior fellow at the Hoover Institution, where he leads Hoover's State and Local Governance Initiative. He formerly served as principal chief economist on the President's Council of Economic Advisers (2019–20) and taught at the University of Chicago's Booth School of Business (2004–9) and the Kellogg School of Management (2009–12). Rauh studies government pension liabilities, corporate investment, business taxation, and investment management. His scholarly papers have appeared in leading journals, his research has received national media coverage, and he has testified before Congress on various topics.

Condoleezza Rice is the Tad and Dianne Taube Director of the Hoover Institution and the Thomas and Barbara Stephenson Senior Fellow on Public Policy. From 2005 to 2009, Rice served as the sixty-sixth secretary of state of the United States. Rice also served as President George W. Bush's national security advisor from 2001 to 2005. Rice served as Stanford University's provost from 1993 to 1999. Rice has been on the Stanford faculty since 1981 and has won two of the university's highest teaching honors. She is also currently a founding partner of international strategic consulting firm Rice, Hadley, Gates & Manuel LLC and an owner of the Denver Broncos.

Douglas Rivers is a senior fellow at the Hoover Institution and a professor of political science at Stanford University. He is also a director and the chief scientist at global polling firm YouGov PLC. Before joining Stanford, Rivers taught at Harvard University, the California Institute of Technology, and the University of California–Los Angeles. He cofounded Knowledge Networks in 1998 to provide access to public opinion survey tools and large opinion panels for conducting survey experiments through WebTV. He later founded the survey research company Polimetrix, which was acquired by YouGov in 2007. Rivers was elected a fellow of the American Academy of Arts and Sciences in 2015.

Jonathan Rodden is a senior fellow at the Hoover Institution and the Stanford Institute for Economic Policy Research and professor of political science at Stanford University. His work focuses on economic and political geography, political institutions, and representation. His books include *Hamilton's Paradox: The Promise and Peril of Fiscal Federalism* and *Fiscal Decentralization and the Challenge of Hard Budget Constraints*. He has been active in debates about the design of multilevel institutions in the European Monetary Union and has worked with the European Parliament. His recent work examines the impact of the great recession, with a focus on differences between urban and rural areas.

Daniel L. Rubinfeld is the Robert L. Bridges Professor of Law and professor of economics emeritus at the University of California–Berkeley and professor of law at New York University. He previously served as chief economist and deputy assistant attorney general for antitrust in the US Department of Justice (1997–98). Rubinfeld has written many articles relating to antitrust and competition policy, law and economics, and public economics. He is the author of two textbooks and coauthor (with Robert Inman) of *Democratic Federalism*. He is a member of the American Academy of Arts and Sciences and a former president of the American Law and Economics Association.

John B. Taylor is the George P. Shultz Senior Fellow in Economics at the Hoover Institution and the Mary and Robert Raymond Professor of Economics at Stanford University. He also directs Stanford's Introductory Economics Center, cochairs the faculty council of the Stanford Emerging Technology Review, and chairs the Hoover Economic Policy Working Group. He has served as senior economist and later member of the President's

Council of Economic Advisers, as under secretary of the Treasury for international affairs, as president of the Mont Pelerin Society, and on the G20 Eminent Persons Group on Global Financial Governance. Among his many awards are the Adam Smith Award, the Bradley Prize, and the Hayek Prize.

Alice Yiqian Wang is a PhD/JD candidate at Stanford University and Yale Law School. Her research primarily concerns executive control over the immigration courts and decision-making dynamics among immigration court judges. She has contributed to the journal *European Politics and Society* and the book *Who Governs? Emergency Powers in the Time of COVID*.

Index

Note: The letter f following a page number denotes a figure; the letter t denotes a table.

ACA. *See* Affordable Care Act
accountability
    for K–12 education, 193, 195–96, 197f,
        198f, 199, 392–93
    related to block grants, 390–91
achievement, student, 180–83, 181f, 182f,
    183f, 184f
Adams, Henry, 69
adaptive infrastructure, 215–16
adequacy court cases, and school finance,
    188
Aduhelm (aducanumab), 288
Affordable Care Act (ACA)
    composition of health financing and
        insurance, 239, 240f
    essential health benefits requirement,
        266–67
    and federal budget outlook, 244–45
    insurance exchange marketplaces run by
        states, 259, 260t–61t, 261–62
    Medicaid expansion under, 172, 274–76,
        306, 309–10
    options for reforming marketplace
        exchanges, 276–77
    public option insurance plans, 262
    Section 1332 waivers under, 256–57,
        257t–58t, 259
    as source of healthcare financing, 237
    state differences in administration
        of, 252, 256–57, 257t–58t, 259,
        260t–61t, 261–63

aggressive use of data, 381–82
agriculture, appropriation of federal funds
    for, 93–94
AHCM (average high cost multiple), 297,
    299–300
aid to individuals, federal spending on,
    89–90, 97–98, 99, 99t, 100f. *See*
    also Affordable Care Act; Medicaid;
    Medicare; social insurance programs
Alaska, reinsurance program in, 257t
alternative payment models for Medicaid
    providers, 278
American Civil War, 67, 114, 115
American federalism. *See* federalism
American Insurance Co. v. Canter (1828),
    108n10
American National Election Studies
    (ANES) Trust in Government Index,
    46, 46f, 60n3
American Recovery and Reinvestment Act
    (ARRA), 218–19, 221t, 222, 307–8
American Rescue Plan Act (ARPA), 311,
    339, 340t
Anti-Federalists, 11, 22–25
Arizona, public's federalism preferences in,
    47, 49–50, 50f
Article 4 of US Constitution, 88
Articles of Confederation, 9
Ashraf, Nava, 214
average high cost multiple (AHCM), 297,
    299–300

balance of payments, 295–96
balanced budgets
    federal, 84–85, 94
    state, 166, 385–86
Balat, Jorge, 218
ballot measures, use of in California, 402
bankruptcies, public-sector, 338–39
Basic Health Programs (BHPs), 259
Baum-Snow, Nathaniel, 219
Bhattacharya, Jay, 4, 286–90
Bill of Rights, 20–21
block grants, 90–91, 282–83, 362, 390–91
Bolick, Clint, 388
Bolotnyy, Valentin, 4, 365, 367
Bonus Bill, 90–91, 109n23
Boskin, Michael J., ix, xi–xii, 4, 63, 64, 117, 171,
    175, 176, 290, 358–59, 369, 371, 379,
    384, 389, 390, 392, 397–402, 405–6
Boston, Massachusetts, 364–65
bottom-up programs, 391–92
bounties, 89–90
Brady, David, 3, 116, 143, 172
Brandeis, Louis, 15, 325
Brown, Jerry, 5–6, 74, 397–406
Bryce, James, 323, 326
Buchanan, James, 13
budget, federal. See also federal spending;
    fiscal federalism
    balanced, 84–85, 94
    deficits, 101, 103–4, 105
    Madison budget, 84, 85, 99t, 101, 102f,
        104–6, 104f, 105f, 106f
    projected deficits, 244
    role of healthcare financing in, 243–45,
        243f, 245f
    state of, 347, 348t, 349–50
budgets, state, 166, 385–86, 401–3. See also
    intergovernmental transfers during
    recessions
Bush, George W., x
Bush, Jeb, 5–6, 383–95

CAA (Consolidated Appropriations Act),
    339, 340t
Cain, Bruce E., 64

Calhoun, John C., 90–91, 109n22
California
    in battle over federalism, 74, 75
    court interventions related to education
        financing in, 187
    Governor Jerry Brown's perspectives on
        federalism in, 397–406
    high-speed rail project in, 13, 211
    Local Control Funding Formula in,
        399–400
    mandated insurance coverage in, 264t
    public's federalism preferences in, 47–48,
        48f
    raisin producers cartel in, 78
    regulations in shifting burdens to other
        states, 14
    state-based subsidies in, 259
    state-level responses to COVID-19
        pandemic, 35–36
    Unemployment Trust Fund solvency
        rate of, 299–300
California rule, 404–5
Canes-Wrone, Brandice, 143–44
capitalism, democratic, 1
CARES (Coronavirus Aid, Relief, and Eco-
    nomic Security) Act, 301–2, 304–5,
    339, 340t
CBO (Congressional Budget Office),
    222–23, 224, 310, 358
central governments. See also federal govern-
    ment; federalism
    optimal degree of centralization vs.
        decentralization, 291–92
    relationships between subnational gov-
        ernments and, xi–xii
CES (Cooperative Election Study), 50–51,
    52f, 53
charter schools, 190–91, 191f, 400
cheap debt, infrastructure spending moti-
    vated by, 206–7
child welfare system in Florida, 385
Children's Health Insurance Program
    (CHIP)
    and composition of health financing and
        insurance, 239, 240f

and federal budget outlook, 244–45

limits on states' authority regarding, 267–68

as source of healthcare financing, 234f, 236–37

state differences in administration of, 246–47

state differences in eligibility for, 251–52, 253t–55t

citizen choices in K–12 education, 190–92, 191f, 203, 364–65

Civil War, 67, 114, 115

Clean Power Plan, 75

Cleveland, Grover, 116–17

Cogan, John F., 2–3, 113–17, 172

collective bargaining, and competitive federalism, 328–29, 329f

Colorado

public option insurance plan in, 262

reinsurance program in, 257t

Commerce Clause of US Constitution, 69, 79, 91

commercial subsidy proposals, 86

common market, framers' establishment of, 32

competence, impact on trust in government

additional pandemic-related data analyses, 140

approval of federal handling of COVID-19 pandemic, 124–27, 125f, 126f, 127f, 128f

approval of local handling of COVID-19 pandemic, 130–33, 133f, 134f, 135f, 136f

approval of state handling of COVID-19 pandemic, 128–30, 129f, 130f, 131f, 132f

copartisanship and rating of COVID-19 handling, 133–37, 137f, 138f, 139f

data used to study, 124

discussion of chapter, 143–44

general discussion, 140–41

highest- and lowest-rated states, 140

overview, 3, 119–21

pandemic as special case study of levels of government, 121–23

perceived competence, importance of, 137–40, 140t

competition in, 15–16

competitive bidding of Medicare services, 269, 271–72

competitive federalism

data on domestic expenditure and sources of revenue, 330–32

developmental vs. redistributive functions, 321, 322–23

discussion of chapter, 359–61

general discussion, 338, 341

lower tiers of government in federal system, 323–24, 324t, 325–27, 325t

overview, 5, 321–22

political pressures for redistribution, 327–29, 328f, 329f

recent developments threatening, 338–41, 340t, 341f

trends in domestic expenditure, revenue sources, and debt, 332–38, 333f, 335f, 335t, 336t, 337f

comprehensive managed care organizations, 247, 248t–49t, 250

confederation, as option for Constitutional Convention, 9

confidence. *See also* competence, impact on trust in government

discussion on levels of and attitudes toward federalism, 63–64

in federal government, 34, 44–47, 45f, 46f

in local governments, 34, 40–42, 42f

by party, 47–50, 48f, 49f, 50f

in state governments, 34, 43–44, 43f

congestion, projects reducing, 212–13, 365–66

Congressional Budget Office (CBO), 222–23, 224, 310, 358

Consolidated Appropriations Act (CAA), 339, 340t

consolidated nation-state, as option for Constitutional Convention, 9

consolidation
fiscal, 349, 354–55
partial, Anti-Federalist arguments for, 11
of school districts, 192–93, 192f, 194f,
203–4
Constitution, US. *See also* framers' view of
federalism
Article 4, 88
Commerce Clause, 69, 79, 91
Fourteenth Amendment, 67–68
general welfare clause, 13–14, 89–90,
91, 92
original concept of fiscal federalism,
85, 91
consumer-directed healthcare, integrating in
Medicare, 269–71
contractors, federal, 175–76
cooperation between state governments,
379–80, 387–88
Cooperative Election Study (CES), 50–51,
52f, 53
cooperative federalism, 328
copartisanship, and rating of COVID-19
handling, 133–37, 137f, 138f, 139f. *See
also* partisanship
Coronavirus Aid, Relief, and Economic
Security (CARES) Act, 301–2,
304–5, 339, 340t
corporate power, and phases of
federalism, 68
cost-benefit analysis for infrastructure
spending, 210–12
court interventions related to education
financing, 186–88
COVID-19 pandemic
additional data analyses, 140
copartisanship and rating of government
handling of, 133–37, 137f, 138f, 139f
data used to study competence and trust
during, 124
drivers of public attitudes toward governments during, 35–36
fiscal relief measures during, 339–41,
340t
impact of competence on trust in government, 3, 119–21, 140–41, 143–44
Medicaid during, 308–9

perceived competence of government
during, 137–40, 140t
public approval of federal handling of,
124–27, 125f, 126f, 127f, 128f
public approval of local handling of,
130–33, 133f, 134f, 135f, 136f
public approval of state handling of,
128–30, 129f, 130f, 131f, 132f
and public attitudes toward federalism,
33, 34, 39, 53–60, 56f, 57f, 58f
as special case study of levels of government, 121–23
unemployment insurance during, 301–2
crises, financial. *See* recessions
Crowder, Enoch, 70
Cumberland Road (Ohio), 86, 88–89
cyclical ratcheting, 145, 291. *See also* ratchet
effect of intergovernmental transfers
during recessions
cyclicity of federalism in America, 65–71

Daniels, Mitch, 5–6, 375–82
data
aggressive use of, 381–82
for cost-benefit analysis related to infrastructure, 210–11
Davis, Steven J., 116
debt
and competitive federalism, 337–38,
337f, 338–39
interest on public, 97, 99t
state and local, 311–12, 312f, 313f,
314–15, 315f
decentralization theorem, 206, 291–92
decentralized decision making. *See* framers'
view of federalism; public attitudes
toward federalism
defense-related expenditures, 97, 99t,
107, 113
deficits, federal budget, 101, 103–4, 105, 244
Democracy in America (Tocqueville), 67
democratic capitalism, 1
Democratic Federalism (Inman & Rubinfeld),
76–78
Democratic Party. *See also* partisanship
and approval of federal handling of
COVID-19 pandemic, 125–26, 126f

and approval of local handling of COVID-19 pandemic, 131–32, 134f

and approval of state handling of COVID-19 pandemic, 129, 130f

and battle over federalism, 75

copartisanship and rating of COVID-19 handling, 133–37, 137f, 138f, 139f

drivers of public attitudes toward governments, 35–36

fine-grained account of trust and confidence by party, 47–50, 48f, 49f, 50f

and intergovernmental transfers during recessions, 166–67

and original concept of fiscal federalism, 115, 116, 117

and perceived competence of government during pandemic, 139–40, 140t

and public attitudes toward scope of federal power, 37–39, 38f, 40, 41f

state-level partisan (mis)match, 50–51, 52f, 53

and trust and confidence in federal government, 45, 45f, 46f, 47

and trust and confidence in local governments, 41–42, 42f

and trust and confidence in state governments, 43f, 44

Department of Defense, 234f, 237

Department of Education (Florida), 385

Department of Labor (Florida), 384–85

DeSantis, Ron, 36

destructive competition for benefits of government, 12–15

developmental function, in competitive federalism

data on domestic expenditure and sources of revenue, 330–32

general discussion, 338, 341

overview, 321

recent developments affecting, 338–41, 340t, 341f

vs. redistributive function, 322–23

throughout twentieth century, 325–27

trends in domestic expenditure, revenue sources, and debt, 332–38, 333f, 335f, 335t, 336t, 337f

diffusion of power, 20–22

direct citizen choices in K–12 education, 190–92, 191f, 203, 364–65

direct relief to individuals, appropriation of federal funds for, 89–90, 97–98, 99, 99t, 100f. *See also* Affordable Care Act; Medicaid; Medicare; social insurance programs

direct state expenditures during recessions, 153, 155f, 157

disaster relief proposals, 86–87, 94, 95, 108n11

disaster response, conflict between different levels of government in, 385

discretionary spending, 243f, 244, 245f

discrimination, racial, 67–68

diverse interests and preferences, responsiveness of federalism to, 11–12

Dobbs v. Jackson Women's Health Organization (2022), 55, 60, 70

domestic expenditure, and competitive federalism, 330–31, 332–34, 333f

double recession of early 1980s, 152–53, 154f, 155f, 156f, 157, 158f

Douglas, Stephen, 70, 75

drugs

benefits in Medicaid, altering regulations of, 279–80

cost of, 286–89

dual sovereignty system

creation of by Constitutional Convention, 9–11

general discussion, 25–26

as preserving "the spirit and form of popular government", 22–25

as protecting "private rights", 16–22

as "securing the public good", 11–16

early 1980s double recession, 152–53, 154f, 155f, 156f, 157, 158f

early 1990s recession, 152–53, 154f, 155f, 156f, 157, 158f

early 2000s recession, 152–53, 154f, 155f, 156f, 157, 158f

early childhood programs, 391

EB (extended benefits) program, UI, 297, 300

economies of scale, 26n8

education. *See also* K–12 education
  accountability system for, 193, 195–96,
    197f, 198f, 199, 392–93
  appropriation of federal funds for, 93,
    94, 115
  changing shape of US schooling, 190–93
  consolidation of school districts, 192–93,
    192f, 194f
  discussion of chapter, 203–4, 362–65
  funding for, 180, 185–90, 185f, 186t,
    187f, 189f, 190t
  general discussion, 199
  higher, 380, 399
  and intergovernmental transfers during
    recessions, 167–68, 174–75
  outcomes, 180–83, 181f, 182f, 183f, 184f,
    188–90, 189f, 190t
  overview, 3–4, 179–80
  perspectives of governors on, 376–77,
    383–84, 386–88, 392–93, 399–400,
    405–6
  trend toward more direct citizen choices,
    190–92, 191f
Education Week, 124
effective federal funds rate, 353, 353f
EHB (essential health benefits) requirement
  of ACA, 266–67
elderly population, increase in, 368–69
emergency response, 385
Emergency Unemployment Compensation
  program (EUC08), 300–301
Employee Retirement Income Security Act
  (ERISA), 263, 266–67, 268, 280–81
employer-sponsored insurance (ESI)
  allowing states greater flexibility in regu-
    lating, 280–81
  composition of health financing and
    insurance, 239, 240f
  ERISA as limiting state authority over,
    266–67, 268
  as source of healthcare financing, 233,
    234f
employment created by infrastructure
  spending, 217–19
enforcement of laws, 22–23
entitlement programs, 98. *See also* Medicaid;
  social insurance programs

enumerated powers doctrine, 85, 87–88,
  91–92
Epple, Dennis, 5, 287, 359, 364–70, 380, 381
equity, in fiscal federalism, 361, 362, 363
equity court cases, and school finance,
  186–88
ERISA (Employee Retirement Income Security Act), 263, 266–67, 268, 280–81
ESI. *See* employer-sponsored insurance
ESSA (Every Student Succeeds Act), 195,
  196
"Essay on Fiscal Federalism, An" (Oates),
  205
essential health benefits (EHB) requirement
  of ACA, 266–67
EUC08 (Emergency Unemployment Compensation program), 300–301
European Union (EU), 77–78
Every Student Succeeds Act (ESSA), 195,
  196
ExcelinEd (Foundation for Excellence in
  Education), 383, 387, 388
exchanges, state-run ACA marketplace, 259,
  260t–61t, 261–62, 276–77
expenditures, federal. *See* competitive
  federalism; federal spending; fiscal
  federalism; healthcare financing;
  infrastructure spending; intergovernmental transfers during recessions;
  macroeconomic aspects of federalism; social insurance programs
experience rating system, in UI program,
  297, 302–3
extended benefits (EB) program, UI, 297,
  300
externalities, 12–15, 78, 212–13

faces of federalism, 65–71, 71f
factional politics, 17–18, 19–20
Families First Coronavirus Response Act
  (FFCRA), 301, 308, 310, 339, 340t
FAST Act (Fixing America's Surface Transportation Act), 221t
federal budget. *See also* federal spending;
  fiscal federalism
  balanced, 84–85, 94
  deficits, 101, 103–4, 105

Madison budget, 84, 85, 99t, 101, 102f, 104–6, 104f, 105f, 106f
projected deficits, 244
role of healthcare financing in, 243–45, 243f, 245f
state of, 347, 348t, 349–50
federal contractors, 175–76
federal courts, and school finance, 187
Federal Farmer (Anti-Federalist pamphleteer), 11, 24
federal funds effective rate, 353, 353f
federal government. *See also* federal spending
accountability system in K–12 education, 193, 195–96, 197f, 198f, 199, 392–93
COVID-19 pandemic as case study for trust in, 122–23
creation of by Constitutional Convention, 9–10
fine-grained account of public's federalism preferences, 47–50, 48f, 49f, 50f
funding of schools, 185–87, 185f, 186t
incentives from, role in infrastructure policy, 216–17
limits imposed on states' authority in healthcare policies, 267–68
number of employees in, 342n5
perceived competence of during pandemic, 137–40, 140t
public approval of handling of COVID-19 pandemic, 124–27, 125f, 126f, 127f, 128f
relation between proximity and trust, 122
trust and confidence in, 34, 44–47, 45f, 46f
federal lands, distribution of proceeds from sale of to states, 88–89
federal medical assistance percentage (FMAP) rates, 307–8, 310–11
Federal Pandemic Unemployment Compensation (FPUC), 301–2, 305
Federal Reserve, 351–54, 352t, 353f, 354f
federal spending. *See also* competitive federalism; fiscal federalism; healthcare financing; infrastructure spending; intergovernmental transfers during

recessions; macroeconomic aspects of federalism; social insurance programs
on aid to individuals, 89–90, 97–98, 99, 99t, 100f
and destructive competition for benefits of government, 12–14
discussion of chapter, 113–17, 172
domestic expenditure and competitive federalism, 330–31, 332–34, 333f
erosion of barrier separating state and local activities, 92–96
funding for K–12 education, 180, 185–90, 185f, 186t, 187f, 189f, 190t
general discussion, 106–7
historical perspective on recessions and, 146–52, 148f, 149f, 186t, 187f, 152f
impact on state and local activities, 96–106, 99t, 100f, 101f, 102f, 103f, 104f, 105f, 106f
impending potential crisis related to, 378, 394
national expenditure from 1993–2021, 324t
original idea of fiscal federalism, 84–92
overview, 2–3, 83–85
vs. state government spending over time, 293, 294f, 295–96, 295f, 296f
Federal Unemployment Tax Act (FUTA), 297, 298
federalism. *See also* competitive federalism; fiscal federalism; public attitudes toward federalism
augmenting study of, ix–x, xi–xii
battle over, 73–75
discussant remarks and discussion of, 73–79, 171, 357–71
Governor Jeb Bush's perspectives on, 383–95
Governor Jerry Brown's perspectives on, 397–406
Governor Mitch Daniels's perspectives on, 375–82
optimal degree of centralization vs. decentralization, 291–92
overview, 1–6
phases and faces of, 65–71, 71f
self-correcting character of, 382

Federalist, The (Madison), 10, 17, 20, 66

federally facilitated marketplace (FFM), 259, 260t–61t, 261–62

FFCRA (Families First Coronavirus Response Act), 301, 308, 310, 339, 340t

50-50 programs, 94

financial crises. *See* great recession of 2008; recessions

financing. *See also* federal spending; fiscal federalism; healthcare financing; intergovernmental transfers during recessions
from federal government, rules related to, 384–85
infrastructure spending through user fees, 213–15
for US education, 180, 185–90, 185f, 186t, 187f, 189f, 190t

Fiorina, Morris P., 2, 63, 75–76

fiscal federalism, 106f. *See also* competitive federalism; federal spending; healthcare financing; infrastructure spending; intergovernmental transfers during recessions; macroeconomic aspects of federalism; social insurance programs
budgetary impact of abandonment of original concept of, 96–106, 99t, 100f, 101f, 102f, 103f, 104f, 105f, 106f
discussant remarks and discussion, 113–17, 359–64
erosion of original concept of, 92–96
general discussion, 106–7
key principles laid out by Oates, 205–6
original concept of, 84–92
traditional theory of, 206

fiscal policy
discussion of chapter, 357–59
federal impact on state and local government policy, 354–55
general discussion, 355–56
getting back on track, 352–54, 353f, 354f
guidelines for, 349, 350–51
monetary policy issues, 351–52, 352t
overview, 347
state of federal budget, 347, 348t, 349–50

fishermen, appropriation of federal funds for direct relief to in 1792, 89–90

Fixing America's Surface Transportation Act (FAST Act), 221t

Florida
Governor Jeb Bush's perspectives on federalism in, 383–95
responses to COVID-19 pandemic in, 35–36

flypaper effect, 145, 172–73, 218–19, 267–68. *See also* fiscal federalism; intergovernmental transfers during recessions

FMAP (federal medical assistance percentage) rates, 307–8, 310–11

Ford, Gerald, 367–68

Foundation for Excellence in Education (ExcelinEd), 383, 387, 388

founders' view of federalism. *See* framers' view of federalism

Fourteenth Amendment, US Constitution, 67–68

FPUC (Federal Pandemic Unemployment Compensation), 301–2, 305

framers' view of federalism
discussant remarks on, 78–79
discussion of chapter, 32
general discussion, 25–26
lack of agreement among framers, 65–67, 77
original idea of fiscal federalism, 84–92
overview, 2, 9–11
as preserving "the spirit and form of popular government", 22–25
as protecting "private rights", 16–22
as "securing the public good", 11–16

free rider problem, 16

freedom of religion, 20–21

funding. *See* federal spending; financing; fiscal federalism; healthcare financing; intergovernmental transfers during recessions

FUTA (Federal Unemployment Tax Act), 297, 298

Garin, Andrew, 218

general fund revenues, 103, 103f

general welfare clause of US Constitution,
     13–14, 89–90, 91, 92
Georgia, reinsurance program in, 257t
Gibbons v. Ogden (1824), 68
Giles, William, 90
Glaeser, Edward L., 214
global financial crisis of 2008. *See* great
     recession of 2008
goods, healthcare expenditures on, 235f,
     237–38
Google Trends, 54–59, 56f, 57f, 58f, 60
governors, perspectives on federalism of
     Jeb Bush, 383–95
     Jerry Brown, 397–406
     Mitch Daniels, 375–82
     overview, 5–6
grants-to-states programs. *See also* fiscal fed-
     eralism; intergovernmental transfers
     during recessions; social insurance
     programs
     to assist states in providing healthcare,
        282–83
     block grants, 90–91, 282–83, 362,
        390–91
     erosion of original concept of fiscal
        federalism, 93–94
     impact of federal government spending
        on state and local activities, 97, 98,
        99, 99t, 100f
     matching grants, 94, 361, 362
     in original idea of federalism, 87
Great Depression, 95. *See also* New Deal
great recession of 2008
     intergovernmental transfers during,
        152–53, 154f, 155f, 156f, 157, 158f
     Medicaid during, 307–8
     unemployment insurance during,
        300–301
Great Society, 96, 98
Grodzins, Morton, 70–71, 119

Hamilton, Alexander, 13–14, 66, 85, 89
Hanushek, Eric A., 3–4, 113, 174, 203–4,
     287, 288, 363–65, 370, 384, 386–88,
     392
Hartney, Michael T., 63, 174
haves/have-nots, 322–23

Hawaii, waiver of SHOP in, 259
health insurance. *See also* Affordable Care
     Act; healthcare financing; Medicaid;
     Medicare
     allowing states greater flexibility in regu-
        lating, 280–81
     composition of health financing and,
        239, 240f
     regulation of by states, 263–64,
        264t–66t, 266–67
     as source of healthcare financing, 233,
        234f
     state-run ACA marketplace exchanges,
        259, 260t–61t, 261–62, 276–77
healthcare financing
     challenges in public funding of health-
        care, 239, 241–46, 241f, 242f, 243f,
        245f
     consequential changes required in direc-
        tion of policies, 281–83
     discussion of chapter, 286–90, 362
     growth in health spending, 238–39,
        238f
     limited innovation by states, 267–68
     overview, 4, 231–32
     perspectives of governors on, 375–76
     reform proposals to address crisis in,
        268–81
     sources of funding, 233, 234f, 235f,
        236–39, 238f, 240f
     state differences in Affordable Care
        Act, 252, 256–57, 257t–58t, 259,
        260t–61t, 261–63
     state differences in Medicaid and CHIP,
        246–48, 248t–49t, 250–52, 253t–55t
     state insurance adequacy regulation,
        263–64, 264t–66t, 266–67
Henry, Patrick, 16–17, 23
higher education
     state role in funding, 380
     Title IX regulations, 399
highest net benefit infrastructure projects,
     prioritizing, 212–13
high-speed rail project in California,
     13, 211
Highway Trust Fund, 223, 223f
Hoffmann, Florian, 368

homeschooling, 191, 191f
homogeneous groups, and adoption of radical policies, 17–18
Hoover Institution, ix
House of Representatives, 24

Idaho, reinsurance program in, 258t
IIJA (Infrastructure Investment and Jobs Act), 220, 221t, 222–25
Illinois, shared projects with Indiana, 380
immigration, 388–89
Immigration Wars (Bush & Bolick), 388
incentives, focusing on in infrastructure spending, 216–17
income dynamics, effect of unemployment insurance on, 305
income eligibility levels, CHIP, 251–52
income inequality, 368, 369
income support, federal spending on, 95. *See also* social insurance programs
income taxes. *See* taxation
independents. *See also* partisanship
    and approval of federal handling of COVID-19 pandemic, 127, 128f
    and approval of local handling of COVID-19 pandemic, 132–33, 136f
    and approval of state handling of COVID-19 pandemic, 130, 132f
    copartisanship and rating of COVID-19 handling, 133–37, 137f, 138f, 139f
    and fine-grained account of trust and confidence by party, 48f, 48–49, 49f, 50, 50f
    and public attitudes toward scope of federal power, 37–39, 38f, 40, 41f
    and trust and confidence in federal government, 45f, 46, 46f, 47
    and trust and confidence in local governments, 41, 42f
    and trust and confidence in state governments, 43f
Indiana, federalism in, 375–82
individuals, federal spending on aid to, 89–90, 97–98, 99, 99t, 100f. *See also* Affordable Care Act; Medicaid; Medicare; social insurance programs

inflation, and monetary policy, 353–54, 354f, 357–59
Infrastructure Investment and Jobs Act (IIJA), 220, 221t, 222–25
infrastructure spending
    and aggressive use of data, 381–82
    discussion of chapter, 361, 365–67
    financing through user fees, 213–15
    focusing on incentives, 216–17
    general discussion, 225
    guiding principles for, 210–17
    inventory of US infrastructure, 208, 209t
    learning from past and preparing for future, 219–20, 221t, 222–24, 223f
    overview, 4, 205–8
    planning for technological change, 215–16
    prioritizing highest net benefit projects, 212–13
    rigorous cost-benefit analysis for, 210–12
    as short-run stimulus vs. long-run investment, 217–19
Inman, Robert, 76–78
innovation in government, as advantage of federalism, 15–16
input-based teacher evaluation, 196, 198f
insurance, health. *See also* Affordable Care Act; healthcare financing; Medicaid; Medicare
    allowing states greater flexibility in regulating, 280–81
    composition of health financing and, 239, 240f
    regulation of by states, 263–64, 264t–66t, 266–67
    as source of healthcare financing, 233, 234f
    state-run ACA marketplace exchanges, 259, 260t–61t, 261–62, 276–77
insurance, unemployment. *See* unemployment insurance (UI)
interest
    net outlays for, 243f, 244, 245f
    on public debt, 97, 99t
    rates of, 207, 353, 357
intergovernmental programs, and competitive federalism, 327, 328f

intergovernmental transfers during recessions. *See also* healthcare financing; infrastructure spending; K–12 education; social insurance programs
    closer look at recessions since 1980, 152–53, 154f, 155f, 156f, 157, 158f
    discussion of chapter, 171–72, 173–76
    evolving role of federal funding, 146–52, 148f, 149f, 150f, 151f, 152f
    general discussion, 166–68
    infrastructure spending, 206–7
    overview, 3, 145–47
    in small states, 146–47, 157, 159–61, 159f, 160f, 162f, 163f, 164–65, 164f, 165f
internal improvements, federal funding for, 92–93, 114–15
international affairs outlays, 97, 99t
Interstate Commerce Commission, 68
Interstate Highway System, 223–24

Jacobs, Nicholas, 54
Jaffe, Jacob, 3
Jefferson, Thomas, 66, 108n10
Jim Crow system, 67
Johns Hopkins Coronavirus Research Center, 124
Juhn, Chinhui, 368
justice, fundamental issues of, 21–22

K–12 education
    accountability system for, 193, 195–96, 197f, 198f, 199, 392–93
    changing shape of US schooling, 190–93
    consolidation of school districts, 192–93, 192f, 194f
    discussion of chapter, 203–4, 362–65
    funding for, 180, 185–90, 185f, 186t, 187f, 189f, 190t
    general discussion, 199
    and intergovernmental transfers during recessions, 167–68, 174–75
    outcomes, 180–83, 181f, 182f, 183f, 184f, 188–90, 189f, 190t
    overview, 3–4, 179–80

    perspectives of governors on, 376–77, 383–84, 386–88, 392–93, 399–400, 405–6
    trend toward more direct citizen choices, 190–92, 191f
Kennedy, David M., 2, 73–75, 76, 79
Kentucky, cooperation with government of Indiana, 379–80
Kousser, Thad, 5, 73–76, 173–74, 402–3

labor disincentives, and unemployment insurance, 304–5
Lastra-Anadón, Carlos X., 5, 359–61
Laurence, Abbott, 89
laws
    and destructive competition for benefits of government, 14
    enforcement of, 22–23
"layer cake" federalism, 70–71, 71f
Leduc, Sylvain, 218–19
Lee, David, 368
Lemieux, Tom, 368
levels of government. *See* federal government; local governments; state governments
liabilities of states, conversion into federal liabilities. *See* social insurance programs
liability rules, and competition among states and localities, 15–16
liberty, protection of as objective of federalism, 16–22
licensure, reciprocity agreements for occupational, 389–90
Local Control Funding Formula (California), 399–400
local draft boards, 70
local governments. *See also* competitive federalism; social insurance programs
    composition and growth of healthcare financing by, 241, 241f, 242–43, 242f
    COVID-19 pandemic as case study of trust in, 122–23
    cuts to intergovernmental grants during recessions, 153, 156f, 157
    debt and unfunded pension liabilities in, 311–12, 312f, 313f, 314–15, 315f

local governments (*continued*)
 direct expenditure by from 1993–2021, 324–25, 325t
 discussion on trust in, 63–64
 drivers of public attitudes toward, 34–36
 effect of intergovernmental transfers during recessions on, 146
 effects of recessions on in small states, 161, 162f, 163f, 164–65, 164f, 165f
 and fine-grained account of public's federalism preferences, 47–50, 48f, 49f, 50f
 and funding of schools, 185–87, 185f, 186t
 impact of federal fiscal consolidation on fiscal policy of, 354–55
 and infrastructure spending, 216–17, 222–24
 perceived competence of during pandemic, 137–40, 140t
 public approval of handling of COVID-19 pandemic by, 130–33, 133f, 134f, 135f, 136f
 recession-induced cuts in public-sector employment in, 149–52, 149f, 150f, 151f, 152f, 157, 158f
 and relation between proximity and trust, 122
 relationship with state governments, 385
 and state budget deficits, 403–4
 state restrictions on debt in, 367–68
 trust and confidence in, 34, 40–42, 42f
localized impact, centralized decision making about projects of, 13–14
"lockdown," Google Trends associated with, 58–59
London transport authority (UK), 365–66
Long Term Trend (LTT) assessment of NAEP, 180, 181f, 183f
long-run investment, infrastructure spending as, 217–19
Louisiana Purchase, 108n10
Ludwig, Jillian, 4–5, 367

MA (Medicare Advantage), 270, 271
MACRA (Medicare Access and CHIP Reauthorization Act), 289–90

macroeconomic aspects of federalism
 discussion of chapter, 357–59
 general discussion, 355–56
 getting back on track, 352–54, 353f, 354f
 guidelines for fiscal policy, 349, 350–51
 impact on state and local government fiscal policy, 354–55
 monetary policy issues, 351–52, 352t
 overview, 5, 347
 state of federal budget, 347, 348t, 349–50
MaCurdy, Thomas, 4, 175–76, 286–89, 357–59, 370–71
Madison, James, 9–10, 13–14, 17–18, 19, 20, 66–67, 85, 89–90, 91–92, 109n23
Madison budget
 balanced, 85
 behavior of post–World War II, 104–6
 federal spending on national vs. state and local activities, 99t
 outlays vs. state and local activity outlays, 101, 102f
 overview, 84
 surpluses, 104f, 105f
 total budget vs., 106f
Main NAEP, 180, 183f
Maine, reinsurance program in, 258t
maintenance financing through user fees, 213–14, 214–15
maintenance of effort (MOE) rules, 283
maintenance projects, as highest net benefit projects, 212
majority factions, tyranny of, 17–18
managed care delivery, Medicaid, 247–48, 248t–49t, 250, 251
mandated insurance coverage, 263–64, 264t–66t, 281
mandatory spending, 243f, 244–45, 245f
MAP-21 (Moving Ahead for Progress in the 21st Century Act), 221t
"marble cake" federalism, 70–71, 71f, 119
marketplace exchanges, state-run ACA, 259, 260t–61t, 261–62, 276–77
Maryland, partisan (mis)match in, 51
"mask mandate," Google Trends associated with, 58–59

Massachusetts
    Boston as example of school choice,
        364–65
    Boston Metropolitan Transit Authority
        user fees, 365
    mandated insurance coverage in,
        264t–65t, 281
    partisan (mis)match in, 51
matching grants, 94, 361, 362. *See also* Med-
    icaid; social insurance programs
math performance, student, 180–81, 181f,
    182f, 183, 184f, 188–89, 189f
maximum out-of-pocket (MOOP) thresh-
    olds for Medicare, 270
McConnell, Michael W., 2, 63, 74, 75, 76–78,
    143, 365, 367, 368
Medicaid
    altering regulations of pharmaceutical
        benefits in, 279–80
    composition of health financing and
        insurance, 239, 240f
    and consumer-directed healthcare, 270
    expansion of under Affordable Care Act,
        172, 274–76, 306, 309–10
    expenditures, growth of, 306–7, 306f
    and federal budget outlook, 244–45
    and federalism, 309–11
    and intergovernmental transfers during
        recessions, 157
    limits on states' authority regarding,
        267–68
    managed care delivery, 247–48,
        248t–49t, 250, 251
    nursing home benefits, 250–51
    options to expand provider networks for
        enrollees, 277–79
    overview, 305–6
    peculiar structure of, 173
    reform ideas for, 390–91
    as source of healthcare financing, 234f,
        236
    state differences in administration of,
        246–48, 248t–49t, 250–52
    in times of crisis, 307–9
Medicare
    and federal budget outlook, 244
    general discussion, 286–87, 288

policy approaches for enhancing com-
        petitiveness in, 269–74
    ratings for doctors providing service
        under, 289–90
    as source of healthcare financing, 234f,
        236
Medicare Access and CHIP Reauthorization
    Act (MACRA), 289–90
Medicare Advantage (MA), 270, 271
medications
    benefits in Medicaid, altering regulations
        of, 279–80
    cost of, 286–89
Medigap insurance policies, 270, 271
Minnesota
    Basic Health Program in, 259
    reinsurance program in, 258t
minority rule, 18
Mississippi Miracle, 387–88
mobility, liberty through, 18–19
MOE (maintenance of effort) rules, 283
monetary policy
    discussion of chapter, 357–59
    getting back on track, 352–54, 353f, 354f
    issues with, 351–52, 352t
    tips for, 355–56
Monetary Policy Report (FRB), 351–52, 352t
MOOP (maximum out-of-pocket) thresh-
    olds for Medicare, 270
moral hazard, UTFs and, 303–4
Moving Ahead for Progress in the 21st Cen-
    tury Act (MAP-21), 221t
Mueller, J. Tom, 53
multistate purchasing pools for prescription
    drugs, 280
municipal governments. *See* local
    governments
Murphy, Kevin, 368

National Assessment of Educational Prog-
    ress (NAEP) scores, 180–81, 182f,
    183, 183f, 188–89, 189f, 386
National Bank Bill, 86
national defense–related expenditures, 97,
    99t, 107, 113
National Flood Insurance Program (NFIP),
    366–67

national government. *See* federal
  government
national health accounts (NHAs), 233
National Labor Relations Act (NLRA),
  342n6
national transportation system, Bonus Bill to
  finance, 90–91, 109n23
national university proposals, 86
nature of representation, 23–24
NCLB (No Child Left Behind Act), 193,
  195–96, 392–93, 399
Nechyba, Thomas, 5, 359–64, 369, 370, 394
negative externalities, high net benefit projects reducing, 212–13
net outlays for interest, 243f, 244, 245f
Nevada, public option insurance plan in, 262
New Deal, 95, 96, 147, 148f
New Jersey, mandated insurance coverage
  in, 265t
New York
  Basic Health Program in, 259
  New York City debt, 367–68
  underground mess of infrastructure in,
    210–11
Newsom, Gavin, 35–36
NFIP (National Flood Insurance Program),
  366–67
NHAs (national health accounts), 233
Nicholas, John, 86
90-10 rule for Interstate Highway System,
  223–24
NLRA (National Labor Relations Act),
  342n6
No Child Left Behind Act (NCLB), 193,
  195–96, 392–93, 399
nonphysician Medicaid providers, 278–79
nursing home benefits, Medicaid, 250–51

Oates, Wallace E., 205–6, 291–92
Obamacare. *See* Affordable Care Act
occupational licensure, reciprocity agreements for, 389–90
Ohio, compact between federal government
  and, 86, 88–89
older Americans, increase in number of,
  368–69
open enrollment periods, 262

Oregon, reinsurance program in, 258t
outcome-based teacher evaluation, 196, 197f
out-of-pocket (OOP) payments for healthcare, 233, 234f, 236
out-partisan effect, 143–44
ownership, infrastructure, 208

P4P (pay for performance) programs, 269,
  273–74, 278, 289
Pandemic Emergency Unemployment Compensation (PEUC), 301
Pandemic Unemployment Assistance
  (PUA), 301
parental choice in K–12 education, 190–92,
  191f, 203, 364–65
Parker v. Brown (1943), 78
partial consolidation, Anti-Federalist arguments for, 11
partisanship, 400
  and approval of federal handling of
    COVID-19 pandemic, 125–27, 126f,
    127f, 128f
  and approval of local handling of
    COVID-19 pandemic, 131–33, 134f,
    135f, 136f
  and approval of state handling of
    COVID-19 pandemic, 129–30, 130f,
    131f, 132f
  and competence, relation to trust in
    government, 119–22, 123, 140–41
  copartisanship and rating of COVID-19
    handling, 133–37, 137f, 138f, 139f
  as driver of public attitudes toward gov-
    ernments, 35–36
  fine-grained account of influence on
    trust and confidence, 34, 47–50, 48f,
    49f, 50f
  and intergovernmental transfers during
    recessions, 166–67
  out-partisan effect, 143–44
  overview, 34
  and perceived competence of govern-
    ment during pandemic, 139–40, 140t
  and public attitudes toward scope of
    federal power, 37–39, 38f, 40, 41f
  state-level partisan (mis)match, 50–51,
    52f, 53

and trust and confidence in federal government, 44–47, 45f, 46f
and trust and confidence in local governments, 41–42, 42f
and trust and confidence in state governments, 43f, 44
pay for performance (P4P) programs, 269, 273–74, 278, 289
payroll tax revenues, 102–3
PCCMs (primary-care case management organizations), 248, 248t–49t, 250
PCPs (primary-care providers), 250
"peek and shriek" process in New York, 210–11
Pennsylvania Turnpike, 214, 366, 370
pension liabilities
  and competitive federalism, 338
  unfunded, 311–12, 312f, 313f, 314–15, 315f, 368, 404–5
perceptions of competence. See competence, impact on trust in government
performance, and trust in government. See competence, impact on trust in government
performance, student, 180–83, 181f, 182f, 183f, 184f
permanent fiscal policy, 349, 350
pervasive fiscal policy, 349, 350
Peterson, Paul E., 5, 32, 114, 115, 171, 176, 203, 359–61, 375–78
PEUC (Pandemic Emergency Unemployment Compensation), 301
pharmaceuticals
  benefits in Medicaid, altering regulations of, 279–80
  cost of, 286–89
pharmacies dispensing drugs to Medicaid beneficiaries, 279
phases of federalism, 2, 65–71, 71f
"Philadelphiensis", 21
Pierce, Brooks, 368
PISA (Programme for International Student Assessment) scores, 183f, 184f
policy. See also competitive federalism; healthcare financing; infrastructure spending; K–12 education; macroeconomic aspects of federalism; social insurance programs

changes in, and public attitudes toward scope of federal power, 37–39
federalism in, 3–5, 357–71
policy professionals, 327–28
political changes, and competitive federalism, 322–23, 327–29, 328f, 329f
political partisanship. See partisanship
Polk, James, 110n26
Ponzetto, Giacomo, 214
popular government, federalism as preserving spirit and form of, 22–25
positive externalities, high net benefit projects producing, 213
postal power, 91
power. See also public attitudes toward federalism
  attitudes toward scope of federal, 36–39, 37f, 38f, 54–59, 56f, 57f, 58f
  corporate, and phases of federalism, 68
  diffusion of, 20–22
  enumerated powers doctrine, 85, 87–88, 91–92
predictable fiscal policy, 349, 350–51
preferred drug lists, 280
prescription drug benefits in Medicaid, altering regulations of, 279–80
presidents, role in use of federal spending powers, 91–92, 93, 107, 116–17
primary-care case management organizations (PCCMs), 248, 248t–49t, 250
primary-care providers (PCPs), 250
principled arguments about federalism, 74–75
prior authorization policies for drugs, 280
prioritization in infrastructure spending, 212–13
private funding for healthcare, 233, 234f, 238–39, 238f
private health insurance
  allowing states greater flexibility in regulating, 280–81
  composition of health financing and, 239, 240f
  regulation of by states, 263–64, 264t–66t, 266–67
  as source of healthcare financing, 234f

"private rights" protection as objective of
    federalism, 16–22
private schools, 191, 191f
products
    healthcare expenditures on, 235f,
        237–38
    Medicare, competitive bidding on,
        271–72
Programme for International Student
    Assessment (PISA) scores, 183f,
    184f
project prioritization for infrastructure
    spending, 212–13
provider networks, options to expand for
    Medicaid enrollees, 277–79
PUA (Pandemic Unemployment Assis-
    tance), 301
public attitudes toward federalism
    approval of federal handling of COVID-
        19 pandemic, 124–27, 125f, 126f,
        127f, 128f
    approval of local handling of COVID-19
        pandemic, 130–33, 133f, 134f, 135f,
        136f
    approval of state handling of COVID-19
        pandemic, 128–30, 129f, 130f, 131f,
        132f
    contemporary, 36–39, 37f, 38f
    copartisanship and rating of COVID-19
        handling, 133–37, 137f, 138f, 139f
    COVID-19 and alterations in, 53–59,
        56f, 57f, 58f
    discussant remarks on, 75–76
    discussion of chapter, 63–64
    drivers of, 34–36
    general discussion, 59–60
    historical, 39–40, 41f
    overview, 2, 33–34
    and perceived competence of govern-
        ment during pandemic, 137–40, 140t
    state-level partisan (mis)match, 50–51,
        52f, 53
    trust and confidence by party, 34, 47–50,
        48f, 49f, 50f
    trust and confidence in federal govern-
        ment, 34, 44–47, 45f, 46f

    trust and confidence in local govern-
        ments, 34, 40–42, 42f
    trust and confidence in state govern-
        ments, 34, 43–44, 43f
public choice theory, 18, 23
public debt, interest on, 97, 99t
public funding of healthcare. See healthcare
    financing
public good, federalism as advancing, 11–16
public option insurance plans, 262, 281
public schools. See K–12 education
public spiritedness, 24–25
public universities, state role in funding, 380
public-sector bankruptcies, 338–39
public-sector employment
    closer look at recessions since 1980,
        152–53, 154f, 155f, 156f, 157, 158f
    and competitive federalism, 328–29, 329f
    discussion of chapter, 171–72, 173–76
    evolving role of federal funding, 146–52,
        148f, 149f, 150f, 151f, 152f
    general discussion, 166–68
    overview, 3, 145–47
    in small states, 146–47, 157, 159–61, 159f,
        160f, 162f, 163f, 164–65, 164f, 165f
pupil-to-teacher ratios, 167–68

Race to the Top program (RTT), 195, 376,
    399
racism, 67–68
radical policies, adoption of by homogenous
    groups, 17–18
raisin producers cartel (California), 78
ratchet effect of intergovernmental transfers
    during recessions. See also social
    insurance programs
    closer look at recessions since 1980,
        152–53, 154f, 155f, 156f, 157, 158f
    discussion of chapter, 171–72, 173–76
    evolving role of federal funding, 146–52,
        148f, 149f, 150f, 151f, 152f
    general discussion, 166–68
    overview, 145–47, 291
    in small states, 146–47, 157, 159–61,
        159f, 160f, 162f, 163f, 164–65, 164f,
        165f

Rauh, Joshua, 4–5, 113–14, 286, 289, 358,
     367, 370, 381, 404
reading performance, student, 180
Reagan, Ronald, 72n11
rebates, negotiating with drug manufactur-
     ers, 279–80
recessions. *See also* intergovernmental trans-
     fers during recessions
     Medicaid during, 307–9
     unemployment insurance during,
          300–302
reciprocity agreements for occupational
     licensure, 389–90
Reconstruction era, 67–68
redistributive function, in competitive
     federalism
     data on domestic expenditure and
          sources of revenue, 330–32
     vs. developmental function, 322–23
     general discussion, 338, 341
     overview, 16, 321
     political pressures for redistribution,
          327–29, 328f, 329f
     recent developments affecting, 338–41,
          340t, 341f
     throughout twentieth century,
          325–27
     trends in domestic expenditure, revenue
          sources, and debt, 332–38, 333f,
          335f, 335t, 336t, 337f
reform proposals to address fiscal crisis in
     healthcare
     allowing states greater flexibility in regu-
          lating health insurance, 280–81
     delegating more authority to states for
          shared financing, 274–80
     enhancing competitiveness in Medicare,
          269–74
     overview, 268–69
regulation(s)
     in cost-benefit analysis related to infra-
          structure, 211
     and destructive competition for benefits
          of government, 14
     of private health insurance by states,
          263–64, 264t–66t, 266–67

reimbursement rates
     for Medicaid providers, 278, 307–8,
          310–11
     for nursing homes, 251
     for pharmacies dispensing drugs to
          Medicaid beneficiaries, 279
reinsurance programs, 257, 257t–58t
relief proposals, 86–88, 89–90, 94, 95, 108n11
religion, freedom of, 20–21
Rendleman, Hunter, 54
Reno, Janet, 388–89
representation, nature of, 23–24
Republican Party. *See also* partisanship
     and approval of federal handling of
          COVID-19 pandemic, 126–27, 127f
     and approval of local handling of
          COVID-19 pandemic, 132, 135f
     and approval of state handling of
          COVID-19 pandemic, 130, 131f
     and changes to concept of fiscal federal-
          ism, 115, 116–17
     copartisanship and rating of COVID-19
          handling, 133–37, 137f, 138f, 139f
     drivers of public attitudes toward govern-
          ments, 35–36
     and fine-grained account of trust and
          confidence, 47–50, 48f, 49f, 50f
     and intergovernmental transfers during
          recessions, 166–67
     and perceived competence of govern-
          ment during pandemic, 139–40, 140t
     and public attitudes toward scope of
          federal power, 37–39, 38f, 40, 41f
     state-level partisan (mis)match, 50–51,
          52f, 53
     and trust and confidence in federal gov-
          ernment, 44–45, 45f, 46f
     and trust and confidence in local govern-
          ments, 41–42, 42f
     and trust and confidence in state govern-
          ments, 43f, 44, 47
republicanism. *See* framers' view of federalism
responsiveness of federalism to diverse inter-
     ests and preferences, 11–12
retrospective cost-benefit analysis, 212
returns on infrastructure spending, 224

revenues
  federal, and federal budget outlook,
    243–44, 243f
  impact of federal government spending
    on state and local activities, 99–101,
    101f, 102–6, 102f, 103f, 104f
  intergovernmental, from federal govern-
    ment, 294f, 295, 295f, 296f
  sources of, and competitive federalism,
    331–32, 334–37, 335f, 335t, 336t
  for US education, 180, 185–90, 185f,
    186t, 187f, 189f, 190t
Rhode Island, mandated insurance coverage
  in, 265t
Rice, Condoleezza, ix–x, 383, 393
rights
  protection of as objective of federalism,
    16–22
  states', 57–58, 57f, 60, 67–68
rigorous cost-benefit analysis for infrastructure spending, 210–12
river and harbor appropriations bills, 93, 117
Rivers, Douglas, 3, 64, 144, 171
road construction proposals, 86
Rodden, Jonathan, 3, 73, 171–72, 173,
  174–76
Rogowski, Jon C., 54
Roosevelt, Franklin Delano, 342n6
Roosevelt, Theodore, 68–69
RTT (Race to the Top program), 195, 376, 399
Rubinfeld, Daniel L., 5, 76–79, 172–73
rule-making powers, 394–95
rules-based monetary policy, 351–52, 352t,
  353–54, 354f, 355–56, 357–58
rural areas, ACA health insurance availability
  in, 260t–61t, 263
rural communities, federalism preferences
  in, 53
Ryan, Paul, 390

salt tax, direct relief to individuals affected
  by in 1792, 89–90
San Antonio Independent School District v.
  Rodriguez (1973), 187
SBMs (state-based marketplaces), 259,
  260t–61t, 261–62
school choice, 190–92, 191f, 203, 364–65

school districts. See also K–12 education
  consolidation of, 192–93, 192f, 194f,
    203–4
  and heterogeneity in schools, 190
scope of federal power. See also public atti-
    tudes toward federalism
  contemporary attitudes toward, 36–39,
    37f, 38f
  influence of pandemic response on pub-
    lic opinion, 54–59, 56f, 57f, 58f
secession, calls for, xi
Second Reconstruction, 68
Section 1332 waivers under ACA, 256–57,
  257t–58t, 259
"secure the public good" objective of federalism, 11–16
Selective Service system, 70
self-funded insurance plans, 266
self-interested government, 19–20
Serrano v. Priest (1968), 187
services, healthcare expenditures on, 235f,
  237–38
SES (socioeconomic status) achievement
  gaps, 181, 183, 183f
Sessions, Jeff, 74
shared healthcare financing, 274–80. See
    also Affordable Care Act; Medicaid;
    social insurance programs
SHOP (Small Business Health Options
    Program) waiver, 259
short-run stimulus, infrastructure spending
    as, 206–7, 217–19
Shultz, George, xi, xii
single-payer systems, state-level, 281
slavery, 67, 70, 114–15
Small Business Health Options Program
    (SHOP) waiver, 259
small states, intergovernmental transfers
    during recessions in, 146–47, 157,
    159–61, 159f, 160f, 162f, 163f,
    164–65, 164f, 165f, 166
social insurance programs. See also
    Medicaid
  discussion of chapter, 367–68
  and federal spending vs. federal revenues,
    98, 99t, 101–3, 103f, 105–6, 106f
  general discussion, 315

overview, 4–5, 291–93
pensions and debt, 311–12, 312f, 313f, 314–15, 315f
spending shares of federal vs. state governments over time, 293, 294f, 295–96, 295f, 296f
state-by-state competition on, 16
unemployment insurance, 296–305
Social Security Act of 1935, 95
socioeconomic status (SES) achievement gaps, 181, 183, 183f
solvency of Unemployment Trust Funds, 297–300, 298f, 299f
special districts, 77, 379–80
spending, federal. *See also* competitive federalism; fiscal federalism; healthcare financing; infrastructure spending; intergovernmental transfers during recessions; macroeconomic aspects of federalism; social insurance programs
on aid to individuals, 89–90, 97–98, 99, 99t, 100f
and destructive competition for benefits of government, 12–14
discussion of chapter, 113–17, 172
domestic expenditure and competitive federalism, 330–31, 332–34, 333f
erosion of barrier separating state and local activities, 92–96
funding for K–12 education, 180, 185–90, 185f, 186t, 187f, 189f, 190t
general discussion, 106–7
historical perspective on recessions and, 146–52, 148f, 149f, 150f, 151f, 152f
impact on state and local activities, 96–106, 99t, 100f, 101f, 102f, 103f, 104f, 105f, 106f
impending potential crisis related to, 378, 394
national expenditure from 1993–2021, 324t
original idea of fiscal federalism, 84–92
overview, 2–3, 83–85
vs. state government spending over time, 293, 294f, 295–96, 295f, 296f

spillovers
in fiscal federalism, 361, 363
and social insurance programs, 292
standardized tests, high-stakes use of, 193, 195
state action exemption doctrine, 78
state activities, federal spending on. *See* spending, federal
state courts, and school finance, 187–88
state governments. *See also* competitive federalism; framers' view of federalism; governors, perspectives on federalism of; intergovernmental transfers during recessions; social insurance programs
Affordable Care Act differences in, 252, 256–57, 257t–58t, 259, 260t–61t, 261–63
budgets of, 166, 385–86, 401–3
changes required in direction of health policies, 281–83
composition and growth of healthcare financing by, 241, 241f, 242–43, 242f
Constitutional Convention decisions regarding, 9–10
cooperation between, 379–80, 387–88
copartisanship and rating of COVID-19 handling of, 133–37, 137f, 138f, 139f
COVID-19 pandemic as case study for study of trust in, 122–23
debt and unfunded pension liabilities in, 311–12, 312f, 313f, 314–15, 315f
delegating more authority to for shared healthcare financing, 274–80
destructive competition between, 12–15
direct expenditure by from 1993–2021, 324–25, 325t
discussion on trust in, 63–64
distribution of proceeds from sale of federal lands to, 88–89
drivers of public attitudes toward, 34–36
and federal accountability system in public education, 193, 195–96, 197f, 198f, 199
federal incentives, role in infrastructure projects, 216–17

state governments (*continued*)
  in fine-grained account of public's
    federalism preferences, 47–50, 48f,
    49f, 50f
  and fiscal need for major reforms of
    health policies, 245–46
  funding of schools by, 185–87, 185f,
    186t, 187f, 189f, 190t
  in healthcare funding, overview of, 246
  and healthcare management and fund-
    ing, 231–32
  impact of federal fiscal consolidation on
    fiscal policy of, 354–55
  and infrastructure spending, 222–24
  innovation and competition in, 15–16
  limited innovation in healthcare policies
    by, 267–68
  lowest-rated COVID response among,
    140
  Medicaid and CHIP program differ-
    ences in, 246–48, 248t–49t, 250–52,
    253t–55t
  normative role for, 76–77
  partisan (mis)match and public attitudes
    toward, 50–51, 52f, 53
  perceived competence of during pan-
    demic, 137–40, 140t
  and protection of "private rights", 16–22
  public approval of handling of COVID-
    19 pandemic by, 128–30, 129f, 130f,
    131f, 132f
  regulation of private health insurance by,
    263–64, 264t–66t, 266–67
  relation between proximity and trust
    in, 122
  responsiveness to diverse interests and
    preferences, 11–12
  restrictions on local debt in, 367–68
  spending by, vs. federal spending over
    time, 293, 294f, 295–96, 295f, 296f
  student performance across states, 181,
    182f
  trust and confidence in, 34, 43–44, 43f
"state sovereignty," Google Trends associated
    with, 57–58, 58f
State Unemployment Tax Act (SUTA), 297,
    298–99

state-based marketplaces (SBMs), 259,
    260t–61t, 261–62
state-based subsidies, 259
"states' rights"
  Google Trends associated with, 57–58,
    57f, 60
  and phases and faces of federalism,
    67–68
"stay at home mandate," Google Trends
    associated with, 59
student performance, 180–83, 181f, 182f,
    183f, 184f
subnational governments, relationships
    between central governments and,
    xi–xii. *See also* local governments;
    state governments
subsidies
  for individual usage of infrastructure, 214
  state-based, 259
supplemental rebates, negotiating with drug
    manufacturers, 279–80
Supreme Court
  and original concept of fiscal federalism,
    91–92, 95–96
  ratification of government's right to
    purchase territory, 108n10
  and restoration of constitutional
    order, 26
SUTA (State Unemployment Tax Act), 297,
    298–99

Tariff Act of 1789, 89–90
taxation
  competition among governments for
    taxpayers, 15
  and competitive federalism, 326, 331,
    334–37, 335f, 335t, 336t
  and destructive competition for benefits
    of government, 12–15
  federal, relation to federal revenues and
    outlays, 102–3, 102f, 103f
  and intergovernmental transfers during
    recessions, 167
  and state budgets, 401
  and unemployment insurance, 297,
    302–4
Taylor, John B., 5, 288, 357–59

Taylor rule, 353–54, 354f

teacher evaluations, 195, 196, 197f, 198f

teacher unions, 376–77

technological change, planning infrastructure for, 215–16

Tennenbaum Program for Fact-Based Policy, 64

Texas
    public's federalism preferences in, 47–49, 49f
    Winter Storm Uri in, 215–16

Tiebout effect, 15

time trend analysis of public opinion during COVID-19 pandemic. *See* public attitudes toward federalism

TIMSS (Trends in Math and Science Study) scores, 183f

Title IX regulations, 399

Title XII advancements, 298, 298f

Tocqueville, Alexis de, 20, 29n36, 67, 322

tolls. *See* user fees, financing infrastructure spending through

trade unions
    and competitive federalism, 328–29, 329f
    public-sector, 168, 174
    teacher, 376–77

traffic congestion, projects reducing, 212–13, 365–66

transfer-dependence. *See* intergovernmental transfers during recessions

Transport for London (UK), 365–66

transportation programs, 391–92

Treasury, direct relief payments from, 89–90

Trends in Math and Science Study (TIMSS) scores, 183f

Trump, Donald, 119, 123

trust. *See also* competence, impact on trust in government
    discussion on levels of and attitudes toward federalism, 63–64
    in federal government, 34, 44–47, 45f, 46f
    in local governments, 34, 40–42, 42f
    by party, 47–50, 48f, 49f, 50f
    in state governments, 34, 43–44, 43f

Trust in Government Index, ANES, 46, 46f, 60n3

Tyler, John, 110n26

unemployment insurance (UI)
    and federalism, 302–5
    overview, 296–97
    in times of crisis, 300–302
    Unemployment Trust Funds and solvency, 297–300, 298f, 299f

Unemployment Trust Funds (UTFs), 297–300, 298f, 299f, 303–4

unfunded pension liabilities, 311–12, 312f, 313f, 314–15, 315f, 368, 404–5

unions
    and competitive federalism, 328–29, 329f
    public-sector, 168, 174
    teacher, 376–77

United States v. Alfonso D. Lopez, Jr. (1995), 69

universal healthcare systems, state-level, 281

universities
    state role in funding public, 380
    Title IX regulations, 399

US Constitution. *See also* framers' view of federalism
    Article 4, 88
    Commerce Clause, 69, 79, 91
    Fourteenth Amendment, 67–68
    general welfare clause, 13–14, 89–90, 91, 92
    original concept of fiscal federalism, 85, 91

US Supreme Court
    and original concept of fiscal federalism, 91–92, 95–96
    ratification of government's right to purchase territory, 108n10
    and restoration of constitutional order, 26

user fees, financing infrastructure spending through, 213–15, 222, 365–67, 370, 381–82

UTFs (Unemployment Trust Funds), 297–300, 298f, 299f, 303–4

VA (Veterans Affairs), 234f, 237

"vaccine mandate," Google Trends associated with, 58–59

value-based programs (VBP), 269, 273–74, 278, 289

vehicle per-mile (VMT) user fees, 222

Vermont
    mandated insurance coverage in, 266t
    state-based subsidies in, 259
    state-level partisan (mis)match in, 51

Veterans Affairs (VA), 234f, 237

veterans' payments, 113

Wabash, St. Louis & Pacific Railway Company v. Illinois (1886), 68

Wagner's law, 145

waivers
    for nursing home benefits, 251
    of Small Business Health Options Program, 259

Wang, Alice Yiqian, 2, 63, 64, 75–76

Washington, DC, mandated insurance coverage in, 264t

Washington state, public option insurance plan in, 262

welfare, state-by-state competition on, 16. *See also* social insurance programs

Williamson, Hugh, 90

Wilson, Daniel, 218–19

Wilson, James, 13

Wilson, Woodrow, 69

Winter Storm Uri (2021), 215–16

Wisconsin, COVID response ratings for, 140

work disincentives, and unemployment insurance, 304–5

World War I, 147, 148f

World War II, 148, 148f

YouGov polls, 47, 120, 124. *See also* competence, impact on trust in government